British Railways Steam 1968

DEDICATION

This book is dedicated to members of the 20.55 Club, especially those deceased friends, Ian Johnson and Peter Barber. Also to the numerous enginemen who made all that is within possible, not forgetting those other railwaymen who not only didn't prevent us from going where we wanted to go, but often were welcoming to those who demonstrated an interest in the work they were engaged in.

British Railways Steam 1968
The Final Chapters

Stephen Leyland

crecy.co.uk

First published 2018

© 2018 Crecy Publishing Ltd

ISBN 9780860936930

All rights reserved. Apart from any fair dealing for the purpose of private study, research, criticism or review, as permitted under the Copyright, Design and Patents Act 1988, no part of this publication may be reproduced, stored in a retrieval system, or transmitted in any form or by any means, electronic, electrical, chemical, mechanical, optical, photocopying, recording or otherwise, without prior written permission. All enquiries should be directed to the publisher.

Printed in Malta by Gutenberg Press Limited

Crécy Publishing Ltd
1a Ringway Trading Estate, Shadowmoss Rd,
Manchester M22 5LH
www.crecy.co.uk

Front cover:
No. 48278 (10F) working the Heysham–Darwen tanks at Hoghton on 20 June 1968. *I.C. Simpson*

Back cover, main:
People milling about on depots unchallenged in any number was a sure sign of the end, as seen here at Rose Grove on 3 August 1968 with 48773 and 48423 spending their last hours in B.R. service; one to live on in preservation, the other not. Note the enormous rejected coal lumps! *Allan Hayes*

Back cover, inset top: The water running to waste from 48773's tender at Bolton symbolises B.R.'s squandering of so-called outdated resources in the years up to 1968. Steam traction could have been modernised along with its facilities for operation, but it was never more than dabbled in. *V.A. Sidlow*

Back cover, inset bottom: As an 8F condemned at Lostock Hall earlier in the summer of 1968, 48646 had no official business at 9K following closure, but it appeared in late August of that year, having run hot en route to the breaker's yard. The observant, however, will note that the engine is in possession of its motion, has a numberplate and is in steam! Hidden coincidences abound. The image dates from the previous year, probably 19 June, when 48646 later in the day worked the 20.40 Bolton–Hull goods as a visitor from Lostock Hall. It was a Hull scrapyard (Drapers) that eventually claimed it, but before that when arrested in its journey there it lay inert on 9K for many weeks in precisely the same position as seen, half out of the coaling tower as if waiting again for its tender to be replenished!
M.S. Stokes

Contents

Thanks and Acknowledgments 6
About the Author 6
Introduction 7

1 Kingmoor's Legacy Intact – A Peak District Priority 8
2 After the First Contraction 68
3 Pastures New and Pastures Old 122
4 Steam Survives in Small Pockets 178

Appendix

I Abbreviations and Railway Terms 236
II Railway Place Names Lesser Known 238
   in the Twenty-first Century
III Summary of Trips Made in 1968 240
IV Explanation of Train Reporting Numbers 242
V Maps and Diagrams 244

Thanks and Acknowledgments

In addition to the various photographic contributors whose names appear with their work, I would chiefly like to thank Vernon Sidlow for sterling and patient work with the images used and for the technical expertise that seems necessary to get a book out in this digital age. The author is famously lagging behind in these advances! Gratitude is also extended to Ian Simpson for advice and encouragement, and to Lee Johnson, who photographed the 'Survivors' images for me.

ABOUT THE AUTHOR

Stephen Leyland was born in Bolton two days before Nationalisation of the 'Big Four'. A spotter from 10 years old turned steam enthusiast, his railway interest post B.R. steam embraced loco activity at the National Coal Board (N.C.B.) and industrial installations as well as the preserved scene. Train timing, more serious photography, continued tape recording and travelling over previously unexplored lines on mainland U.K. remained prominent in his life through most of the 1970s, as did German steam. His interests within the sphere of the older railway extended to travels in southern Africa during the decade up to 1990. In more recent times his research and writing have played a bigger part, contrasting with the more practical side of preservation, including major involvement in the restoration of ex Bolton loco, 73156.

The author spent twelve months with B.R. in signalling during 1967, but otherwise worked in textiles and electrical goods. Early retirement allowed him to become a carer for his elderly father and more recently he spent ten years as a working volunteer in the East Lancashire Railway's Steam Department. Having remained single and never moving from Bolton, he has also enjoyed other foreign travels, cycling, singing, amateur dramatics, alternative music, walking, the seaside and sunshine, as well as looking after his 40 year-old Ford Capri.

Introduction

This book is all about how (chiefly) four Bolton colleagues got out and got what they could of the fast-shrinking steam scene on B.R. up to August 1968. We four had, over the few preceding years, whilst absorbing the constantly changing railway scene, ingratiated ourselves with the Bolton loco shed staff by also cleaning and greatly improving the appearance of many engines allocated to the 9K-coded loco depot, thereby gaining trust and assurance during as near a continual presence as was possible that we meant only good (see Appendix V, Diagram 3).

This personal account is a slightly modified version of a final volume (of four) that I wrote some time ago, covering the period September 1964 to August 1968 and entitled *After the Stripe*, but which was not published beyond various friends. The last year of steam opens with most of the headlong dash to eliminate it completed, countless line closures effected and the near total loss of loco-hauled carriage comfort on all but expresses to that apology of a replacement, the despised diesel multiple unit. Smelly, vibrating and unreliable, and deservedly dubbed 'bog units' or 'bog carts', they were loathed by enthusiasts of the traditional, dignified railway for what they had replaced. To the reader who went through similar pursuits, following steam in '68, I hope it will strike chords of recognition during that unrepeatable time we experienced, To those too young to remember, or even be there, but wonder – 'enjoy'!

1

Kingmoor's Legacy Intact – A Peak District Priority

1 January to 4 March
Up to the Buxton, Trafford Park and Northwich depot closures.

1967 was a hard year to say 'goodbye' to for enthusiasts in the North-west. It had given us so much, though much too was taken away. 'Glorious'? For me, oh yes! We were used to the encroaching dieselisation from the south and had somehow weathered the enormous blow to steam-worked passenger traffic at the end of the summer timetable. Locally too at Bolton, the effects late in the year of Springs Branch steam shed's closure merged with doomy hints at what was happening at the seemingly unshakeable and far-reaching Kingmoor motor power depot (mpd). A lot was in the air during those last weeks. I'd gone back to train booking at Bolton East Jc. box in early October 1967, a fortnight after a disastrous 'career move' hiatus prompted partly by signalmen's well-meant advice to get off the railway they saw no future in.

It was wonderful to be back at the box, but I knew that the end of 1967 would see me at the age limit for train register keeping for the able-bodied. Holiday dates for 1968, issued just before Christmas, I considered would be too late for steam chasing. There were no signal boxes on the vacancy list to attract me, and neither did platform work. A job offer in textiles again, plus other considerations, saw me down the East Jc. steps once more, and for the last time whilst employed there, on 11 January 1968 (see Appendix V, Diagram 4).

On the last afternoon of 1967, a Sunday, I worked with the Bolton volunteer cleaning gang on home engines 45110, 73040 and 44664. New Year's Eve personally meant three church services too, and with some of the choir to which I belonged, after Watchnight, this recently turned 20-year-old, unversed in many ways of the world, shy and reserved in certain (mainly female) company, attended a party. Any related reluctance to accept was overcome by a legitimate 'escape' clause limiting me to an 01.00 departure as I had to be at the box by 6am. Despite being New Year's Day with its far from fully restored weekday service, a booker was called for. Soon after arrival it snowed heavily for an hour without adversely affecting the Up 'Belfast Boat Express', which left Bolton perfectly to time at 07.50 behind Carnforth's 45342. How very appropriate that my first steam sighting of 1968 should be of that working in view of the train's growing significance and importance during the coming months to North-west enthusiasts, as will be seen. The early turn that morning provided very little indication of how things were going to be under the new Carlisle Kingmoor diesel diagramming, as non-passenger traffic made a very slow start. Complex diagrams over several days, even with steam, had permeated all the North-west. In the build-up to steam's year end demise at Carlisle Kingmoor (12A) we'd seen the signs in some fully dieselised workings and the odd one for crew training only that reverted to steam later. Now we braced ourselves for the worst.

Monday, 1 January
Later morning on 1 January brought good and bad news in the dieselisation of the 07.40 Barrow–Manchester parcels, 3J03, MO (09.30 from Heysham MX), but the continuation of steam on the Manchester portion of the 08.25 Glasgow–Liverpool, 1J42, which appeared almost on time behind 45420 (9D). The 'Boat Train's two middle of the day workings remained unaltered, but 45342 (10A) was uncharacteristically well late with the 09.15 Manchester Vic.–Blackpool North parcels, 3P04. What happened with the next leg (13.50 Blackpool–Manchester parcels) is not known, but a type 4 diesel on the evening 'Boat' did not bode well and we didn't know what to think. Thankfully, however, there was no cause for alarm and Carnforth stability with steam resumed the next morning, ruling the roost without a single known interruption by modern power until the true takeover in early May. Later foreknowledge of this permitted the event to be fully commemorated.

Eight loco-hauled goods, parcels and newspaper trains through Bolton alone during what might be termed 'daytime' that weren't fully diesel worked up to Kingmoor's closure, plus a probable four night-time parcels, news and mail jobs were off the steam list from 1 January 1968. A similar impact could be felt throughout the remainder of the partly steam-worked L.M.R. Tebay and Workington sheds had gone at the same time, but with far more local effects.

Locomotive withdrawals at Kingmoor, heavy even in the summer, had been stepped up during the autumn of 1967, reducing the allocation of just over 100 at the end of June to forty-five, which were disposed of from the beginning of December. Many of these were there at the end itself when the twenty that were not condemned moved south to pastures new. 'Black 5s' in ones, twos and threes went to Stockport Edgeley, Newton Heath, Bolton, Lostock Hall and Rose Grove, whilst Speke Jc. and Carnforth each received three 9Fs. The surviving 'Brit', 70013, found a new home at the latter. From Tebay, where the bankers had been replaced by Type 1 diesels, three 75XXX escaped to Carnforth and the same number

The sprawling and busy Carlisle Kingmoor mpd had an impact partly on the whole of the still steam-worked North-west when it closed at the end of 1967, setting the scene for what followed and for what is portrayed in this book. Its proportions are more than suggested in the panoramic view of the north end of 12A, whilst a few latter-day loco types at the south end are more closely shown in the second image. *Alan Gilbert/M.L.S. collection*

Earlier in December 1967, Springs Branch mpd also succumbed to direct dieselisation with its own purpose-built premises even closer by than Kingmoor's. The difference was that the Wigan set-up was for diesel maintenance and not a running shed. Thus, diesels in service used the old shed yard, rubbing shoulders initially after the change with visiting steam locos. These could be, and were, serviced there for some weeks and even into early 1968, but they all originated from other depots. The new and old are seen here on 18 November 1967, just a fortnight before steam allocated to 8F finished. *P. Barber*

A probably unique photograph of the interior of Bolton East Jc. signal box, showing almost the entire frame, looking towards Burnden Junction. Lever No. 140 is on the right. By the time that the author worked there some of the block instruments had been replaced by more modern types and there were a few more spare levers, but two signalmen and a train booker occupied the box on most turns until well after the steam era. The booker's desk and telephone exchange is just beyond the seated gentleman's feet. Date and photographer unknown. *Author's collection*

Bolton East Jc. signal box; an exterior view showing the wider scene from the old cattle dock towards Orlando footbridge. One could not ignore rumours, and a strong one cropped up regarding the end of steam on the 12.17 Preston–Manchester, 1J42, at the beginning of November 1967, even though not linked to an influential shed closure. That is the reason for this photograph, supposedly of the penultimate with steam, on 2 November 1967. For the last, as we thought, I made a tape recording of the event instead. The engine here is 44920 (8F), which was withdrawn for scrap in the week ending 2 December 1967 when 8F finished with steam, though happily 1J42 survived well into 1968 before the diesels took over, as will be seen within. The RH signals are for the express and the extreme LH ones for the 12.00 Liverpool Exchange–Rochdale dmu. Simultaneous departures around the front and back of the cabin were common in those days. *S.A. Leyland*

were condemned at 12E. Workington was down to the same size of allocation at the end and three Ivatt 4s were despatched to Lostock Hall, two 'Black 5s' to Bolton and one to Trafford Park, though I suspect the latter to be an error, as will be seen.

The new northern limitations on steam workings were Barrow, Oxenholme (except for the Windermere branch tripper and thrice weekly cement train to Shap – details later) and Settle Jc., a few Heysham–Leeds oil trains behind steam marking the boundary there. Of course, certain infrequent exceptions and infringements were reported from time to time, but to all intents and purposes, steam was kept within the receded northern limits and off the newly dieselised workings. Steam servicing facilities at Normanton mpd were discontinued at the same time, eliminating the stabling overnight (or longer) of visitors to Yorkshire. I don't think that surviving trans-Pennine steam freights were greatly affected by this and the magazines did report steam continuing into 1968 on the 03.32 Leeds–Halifax and 04.38 Halifax–Manchester passenger trains, for a time at least.

I have acknowledged above the transfer of the sole surviving 'Britannia', 70013, to Carnforth, but this engine was set aside now for special use only. Enthusiast railtours had been in a state of suspension since late November 1967 after a ruling by B.R.'s vice chairman, Philip H. Shirley. His departure on 1 January 1968, particularly coming shortly after that of the 'fiery, iconoclastic' Sir Stanley Raymond as B.R. Chairman (to Cunard), permitted the steam ban to be lifted from 17 March 1968, from which date the floodgates were open during the ensuing few months left to the old motive power. Stanier 'Black 5s' and 8Fs as at 1 January 1968 constituted 84% of the standard gauge steam stock. Remarkably, there were now 150 of each type in service. The Ivatt 4 'Piggies', six remaining, were all Lostock Hall-based now and nearly all of the twenty-three B.R. 5 4-6-0s were at Patricroft mpd, as had been the case for some time. Carnforth had on its books the ten 75XXX that remained in stock and some of the surviving eighteen 9F 2-10-0s. The others were allocated to Speke Jc. The total as 1968 opened was 357 steam locos. 'Black 5s' and 8Fs were distributed generally

The complete railway at Bolton East Jc. looking towards Burnden Jc. and Manchester with 'A' Sidings on the right and Haslams in the centre as Bolton loco 48380 struggles to drag a goods off the Bury line at 08.28 on an initially frosty 28 March 1968. The 8F had literally inched its way up the 1 in 100 from Darcy Lever viaduct, emulating a formerly more frequent incidence of goods trains stalling in the course of this same manoeuvre. Even in 1967 from East Jc. box the author saw only one come to a stand amongst many valiant and successful efforts. *V.A. Sidlow*

to eleven of the remaining thirteen depots. Northwich and Buxton operated 2-8-0s only. The depots, with their codes, were as follows:

8A Edge Hill	9E Trafford Park	10A Carnforth
8C Speke Jc.	9F Heaton Mersey	10D Lostock Hall
8E Northwich	9H Patricroft	10F Rose Grove
9B Stockport Edgeley	9K Bolton	
9D Newton Heath	9L Buxton	

Upon that ever diminishing total of 357 was focussed not only the 'spotlight' illuminating the concluding act of many who chronicled the decline of that most affectionately held form of motive power, but the gaze too of an ever-increasing audience. In its midst sat yours truly. A good seat doesn't necessarily make a good reviewer, but what he saw of that drama as it unfolded to its inevitable conclusion will be related as faithfully as knowledge and ability permit.

Tuesday, 2 January

Tuesday the 2nd saw everything back to normal in terms of traffic levels, and the new shape of things on through workings for early 1968 showed their true colours on this rather dark day of diesel discoveries. The partly anticipated, but in some cases, shock instances of dieselisation and other changes for the worse, did have a negative effect on morale that was most keenly felt upon realisation. The following table summarises the sudden changes to Bolton's steam-hauled traffic. These are in addition to certain trains that had lost their steam traction as Kingmoor workings during the closing weeks of 1967:

4P50	05.25 Brewery Sdgs–Burnley SX (Blackburn SO)	Ceased to stop at Bolton to set down. Sometimes diesel hauled
5J14	04.05 Carlisle–Moston	Became diesel hauled
5P30	07.45 Brewery Sdgs–Burnley SX	Discontinued
8F37	08.30 Brewery Sdgs–Carlisle SX	Became diesel hauled
3J41	08.05 Carlisle New Yard–Red Bank empty vans	Became diesel hauled
3J03	07.40 Barrow–Manchester parcels MO	Became diesel hauled
3J03	09.30 Heysham–Manchester parcels MX	Became diesel hauled
3P05	16.30 Manchester–Blackpool N. parcels SO	Became diesel hauled
3P05	18.05 Manchester–Blackpool N. parcels S	Became diesel hauled. Ret. Wkg. of 3J03
1P14	20.30 Manchester–Heysham News SO	Became diesel hauled. Ret. Wkg. of 3J03
5J10	19.05 Burnley–Moston SX	Diverted via Castleton. Still steam

Apart from the 'Belfast Boat Express', regular steam-worked passenger trains in Lancashire by now were all portions of longer distance expresses to or from Glasgow to Manchester or Liverpool, steam south of Preston or Wigan, plus trains ex Euston with Blackpool portions steam-worked west of Preston. Here, Carnforth loco 44709 brings the 12.17 Preston–Manchester out of Bolton under the Burnden Jc. signal gantry. This three-train loco diagram (Mon–Fri) was taken over by Newton Heath when Springs Branch closed, but foreign locos were not infrequently used, as witnessed here. In fact, 44709 could not have worked the 21.25 Preston–Liverpool that night (31 January 1968) as booked for it was seen heading LE through Bolton at 20.33 and taking the Blackburn line, probably being returned home via Hellifield. *I.C. Simpson*

The day of these revelations ended on a much cheerier note though, as if the fiery spectacle of 44894 (10A) approaching Green Lane bridge (just north of Moses Gate) on the evening 'Boat Train', with sound effects to match, had been divinely sent to counter the mood brought on by earlier events. 1P02 seemed determined to eradicate its quarter of an hour lateness that night!

So, what was left for the steam enthusiast on our local scene? During my year at the box the old order on through traffic and principal trains starting from, or terminating at, Bolton, as opposed to pilot and trip workings, had nearly halved for various reasons, chiefly dieselisation and discontinuation. Still steam worked at the start of 1968 were the following, which I list in the knowledge that many will not necessarily receive further mention on account of my imminent departure from Bolton East Jc. (see Appendix V, Diagram 2). The booked time at Bolton is on the right.

6P22	23.20 Brewery Sdgs–Ribble Sdgs SX	00.10/00.18
5P05	22.30 Ancoats–Heysham SX. Worked by 10A 5MT ex 3M1	23.32/00.12
	Full diagram: 7J32/LE to 9K/Next day's 9K Ballast wkg./3M13/	
	LE Rochdale to Ancoats/5P05. 9K men with relief at Bolton	
3J05	21.45 Blackpool N–Manchester parcels	00.43/00.53
		(pass 00.41 SuO)
7J85	21.15 Wyre Dock–Moston SX	00.38/01.10
6P59	23.38 Brewery–Blackburn SX. Return working of 5J10	00.23/00.48
7J82	01.43 Farington–Brewery MX	02.33/02.58
3P01	03.05 Manchester–Blackpool N. parcels	pass 03.24

6P23	03.25 Brewery–Blackpool T Rd. MX. Worked by 9H class 8F	relief 04.15/04.17
6P23	03.40 Brewery–Blackpool T Rd. MO. Worked by 9H class 8F	relief 04.28/04.30
1P97	03.45 Manchester–Colne News MX	04.02/04.05
1P97	03.42 Manchester–Colne News MO. (Return working of 3J20 – engine and men MX. Also 9K relief at Bolton MX)	04.02/04.04
6P69	03.55 Brewery–Blackburn MO. Worked by 9D power. (see SX version)	pass 04.41
3P14	05.00 Manchester–Colne parcels	05.20/05.28
8M05	03.05 Healey Mills–Bolton (Burnden) MX. (Return working of 5N12)	arr 05.30
8P36	05.25 Castleton–Workington SO. Unsure about steam on this now	pass 06.02
4P50	05.25 Brewery–Burnley. Sometimes diesel. Via Clifton	pass approx 06.00
1J05	06.10 Heysham–Manchester 'Belfast Boat Express' MX	07.46/07.50
1J05	06.30 Morecambe–Manchester MO	07.46/07.50
1J05	07.15 Heysham–Manchester 'Belfast Boat Express' SuO. All versions of 1J05 worked by 10A 5MT. For diagram see 3P04	08.48/08.52
3P04	09.15 Manchester–Blackpool N. parcels SX. Diagram: 1J05/3P04/3J06/1P02	10.11/10.23
3P04	09.30 Manchester–Blackpool N. parcels SO. Diagram: 1J05/3P04/LE 9D/1P02 (3P04 ran via Castleton)	10.11/10.23
8J50	09.20 Abram–Halliwell SX. Motive power source uncertain	
7N55	12.35 Halliwell–Healey Mills SO. Worked by 9K 5MT or 8F off shed	
1J42	12.17 Preston–Manchester. Portion of 08.25 Glasgow–Liverpool SO. Usually diesel SO (main train engine) now, but mainly steam SX (9D loco) with decreasing incidence until end April	12.45/12.47
3J83	13.25 Colne–Red Bank empty vans SO. Worked by 10F 5MT. Occasionally an 8F	pass 14.38
3J06	13.50 Blackpool N.–Manchester parcels SX. (For diagram see 3P04)	15.22/15.36
5J13	16. 40 Burnley–Moston SX. Worked by 9D 5MT	Usually passed Bolton 18.15-18.35
7J32	16.50 Heysham–Burnden SX. Worked by 10A 5MT. (For diagram see 5P05)	arr. approx 19.00
3M13	20.20 Bolton–Bedford parcels SX (via Castleton) Worked by 10A 5MT (9K men) to Rochdale. For diagram see 5P05	dep 20.20
3J20	17.45 Colne–Ashton Moss parcels SX (via Clifton) Worked by 10F 5MT to Bolton then 9K 5MT	20.23/21.45
3J28	20.57 Bolton–Guide Bridge parcels SX (via Clifton). Worked by 10F 5MT ex 3J20	
1P02	20.55 Manchester–Heysham 'Belfast Boat Express'. (For diagram see 3P04). Worked by 10A 5MT	21.12/21.20
1P02	20.55 Manchester–Morecambe SuO (via Pendleton Broad St.). Worked by 10A 5MT ex Up 'Boat Train'	21.14/21.20
5J44	18.45 Heysham–Ardwick East Yard SO. Worked by 9K 5MT LE to Heysham	pass 20.56
5J10	19.05 Burnley–Moston SX. (via Castleton). Worked by 10F 8F	pass approx 21.40
3P03	21.05 Oldham Clegg St–Blackburn parcels SX (via Clifton)	22.00/22.33
5N12	22.16 Bolton–Healey Mills SX (via Clifton). Worked by 9K 8F	

All Moston- and Brewery-related workings not so designated were routed via Castleton, except during a temporary arrangement to be described shortly. All the above, with only modest Bolton mpd involvement, are trains from the Working Timetable, that 'bible' of main line duties. Contributing more prominently to steam activity around Bolton and 9K depot's sphere of operation were its trip workings and pilots that only appeared in the periodically issued 'Shunting Engine and Local Trip Notice'. The contents for early 1968 applying to Bolton mpd can be summarised by the following listing:

- Brewery–Horwich goods, passing Bolton approx 08.30–10. 00. SX.
- Horwich–Moston goods, return working of the above in the later morning. SX.
- Brindle Heath–Horwich goods in the early afternoon SX.
- 18.05 Bolton Rose Hill–Moston goods SX. Usually class 8F.
- Bolton station pilot.

- Patricroft (Astley Green)–Crumpsall coal.
- 04.00 Bolton (Burnden)–Moston and assist Patricroft–Crumpsall.
- Castleton pilot.
- Continuous pilot (Trip and shunt locally as required).
- 06.05 Bolton–Bamfurlong/Bamfurlong or Abram–Halliwell goods.
- Rawtenstall pilot (unsure if this job still existed).
- Brindle Heath–Agecroft–Moston trips MO.
- Heap Bridge trip SX.
- Bolton area ballast SX (men only).
- Kearsley pilot.
- 'Special Trips' SX.

Thanks to sufficient surviving paperwork from the depot during a lengthy period up to the autumn of 1967, the many and often complex changes to the 9K trip and pilot work could be monitored and followed in considerable detail. Since this paperwork 'dried up', a close watch on developments has not been possible, but the above is submitted with a high degree of confidence, nevertheless. To fulfil the above listed work Bolton shed currently had at its disposal an allocation that had fallen to no more than twenty-two engines of three classes. The 'Black 5s' ranged in seniority at 9K from very recent arrivals to the far off days (or so it seemed) when 26C was the code for Bolton. Here they are at the start of 1968, showing the date of arrival and depot from which they came:

44664 – 14/10/64 ex Blackpool Cen.	48111 – 15/10/66 ex Agecroft
44728 – 5/10/64 ex Blackpool Cen.	48380 – 1/11/66 ex Colwick
44802 – 5/1/68 ex Carlisle Kingmoor	48504 – 25/5/66 ex Nuneaton
44829 – w/e 21/1/68 ex Workington	48559 – 12 or 13/8/67 ex Crewe South
44947 – 23/9/64 ex Blackpool Cen.	48652 – early June 1965 ex Bury
45104 – 10/4/65 ex Bury	48702 – 22/8/64 ex Northwich
45110 – 20/7/65 ex Stafford	48740 – 31/8/64 ex Northwich
45260 – 16/2/65 ex Coalville	48773 – 21/9/64 ex Buxton
45290 – 10/2/62 ex Newton Heath	73040 – 4/5/66 ex Croes Newydd
45294 – by 3/1/68 ex Workington	73069 – 5/5/66 ex Tyseley
45318 – 10/4/65 ex Bury	
45381 – 11/4/65 ex Bury	
48046/200 – 31/12/67 ex Newton Heath	The above are actual, rather than official dates
Above two never used – withdrawn immediately	1968 arrivals were officially Bolton by 1 January 1968

Having set the scene, locally, and to an extent further afield, we can return to observed traffic and very early New Year events, but not until I have clarified that only non-Bolton engines mentioned herein will be accompanied by their shed code, except when 'foreigners' are referred to in quick succession. Back-pedalling briefly to Tuesday, 2 January, and its early turn irregularities, 44894 (10A), which had taken up the 'Boat Train' diagram for three days, left Bolton half an hour late on the Up. This was unusual, even though the train's punctuality relied heavily on that of the sailings from Belfast. Its average lateness at Bolton on fifty-one known dates in 1968, and whilst still steam worked, was only 6.57 minutes. A Lostock Jc. train register has assisted greatly in producing this statistic. The now wider-ranging Ballast loco, 45095 (10A) on 2 January, was detailed for work at Crumpsall, illustrating a location outside the old Bolton/Chorley area alternate designation of the turn that was formerly the norm. The 'freelance' 9K engine that often had its hand turned to coal empties, today 48559, was given a Rochdale–Healey Mills run. The dinnertime Glasgow (portion from Preston) made an unusually good start to the year, time keeping-wise, that on 2 January providing the week's only blemish to speak of when 44780 (9D) made a thirty-six-minute late appearance.

Wednesday, 3 January

Early next morning, amidst a deep, but short-lived fall of overnight snow, the diesel loco off Shrewsbury–Bolton empty parcels vans (a new train from 6 September 1967, said to be 3L32, but timings never discovered) happened to be D5000. It was next specially detailed to take 73014, clean and green, but long withdrawn at 9K, from the depot on the first stage of its journey to Cashmores of Newport for breaking up. It had achieved celebrity status in the spring and early summer of 1967 on special passenger workings, but now both of our green B.R. 5s had gone. Newton Heath was the next port of call, where more scrap locos were probably due to join the cavalcade.

In the absence of a special notice about the movement at East Jc. I deduce that it travelled direct from 9K, and that I'd asked Burnden Jc. the departure time (06.54, i.e. long before dawn), but not to save me the notice. Such things were instant scrap paper once the train had gone and lit many cigarettes until I started to save them for posterity at East! A different Type 2 the next day had very similar orders and though I didn't know which loco(s) it had been

Above: No. 73014 in better times, just a few months earlier, passing the by then closed mpd at Mirfield with the 10.48 Filey–Manchester summer Saturday train on 24 June 1967, booked return work for an earlier Scarborough-bound train that on that date had started specially at Bolton. The author was on the footplate at this point. *Barry Mounsey*

detailed to pick up, an informed guess would be 44927 from the considerable scrap content at 9K. Meanwhile, on the 3rd at East, nothing beyond the very late running of the surviving Brewery–Burnley goods, 45202 (9D) today, stood out on a reasonably busy early turn. By this time, local duty Halliwell pilot had ceased to be, requisite shunting being performed, it seems, by the trip engine. No. 45318 spent at least two hours there that morning, for instance, in between working trains to and from the goods yard.

As 1968 opened, all of Bolton's 'Black 5s' except the three received via the twelve division sheds upset were fairly long-term residents. Here, 45318, ex Bury in April 1965, is positioned under the coaling tower at 9K on 3 February 1968. *V.A. Sidlow*

Above: No. 44802 heads towards Bradley Fold and the east on 3 February 1968 with the lunchtime Halliwell–Healey Mills, crossing the Raikes viaduct immediately out of Bolton.

Bradley Fold station, looking west, shortly before closure in 1970, but just as it was on the author's first evening trip of 1968. The Up loop was out of use even then. *S.A. Leyland*

The snow's enemy had been rain, followed by high winds, the latter of which may well still have raged during a splendid evening I spent at Bradley Fold station. The interval of two hours from 18.20 featured five goods workings plus Bedford parcels. Both Bolton–Mostons ran that night on loads of 44 and 37 respectively. The second train, 7J13, about which I'd had doubts for some time, and therefore not on the 'master' list, was hauled by 45294, my first sighting of the loco as a transfer from Workington to Bolton. 45202 (9D) on the earlier Burnley–Moston had preceded it and indicated the return working of that morning's Brewery–Burnley (see above). Two Castleton–Boltons ran with local 8Fs, but all else went eastbound, the best direction for tape recording steam at work. I didn't have my trusty Philips Cassette with me that night, maybe on account of the winds, but taping, quite seriously since November 1966, had progressively become my favoured medium of capturing the steam scene, over photography. The latter, however, just about kept going until the end.

As activity and variety at our home depot lessened and even the most 'unlikely' foreign loco visitors caused little wonder, compared with the mid-1960s, more evening time came to be devoted to other locations where the engines could be seen and heard working. The Bury line was certainly the best bet locally since the two Carlisle goods had gone out of the running, and for that reason Entwistle was thrown over for Spring Vale or Darwen as the southbound climb to Waltons Sidings (Sough) still had its attractions, as will be seen from the spring onwards; Broadfield bank too in the lengthening hours of daylight.

Thursday, 4 January

Snow on Thursday the 4th began at just the time that Wednesday's had gone by. Long before that my penultimate sighting of 6P23, Brewery–Blackpool, well late at 05.53 saw 48491 (9H) bring its thirty-two wagon load off the 'branch' (as the Rochdale line was called) as I turned up for work. Unsurprisingly, this train was seen infrequently. Later, amongst regular movements, two light engines ex 9K set off for their places of work more deviously than usual, suggesting a problem with the shed turntable. No. 48702 on Kearsley pilot reversed at our points and again at Rose Hill to traverse the fork whilst 48111, sent specially to shunt at Bury, would normally have used the fork without changing direction.

The Glasgow portion for Manchester at dinner conveyed only four coaches (45397 – 10F) today, and soon afterwards 73069, after being sent to Horwich for the purpose, dragged one of the Works shunters, D2214, back to 9K. At home I discovered that I'd been offered a job in foam lamination that I had applied for and decided to accept it, tendering my notice to the railway next day.

Doing so seemed to heighten my awareness of being where I was, and that this time the severance would be permanent. The voluntary giving up in an absolute and final way of something one has loved or held very dear, for an alternative to it that is supposed to improve one's lot, but which is still very much a mystery that has yet to prove itself to be better, often imparts to that original object of affection a renewal of the charms that captivated one in the first place, but which had perhaps been dulled by time and repetition. Evening time I went to tell my friend, Paul, about a most unusual out-of-gauge-load running tomorrow, and after choir practice walked, perhaps reflectively, down to the shed.

Friday, 5 January

A surviving reaction to the above is that my notes for those last few days at East took in greater detail than of late. So far within these pages little more than irregularities have featured, but those reproduced below for 5 January illustrate well an early turn just after the Kingmoor 'shake-up'. All steam shed codes are included.

45110 (9K) LE Rawtenstall	05.58
48282 (9H) 03.25 Brewery–Blackpool (43) MX	06.11
D5030 Shrewsbury–Bolton parcels engine (arrived)	–
44845 (9D) 05.25 Brewery–Burnley (16) SX	06.53
48380 (9K) Engine and brake van (EBV) Bamfurlong	07.06
45445 (10A) Ballast engine to Bullfield	08.04
45134 (10A) Up 'Belfast Boat Express' dep.	08.04
48702 (9K) Kearsley pilot engine (via fork)	08.07
44802 (9K) LE Bolton mpd	08.59
D1621 09.00 Manchester–Glasgow, 1S45	09.19
Type 2 04.05 Carlisle–Moston (17=32)	09.42
Type 2 Millerhill–Oldham Glodwick Rd	09.56
45445 (10A) Ballast EBV Peel Hall (Walkden H.L.)	10.07
D7506 08.30 Brewery–Carlisle (37) SX	10.12
48111 (9K) Brewery – Horwich (14) SX	10.20
D5285 Mold Jc.–Bolton van special	10.25
45134 (10A) 09.15 Manchester–Blackpool parcels	10.49
D338 Red Bank–Barrow special ECS, 3T40	11.06
45318 (9K) Haslams Sdgs–Halliwell (22)	11.31
48551 (9F) 07.20 Hellifield–Stafford special, 8X46	11.12/11.34
44664 (9K) LE Horwich	12.00
D1631 09.30 Heysham–Manchester parcels MX dep.	12.09
44818 (9D) 12.17 Preston–Manchester (Glasgow portion)	12.49/12.51
Type 2 07.20 Carlisle–Glodwick Rd. (40)	12.34
D328 08.05 Carlisle–Red Bank empty pcls. vans. 3J41	13.05
48111 (9K) Horwich–Moston (28=48)	13.15
45318 (9K) Halliwell–Burnden (12)	13.17
48380 (9K) Halliwell–'B' Side (Rose Hill) (6)	13.27
45318 (9K) Haslams Sdgs–Bullfield (12)	13.47

Goods train wagon loadings are in parenthesis after the description. At East Jc. we wouldn't normally have seen the engine for Rawtenstall and Kearsley pilot was still making its roundabout start before heading south. No. 44802 constituted Bolton's sole acquisition from Kingmoor and the above observation marks the arrival of an engine that did at least stay the course at 9K and was granted more attention by we cleaners than any other latecomer. Of great interest was the special, 8X46. The old mpd at Hellifield was used to house certain historic railway vehicles not on public display. Up to that morning, ex L.N.W.R. 0-4-0ST No. 1439, preserved coach M282494 and B.R. snowplough 900566 were amongst those kept therein. Despite the Heaton Mersey loco actually used to transport this varied stock under a host of operating instructions, Lostock Hall provided the power and men. These and the Hellifield guard were relieved officially at Bradshawgate (first box up the Blackburn line out of Bolton) by 9K men, but they probably took over at Orlando Bridge (O.B.) or the station as the train halted there for some time, as seen. The little 0-4-0 was, perhaps surprisingly, hauled dead on its own wheels and the whole continued via Castleton to Stockport at 20mph maximum. Fresh men and a loco change took place at Heaton Norris Jc. The increased incidence (since late 1967) of diesel utility on regular and special traffic can be seen from the above. There's a suggestion too that the identifying of diesels did not command the same dedication as that of their predecessors!

After that early turn I went to buy a new cassette tape and batteries, and our good turn at the shed in the evening was to report what seemed like some suspicious behaviour to the foreman on duty, Mr Arthur Hulton. He'd long become reconciled to our presence at 9K providing we didn't stray up the shed yard towards the turntable.

Saturday, 6 January

On Saturday morning, the 6th, 45260 took a brake van to Bury (still via Bolton East Jc.) and just over an hour later returned with a train bound for Preston, fourteen wagons, equal to twenty in length the circuit said, conveying redundant signalling equipment and the like. Clearly the accumulating and loading of this had been done beforehand. Another two hours and a bit saw the engine back to shed and finished. Forty minutes later I finished too, shortly after Halliwell–Healey Mills had clattered by (4538l) on forty empties. Relief at the box on Saturdays was at 13.00, an hour sooner than usual, maybe having its origins in the Wanderers home matches. One of the signalmen I'd worked with that week was Bob Middlewood, slightly rotund, congenial, a cardigan wearer with a crew-cut. He often ran me home in his car when our hours coincided. The other 'bobby', John Winward, another gentleman, had musical Salvation Army connections. He went driving for N.C.L. in a couple of years' time, from being a relief signalman. The box was double manned except for twenty-four hours from 22.00 Saturday and was among the biggest on the old L&Y Railway, with a frame of 143 levers. Since Bolton Station Down box had closed in September 1966, ninety-five levers were still in use at East.

I could write (and have done in the past) pages about Bolton East and my employment there, but this seems inappropriate, as I was on the verge of leaving. Another reason for doing so was in order to have a full Saturday a week to go out and take in the wider steam scene, often, as it turned out with my friends. Since going back to the box in October 1967 I'd only taken one rest day. Though entitled to one a week, we were encouraged to work them as there was no bookers rest day relief. Last summer

Say 'Woodhead Electric' to any enthusiast, young or old, and a very high percentage will immediately know what is meant. This view in advanced dusk at Godley Jc. evokes the author's uncharacteristic, but enjoyable fill-in run of 6 January, at odds though it was with the pursuits that make up this book. A concession to non-steam loco-hauled travel will be detected occasionally within it.
F.J. Gradwell

I'd fared better, as there was some relief then, and I was more insistent if necessary. Actually 'having' to work was never a hardship, it must be conceded, as I was surrounded by a railway 'world' that I'd come to love, and even felt in quite an exalted position. True, one could make a 'go' of it of sorts, trip-wise, after an early turn, but by early 1968 most of the steam action was on non-passenger workings and Saturday mornings were the best. This very day, 6 January, I'd have joined my friends' trip to Gowhole and Buxton, given the choice.

The new job was supposed to give me Saturdays off on a regular basis, but making a 'go' of it today I went straight to Manchester on the 13.45 with the slightly odd, but deliberate intention of photographing the Victoria pilots. Before long, however, the three 9D 'Black 5s' there, plus 73010 (9H) at Exchange no longer held my interest sufficiently, perhaps due to a low level of activity. This gave rise to a move that superficially was at odds with the whole steam enthusiast mentality as herein portrayed as I opted for the novelty of a run to Sheffield via Woodhead.

An awareness that my 'priv' rate fare facility would before long expire as surely as Cinderella's finery may well have had a hand in this decision to 'go electric' for a mere 5/9d return. The old electrics had been at Piccadilly ever since I'd first beheld the station as London Road, and funnily enough it was 27003 (then not named *Diana*) that linked that almost ten-year gap. Whisking me across the Pennines on the 16.10, it combined the fast time of fifty-two minutes (making two stops) with a matchless style of transportation in which one was conveyed more as an individual. In compartment comfort one felt much more in control of things than in the communal strip-lit units of the twenty-first century, smart and snappy though they may be. Indeed, the sole common feature linking my run on 1950s technology with a Manchester–Sheffield journey in the present day was the time taken. What has been gained? Yes, it was an impressive clatter over the many junctions of each city's suburbs and an incontestably splendid service on what has become one of the country's most lamented main lines. I returned several times after steam had finished to enjoy it again.

Meanwhile, returning with 26050 *Stentor* on the 17.45 still gave plenty of time before the evening's main attraction. I'd drawn a line under the 3,900 or so miles I'd travelled with steam in 1967, knowing full well that the year after would afford drastically reduced opportunities in that field, though I think the broad conception of those opportunities that we'd formed at the time painted a far gloomier picture than the one that actually emerged. B.R. had been vowing to ban steam on passenger work for almost eighteen months now, without succeeding, but nobody expected those intentions to remain unfulfilled until the end itself! True, the scope for enthusiasts on such traffic narrowed as the year wore on, and as it did, more and more devotees of steam emerged onto the contracting scene, rendering the prestige workings and locations all the more populated!

One naturally targeted train was, of course, 'The Belfast Boat Express', Britain's last steam-hauled titled train. The seasonally boosted patronage by enthusiasts out for the recent Christmas reliefs had tailed off to 'normal' in early 1968, but the trend in that respect could, and did, go only one way as the threat of dieselisation loomed ever nearer.

Contrasting running standards on the 'Boat' were nothing new, but if anything seemed more pronounced as runs were being evaluated more frequently than before, not just personally, but by others who came to be almost regular patrons of 1P02 south of Preston, and with whom friendships were struck through the common interest. On 6 January, 45134 (10A) had started a six-day session on the diagram and its performance going north included some smart features. The train was a full fifteen minutes late out of Victoria with seven coaches plus a long wheelbase van, equal to seven and a half in weight really. The start was none too good with only 48mph by Agecroft Jc. and this fell to 43 passing Clifton, but, with more vigour and sounding curiously like a 3-cylinder engine at such speeds (an opinion held by more than myself), the 4-6-0 accelerated to 48/50 and held it to Moses Gate on the average 1 in 200 rise. As commonly happened, the seven-minute allowance to Clifton was nowhere near kept and the far less demanding ten minutes in from that point were not sufficiently capitalised upon. Most runs that did maintain the seventeen-minute schedule to Bolton (and there weren't that many) balanced these two losses and gains more effectively.

The eight-minute allowance at Bolton, rarely needed in full, was, I suspect, a factor in many poor journey times to that point. Tonight we were stationary for only two and a half minutes, then away again, steadily into speed up the slight rise to beyond Lostock Jc. And, with a not too common 70mph on faintly favourable grades through Adlington, gained nearly a minute to Chorley. Smart station work here saw 1P02 just six minutes late away, but further efforts to pull anything back were ruined by a dead stand before Euxton Jc. and checks on the main line limiting the highest rate to 47mph. Arrival in Preston was eight and a half minutes down. A normally comfortable fifteen-minute connection here permitted us to get home the same night, but this was the last train in winter at 22.10.

Sunday, 7 January

Sunday cleaning at 9K on 7 January focussed on 'a lot of 44802', the 'new' engine, and the driver's side of 48504, both being fresh subjects. The week just gone had been wintry enough with its intermittent snow, but that to come was bitterly cold throughout. Working on the 8F in particular was therefore carried out in extremely unpleasant conditions. It didn't 'clean' too well either, in the proper sense and much of the exercise took the form of a light oiling, once it had been found that the dirt wouldn't come off properly. Hands, gloveless and aching with cold, either held on to the steel rail or applied

One of the earlier cleaning sessions on former Kingmoor loco 44802 at Bolton. Left to right are Keith Pendlebury, Stephen Leyland and an unremembered younger enthusiast.
Photographer unknown

paraffin to the generously proportioned boiler, smokebox and the seemingly endless expanse of firebox side. Ladders were, of course, needed to reach the tender's upper regions. A brazier burned adjacent to the water column next to 48504 and with each descent from running plate level to replenish rags or paraffin, hands were held literally, but fleetingly, in the yellow flames themselves to restore some feeling! The contrast between these conditions and those of cleaning an engine in steam, inside the shed building and in summer heat, whilst not ideal themselves, were doubtless brought longingly to mind! I have less vivid recollections of how the 'Black 5' came up on that inaugural session – not overly well I think. Of the two, only it received further attempts, which reaped better rewards, but 48504 was at least sought out photographically the following day.

Monday, 8 January to Thursday, 11 January

An iron grey, yet frosty morning of rather poor visibility saw Paul and I at Kearsley soon after 09.00 looking for 48504. Just three minutes after 4P50 (Brewery–Burnley) with 44845 (9D) had opportunely emerged from the mist with its fully fitted lamps in place, our 8F first took a short Burnden–Clifton Jc. trip before returning to work Kearsley pilot. Its chief duties were rearranging traffic in the yard close to the substantial Branch Sidings ground frame of that name and transferring coal wagons to and from the Linnyshaw Moss N.C.B. exchange point. Phil Platt, my long-term friend from earliest secondary schooldays who had gone straight to working at the shed from the classroom, was firing 48504 today and he was surprised, but pleased, to see us deliberately seeking out this very ordinary job. As ascertained from large-scale maps, the 0.9 of a mile from ground frame to Linnyshaw Moss averaged 1 in 47½. Drawing part way up this bank with at least one substantial rake, to change roads, provided less of a spectacle (but lots of gentle slipping) than might be thought. A couple of light engines went by while we were there and the local ballast engine, 44672 (10D) arrived with its brake van.

My final week at East, on lates, was with Harry Wood and Sam Thomasson. The former was a gaunt, angular man of about 55 upon whom the ravages of Capstan Full Strength had steadily taken their toll.

To me, his most irritating habit was, even on the coldest days, to bung up the cabin stove nearest my desk and shut the doors, wasting a huge amount of heat on the pretext that that was how they were supposed to be kept. He lived quite near to me in Greenland Road and, like about half the signalmen, had a car. Harry was also treasurer of the B.R. Staff Association Club in Green Lane. He and regular mate Sam had a sideline in firewood and at quieter times between them would manhandle large pieces of wood, even the odd old signal post, into the box and set to work with the two-handed saw. It's surprising what they found in the adjacent sidings! Of course, both of them leaving the cabin together flew in the face of the rule book, but I managed somehow on these occasions. Sam, a big man from Morecambe originally, possessed rather more subtle idiosyncrasies. I don't think either had much interest in railways outside the job.

That last Monday, the 8th, saw a small number of changes to timetabled traffic, but virtually no specials, even all week. The ballast engine we'd seen at Kearsley was first to appear, heading for Bullfield with three on. No. 45104 was turned off 9K mid-afternoon to replenish the area's frost fires. Noticeably substantial was the Halliwell–Burnden tripper's load of fifty, with 45110. The 16.50 Heysham–Burnden's engine, 45342 (10A), instead of repairing to 9K for the night, later (20.41) took out the 19.32 Bolton–Moston, 7J13, hitherto a separate 9K loco duty. This wasn't due to a failure or anything as the same arrangement applied on the 9th, too. By the third night, the train was coming into Bolton circuited as 'Heysham–Moston', i.e. one train, albeit with a lengthy traffic stop at Bolton, but doing away with 7J13, for that's how it continued. It continued via Clifton too, not Castleton, and often with a heavy load south of Bolton. The loco still returned to 9K after finishing at Moston and the diagram (see 5P05, page 13) remained otherwise unaltered. The re-routing applied to certain traffic that normally used Castleton South curve, which was closed for several weeks to permit the completion of bridge work there in connection with the M62 motorway construction. Some trains reversed at Castleton East Jc. instead.

So, for some time, evening steam levels on the Bury line were well down. On the 9th I actually noted four goods sent the new way (including both Horwich–Moston mid-afternoon, a mere four minutes apart, 48380 and 48702 with thirty-nine on between them), but not the second Burnley–Moston, 5J10, so this must still have been booked via Clifton. In the early spring when Castleton curve was open for business again, this train too joined the evening procession up Broadfield bank. The Heysham–Burnden and second Bolton–Moston that were about to be recognised as one train were both powered on 9 January by 44715, an ex

Responding to the unexpected attentions to his lowly duty (Kearsley pilot), Phil Platt puts on a little smoke as the crew await the next move. The distorted rear part of the LH running plate on 48504 is discernible. The date is 8 January 1968.
S.A. Leyland

No. 48773 stands at Kearsley Branch Sidings as pilot there. On 16 July 1965 the locomotive became derailed there after being unable to control the load behind it down the steep gradient from Linnyshaw Moss. *Ray Farrell/M.L.S. collection*

Workington loco that, because of the following evidence we mistook, hook, line and sinker, for a transfer to 9K. It returned to Bolton shed after 7J13, but instead of fulfilling the diagram was tried out on station pilot on the 11th and 12th. After that it was not seen running again and the 4-6-0 had certainly been taken out of use by 21 January (officially by 27 January) and dumped at 9K, where it remained until sold for scrap. When the national magazines finally caught up with actual events, their listings showed it as reallocated 12D to Trafford Park, which we took to be an error or misprint. The British Transport Enthusiasts Guild, to which I remained a member for its bulletins, though I'd long since ceased to participate in shed visits with them, had the loco as withdrawn from Workington, also obviously a mistake. Had it ever reached 9E between New Year and my 9 January observation? I'd think not. Why didn't Bolton despatch it to the Manchester depot instead of appropriating it? No. 44715 was a curious case, but present day research is a wonderful thing, and through the good offices of Mr Richard Strange, the scrap sale paperwork is known to acknowledge its physical location (9K), whilst stating its official base as Trafford Park.

A Bolton 8F, 48559, which I'd last seen at work hauling Brindle Heath–Horwich on the 3rd, was condemned at about this stage in the current week. A Rugby engine for many years, it had become Crewe South based in August 1965, prior to making the move to 9K two years later, so it hadn't been with us for so long.

The cabin coal that afternoon of the 9th had become a frozen, solid mass under the snow and a right old job to break up and bring inside. Harry Wood, mentioned above, often offered me a lift home in his Ford Anglia. By the time we'd walked to it and were ready to move off on winter nights the time gained was negligible! His foot-to-the-floor revving, the moment the engine fired in such cold conditions had even I, who had no interest in cars then, or for long after, taking pity on the poor old motor! It was minus 2½°C when I got home that evening. Though still under foot, we'd had less snow than much of the country but more fell locally on the 10th with the rest of the week staying largely sub-zero.

My last two evenings at East adopted that superficially curious trait of being noticeably busier than usual, without the contents of my notebook bearing this out. It's my diary that says so. The latent activity in cases like these lay in shunts and pilot movement, which required, by regulation, to be recorded on the instruments and therefore in the register. Blocking back, inside or outside the home signal and shunting into the forward section were common manoeuvres at East that carried their own associated bell codes and respective cancelling codes when each movement was completed. No. 45110 doubled up as 'B' Side pilot for a time on the 10th, as well as one of the afternoon trippers. The first Heysham–Moston 'through' train was worked by 45001 (10A), which arrived hauling only twelve vehicles, but loaded to 41=46 at departure. Goods train loadings were 'circuited' from box to box by phone. In this example 41=46 means the actual load of 41 wagons was equal to 46 either in length or weight. One's own observations could only quote the actual number with accuracy. For me to have known this second statistic the re-marshalling must have been carried out in 'B' Side (formerly at Burnden) and the new formation reversed down the back of the box towards O.B. in order to clear the points for turning it out onto the Manchester line.

Whether due to a sense of occasion or not I can't recall, but on the morning of my last day, the 11th (Thursday), I took a couple of photographs from the old cattle pens off Moncrieffe Street that featured the signal box with mid-morning workings there. Against the source of pale sunshine with snow underfoot are preserved on 'enprints' of the day the first two steam entries on the following list, which (after lunch) show a representative late turn of the immediate period.

That Halliwell–Healey Mills run, an incidental extra to the SO train, 7N55, was the last I ever saw mid-week. It will be noticed that the non-appearance or non-availability of 45001 (10A) ex Heysham–Moston of the night before caused 9K locos to cover the Ballast and Bedford parcels duties. My notes of the time, transcribed here very many years later, fail to explain the almost simultaneous departures of 45444 and 44664, depending just where the Moston goods set off from after attaching, but this is of little importance.

A departure of personal importance from the box that night at 22.00 proved to be nowhere near as final as I expected it to be, though I wouldn't return as an employee again. It was a measure of the kindness and friendliness of some of the men in particular that I would be welcomed to that narrow interior on a not infrequent basis for almost twice the length of time that I'd worked there. Disproportionate it seems, until one recalls the kindred spirit that railwaymen had for one another, and some may still have in that vastly changed industry. Could it be that I'd been considered one of them?

D7610	04.05 Carlisle–Moston goods	10.24
44715 (9E)	Station pilot	
D222	08.30 Brewery–Carlisle SX	10.45
D7634	Millerhill–Glodwick Rd. Vans	10.57
48740 (9K)	Brewery–Horwich (28) SX	11.20
48652 (9K)	Halliwell–Healey Mills (50) Normally SO	11.35
(Break for lunch – late turn observations follow)		
48702 (9K)	Brindle Heath–Horwich SX	13.47
D5292	Trackliner to Nuneaton	13.52
D5136	Carlisle–Ashburys vans 5H17 (51) SX	14.21
45381 (9K)	Ballast to Bullfield (3) SX	14.22
45318 (9K)	Haslams Sdgs–Halliwell (29) SX	14.34
48740 (9K)	Horwich–Moston (39) SX	14.42
45342 (10A)	13.50 Blackpool N–Manchester parcels SX	(time not noted)
45318 (9K)	Westhoughton–Burnden (15) SX	16.15
45318 (9K)	Halliwell–Burnden (40) SX	17.10
45284 (8A)	16.40 Burnley–Moston (12) SX	17.55
D5142	17.45 Manchester–Preston 1P33 (Glasgow portion)	18.03
D5203	18.05 Manchester–Blackpool N. parcels SX	18.24
45444 (10D)	16.50 Heysham–Moston (31/45) SX	19.23/20.32
D5153	20.05 Bolton–Wigan parcels 3F17 SX	(time not noted)
44664 (9K)	20.20 Bolton–Bedford parcels SX	dep. 20.33
45382 (10F)	20.57 Bolton–Guide Bridge parcels SX	dep. 20.53
Cl. 8F	19.05 Burnley–Moston (25) SX	20.58
45342 (10A)	20.55 Manchester–Heysham ('Boat Train')	21.16
D5151	20.00 Ancoats–Carlisle 5P18 (17/29) SX	(time not noted)
44947 (9K)	17.45 Colne–Ashton Moss parcels SX	dep. 21.46

Just how fleeting had been my own involvement is brought to mind by a last reflection on that topic. The men at East used to maintain that the only driver capable of leaving Haslams Sidings with a train to speak of that would never cause his engine to slip was Jack Byrne; a small, quiet man of long experience who did think about his work.

He lived just a bit further down Walker Avenue to myself. Because he was known universally at the shed as Jack 'Bryn' I took this to be his real name. He never corrected me whenever I not infrequently shouted 'Hello Mr Bryn', thinking perhaps 'cheeky teenager' (though I wasn't), or suspecting where I'd picked up the derivation, forgave me. At least two other lifelong railwaymen lived on Walker Avenue; Mr Fred Greenfield, one time Station Master at Great Moor Street, later at Trinity Street, and only next door to me resided retired goods guard Ernest Meadowcroft, who had a long service plaque, which I only saw when his granddaughter cleared out the house.

So what was my twelve months to their service and that of countless others? Despite the obvious answer, the year that not much more than chance had sparked off meant more to me than I can adequately express here. It had enriched my appreciation of and passion for a railway that had changed so much in 1967, afforded a glimpse at least from a rare standpoint of the real railway world, from the inside, been educational, and introduced me to signalling and to many splendid characters too. So, it's 'au revoir' to East, not yet 'goodbye' as it will play a minor part in this portrayal of steam's last phase through the eyes of one now on 'civvy street'.

Leaving the railway also meant making sacrifices, though having carefully weighed up all the things that would change as a result, I clearly was prepared to accept this and considered the move to be beneficial overall for reasons explained. I finished on the Thursday night, the 11th, having a rest day and one day's holiday to my credit. One of the sacrifices just alluded to was privilege travel and I used up the facility next morning on two returns to Preston and Manchester (valid one month) before handing in my uniform and 'priv' card. This purchase was to cover known journeys I would make on Saturday too and to which I was entitled. Reasons for non-production of the card, should it have been requested, would have been easily verifiable.

Friday, 12 January

For Friday the 12th I'd decided to sample the 12.17 ex Preston, dinnertime Glasgow, while the opportunity presented itself (no other weekday would, as I probably

Steam abounds around 45345 (10D) at the long-vanished Liverpool Exchange station before it departs with the SuO 09.50 to Preston (portion for Glasgow) on 21 January 1968. Its return working would be the 16.53 Preston–Liverpool Ex. On weekdays the 09.00 version of the train depicted gave its engine to the 12.17 Preston–Manchester, already encountered and seen again in the next photo. *P. Barber*

Some weeks later than the author's 12 January 1968 run on the 12.17 Preston–Manchester, 44735, as seen here, worked the train on 1 March. Hurrying along the Up Fast at Farington Curve Jc., this engine was still officially based at Trafford Park until the forthcoming weekend closure of that depot brought it to Newton Heath's door. *I.C. Simpson*

realised), and for which the first set of tickets was procured. In Preston by 11.30 without having seen anything out of the ordinary, I noted the loco for 1J42, as expected, stabled in the Up bay adjacent to platform 6. Newton Heath engines at this time (like most others) had a particularly drab uniformity in their appearance. Quite recently, many 9D 'Black 5s' had been given a smokebox repaint. The shine had not entirely disappeared under the dirt of their environment. Since the repaint nobody had redone the numberplates in white, or the shed code, and that near anonymous front end was the 'Newton Heath look' of late 1967 into 1968 that everyone got to know so well.

Before the train I awaited came in, a northbound goods passed (amongst others), which had become unique as the only regular steam working since New Year north of Oxenholme on the main line. This was the 09.15 Clitheroe–Shap, 5P14, Scheduled MWFO (and an hour late today with fifteen wagons). This loaded cement train used Lostock Hall motive power, 44683 being the loco I saw. It returned from Shap soon after arrival with empties as 5P16, due through Preston at 16.50. It did not, I understand, retain steam for too much longer.

With a clear road passing Bolton engine shed, the 12.17 Preston–Manchester gets smartly into speed, hauled by an unknown 'Black 5'. Date not recorded. *P. Salveson*

1M27 from Glasgow arrived punctually and the rear portion for Manchester, 1J42, was able to leave at 12.18 with seven coaches. The engine, 45076 (9D), about which I wasn't too optimistic, accelerated to a respectable 53mph through Leyland, but still lost two minutes on the impossible seven-minute booking to passing Euxton Jc. Climbing the 1 in 134 of Chorley bank at 45–48mph to the station conspired to further prove me wrong about our loco and the 4-6-0 ran very well from this point too, 64 through Adlington getting up to 71mph after Blackrod on the lightly falling grades. The 40mph onto the Slow line, as booked, at Lostock Jc. was adhered to and despite a check to 10 approaching the short Moor Lane tunnels, the express stopped on time at Trinity Street after a slick twenty-seven-minute run. Held two minutes over at Bolton, on to Manchester 64mph was the fastest speed, a slowing to 20 at Agecroft Jc. preventing a strictly punctual arrival, though we were less than a minute in arrears finishing. I'd picked a good one after all!

I can't think of a better way to illustrate how the place of one's abode influences the life one leads. Had I been brought up in Ullapool or Caister-on-Sea, for example, how would 1968 have panned out for me? Would steam still (or have ever been) be influential in my life, or even dominate it as was the case? In the whole scope of place-to-place distances in the British Isles, we in Bolton were so fortunate to be a mere 20 miles or so from the final epicentre of steam activity on B.R.; and now, as the year opened, in as good a place as any. This was where it was at, to coin an 'in' phrase of the times. Preston had provided varied steam activity in the half hour or so over midday.

After departure we'd crossed Caprotti 5, 73134 (9H) on northbound coal at Euxton Jc., encountered 73067 (9H) on a Windsor Bridge shunt soon after noting our own 48702 on Brindle Heath–Horwich in the loop at Pepper Hill and 73040 LE home through Manchester Vic., as well as the pilots (two 'Black 5s') there. Another 9K stalwart, 48652, headed the same way with empty coal and only eight minutes later Patricroft's 48491 with a longer goods; nothing unusual really for the period. A lot of steam enthusiasts noted only the action with that motive power. Pretty well all of the alternative these days, well into the twenty-first century, comes under the category of 'Heritage Diesel Traction'. We didn't see it like that then of course, but I've never regretted excluding only dmus from my written records. The 09.50 Newcastle–Liverpool dropped into Exchange station that day on time, as well it might with 'twin-Peak' haulage of D40 and D188! Final observation of the trip, however, proved to be of the slightly odd circumstances (see 8-11 January) of 44715 (9E) on its last day of operation as it fulfilled Bolton station pilot.

During an earlier session at Manchester Vic. following a 12.17 run, 45271 demonstrates the 'Newton Heath (front end) look' as one of the Victoria pilots, whilst Bolton's 48166 runs up to the east end thirteen hours after leaving 9K for the duty known as Patricroft–Crumpsall. On this occasion the banker for this train was 45246 (9D). *S.A. Leyland*

I'd been a member of the Bolton Youth Orchestra for several years. Rehearsals were on Friday evenings at Derby Street school and generally enjoyable to one degree or another. Thursday was choir practice at St Simon & St Jude, where my Dad was organist. Signal box hours during 1967 had restricted me to every other week at best attending these musical alternatives to the railway. In 1968 I quickly got into the routine of heading for the sheds or station straight afterwards to catch up on what was happening and on Fridays to discuss Saturday's trip with my friends, usually Paul, Vern and Keith, until the gathering enlarged as the winter wore on with new acquaintances who'd 'done' the 'Boat Train' to Bolton. Sometimes I didn't make it in time to see the 'Boat', as per tonight, the 12th. Northwich was decided, though in the event only Keith and I went. Certain irregular railway attractions sometimes pulled at my conscience over orchestral obligations. Age-wise I was nearing the end of 'Youth' and could with dignity have left on those grounds alone, and in fact did so, but not until just before the end of steam. The choir retained my loyalty.

Saturday, 13 January

In the forthcoming few months, utilisation of the Up 'Boat' as a springboard for trips within or beyond Manchester for we Boltonians increased dramatically. Whilst the train didn't provide the earliest possible arrival on the scene (always an advantage with freight-orientated objectives on a Saturday), it did run early enough not to jeopardise those objectives. The steam haulage proved irresistible in the majority of cases, though the day's destination was generally reached an hour or so later than the first service train from Bolton permitted. Waiting for the 'Boat' on the 13th, however, did jeopardise our connection at Manchester Central as the Heysham had been delayed by a derailment at Bay Horse and, with 45342 (10A) ended up thirty-one minutes late leaving Bolton. A poor road between Farnworth and Clifton Jc., probably due to something ahead, extended the journey time to more than twenty minutes and kept the top speed down to 53mph, but we just caught the intended dmu to Northwich.

Opposite: Water columns come in many and varied types. This clever design at Manchester Victoria's platform 17 enables the fireman of 45420 (9D) to operate the valve from where he is standing. The engine was one of the pilots on 30 March 1968. *T. Heavyside*

Above: The I.C.I. block limestone hopper trains went over to Type 2 diesel haulage in 1964, so it is likely that 48036 (8E) is covering for one out of service. A banker, 48617 (8E), has been taken for the climb out of Northwich during the frosty dawn of 4 January 1968. *I.C. Simpson*

Without the availability of banking engines at the steeply uphill beginning and end of the loaded limestone runs, the Type 2s in my opinion could not have managed. For the 10.06 Tunstead–Oakleigh on 13 January 1968 assistance is given to D5275 as 48727 (8E) shoves mightily whilst the train crosses the A533 Middlewich road. The author's notes suggest that the cold weather had got the better of his ability to write anything down by this time as several lines are in another hand! *S.A. Leyland*

A measurable depth of snow lay underfoot. It had lodged too in the horizontal pointing of the Dane and Weaver viaduct, around which we spent an encouragingly busy morning for traffic. The loadings of goods trains seen varied rather more than the types of steam locos used to haul them, there being a not unexpectedly near resident 8F monopoly. In the two hours after our 09.40 arrival, seven freights were noted with steam and slightly less than that diesel worked, but in addition were several light engines and EBVs in the former category. Such activity until just after dinner created a diversion from the cold. Despite the leaden skies I doubt that it got above zero all day and I couldn't prevent the cutting, but not particularly strong, wind out of the east from interfering with my recordings at times, even at ground level. After dabbling with a £5 portable Japanese spools recorder since 1963, I'd been seriously tape recording the sounds of steam on a Philips model 3301 cassette machine since November 1966. This medium was rapidly taking precedence over photography on a personal level and was only a month away from eclipsing it completely until mid-summer.

The most industrious of several locos observed at Northwich was 48727 (8E), seen on two goods and on banking duty, too. The heaviest steam-hauled job, a mixed goods of fifty-six wagons, came south behind 48639 (8E). The 2-8-0 took what little run it could at the 1 in 100 over the viaduct but soon slowed to walking pace, experiencing frequent though brief wheelslips as its long train straddled the steepest grade and the broken and less severe slope on towards Hartford East Jc.

We trudged east along the Weaver's bank to vary the day's photographic efforts, amused by the railway-style semaphore signals by the lock gates there, then back to see at closer quarters one of the block I.C.I limestone trains, 5F66 (10.06 Tunstead–Oakleigh) banked vigorously out of Northwich by 48727.

This train was not booked for assistance, but I've always thought that those Type 2s (D5275 in this case), doing the work of regular class 8 steam, must have had little or nothing in reserve, except downhill. These hopper formations, which we saw a lot of in the coming weeks, seemed to be the preserve of a near consecutive batch of six engines. Later still, with traffic tailing off, we found Hartford North Jc. box (controlling access to the massive I.C.I complex at Oakleigh) and were grateful for being permitted inside for an hour or so, not the least for the warmth offered. Unable to resist mentioning my very recent departure from signalling, this brought forth an offer to work some levers and bells, bringing a special and unexpected feature to the day.

In the yard of the Stanier 8F monopolised allocation at Northwich mpd plenty of engines are lit up for work in this Sunday view from mid-1967, as well as of the industrial backdrop that justified their existence.
Peter Reeves/M.L.S. collection

Still to be had, once more exposed to the elements and getting on for mid-afternoon, were the return working of 48639, which sounded as if a hot box had developed part way along its train, 48036 (8E) on coal empties up the bank with a terrible bang in its motion, or more likely axle boxes, and 48746 (8A) LE home from Oakleigh off an arrival we seem to have missed. Despite possession of a current Working Timetable (WTT) on the day, the identity of most steam-hauled freights could be not much more than guessed at and Northwich trip workings weren't, of course, included in the book. Two goods via Northwich that became prominent in our endeavours during the spring were not knowingly seen today, probably due to late running, to which both, it transpired were prone.

Soon wearied again by the cold and (I suspect) inadequate footwear, and clearly with the best activity behind us, Keith and I found a cafe for an early tea, where we became the focus of some curiosity for a couple of girls. After that the journey back to Manchester still left us with a three-and-a-half-hour wait at Victoria for the evening's 'Boat' and the wonder is that we'd not visited Northwich shed where welcoming and warm, but slowly cooling, footplates beckoned in a probably deserted depot. Eighteen months earlier, and with the same colleague, a planned trip to that same shed was as perverse an objective on a June Saturday as omitting to do so had been now! This view is expressed nearly fifty years later, but I stand by it. And so, on 13 January 1968 the wait on Victoria was alleviated by alternate games of cards and football, until, most likely, others began to arrive for the run.

The express was a full twenty minutes late away that night, 45342 (10A) having seven coaches and a long van. A fairly good 48–49mph after Clifton Jc. was cut short to less than half that after Farnworth, putting paid to any recovery there might have been in running to Bolton, where 5five and a half minutes were gained on the stop. Similarly, on to Chorley, a brief stand approaching Lostock Jc. wiped out sure gain as we reached a fine 69mph after Adlington. Why did keen drivers so often not get the chances they deserved? Despite station cuts again, the theoretical turn round time at Preston for the last train back (22.10 in winter) was down to one and a half minutes. Rarely was this 'connection' cut so fine when enthusiasts had to gamble on getting home or not, but the 'extra' (but really expected) steam mileage weighed heavily against a half-hour wait at Chorley, especially for those holding tickets! Providing even a slender chance existed, most tended to stay the course, as will be seen in future

Above: No. 92218 (8C) on Northwich loco shed on 2 March 1968, prior to working the 11.15 Oakleigh–Corkickle I.C.I. soda ash hoppers (covhops) on the last day of steam operation from 8E depot. *I.C. Simpson*

cases. In this instance no one was stranded as 45342 picked up just the one-minute recovery time laid down in the Working Timetable (WTT) without any sign of the big displays that drivers were occasionally given to on this potentially fast section. Lostock Hall's 43033, one of several still in use from that class at 10D, performed station pilot duties at Preston that night. These Ivatts seemed to enjoy a popular run thus engaged, then disappear forever, but this was to some extent just an impression gained.

Illustrating the proximity of Northwich mpd to the station is this 25 February 1968 view showing 48224 (8E) and another 2-8-0. *T. Heavyside*

Inside Bolton mpd and withdrawn five weeks earlier stands 73156 on New Year's Eve 1967. In the middle is 45001 (10A), which will power Bolton Ballast working at West Jc. the next morning, and on the right 44664 still has some useful time ahead of it. *Peter Reeves/M.L.S. collection*

Sunday, 14 to Friday, 19 January

Sunday afternoon I was down at 9K, but not to clean, perhaps the others were. I was also not there, it seems, to make any permanent record of the shed's contents and current loco status, a lamentable trait of mine during 1968, especially in view of the useful and detailed listings compiled since October 1966. Oh, how do those far too spaced out latter-day entries contrast with earlier times, and even more so the few blank pages at the end of that little file! What made me almost desist from making these records in the closing months of the depot's existence I've never been truly able to fathom. In all other 'departments' except photography my chronicling of the diminishing scene went on as before or improved in detail.

Local observations of mine through the remainder of 1968 were, by necessity, in the evening or on Saturday or Sunday. Particularly as the evenings lengthened, we increasingly went out of town for steam action because the longer hours of daylight ran in proportion to the declining attractions on our immediate doorstep. It could still be busy at Orlando bridge after tea (probably the best time to be around), but by May a large part of that traffic was diesel worked. The trends as we combated this progression through the spring and summer, plus the alternative locations in vogue, will reveal themselves in due course.

So, here I was at the other end of 1967, overlooking the other side of the railway at Bullfield from a different mill; a sort of mirror image of the situation before my year on B.R. In part of the giant Atlas spinning mill complex, Mornington Road, which had closed to its intended industry at intervals during the 1960s, a new kind of textile process had come to inhabit one (and later two) of the gaunt and empty floors, but still only a tiny part of that once taken up by Musgraves. The flame lamination of foam to a wide range of fabrics was the business of W.W. Chamberlain, a company based in the Midlands. The firm underwent two name changes in the next seven and a half years and with the second I was compulsorily out. Impressions on my first day, 15 January, were lukewarm. Hours worked on occasion in the opening months would clash with my new and vital plan to be free to follow steam at weekends. Just as at Eagle Mill, endeavours to establish the presence of steam on certain workings by carefully timed gazing in the right direction never came to anything; not even a reprimand for loitering!

The dark weekday evenings of early 1968 soon re-established a pattern of very local steam observation personally. My friends carried on as they had done. The only night I missed that week commencing 14 January was Tuesday when we congregated at Paul's house – he lived nearest to Bolton shed – to trace earlier allocations of many 26C and 9K engines; a mistimed exercise, maybe? Monday had revealed 73156 as sold to Woodham Bros., of Barry, but it wasn't to depart just yet. On still active machines I painted a buffer beam 'Bolton', the last it seems of a protracted practice of mine. No. 48702 was never eligible for this small adornment and 73040 neither with our home shed name, but along with a coloured numberplate background scheme of around

33

Less well known than 73069 generally, 73040 in decent lined black was looked after by the unofficial cleaners at 9K too, though in 1968 it fulfilled little other than station pilot until the pair went to Patricroft in April. *P. Barber*

Several minutes after our worthwhile but unidentified 'Black 5' sighting at Green Lane bridge on 17 January, Pete from Gorton, still unknown to us I think, alighted at Bolton from that same 'Belfast Boat Express' and took this photo of 45390 (10A). Only very many years later when compiling a motive power list for the train did this identity come to light. On the opposite platform a dmu works the 20.02 Liverpool Ex.– Manchester Vic. In the summer of 1965 we were seeing this train as an Agecroft steam working with timings at most a minute different from those applying in 1968, as far as Bolton.
P. Barber

two years earlier, authenticity took second place to distinction. A few Bolton locos *had* been through Cowlairs Works over the years and returned with the 'real McCoy' confirming their allocation. Wednesday's walk to Green Lane bridge for the 'Boat', its engine's customary shutting off point, was worthwhile for a lively enough approach, even if 1P02's steed was unidentified in the darkness. 45382 (10F) on Bolton–Guide Bridge parcels and 44758 (10A) with forty wagons on Bolton–Moston also appeared in the twelve minutes just after 9pm. The 'Boat's' anonymity persevered the night after too as it passed the mpd, where a failed 44971 (10D) had found refuge. On Friday the 19th after orchestra rehearsal we telephoned Lostock Hall and Carnforth depots, maybe for a specific reason as to Saturday's workings, but Paul and I elected to visit Peak Forest the next day.

Saturday, 20 January

A 'Boat Train' start to the day saw Carnforth's 45390 (perhaps the anonymous loco of midweek?) on seven coaches leave Bolton virtually to time and make quite a smart run, getting up to 66mph before Clifton Jc., taken at 64, and reaching Manchester just ahead of schedule, despite a mild signal check. Apart from engines at rest on Bolton and Stockport depots, the only other steam in action en route proved to be 73134 (9H) taking out the empty stock of the still steam-worked 05.45 Wigan NW–Manchester Exchange, 1C50, a portion of the 23.55 Glasgow–Liverpool. The Patricroft engine that worked 1C50 was booked LE to shed upon the train's 06.20 arrival. Sleeping car passengers were permitted to remain in their berths until the more civilised hour of 07.30, hence the stock not being taken up to Red Bank C.S. by the Exchange pilot until close to the time noted today, 08.09. This move and that of the Heysham stock ensured a fine show up the tough, curved and steeply graded immediate climb from the platform ends, and one that we subsequently took advantage of a number of times by rushing on foot to a thoroughfare also known as Red Bank at the end of the 1 in 59 section, where the sound effects never disappointed!

Buxton mpd of late had been getting by on the steam side with just a handful of 8F 2-8-0s and the latest end of steam projection included 9L in the next round of depot closures, not that time spent at the well-known Midland main line summit restricted one to locos based solely at the nearby spa town. Unfamiliar with the environs of Peak Forest itself, beyond what could be gathered from a passing, or even a stopping train, the trip of 20 January was to 'grab' me in no uncertain way and ensured a number of returns in the little time that was left. I probably expected to be 'grabbed' as a particular fondness for the rugged locale had its origins in previous journeys over the Midland route, to Buxton or further afield.

Dove Holes by then was (and still is) the closest open station to Peak Forest. Today's schedule got us on the scene at going up for 10am; late, but this stone and ballast quarrying district ensured that all four trips made pulled steam activity 'out of the hat' somewhat later in the day than could be reasonably expected at many other locations on a Saturday by then. A wide, grass-covered ledge on the Up side of Peak Forest's largely sheer rock cutting, halfway between Dove Holes (Midland) tunnel's southern portal and the summit, and above chimney height, made an ideal base from which to tape record southbound trains on the 1 in 90 grade. First up was 48620 (9D) under fairly light steam (I suspect he'd eased) with thirty-four iron ore empties on 7H57, the 08.29 Dewsnap–Buxton.

Only the Down line was currently open through the tunnel due to work being carried out within. Though this turned to the advantage of the tape recordist in general, Up trains were shutting off steam a short way after our location to drop off pilotmen and negotiate the crossover at Peak Forest North box.

No. 48191 (9F) enters the magnificent Peak Forest cutting on 17 February 1968 hauling the 12.00 Tunstead–Runcorn. Five exposures by the author that day represented his last photography for more than four months in favour of tape recording only. The ledge occupied on 20 January for that purpose can be seen on the left. *S.A. Leyland*

Fully discovering the late Peter Barber's photographs late in the year 2017 has expanded more than one pleasant coincidence from nearly fifty years earlier. Our paths fleetingly crossing at Dove Holes station during my successful retreat to Peak Forest on 24 February, he left no recorded note of his own observations, but here on that day in glorious sunshine is another view of the 12.00 Tunstead–Runcorn, passing by Peak Forest North signal box, hauled by 48252 (9F). *P. Barber*

Well over an hour elapsed before the next steam working, but then 48465 (9L) blasted beneath Paul and I with great vigour on a load of coal, providing the sort of action with which I associated the line. Shopping Proposal forms for 8Fs (and probably other goods engine types) that regularly worked in the Peak District were endorsed with a rubber stamp to that exact effect, as if to inform the workshop concerned that such locos lived on the whole a more taxing life in the rugged terrain and long, steep climbs for which that part of Derbyshire was famed. At least that's how I interpreted it. Following the coal train, tender first and hopelessly late, came 48252 (9F), the engine for 8F56, the 12.00 Tunstead–Runcorn, a SO train of 'covhops' for which Heaton Mersey provided power.

On this first trip to Peak Forest, outside the I.C.I, limestone hoppers structure, diesels were absent on timetabled goods, except for the banker down at Great Rocks. The line hung onto its main line status, for although the 'Peak' hauled St Pancras expresses had recently been diverted away from Manchester Central to Piccadilly, they (until later in 1968) still ran via Matlock. The attractive maroon and white enamel sign, '985 Feet Above Sea Level' therefore continued to inform passengers of their altitude and by inference the reason that their train had not been travelling very quickly over the last few miles. This latter trait, however, was less noticeable with contemporary power (D76 on the 08.00 from St Pancras for example) on six or seven coaches than with the somewhat heavier average loads hauled by class 6 or 7 steam a few years earlier.

Shifting position now on this grey, but not particularly cold day, we called in at Peak Forest South signal box where the friendly 'bobby' divulged various information that led to our walking by an unrecalled route to Great Rocks, further down the 1 in 90, but the provision of D5139 as banker on 8F56 (see above) at 14.12 ensured an undelayed return to the summit. A Buxton-based Type 2 on that duty (though maybe not known to us in advance of the trip) had evidently been the norm for some time. Thereafter we generally kept our distance from those rasping, discordant air horns. Though it proved impossible to escape the sound completely, bankers at least tended to drop off far enough from the summit to have minimal interference with tape recordings made around the closed Peak Forest station itself. Less unpalatable from afar and heard repeatedly in the course of a full day's trip, those air horns, given the acoustic treatment peculiar to that craggy locality, quickly imprinted upon my mind their distinctive muted raucousness as being unique to an area of which I was rapidly becoming very fond.

Viewed from aloft, Peak Forest South, including the signal box, is host to 48191 (9F), which has steam on just over the actual summit with a goods towards Buxton. The front brake van appears to have a number of 'passengers'. *P. Stamper*

Whilst briefly down at Great Rocks we attempted to investigate a derailed 8F that the South signalman not only mentioned to us, but phoned up about to check the latest. It was still there, though we didn't get close enough for identification or persist further as live steam was the objective. On the subject of sound association at Peak Forest, joining that of the Type 2s was a low, almost imperceptible hum from the lime works just north of the station. Somehow, because it was so subtle and an integral part of the district's industry, I never considered it obtrusive or a nuisance while tape recording there. It even achieved more than acceptability because of the affection I held for the place.

No. 48620 (9D), seen earlier, had been retained to work a ballast back towards Manchester, doubtless in readiness for some Sunday P-Way work. The necessity of stopping to pick up a pilotman at the summit (actually North box) enabled two recordings to be made from the limestone works. The 8F's sedate ascent contrasted with a vigorous restart that included a 'heavy duty' wheelslip that lasted for just two exhaust beats and an elaborate 'crow' whistle to anyone inside the tunnel. Waiting another hour and a half until around teatime produced only modern power on regular block loads and the return of D1810, seen earlier on an anonymous 7Z70 towards Buxton. It now reappeared on what we in due course discovered to be part of a protracted series of special trains conveying massive limestone boulders for a dock extension at Port Talbot. We were lucky to get one steam-hauled a month hence, when I will provide full details. Despite not more than 25% steam on the traffic seen, we returned very happy about the day's action.

Ample time remained before the by now customary evening activity to call in at Stockport Edgeley mpd, a diversion that must have involved an illicit break of journey on a day return ticket. Stockport's allocation was now down to twenty 'Black 5s' and 8Fs only. A few were missing, but countered numerically by local (mainly Heaton Mersey) visitors. No. 92218 (8C) was the only engine I marked down as in steam, though others were doubtless in the advanced stages of cooling down. The seven condemned machines on shed were not all resident. This turned out to be my last visit to 9B of quite a number over the previous few years. Shed visits, except for Bolton, were few and far between for me during 1968.

The subsequent 'Boat Train' run that evening was low on excitement, 'but I stayed on to Preston', which implies that I'd not pre-purchased a ticket first thing as I often did

Though taken just prior to closure, a similar sight would have greeted our 20 January call at Stockport Edgeley on the way home from Peak Forest. Home engines 45046 (left) and 45200 have finished for the weekend on 27 April 1968. *I.C. Simpson*

A daytime view of Stockport shed a few weeks earlier showing, in the yard at least, a roughly 50/50 diesel and steam split. *P. Barber*

The imposing presence of the old L & Y train departures indicator greeted one as the subway steps led onto platform 12 at Manchester Victoria. Here it is after dark on 13 January 1968, confirming to the photographer, as well as to Keith and I after our prolonged wait, that the 'Belfast Boat Express' did indeed leave from there as usual, SuX. *P. Barber*

now when intending to finish the day that way. On paper, 45390's (or should it be the driver's?) efforts look OK – five minutes late from Vic., two late into Preston, but it was the cutting of station times that 'rescued' poor running. A top speed of 50mph by Agecroft Jc. fell off to a dire 37 by Moses Gate, followed by 61mph maximum only on to the Chorley stop, and about the same near Farington after a check. Without the check 1P02 would have been virtually punctual into Preston, but should a driver stake everything on keen platform staff and a clear road to ensure the desired effect? Of course, this is all assuming that the driver has enough steam and that the engine isn't a very rough rider, to name just two factors hidden from the general passenger inclined to complain. No. 45390, though far from prominent on the diagram in recent times, had put in a complete week as recently as November 1967, so wasn't in the 'never used' league of Carnforth's worst.

British Railways Steam 1968

With smokebox facing the station, 73040 shunts in 'A' Side in the course of Bolton station pilot work, to which it was so accustomed by 28 March 1968 when this view from the footbridge was taken. *V.A. Sidlow*

Sunday, 21 and Monday, 22 January

We'd plenty of work on the afternoon of the 21st (Sunday), cleaning 73040, 73069 and 45110. Vern joined us part way through following a fruitless jaunt that would have appealed to all, had we known of the opportunity. A series of small blackboards were used to line the sloped approach to Preston's No. 5 and 6 platforms. During his Saturday trip in that direction they'd told of Sunday diversions to Wigan via the Adlington Jc. to Boar's Head Jc. Line, which was rare track indeed now, and on our doorstep, too. However, no 'grice' was had because the train Vern boarded at Preston simply went direct, suggesting P-Way work cancelled at the last minute, or completed earlier than intended.

A late arrival at 9K from Workington was 44829 and though I can't pinpoint its arrival with much accuracy, it almost certainly occurred during the week ending the 21st, rather than earlier. It had been officially Bolton-based for all of January to date, its working span here amounting to fourteen weeks. My old spotting club, the B.T.E.G., was due to include 9K as part of a 'Manchester' tour that Sunday afternoon, but we didn't see them because it had been postponed until February and the coach picking up points were revised to fit in with an unexpected stipulation by B.R. that participants had to travel at least part way by rail for the society to be granted shed permits, which still weren't free! The coach fare was high at 15/- (or 75p) to offset the £2 permit charge per depot. February was deemed a successful month by the Guild because that tour did run. How things had changed!

Of our two remaining BR 5s from the dozen we received in mid-1966, 73040 was in the least sparkling condition mechanically, though the lined out black paintwork was good. It therefore spent a great deal of time between late January and early April on Trinity Street pilot. In this last

40

year of steam I actually saw it on no other duty until we lost both Standard 5s to Patricroft in a curious rumour reversal. No. 73040's movements in the aforementioned capacity during the evening of the 22nd were almost continuous and I went home (eventually) well pleased with the activity, sometimes integrated with other traffic as captured on tape from Orlando footbridge. Even Paul's rather battered machine was given an airing that night!

Conversely, 73069, the last BR 5 to go through the Works (Crewe), was probably the best left in service and was currently a favourite choice for Ashton Moss parcels (as was the case that night) and the Manchester–Colne News early the next morning. A dead 8F 2-8-0 trundled through hauled by a 'Black 5' (both unidentified), we thought to Bolton mpd. It ran as an unfitted goods train (1-4-4) off the Lostock line, so my still well-tuned ear to the very nearby East Jc. box block bells interpreted. It was the only out of course working seen at O.B. Later, at the station, unexpected loco 44848 (10F) had done well on the 'Boat', being in for 21.12. Although at least one newly found friend from the evening Heysham, Peter Barber of Gorton, had alighted at Bolton, I made no lasting record of his impressions of the run. No. 44848, which made quite customary slips upon restarting, heralded a week of unsettled 'Black 5' power on 1P02 and no doubt the rest of the diagram. That loco's own solo appearance on the working came within a month of the 4-6-0's withdrawal.

The meeting of new colleagues off the 'Boat' as the train's enthusiast clientele picked up in 1968 became an added feature of the nights we didn't travel or were elsewhere for steam. At an embryonic stage were various friendships that no one expected to last what looks like being, for the majority that are still with us, a lifetime. For those no longer with us, that's what it was, albeit a short life.

So, over on the Up platforms as Pete considered a train home, we had gratuitous whistles from 73069's crew on Ashton Moss parcels, unconcerned at what the men in East Jc. thought, and Burnley–Moston's 48393 (10F) clanking through like a rough WD 2-8-0. Despite this it stayed the course until August. Around 10pm I saw Derek, the booker from East finishing, and Sam Thomasson going on for nights. New colleagues and old ones too it had been.

Tuesday, 23 to Thursday, 25 January

Paul and I walked to Bullfield West on Tuesday the 23rd for the evening 'Boat'. The flat-roofed cabin that in 1957 replaced the old box wrecked in a smash, had an immaculate interior. It was the turn of 44894, a Carnforth engine lesser used on the train in 1968, and it made what might be termed regular progress out towards Lostock Jc. Suggestive of a different driver was the 'fantastic firework display' at Green Lane the next night, now with 45212 (10D) working the first of two consecutive appearances on 1P02. This prompted Bullfield again on the 25th, also to see if the Special Traffic Notices (S.T.Ns.) had anything to offer, Thursday being the day they were generally distributed for Saturday and the coming week. Anyway, they hadn't arrived, but 5212 didn't disappoint as it hammered out of Bolton, the adjacent Randolph Street liberally showered with glowing cinders from its chimney. Of course, I'd had my tape recorder on the wrong night!

In somewhat earlier times when Vern and I both worked within easy dinnertime reach of Orlando bridge we often met to take in the activity. In continuing this laudable habit alone into 1968, his brief vigil on 25 January proved particularly fruitful, involving not the tidiest of East Jc. traffic build-ups, chiefly caused by the inopportune arrival of a fifty-wagon van special. On the Up too were 3J41, the daily, lengthy Carlisle–Red Bank empty parcels stock and the late-running 1J42 Glasgow portion for Manchester. On the Down, 45294 got out of Haslams with a Horwich trip goods just before the express left at 13.09 behind 44891 (9D). Because the van special (tender-first 73134 of Patricroft) had to draw forward off the through line to Burnden, propel onto the Down and finally draw into 'A' Sidings, the E.E. Type 4-hauled Red Bank vans had most unusually been sent forward on the goods loop. The train was then held at Burnden Jc. for some unknown reason, causing the rear of the train to foul the Bury line at East Jc! Fortunately, no conflicting passenger trains were due. In little more than fifteen minutes a lot had happened, especially when one includes station pilot (73040).

The van special was the first I knew about to be steam-hauled since Springs Branch had lost its allocation of that traction. To satisfy Bolton's burgeoning parcels and mail order business, van specials had been a feature of my year at East Jc., always off Western Lines from Wigan with a reversal at De Trafford Jc. (Hindley), when the banker became the train engine to Bolton. Points of origin of the specials were Mold Jc., Coton Hill (Salop), Llandilo and occasionally Willesden, the most intensive period I witnessed being over four days during the week ending 28 October 1967 with 242 vans in five trains; three specials plus two scheduled trains to Oldham Glodwick Road made to terminate at Bolton. Despite the obvious need for vans, Bolton never had any timetabled to supply it, only the specials, unlike Oldham. No. 73134 in this latest instance, as a visiting loco to Springs Branch, was clearly put on the job and unusual in arriving tender first. We'll meet another of these trains in late spring.

No portrayal of the whole story behind the following of B.R. steam in 1968 would be complete without relating the extremes of feeling brought about on a personal level; the difficulties, the trials and tribulations, excitements, disappointments, apprehension and deep satisfaction that were all part of steam railway enthusiasm and appreciation during those closing months. They always had been, I suppose, but now it was all coming to a head. Values were soaring and chances missed were sometimes unable to be repeated. Novice enthusiasts were arriving on the scene every day. Sparsely represented, even until the end of 1967, except on railtours and summer Saturdays, the breed in general began to increase in number on the remaining passenger workings, partly as there were fewer of these to patronise; also at the more favoured lineside locations where steam on lower-class duties could be observed to good advantage, though the latter very rarely produced the same concentration of enthusiasts in one place. Reasons for this were the unpredictability of such work and, chiefly, its more limited appeal. Non-passenger traffic powered by steam seldom caused large numbers of people to congregate by the lineside in outlying districts, even towards the very end.

The rewards at lineside positions in relative solitude, amongst considerate friends with the same objectives, could be very fulfilling if those objectives materialised in the way hoped for, but they didn't always, of course. Waiting for specific workings by the line, away from well-known and popular centres was fine for those prepared to sacrifice more steam activity for a particularly desired and/or more spectacular single event, but this introduced a considerable element of risk to the venture, depending how familiar one was (if at all) with the objective.

A freight might be so long in coming that the indications were it wasn't coming at all. Deadlines had to be considered. What was the latest time one could leave the location and still catch the last train home or to another priority? Perhaps there had been insufficient traffic for the train to run throughout, or at all. Maybe there were crewing difficulties; possibly the engine had failed or been required for another job. Had it run very early instead, or been incorrectly identified, or even been diverted? All these conjectures are related through real-life experiences, as the coming weeks will reveal. When workings failed to materialise, if a signal box was not close to hand or accessible, a phone call to the mpd responsible for motive power could be the only recourse, but time spent away from the line was risky.

Friday, 26 January

I am certain that it was the growing south Manchester contingent, brought to Bolton on the 'Boat', that alerted us to a location where none of the above uncertainties were likely to crop up. The communicator, to our enormous benefit in the coming weeks, was most likely to be John, a youthful avid of the old order, best known on account of his unbroken and at times overused voice, 'The Skelton Whine'. The location, Skelton Jc., was hardly isolated and produced goods trains practically to order! The 3.55 miles east of there to Northenden Jc. were something of a bottleneck, fed from the east by three distinct routes or traffic flows, i.e. Mottram and Godley, Guide Bridge, also Tunstead and Gowhole, the latter actually trailing in earlier at Cheadle Jc. Skelton Jc. dispensed three lines, too. On the right, Northwich-bound trains described a long anticlockwise arc on a falling gradient of 1 in 86 to join the electric line from Manchester at Deansgate Jc., while the middle route to Glazebrook and the left-hand one to Arpley made short, sharp ascents to fly over the Northwich on fairly straight courses and grades of 1 in 72 and 1 in 86 respectively. Trains came from and went to a multitude of points other than those named. Skelton Jc. box was a tall affair with thirty-five steps from ground level and it controlled some tall signals too, all in the interests of sighting and visibility, of course. From it those three freight-only lines fanned out into open and seemingly common land, though the footpath that crossed all three was the only true public way. The path went under the two ascending lines, then up onto a long concrete bridge that took it over the one to Northwich, a seeming extravagance, but in times past it had spanned sidings and a turntable. Little or no evidence of this remained, even in 1968.

Saturday, 27 January

I should divulge no more until we ourselves had got there on that first trip and the reader has done so in imagination via what is set down here. The usual late Friday meeting had come down in favour of Skelton Jc. for Saturday the 27th with all the Bolton four. No. 45342 (10A) had returned to the 'Boat' for a few days. Leaving three minutes late on seven coaches, it provided an uninspiring run to Manchester, which, despite speeds mainly in the mid-50s (max 58mph) nevertheless recovered half the arrears. Half a minute after arriving, 73142 (9H) took out the Glasgow ECS for Queens Road. We probably waited for the boat train's stock to head the same way, but neither were tape recorded.

An emu run from Oxford Road to Timperley got us to Skelton Jc. shortly after 09.00 and we joined the clutch of enthusiasts that generally congregated just off the footpath a little below rail level, but not far from the summit flyovers. Though less of a vantage point, it was less exposed than the bridge at this time of year. Tuesdays to Fridays, the busiest time, there was a goods scheduled through the junction on average every 10.1 minutes in each twenty-four-hour period. The three Saturday mornings I spent there produced in the region of twenty trains (similar to the number scheduled) and a steam percentage of just over 40%, except for today when it stood much higher at 60%. None of the most commonly represented depots, i.e. 8A, 8C, 8E, 9B, 9F and 9L, had more than ten weeks left to them; half that in some cases, so we were in the right place. By this stage even the lower-classed freight work was susceptible to either form of motive power.

Earlier I described the location as if facing west because it was the westbound locomotives attacking their respective 'ramps', chiefly on loaded hauls, that provided the elemental interest and excitement. Trains for Northwich and beyond, often under cautionary signals protecting Deansgate Jc., usually trundled round slowly when not actually halted. The splendid steam frequency

Opposite: Star performer at Skelton Jc. on 11 February was 44871 (9B) as described in the account of that day. Here, it ascends the tough rise on the Arpley line. *V.A. Sidlow*

No. 48727 (8B) is out of sight at Skelton Jc. with this Gowhole–Northwich goods as it meanders qround to Deansgate Jc. and the continuing C.L.C. route south on 27 January 1968. The other two routes head towards Glazebrook (middle) and Arpley. *S.A. Leyland*

No. 48727 again, on the same train, taken from the concrete footbridge and looking back towards Skelton Jc. Sidings on 27 January 1968. They are all long lifted, but the turntable pit can still be seen. *V.A. Sidlow*

at Skelton Jc. could hardly do anything for loco variety beyond featuring one or more of Speke Jcs. nine remaining 9Fs. This it did, however, and by early 1968 this roughly equated to getting a 'Jubilee' on the Settle & Carlisle twelve months before; in other words the best one could hope for at the time.

As would be expected, 'attacks' on the 500-yard inclines varied between solid rousing efforts begun well back on near level track east of Skelton Jc. and graphic demonstrations of deceleration as if the bank had been overlooked until unrelenting drag on the loco reminded the driver that he wasn't even in main valve!

Most, however, were worth tape recording for exhaust noise, though some efforts I retained if they were my first audio record of the engine in question. Short though the banks were, even the most lively runs at them could not maintain initial speed. Positive train identification from the W.T.T. amongst those steam-hauled was very difficult due to the anonymity of mineral runs, their propensity to deviate from the book based on experience elsewhere and apparent illogical motive power base usage without full diagram knowledge. If any of the following steam-hauled trains were wrongly identified, the list nevertheless illustrates the type of traffic that could still be thus worked;

a 'common user' system that deprived main line diesels of a dedicated base in favour of a small number of 'Divisions' or 'Lines', e.g. Western Lines. So nebulous did this render the engines' 'base' that the value of quoting it in my opinion evaporated. It is even less relevant to the subject tackled within these pages and so I make no apology for the omission.

From the above listed traffic, the liveliest assault on the bank came from 48060, which forged over the hill and on towards Sinderland Crossing with great vigour. At the time, and for long after, I took Sinderland to be spelt with a 'C' and thought what an entirely appropriate and wonderful name, in view of such unavoidable chimney emissions so nearby! True to form with 48060's superior display, I unsuccessfully tried to fit the recording on the end of a cassette and ran out of tape! Attempting economy in the face of generally increased tape usage could be known to backfire! I tended to keep away from the congregated enthusiasts when steam approached from the east to minimise voice and (when necessary) wind interference. I didn't get to know all the regulars there, though some were 'Boat' patrons, too. One always struck me as the 'leader' somehow at Skelton; one that was looked up to, a young man from very nearby, quite

D6868	06.05 Healey Mills–Oakleigh 7M50	09.35
D5279	09.25 Wallerscote–Great Rocks 5H41	09.35 (empty limestone)
92218 (8C)	06.10 Rotherwood–Garston MX 8M59	09.44 (coal)*
48292 (9F)	06.27 Avenue Sdgs–Garston MX 8M33	09.54 (coal)+
D1842	Unknown working	10.00
48503 (9F)	06.45 Tinsley Yd.–Edge Hill 8M90	10.10 (coal)*
48107 (9B)	LE towards Northwich	10.14
D302	08.00 Stanlow & T.–Wombwell 5E20	10.15 (oil)
D346	07.40 Healey Mills–Oakleigh 7M51	10.20
48117 (9F)	09.00 Mottram–Widnes 8F12	10.24 (coal)*
D5274	08.50 Tunstead–Wallerscote 5F64	10.50 (limestone)
48424 (9L)	Coal towards Glazebrook	10.28?
48727 (8E)	09.05 Gowhole–Northwich 8F90	10.55 (mixed)
45253 (9F)	LE Heaton Mersey	11.00
48465 (9L)	Coal towards Glazebrook	11.19
48503 (9F)	LE Heaton Mersey	11.22
48546 (9F)	Coal towards Glazebrook	11.26
48060 (8C)	Coal towards Arpley	11.43
D5276	10.30 Oakleigh–Great Rocks 5H79	11.46 (empty limestone)
48329 (9F)	09.35 Birkenhead–Ilkeston 8M85	11.50 (empty coal)*
D230	Unknown working	11.58
48424 (9L)	LE eastbound, (home?)	12.04
48201 (9F)	Goods towards Arpley	12.10

Key: * Steam-hauled west of Godley Jc.
+ Steam-hauled west of Cheadle Jc.

The reader may have already noticed the absence of allocations against diesel engine numbers. The L.M.R. early in 1965 abandoned depot allocation specifically for

well known as a railtour organiser with one of the major south Manchester societies. Quiet spoken, with a naturally dark complexion and a certain air of mystery, we

On top of the Glazebrook line flyover, another 8F hauled goods has just passed beneath, bound for the Northwich route on 3 February 1968. *S.A. Leyland*

knew that his family was in the wine business but little else and this detached him in a slightly superior way from we ordinary lads, but only to a degree. He was not unapproachable and did fraternise with us superficially, was well informed and a true steam enthusiast. He and 'The Skelton Whine', with his seemingly unsuppressible schoolboy boisterousness, stood out from the crowd.

Paul and I left Skelton Jc. earlier that day than a natural tailing off of traffic would have dictated because we had a 'promise'. Arranged by Paul, it took the form of a footplate run on 9K's SO light engine to Heysham and back with the 18.45 Heysham–Ardwick fitted goods. Noting on the way back only 73050 (9H) on Exchange pilot and our own 48504 with an Agecroft–Healey Mills run of empties and 48111 light near Pepper Hill, disappointment loomed.

Turning up at the shed, it turned out that the booked driver, Tommy Whittle, whom I only knew by sight, had changed his mind about taking two on the engine, so I let Paul go and didn't see Morecambe Bay that evening after all. The loco for this job was the quite recently acquired 45294.

To combat the real setback of that afternoon, I later headed for the other 'Heysham', 1P02, which beckoned, reaching Victoria mid-evening when no fewer than five of Newton Heath's 'Black 5s' were engaged on pilot or banking duties! No. 73134 (9H) represented Patricroft on parcels stock movement – the third BR 5 seen on such work that day. Over on platform 11 Middle and its extension into Exchange station, vigilance on foot from mid-evening was still advisable to avoid, or even dodge, the frantic antics of trucks engaged in the making up of still numerous parcels, news and mail trains for all points into the early hours, Sunday being no exception at all. The nearly non-stop 20.30 Heysham News SO, as the only one I was familiar with and diesel-hauled from New Year, had D5203 as its power that night. Four minutes after its booked departure, the Heysham passenger ('Boat Train') pulled into No. 12 at 20.34, in good time for an 8.55 start, one would have thought, but it was consistently late away on Saturdays due to picking up a van on 11 Middle. Tonight I noted the sequence of events. Within a minute of arriving, Victoria West box had the peg off for the loco to draw forward. However, 45342 (10A) didn't shift until 20.40 after hooking off. Having got to 11 Middle across the through lines and been attached to the van, an immediate return was prevented by the passage of the train I should have been on – the 18.45 Heysham–Ardwick – which had a clear road through at 20.51 behind 45294. I don't recall seeing Paul on the engine. He may have had to get down (out of sight), as was commonly requested by drivers approaching places of importance to avoid the risk of being reported for granting unauthorised footplate rides. After 45294, a Hull–Liverpool unit, due into Exchange at 20.57 and the usual source of delay to the 'Boat Train' engine and van, was given preference. 1P02 was therefore not re-engined until 21.01 and the train whistled away eleven minutes late at 21.06. There must have been a good reason for not attaching the van to the Heysham News, which would have saved all that trouble.

In actual running, 45342 on the usual load, despite being quite strong on initial starts, lost more time overall to Preston, a slight gain being made only after Chorley, and it again fell to the economised station stops to recover arrears. A top speed of 50mph at Agecroft Jc. dropped to a mediocre 42–44 after Kearsley, while 63 was attained to Chorley and 65 at Farington Curve Jc. With a total of twenty-four minutes allowed stationary at Bolton, Chorley and Preston, it's little wonder that so few runs excelled between these points. On-the-day comment for tonight's effort was 'not good in general'. I'm almost shocked now to read such critical and even depressing summaries of how I (and maybe 'we') felt at the time in the face of so much steam action on our doorstep! The accumulated negative aspects of 27 January – failure to properly tape record 48060, being out of position for another 'superb one' at Skelton Jc. when we briefly looked for an alternative spot, the failed footplate ride and less than completely satisfying 'Boat Train' run elicited a final diary line, 'Thank goodness today is over in a way'! If I thought this was bad, worse was to come, but so was plenty of the opposite. As the Heysham arrived at Preston that night, a different Ivatt to those seen so far on station pilot was noted, but 43008 (10D) was close to the end of its life.

Sunday, 28 to Wednesday, 31 January

The following afternoon, Paul and I cleaned 44802 on 9K to a very satisfying standard for an early effort on the machine; 'superb' was my verdict. Although my abiding memory of this session is of the two methods employed, both were essential for the end result. The tender on this loco was covered in a layer of very stubborn muck, the full removal of which would have taken a huge amount of time. Paul went over all of the tender in the conventional way with paraffin except for one side under the bottom row of rivets, on which I was employed. In the same length of time I found that only sheer pressure with the rag would get down to the paint, but the rewards made it worthwhile. The finish on that section could be restored

The Bolton BR 5 to most narrowly miss surviving as a working unit into 1968 was 73156, since preserved, but here as far from that status as could be, being hauled away for scrap through Manchester Victoria. Condemned on 25 November 1967, its departure from 9K was almost certainly on 1 February 1968. Towed by D5024, this looks very much like another case of the Shrewsbury–Bolton parcels engine being utilised to pick up a withdrawn loco from Bolton that was sold to a breaker in the Salop direction. How the formation came to be this way round in the (northbound) platform 13 is something of a mystery. *Bob Hunter/Bolton Steam Loco Co. Ltd collection*

every week or so in a couple of minutes, whereas the comparatively course and dust-attracting surface of the remainder, a legacy of perhaps years without being cleaned, would deteriorate much more quickly. On 44802, however, the lining was good throughout and the engine came up very well; the tender too with further attentions up to early March, though the concentrated rubbing it required was more difficult and tiring higher up on ladders than at ground level.

I was later than usual arriving at the station on the 29th through making some of my recordings available to a local amateur dramatic society, which was putting on *The Ghost Train*. My interests being known outside immediate railway circles and family, I was happy to assist; at ease too at the director's house when it became clear his daughter wasn't there – only her tape recorder, to which we transferred the sounds. Half of me wished she had been.

Very often around mid-evening now, a second engine had taken to fussing about on the Up side of Bolton station whilst the dedicated pilot was engaged on the Down. The former was most likely a continuous pilot helping out in this busy period part way through its rostered work elsewhere or at the end of its cycle. No. 45104 was thus employed on 29 January while all else was normal. Ancoats–Carlisle (goods) and Wigan–Bolton–Wigan parcels, which both succumbed to diesel haulage in late 1967, had almost consecutively numbered Type 2s, D5200 and D5202 that night.

At the time of writing, with just over thirty years' varied involvement in the restoration of former Bolton engine, 73156, this is the moment to record its departure from the depot for Woodham Bros., Barry. Last seen at 9K on Sunday, 28 January, it is known to have reached sidings at Sutton Bridge Jc., Shrewsbury by 3 February. This single departure (as far as is known) made little impression on the ranks of condemned engines awaiting disposal at Bolton. Because the working allocation was so low now, the proportion of scrap on the premises stood higher than ever. Over on the roads nearest to Back Crescent Road in the open and perhaps one or two elsewhere were thirteen engines after 73156 had gone. Non-Bolton oddities were 44715, the recent ex Workington transfer that never made it to Trafford Park; 44866, also 9E funnily enough, which had a strange story in the railway press about it in the late summer of 1967 and since when it had languished at 9K; plus the following home locos that had met their end over the previous five months:

44728/5377/415, 48046/200/313/425/436/469/764, 73004.

On 30 January, our own 45110 had got onto Heysham–Moston (46), 45290 interrupted 73040's station pilot run and 9K used a Newton Heath machine, 45420, for Ashton Moss parcels. All appeared normal the last night of January when 45017 (10A) had taken up the 'Boat', long before the arrival of which we'd abandoned O.B. in favour of the station to avoid the wind and rain. Bedford parcels that night had gone behind 45424 (10A), which was the last steam loco in service to the best of my knowledge still bearing the old-style crest on its tender. The by now depleted but established ranks of engines from Rose Grove, Carnforth and Newton Heath that could be allocated to workings through Bolton were generally familiar to ourselves through frequent, if not constant, observations. Every now and then, however, for no other reason than chance, one came along that did not 'ring a bell'. No. 48544 (10F) hauling the second Burnley–Moston on 1 February was an example. Release from long-term storage could explain the foregoing, but it's very unlikely that anything was emerging so late in the game.

Thursday, 1 and Friday, 2 February

A forewarning on the evening of Thursday, 1 February through not heeding set up soon afterwards a top entry in my 'Catalogue of Missed Opportunities'. I arrived from choir practice that night as the 'Boat' already stood at platform 3, its engine more often than not at an angle to and just away from the edge on the blade of the scissors crossover, by which means the train, if on time, got round the 21.25 Liverpool dmu stationary at 3 West. No. 45017 (10A) had come to a stand at 21.11½, virtually proving a very smart journey time. Whether followed up or not (and it must have been) with 'the lad on the Heysham' with whom we had 'a good talk', no further details of the run survive in my notes. Which friend was this, whose name I did not yet know?

After a poor day at work on Friday I ducked the orchestra rehearsal and stayed in watching TV until about nine, then went down to find I'd missed a probable record run from Manchester on the 'Boat', again with 45017. The precise time from Victoria, I subsequently discovered, was 14'-12" (14 minutes 12 seconds). Unlikely ever to be bettered, I could so easily have been one of the jubilant few! Why hadn't the previous evening's fine effort spurred me into making an effort myself? Patricroft driver Jack Sullivan met with instant hero status after this run, which would have proved a tough one to match for the diesels that continued to loom, but no more than that.

Saturday, 3 February

It had snowed in Bolton before midnight, but Saturday dawned clear and frosty. Some recompense for the still keenly felt lost chance with 45017 came the way of Keith and I as we set off for Skelton Jc. again, but not before I saw an 'old friend' for what transpired to be the last time. It was the 05.25 Brewery–Burnley, 4P50, running well late with fifteen on behind 44891 (9D). The Up 'Boat' pulled into Trinity St station and was four minutes late away. An exhilarating start merged into rapid acceleration to 71mph through Kearsley in only four and a half minutes! A top speed of 72mph before slackening to 59 through Clifton Jc. preceded an unusual burst up to 70 over Agecroft Jc., and a clear road into the convergence of lines at Windsor Bridge No. 3 was followed by a sprightly pace round the curves to Salford. 1J05 stopped there in 11'-28", the smartness of the run prompting me for once to record the journey time to the nearest second, rather than my still and rather curious eighths of a minute system. To my knowledge this was the fastest sprint time to Salford in the latter days of steam over the 9.91 miles, though a very interesting competing run will emerge in the weeks to come. On briefly to Manchester Vic., unchecked saw us terminate less than a minute in arrears.

After briefly taking in the considerable (but for the period, unexceptional) Victoria steam activity, including 73034 and 48033 (both 9H) on the ex Glasgow ECS for Queens Road and a goods up Miles Platting bank respectively, we reached Skelton Jc. on the same schedule as the week before. As the morning progressed, a lower steam utility that turned out to be 41% emerged, but there was no discernible further trend on such traffic in the coming weeks. On affiliated lines it was possible or even usual to get more than 50% steam up to the early May depot closures, as will be seen. This was largely due to the dominating depot, Heaton Mersey, remaining open until then with ample power. Of the forty-four steam-hauled goods of any type seen during my four trips to Skelton Jc., the locomotive shed representation was as follows:

Edge Hill	2%
Northwich	4%
Newton Heath	4%
Trafford Park	7%
Buxton	7%
Stockport	11%
Speke Jc.	11%
Heaton Mersey	54%

During the period of the day that we spent there on the 3rd, up to mid-afternoon, much more goods went west than east, countered up to a point by light engines returning. Overall, during the week, westbound traffic did outweigh the other in the W.T.T., but not alarmingly. The Arpley route had a corresponding 1 in 86 drop after flying over the Northwich line, whereas that to Glazebrook fell away much more gradually. The few steam-worked trains we saw from the Arpley direction therefore (usually empties) could still have their engines opened up over the top, but never enough to induce me to record in that direction.

On the 3rd, both steam-worked freights for the Northwich line were halted by signals approaching Deansgate Jc. Soon after came the day's outstanding highlight as 48433 (8A), hauling in the region of 1,100 tons, pounded away, gaining some momentum before the 1 in 86 and with a blasting exhaust sure-footedly surmounted it, slowly but confidently. Once over, and after the sound of fifty-four loaded coal wagons had passed, the engine's still deep and forceful sound effects rose and fell, carried back on the prevailing breeze; a breeze that having turned to face it I could not prevent from imposing some unwanted rumble on the finished recording. With such a massive weight on the drawbar, 48433's gravity-assisted acceleration soon levelled out with the track and even slowed slightly before the exhaust sound faded away. The loading of this train was getting towards the maximum of 110 basic wagon units that a single 8F was permitted between Heaton Norris Jc. and Arpley, and if from Mottram or Guide Bridge I'd say it was at the limit for those earlier sections. Most trains were considerably lighter than that, but after sundry other workings and a flurry of 8Fs returning LE towards Manchester another fifty-four wagon rake made an equally powerful attack on the Arpley line bank. This was 48678 (9D), which had gone east on empties more than two hours before reappearing so impressively at 13.15. There'd been more diesel variety than steam, class-wise, so far that day with a 'Peak', D126, on Warsop–Edge Hill, 8M21, one of many jobs not wholly given to modern power west of Godley Jc. Examples of the usual I.C.I. Type 2 hoppers stud and no fewer than eight different E.E. Type 4s put in an appearance up to 14.19. 'Black 5s' were naturally rarer than the 8Fs, but we finished with 45392 (9F) on thirty-one of coal to Arpley at 13.58.

Having done well there, Keith and I agreed to catch a bus to Northenden Jc. to vary the day a bit, but were told that first we'd have to get a train to Altrincham and therefore did. No 2-10-0s had yet been seen until fate decreed that we should cross one during this shortest of journeys, at Navigation Road! The 9Fs held the power by then to change our plans, so, calculating the most likely route of the glimpsed loco and its train, we embarked on a series of frustrating bus rides in the general direction of Godley Jc. via Stockport and Hyde. The futility of such a venture was suppressed in our minds at the time by the remote chance of success, a sort of blindness by intention, illustrating the degree of determination against great odds that a certain situation could spark off, galvanising one into taking desperate, if not actually irrational, measures. The identity of our illusive objective was most likely the eventually celebrated 12.25 Runcorn–Spink Hill coal empties, 7E81. We gave up the 'chase' after finally reaching Woodley, but defeat proved to be not absolute as 48744 (9L) plodded through shortly after 17.00 with empty iron ore hoppers from Dewsnap. With steam workings very sparse by teatime on a Saturday, as I have said, this revived our spirits considerably. Though not forsaking Woodley until nearly 8pm, probably wondering if the 9F would reappear, no more steam did. In the dark at Woodley, in more ways than one, and at a quiet time, its full potential for the sort of steam action we sought was not yet realised. On balance I ended up preferring it to Skelton!

Demonstrating the advantages of a fast start (to Agecroft), 45017 (10A), ten minutes late away, just beat the B.B.E. schedule to Bolton that night, despite a check to 25mph at Clifton Jc. The run's best features were a 'no-nonsense' start to Salford, passed at about 8mph faster than usual, a very fine speed of 56mph over Agecroft Jc., then quite brilliant acceleration away from the Clifton check with only an initially noisy exhaust. Thereafter he maintained 48–50 to an unhindered approach to Bolton. In great contrast, the section to Chorley was curiously the most sluggish I've ever recorded on the 'Boat', or any other train, with nothing higher than 53mph at Adlington! 1P02 could have been on time from its second stop, but the three minutes needed were lost in running. On to Preston, performance improved a little, though arrival came four minutes late after a top speed of 64mph passing Farington Curve Jc.

Sunday, 4 to Friday, 9 February

The general result of Sunday cleaning at 9K during early 1968 was a presentable stud of five or so locos, most of which were not unaccustomed to their condition. Nos 45110 and 48773 on the 4th were the latest to receive attention. The next evening I drove 44664 down a snowy shed yard and into the building at 9K, unaware that it would be condemned (as far as the shed staff were concerned) just two days later. I'd been talking that evening to my old school friend Phil Platt, who'd gone to the shed straight from our secondary education and suspect that his seeing to the disposal of 44664 led to my being allowed to shed the engine. Apart from what one saw for oneself, or was told by shed staff, keeping up with loco withdrawals meant a reliance on listings that appeared in all the major railway magazines by now, plus some society publications. No. 44664 provides an extreme example through our being 'well in' at the depot of advance notice of a withdrawal and it appearing in print for the enthusiast fraternity. The 9K staff considered it finished now, in early February and it ceased to be used, but the internal paperwork would reflect a date of week ending 8 May 1968 and the glossy magazines didn't catch up until their August issues! In the interim forward from 7 February its status would really have been 'stored', probably 'unserviceable' unless 'pending shopping', but everyone knew that didn't apply in real life now.

The exact opposite of 44664's circumstances described above came about only the night after, though again it was impossible to be aware of it at the time. There was no let-up in Tuesday's (the 6th) snow until late afternoon and it froze by evening, when Heysham–Moston was the first attraction, 45390 (10A) maintaining the train's good loadings with forty-nine on. The only non-standard 'Boat Train' loco seen during that first full week of February, 45133 (8A) appeared with a drama concealed from all. Magazines would subsequently inform us that this engine was withdrawn between 27 January and 24 February, our observation providing proof of its use on class 1 work very close to the end of its life. This prompted me to ascertain a more precise date via the archive services of Mr Richard Strange, to whom I am indebted. These revealed that

No. 44664 on Bolton shed in somewhat more rosy times for the engine, soon after a cleaning session in October 1966. *Peter Reeves/M.L.S. collection*

45133 had in fact cheated time, being condemned officially during the week ending 3 February 1968! Clearly, it had found its way onto 1P02 as a stray of maybe several days, hence remaining unclaimed by Edge Hill mpd at the time of its expiry. For sure, were this to have been known at the time, hearts would have gone out to a machine evading those that sought to reduce it to so much scrap, defying both authority and its implied condition by approaching Bolton well up with the clock on express passenger! Three and a half years earlier it had given me a fast run to Manchester when I attended an interview and exam at Hunts Bank for railway clerical work and 45133 was remembered for that, too.

Of two 8Fs we were expecting from Newton Heath, 48026 and 48090, the former arrived on the 6th and was fired the day after, but the latter reached 9K on the 8th. Both were a few days late. No. 48090 lasted a shade under two months and 48026 a little longer in reality, but here would be another out of use before its official date of condemnation. It seems more appropriate to record 44664's demise upon its physical departure from circulation than with the official date. From being Nottingham-based at the beginning of the decade, the 4-6-0 spent just a month at Leicester Midland up to October 1961, then went to Derby mpd for nearly a year and a half. In May 1963 Blackpool Central acquired the loco, where it remained based until transferred to Bolton in September 1964. It reached 9K on 14 October after an overhaul at Cowlairs Works. A steady member of the 9K stud, it did become the focus of one or two early cleaning sessions, but otherwise remained fairly low key at Bolton apart from becoming known among the men as 'Victor Sylvester' on account of the dance maestro's famous 'slow, slow, quick, quick, slow' trademark step, which matched the engine's number phonetically. It lingered long at Bolton shed until after the end of steam itself, not just at 9K, ending up eventually at Drapers scrapyard, Hull.

Very late for a weekday, 45342 (10A) with the 'Boat Train' didn't reach Bolton until 21.36 on the 8th. Delayed too was Ashton Moss parcels, its engine 73069. The inter-platform movements of whatever sized group of enthusiasts had got together at Trinity Street that evening had not escaped the notice of a certain morose ticket collector who came to be known as 'Grumpy'.

That part of the bridge that ran in front of the ticket barriers connecting the Up and Down platforms was not really for the public's use and on this occasion one 'Boat' patron and 'Grumpy' had quite an argument over details that are long forgotten!

By weekend the 'Boat's' engine had changed again to 45025 (10A). The night before, 44683 (10D) had put in its only appearance of 1968. I hadn't seen 45025 on the duty since mid-1966, but once established on the train during its long run up to dieselisation 5025 dominated it with fifty-eight out of eighty-six possible appearances! Needless to say, some impressively lengthy periods of uninterrupted service at 210 miles per day (SuX) were put in by this 34-year-old 'Black 5', the first being of exactly two weeks duration. On Sundays, with no middle part to the diagram, the mileage was only 116.

Saturday, 10 February

Resulting from the Friday night meeting on the 9th (at the shed unusually by now), 10 February was one Saturday when 1J05 left Bolton with ourselves travelling in the opposite direction. It had been decided to intercept 9K's returning Bamfurlong job as it negotiated the gradients during the reversal procedure at De Trafford Jc.; gradients of which I never ascertained the exact degree. Since the snowy start to the week it had remained cold and fine locally until Friday when much had thawed, but as Saturday dawned cold again and grey there still remained more than traces underfoot. We reached the freight-only junction at

De Trafford Jc., named after the eponymous and nearby house and cottage. The signal box's size belies its importance as part of the Hindley railway map in routing trains away from Wigan itself via the Whelley line to and from Standish Jc. It was the scene of our partially successful vigil on 10 February. *S.A. Leyland*

Similar to what we narrowly missed seeing at Littleborough on 10 February through classic mistiming, 44888 approaches Summit Tunnel with 7N95, the 14.30 Halliwell–Healey Mills, some months hence on 28 June 1968. This SX train was new work for Bolton from early May, it would seem. *I.C. Simpson*

De Trafford (Hindley) by 08.30, pondering how long a wait we'd have. In the next hour and three quarters we mostly hung about just outside the box without any objections or challenges from within, nor, as I recollect, any liaison either. During that time we observed one Long Meg–Widnes anhydrite train, 6F38, diesel-hauled (D390), of course.

The subject of this part of the trip made the same movements as those of many van specials for Bolton, as described in the 23-25 January entry. At 10.10 the intended working came into sight from the Amberswood direction, D7628 leading and 45110 acting as banker until the point of reversal. No. 45110 had a perfectly even exhaust and was in fact a superb engine, but it slipped quite often here on the damp rails. The load was one of coal, thirty-one wagons and a brake at each end. With the train's reversal, roles were too and the 4-6-0 became smokebox first. The signals cleared to give access to the Bolton–Wigan line and as we now expected, the restart, with a diesel banker was by no means laboured and the sound of 45110 only began to blow back as the goods got towards Crow Nest Jc., too late for where we were and I kept only the approach recording.

Partly because the dmu age overlapped the demise of the express, semi-fast and stopping train structure on such services, nothing in those days stopped at Hindley for Bolton between 08.23 and 11.43! During the next long wait, therefore, we tried to light a fire in the waiting room and contacted 9K by phone with an enquiry regarding the 12.35 Halliwell–Healey Mills, 7N55, encountering Ossie Leigh of all acting Running Shed Foremen. Ossie had never accepted us as anything but infiltrators and trespassers at the shed, unlike just about everyone else, and true to form he was fairly obstructive and left us little the wiser. Notwithstanding this, it was resolved to continue with the day's plan and reach Littleborough in time for 7N55, changing first at Bolton. The dmu from there to Rochdale (via Bury of course then) unfortunately connected with a Yorkshire-bound train that was first stop Todmorden, though a fairly good turn round time at 'Tod', back to Littleborough, encouraged us to proceed eastwards.

Eventually arriving at Littleborough worryingly close to the time 7N55 could be expected, we were somewhat troubled very soon after by the passage of the second of two diesel-hauled trains of empties in quick succession. The first was a special and though the second one carried the wrong reporting number for the Halliwell starter, the signalman's response to Paul's enquiry maintained that it had originated there. Seeing wasn't always believing and I remained unconvinced, but getting on for an hour later with no further action it was agreed to phone Bolton mpd again, by which time Vern had abandoned. Knowing that Ossie Leigh's turn was over we'd just crammed into the nearby phone box when came the fateful blow of the day as 44802 steamed through! Desperation set in immediately. Clutching at the slenderest of straws, buses to Summit were seriously considered, even though little more than a mile away, but if there'd been a bus we'd have been on it!

The station staff, one man only, who had no understanding of our motives, became suspicious of our haste in trying to get east by any means quickly. This resulted in a fearsome and complex argument over incorrectly issued excess tickets, obtained hurriedly during our flying visit to Todmorden earlier.

Aggravating the effect of all things that had gone wrong so far on this trip was the sight (on the 15.25 train) of two other Bolton engines still at work near Moston, but this was only so due to our inability to take advantage of them imprisoned on a dmu! Good news steam-wise therefore became 'bad' in a way. One, 48380, soon after returned LE to 9K via Victoria and the other (48773) via Castleton maybe.

Exposing the risks of going for isolated workings, this trip, on the simple ratio of steam activity successfully tracked down to time spent on trains or waiting around, was regarded as one of the least fulfilling and most demoralising of the year, but only in terms of capturing steam in the intended way. We didn't think of rejoicing that both targeted workings had materialised with the right power!

Back at Victoria by 16.00, just Keith and I elected to sit it out until the 'Belfast Boat Express' more than four hours hence, rather than go home in the interim. No clues beyond isolated observations up to 18.00 as to how we filled the void survive, no local shed visit as the most likely attraction or diversion lured us out of town.

As with a week earlier, 45025 (10A) on the 10th passed Agecroft Jc. on the 'Boat' at a very good 56mph, but the working into speed had been more gradual. Tonight the train had been only a minute late away. A respectable 53 at Clifton and 49 through Moses Gate preceded a checked approach to Bolton by missing the distant at Green Lane. Whilst the train waited time, 44947 clattered through with its containers on the SO Heysham–Ardwick; a light load tonight of eleven only. Now on time, 1P02 pulled out towards Bullfield, where a PW check to 23mph cost only half a minute or so due to a good following response. The highest rate to Chorley was 64mph and, despite a cautious entry to the station, the allowance was kept. The express was allowed to leave three minutes early according to my watch (which admittedly had been troublesome of late), so in spite of early braking for Euxton Jc. and into Preston too under clear signals (an apparent trait of this driver), and only 61mph on the main line, he stopped ahead of schedule.

Sunday, 11 to Thursday, 15 February

Through communication with others now better informed than ourselves on such topics, we'd learned that there was to be a run of special freights on Sunday the 11th. Skelton Jc. beckoned again, therefore, and though other locations could have been tried, they may not have yielded the same concentration as that enjoyed. A later start was unavoidable on Sundays, of course, the first train to Manchester being the 'Boat' timed to leave at 08.52.

On one occasion in 1968 while that train still sported steam haulage, a lady passenger standing in front of me on Bolton's platform 2 exclaimed in a deflated tone upon seeing a 'Black 5' appear at West Jc. 'Oh, it's one of those old-fashioned trains'. Such was my strength of feeling then, not just about steam and diesel, but a detestation of 'carts' in their current condition in relation to what they'd replaced and the whole 'modern image' thing that I all but took her up on it, incensed, whilst saddened too at finding one so irretrievably duped. The irony was that for passengers in many areas it *was* only an image of improvement. British Rail (the new name still made me nearly retch) had won this lady over to preferring smelly, worn out, shuddering dmus to the dignity and real comfort of a loco-hauled coach. Clearly, her unthinking and undiscerning mind had absorbed and accepted the dictum: Steam = Old = Bad; Diesel = New = Good. That's as deep as it went, and yet she had mastered a form of Mind Over Matter – 'I think I am comfortable, therefore I am'. Whether or not the blame or criticism is justified in the eye of the reader is less important than recording how the situation affected me. Entirely undocumented at the time, the fact that I remembered the incident nine years after the event when writing the first version of my 1968 memoirs itself says something.

Had 11 February been the morning I encountered her (and the chances are it wasn't), she'd have experienced a slower than average run to Manchester on the 'Boat' with 45025 (10A), four minutes late from Bolton, 57mph maximum, two checks to 40 and the Salford stop omitted as usual on Sundays. The vagaries of rail travel on such mornings delayed our arrival at Skelton Jc. somewhat with single-line working on the electric unit from Oxford Road, but once there the motive power weighed so heavily in favour of what was desired that it didn't seem like 1968 or Sunday! In total contrast to the rest of the week, scheduled goods traffic amounted to absolutely nothing, so all seventeen trains seen were specials, and again, predominantly westbound. Unlike the trans-Pennine Sunday pushes of late 1967 (which could be simply enormous operations), today's was less exclusively for coal movements. Six steam depots were represented and today, too, the 8Fs were outnumbered by 'Black 5s' and a comparative abundance of 9Fs. This most welcome aspect, however, proved less of a surprise than the 94% steam presence!

The most audibly impressive engine was 44871 of 9B on coal towards Arpley. Its powerful and even exhaust indicated an engine in very good shape as it pounded up the 1 in 86 from a low initial speed. All eight coal runs seen hauled loads of between twenty-nine and thirty-three. The driver of 45312 (9B) almost let his train stall on the Glazebrook bank through lack of the effort needed, though the loco was back sharply enough three-quarters of an hour later on empties. A third 5MT, 44807 (9E) preceded the first 2-10-0, 92218 (8C) which pranced towards us just after 12.00.

Exercising some selectivity in which trains I tape-recorded, a couple of mixed goods threaded the junction before 92054 (8C) double-headed 44815 (9E) eastbound from the Arpley line on an unusual load of sawn timber – 'planks from Arpley'. The class 5 was condemned by 24 February. Sundry

Emphasising the height of Skelton Jc. signal box and that eastbound signal, this low-angle view of the 12.15 Guide Bridge–Garston coal train features 92069 (8C), one of that depot's 9Fs that did not escape the closure of its home shed, Speke Jc. which ceased steam operation on the day this photograph was taken, 4 May 1968. *I.C. Simpson*

The first of three 9Fs encountered on 11 February was 92218 of 8C, seen here approaching Skelton Jc. at midday with coal for the Arpley line. *V.A. Sidlow*

other workings filled the next hour with never long to wait, until the day's third 2-10-0, 92223 (8C), the engine that hit the headlines in 1964 when the W.R. tried to scrap it, appeared on coal to Glazebrook. This was no 9F ghost though, as an outcry against the Western's ruthless tactics put it through the Works, transferred it to somewhere safer and in due course enabled today's sighting. Although now among the last of the class, it was still too young for the 'torch'. Being situated below rail level at this location as the trains climbed above us often ensured that westbound locos came into earshot before they were seen. With 92223, the distinctive thin wailing whistle and later the rather hollow double-chimneyed exhaust of 9Fs so fitted quickened the pulse a touch only seconds before the sight of smoke deflectors had chance to. One more goods marked the end of the busy period. My Bolton friends had gone on foot to Gatley for a change of scenery. I stayed put after 48252 (9F) went by at 14.00 on mixed to Arpley, but another two hours elapsed before the last of the day was seen behind 48723

(9F). Northwich and Buxton power also had played its part in the excellent proceedings witnessed.

From one apparent act of defiance by steam against its undeniable decline we fly to another in the middle of a fairly ordinary week locally, but 'apparent' is the key word. It concerns a by now very rare example of my fully recording a 9K depot visit. This late winter illustration is from 13 February 1968 at 20.30 when thirteen home engines stood in steam and one (73040) was newly fired. Rather amazingly, none were stopped or under repair, and the missing seven locos therefore made up the current allocation of twenty-one. If we assume, quite reasonably, that some of those not present were out in traffic (say four minimum to cover known jobs), how does this active total compare with the falling locomotive requirements through the latter part of 1967, a trend easily followed and proven from surviving depot records? Those figures, which are incontestable, had, by the year end dropped to fifteen or sixteen locos required daily (SX). Had some mysterious recovery brought them into the upper teens again, or were the statistics for 13 February inflated for another reason? I tend to suggest the former, but the lack of 'inside' information of the kind available for most periods prior to October 1967 mean it can only be a suggestion, albeit a serious one. In truth the 13 February figure is slightly high due to the newly fired 73040 taking a day off from station pilot for washout, whilst one of the engines missing from shed covered the job, so two locos have been counted for a single duty.

The 13 February total in use is therefore twenty, absolute maximum, but far more likely seventeen or so. To find a comparable weekday evening in 1967 from my records we have to go back to the end of September (the 26th) when, at the same time of day, seventeen locos were in steam (all resident) and four absent, all of which would have to have been in traffic to cover known jobs. The active mid-week quota for mid-February 1968 was therefore around four engines fewer than for late September 1967, reflecting the modest job losses since then, but apparently better than at the end of that year. A steady decline in steam engine requirements during 1968 through further job losses and encroaching dieselisation would be the expected progression through this last phase. Steady, however, it was not at this particular depot as Bolton held its head up surprisingly well through the spring, with further causes for speculation on a mini-revival from 6 May.

Since 9K's allocation had dipped into the twenties from autumn 1967, and particularly since the last stored engines were released during October, the stud was operating more efficiently with fewer locos stopped or spare and a reserve close to minimal. It's probably true to say that Bolton's locos were now in better condition than during most of 1967 on average, and even earlier, partly through the worst BR 5s having been gradually weeded out and the retention of all its former stored machines. So, although 9K's fortunes did not alter drastically in the coming weeks, those of steam in general did for sure and it was the areas set to finish first, or next, that dictated enthusiasts' priorities.

I said earlier that it was an ordinary week in motive power circles with no surprises seen out in traffic. Very much out of traffic, 48425 and 73004 were noted as marked up for the Newport (Mon) scrapyards of Buttigieg and Cashmore respectively, amongst ten other steam locos awaiting disposal on 9K. I say 'steam' because a local firm, probably Willy Hatton, had started to cut up the odd diesel shunter on site and by the 13th D2864 had been reduced to bits. Shunters in particular were taking a hammering now because of yard closures and the still slow transition to block loads.

Friday, 16 and Saturday, 17 February

On the first of three consecutive Friday nights that I didn't attend orchestra rehearsal that month, that of the 16th revealed an unprecedented (for a normal evening) crowd of enthusiasts on the 'Boat', including Mr D.T.J. Rollason. Small in stature, but larger than life and owning a stentorian voice often turned to regaling and entertaining his cronies and hangers on, 'The Wellington Mouth' was already a celebrity. We'd first encountered this amiable school teacher from the Shropshire town eponymously prominent in his nickname the previous summer. With steam now well north of his old domain, all his available time seemed spent in pursuit of surviving class 1 workings on extended 'bashes' with a marked accent on minimal expenditure. From the old school of enthusiast, but strangely apart from that stereotyped mould, he'd contributed to *Trains Illustrated* magazine since late 1951 and in time adapted to the post-steam railway with undiminished fervour. Some of the crowd on the 'Boat' that night (45025 – 10A) doubtless went beyond Bolton and it surprises me how rarely I got on the Down train at my home station. The customary discussion regarding Saturday went in favour of Peak Forest again, though only Keith and I went in the end.

So, the Peak Forest No. 2 trip took place on Saturday, 17 February and was regarded as very successful; enjoyable too, despite some lengthy waits. The steam run to Manchester on 1J05 was waived for once in favour of an earlier start on the 06.55 from Bolton in expectation and hope of additional activity at the Midland summit. The one hour gain, however, yielded only predictable diesel workings, plus one (D1747) with the very late running 04.30 Arpley–Buxton, 7H79, MX, booked for water at Cheadle Heath South Jc. in the current WTT, so maybe still steam sometimes. We whiled away more than two hours in the deep snow at the bottom of the deeper rock cutting. Bolton had had a lengthy and heavy shower of the white stuff earlier in the week, but not to compare with this exposed and lofty location, judging by what remained. Eventually, 48532 (9L) ground out of Dove Holes tunnel at barely 10mph on about twenty of coal for Buxton; the time, 11.09 and we'd been up since six! With two northbound diesel-hauled reliefs over dinnertime, passenger traffic was boosted that day. Notwithstanding this, the 12.00 Tunstead–Runcorn followed the first of the reliefs, thereby turning up an exceptional twenty minutes early, close to its starting point at least. Hauled on this occasion by 48191 (9F), we were still north of the summit for its passage. An hour later a mixed goods towards Buxton passed behind the rare combination of D219 and 48365 (9F).

Although cold and windy, it had turned into a very bright February day. Consequently, the most suitable point to make tape recordings of trains leaving the loop at Peak Forest South was on the platform of the closed station where the buildings afforded some protection, not only for personal 'comfort', but as a means of avoiding wind in the microphone. A snippet in *Railway Magazine* for November 1967 had said (amongst other detail) that daily trains of limestone 'blocks' were being transported from Cauldon Low, Derbyshire, to Stoke and eventually in larger made up formations to Port Talbot for a dock extension construction job. I mentioned this briefly with the Peak Forest No.1 trip

Coal and other commodities are brought Buxton-bound through Peak Forest behind the unusual combination of 48365 (9F) and D219 'Caronia' on 17 February 1968. This view is at Peak Forest North, the summit of the line. *Peter Stamper*

account. Such news from the magazine would have gone in one ear and out of the other as no steam involvement was suggested or seemed likely. What we next witnessed at Peak Forest next was clearly a revised form of that 40,000-ton contract, which from Caldon Low (actually in N.E. Staffordshire) could not have been directed over Midland metals in its neighbouring county.

Ignorant of all this at the time, we therefore next observed, backs to the faintly warmed south-facing stone of the station building, two 8Fs restarting forcefully from Peak Forest South. A distant trumpeting blare signalled that the Type 2 banker had dropped off before the pair of 2-8-0s pounded through the platform hauling twenty-seven plate wagons, each with a massive rough-hewn boulder (not 'blocks') chained to it. The train, with a brake van at each end to facilitate reversal, drew to a halt at nearby North box to pick up a pilotman (for the tunnel was still effectively single track) and to detach the leading engine, 48775 (9L). The stone was clearly now coming from the Buxton area. With such a tiny allocation in 1968 I'd be surprised if the depot could have fielded power (two engines) for such a special during the week. No. 48424 (9L) alone now, got the train under way again with one wheelslip on the briefly easier (than 1 in 90) grade before plunging down to the Dove Holes portals where rock enclosed rock for the next 2,984 yards.

The brightness, snow and maybe advance news to those 'in the know' of the freight with its unusual load had brought out quite a lot of photographers. Keith and I were fortunate to be offered a lift by car with one of them over a spectacular whitened and lofty landscape to Edale, where 48424 was expected to come off. Haste was not essential, however, and we could almost have walked the 7 miles in the time available, as it turned out. Such was the scarcity of traffic from the Peak Forest route requiring to gain the Hope Valley line towards Sheffield that the direct chord line (Chinley South to East junctions) had been closed a few years earlier. Currently, a single timetabled goods in each direction, MX, and the special we followed now had to run down to Chinley station, its engine running round the train in order to head east. If steam-hauled, the loco had to turn as well and this alone, I believe, ensured the Chinley station turntable's survival. I was familiar with this interesting operation, having experienced it on the footplate of a Bolton BR 5 on railtour duty the previous November.

The crew of 48424 and the boulders special's guard didn't seem to be in any rush to finish, even allowing for the above described manoeuvre. I positioned myself at the eastern portal of Cowburn tunnel to capture the class 8's last exertions. It emerged soundly enough a good two hours after we'd seen the Peak Forest departure. Travelling slowly, steam was shut off the moment that gravity could take over.

High above the A6 road that follows the same course as the railway through Wye and Ashwood Dale, east of Buxton, 48191 (9F) brings a goods up the 1 in 100 gradient in early 1968. With the road turning four times under the line in the short distance from Peak Forest Jc., the two are almost intertwined. *Peter Stamper*

Waiting to take over at Edale was an engine that raised an eyebrow or two even amongst the steam enthusiasts who were milling around. It was Landore-based D1665 *Titan* and it was here that we learned of Port Talbot as its destination. Hardly possessing the equivalent 'wow' factor as the 'Grange' that once worked through to Huddersfield, whatever working, LE or empties earlier, had brought this diesel to Edale, some condition or other seems to have barred it from crossing this unlikely frontier.

No. 48424 was booked to take a ballast train back to Peak Forest, providing us with a good reason to return there, courtesy of another lift, by which time darkness encroached and all the daylight enthusiasts had retired. To me this was Peak Forest in its most attractive mood with only the occasional car, the almost imperceptible hum from the limestone works and the crunch of freshly frozen snow under foot to break the silence. Shortly before 18.00 a fourth sound was perceived; that of a steam engine distantly ascending the 1 in 90 towards Dove Holes tunnel. This early warning through the clear Peak air gave me barely sufficient time to run from the station, round the knoll to the cutting's lip by the roadside, but I made it and the 2-8-0 blasted into the open, chimney first again and a chimney throwing a fair bit of fire into the gloom below me. Lack of light it was that caused me to marginally over-record 48424's exertions – 20mph plus, but on a load not possible to evaluate, but a very good finale to the day there. It may even have been that engine's finale too, being condemned by the 24th, denied the last rites of its home depot by just a week or so.

Even the opening two sections of the 'Boat Train's' run that night were better than most, and the third almost spectacularly so, as respectable speeds to Chorley did not prepare travellers for the display north thereof! 'Usual engine, usual load (seven + van), usual lateness away (seven minutes)' could sum up what might be termed the

Opposite: The Port Talbot limestone rocks special is double-headed upgrade to Peak Forest North where the pilot loco, 48775 (9L) is removed, leaving fellow Buxton 8F 48424 to continue unaided. After descending to Chinley, where 48424 would turn and run round the train, that single engine would then face 2½ miles of the same adverse grade that was earlier deemed to need two locos, until it dropped down to Edale. *Peter Stamper*

constants for this period. No. 45025 (10A) was just halfway through a fortnight's uninterrupted service on the diagram. After 54mph over Agecroft Jc., the upper 40s (max 50) were sustained to Moses Gate and the seventeen-minute allowance to Bolton was just exceeded. Sixty seconds after booked time away, the Bullfield West slack to 20mph still applied, but thereafter speed built up to 66 north of Adlington. A slight check coming into Chorley knocked punctuality back a bit again, but 1P02 left mid-point between the public time of 21.40 and the working one of a minute later.

No. 45025 restarted quite normally until clear of the station, then was really opened up to produce showering cinders and rapid acceleration down the 1 in 134 bank, though no unusually high speed was reached before the main line. Once over Euxton Junction's 25mph limit, similar tactics were employed and, descending the 1 in 100 to Leyland, the 4-6-0 developed a clear and percussive exhaust. The driver opened the 'Black 5' up intermittently on the more gently falling grades with a well shortened cut-off as the train lurched and clattered over the junctions approaching Preston, where the highest rate of 74mph was achieved. On still jointed track here and there and with all the Fast to Slow pointwork as well, it seemed even faster. It must too be borne in mind that after Euxton Jc. only 3½ miles were available before braking commenced and on this occasion we had no distant at Skew Bridge.

Still, the train arrived two minutes early after a very exciting finish. We were gradually 're-spotting' Lostock Hall's Ivatt 4s by arriving thus each Saturday and this evening 43027 officiated on the station pilot. Back at Victoria I'd noted five 'Black 5s' so engaged, though I think four was still the official quota for that part of the week.

Sunday, 18 to Thursday, 22 February

Sunday's 9K visit was devoid of any recorded detail whatsoever, but I wouldn't have been likely to clean anything due to having blistered my hands fanning a garden fire at home earlier. I'd tried rubber gloves once and once only, and can remember them disintegrating on the tender of 73014. I can also remember my mum recommending Lanry, which must have been bleach, as a means of getting my fingernails decent again and it did have some beneficial caustic effect. Fifty years later, as a volunteer at the East Lancashire Railway, Bury, a nailbrush, soap and hot water are as effective as anything, but to return to 1968, we avoided the depot during the coming week on account of Ossie Leigh acting as Foreman in the evenings. Though aware that Ronnie Horrocks was the driver on Bedford parcels all week, no effort to witness lineside action in keeping with his reputation transpired outside the confines of Bolton station. On Wednesday night the 'Boat' rolled in, still with 45025, in the mightily impressive time of fifteen minutes from Victoria, according to my local notebook. I'd fixed my watch again, and besides I would not have recorded such an exceptionally early arrival without verification.

Later on I bumped into signalmen Hofton and Halliwell from East Jc. The regular evening traffic yielded nothing beyond the norm all week really, but drama there was on the streets as on a cold and foggy Tuesday 'They got Ian Horton the killer on Park Road'. This must have been quite a thing as current affairs hardly ever found their way into my little journal, but Park Road was on my way to work. The next day, the 22nd, I trod it at midday too to reach Bullfield West, quite lucky to see a Down and Up trip freight behind home engines 45318 and 48652, plus the now diesel-worked Carlisle–Red Bank, 3J41, which had D244. A Lostock Jc. train register acquired in recent times shows that I'd just missed a van special from Willesden, but again almost certainly diesel-hauled. The register proves that such specials were still feeding Bolton frequently with twenty-one trains in the month up to 13 March. Willesden seemed to lead the field as regards points of origin now. Llandilo didn't figure at all, whilst Camden and Stoke Gifford, completely new to me, got a mention or two towards mid-March when the register expired. The three trains I did observe at Bullfield all came in two minutes, but I never repeated this dinnertime jaunt.

After the Thursday (the 22nd) rehearsal of our church choir, which marked my tenth anniversary as a member of that body, I joined friends at Trinity Street where several of us had a ride into 'A' Side on the pilot, 45294. Surprisingly, Ronnie Horrocks was still about on Bedford Parcels engine, 45017 (10A) and I ventured to ascertain the chances of travelling with him the night after. All was agreed! A Bolton job rarely observed was the 22.16 goods to Hull, 5N12, worked by 9K to Healey Mills, but that night it was seen leaving Burnden (via Clifton) behind 45110.

Friday, 23 February

I'd picked a Friday night for the footplate run with Ronnie, expecting to be back in the early hours. When I turned up in good time for 3M13, due out at 20.20, it was to find not the usual 10A machine, but our own 44802 and the guard nowhere about. This may have accounted for the parcels being so late away the previous evening, I can't be sure, but he was given a sound berating in his absence by Mr H in a largely unprintable diatribe on tardiness and working practice during a confab involving our crew, myself and the men on Upside pilot, which stood adjacently, cab to cab, for some time. The pilot's young fireman in turn bewailed the clinkered state of the fire on his engine that had reputedly 'bin art since two o'clock yesterday mornin''. Considerable banter revolved too around justification for Ronnie's nickname of 'Sparky', including our own fireman's assertion that 'Fire Brigade' (the latest hit record by The Move) had become very popular in Rochdale that week!

The guard finally arrived and with an unconvincing 'I hope he's in' from Ronnie, we were away, sixteen minutes late. Initially there was a lot of slipping (more good-natured groans from the fireman) until clear of East Jc., then, taking advantage of the dip to Darcy Lever viaduct, 44802's regulator was wrenched open and the 4-6-0 hammered out past Rose Hill, accelerating rapidly to around 45mph. The nineteen-van train roughly maintained this rate up the rise (variously quoted as 1 in 170 or 193) to Bradley Fold, where that station cabin's adverse distant caused a reduction to 30. Nevertheless, Bury was reached in 11¼ minutes. Just over a quarter of an hour was allowed for shunting here and I took up the offer to drive the loco during these moves, which increased our load to one of twenty-five vans. The train weight I failed to ascertain, but 3M13 consisted of the smallest vans so we were probably equal to about nine coaches.

I'd been tape recording my own efforts at shunting with 44802 and now Ronnie stood to one side with an unnecessary reminder of the Broadfield bank ahead. I think I got the train going quite well for an amateur as there was no interference from the official driver and we settled down to about 25mph on the 1 in 82, 44802 blowing off briefly near the top. We arrived at Rochdale just inside the time allowed of fourteen minutes, but still a bit on the late side.

After further shunts our engine worked the train no further, but gave way to a Newton Heath 'Black 5', which coupled to the rear in order to proceed via Castleton, Newton Heath, Philips Park No.1, Ashton Moss and Guide Bridge to Gowhole, where 9D steam and steam in any form came off. In the earlier 1960s and when the destination was Leicester, Bolton men used to work the train, differently routed, to Marple. We, however, now were booked light engine to Ancoats to provide power for the 22.30 Ancoats–Heysham, 5P05. Although 44802 was only three minutes behind its scheduled arrival time, it wasn't possible to get the nineteen-container wagon freight away punctually. This rake, fully fitted, was propelled upgrade to the 'new' Ancoats Jc. (formerly Ashburys West Jc.), then given rightaway engine first, uphill again as steep as 1 in 60 to Philips Park No. 1, but a halt was enforced at No. 2 box. Late at night the area was littered with goods and parcels traffic, and 5P05 made uncertain progress all the way down to Manchester Victoria, stopping there too and opposite Exchange station for six minutes in total.

Starting again at 23.24, Ronnie adopted the tactics for which he was renowned, setting the controls for a noisy journey to Bolton with the reverser only a couple of turns away from full forward gear and the regulator not quite fully open on the quadrant. The freight surged forward in response, reaching about 35mph before slowing to gain the direct line to Bolton at Windsor Bridge No. 3, after which we were blazing away with a clear road. The heavy demand for steam was met more than adequately and the speed curve on this final unhindered section resembled that of passenger trains. We just exceeded 45mph on the easy road to Agecroft Jc., thundered through Clifton and under the new M62 bridge still on the right side of 40 and didn't fall below this until approaching Kearsley, where the signalman presumably discerned our whistled request for water at Bolton (a long and three shorts) above the roaring exhaust and passed on the information. Approaching Moses Gate, comparative silence descended with the closing of the regulator as 5P05 slowed to take the loop line to Burnden Jc.

Despite the earlier stops we'd picked up four minutes to Windsor Bridge and twice that on to Bolton, partly through being scheduled via Brindle Heath Jc. as a legacy of when the train (until 2 October 1967) used to call at the Down Sidings there and partly through fast running. The new booking was twenty-one minutes Windsor Bridge No. 3 to Burnden, whereas we'd taken just over nineteen from Manchester Exchange. So, only eleven late at Burnden and nearly half an hour to departure time, 44802 went on shed 'to cool off' in the driver's words before continuing with another Bolton crew. Afterwards, in the foreman's office (Ossie Leigh must only just have gone home!) Ronnie stayed behind to listen to the forty minutes or so of recordings I'd made, encouraged the playing of them in fact, prompting mainly derogatory comments from the other men, light heartedly, regarding his 'technique'. He relished both nevertheless!

Saturday, 24 February

As I'd not got home until 01.20 on the 24th, I abstained from the early start, intending to join up with friends soon after midday. There 'd been talk of some Bolton-worked special trips to Ashton Moss that seemed worth making an objective of and accordingly I caught the diesel-hauled 12.17 Preston–Manchester (D1960) to Victoria. No. 45110 went LE to Halliwell as I waited at Bolton and was quickly back, still light as the 12.17 pulled in on time. No. 44802, seemingly fresh back from Heysham, stood on the 9K pits as we passed at 12.47, whilst 45110 tailed the express clearly at express speeds as it reached Victoria at 13.02! For what purpose I never found out, being on the 13.05 to Droylsden. There certainly seemed to be substance to the 'special trips' rumour as I'd also passed at or around Windsor Bridge three coal trains headed by 9K machines 45104, 48026 and 48090, but, I suspect largely through insufficient information I drew a complete blank in terms of capturing any action in the desired way. Passing 44836 (9B) on Manchester-bound vans at Philips Park, nothing came through Droylsden in the hour from 13.19; nor was Paul about, as arranged. The only made-up trains I'd seen had been through glass and the trip was looking bleak.

Abandoning the idea and the area, it was with differing degrees of faith and hope, sprinkled with intuition, that I opted for Peak Forest, a gamble certainly at that time on a Saturday, notwithstanding past trends, and I just missed a suitable train at Piccadilly!

Coming onto Dove Holes station in the process of leaving Peak Forest as I arrived was Pete Barber, who reported an unexceptional day there. What was gone was

Earlier during the day of our chance encounter at Dove Holes, Peter had spent some time at Gowhole where, amongst other activity, 48533 (9D) appears between the bare branches affording a view of this one-time busy marshalling yard. *P. Barber*

gone, though it didn't boost my hopes of something to save the day. I was finding out, however, that the short series of trips to this location always ended with a late ballast working, all different though, and all by chance. To my delight and relief, at 17.17, 48115 (9F) trundled tender-first down towards Tunstead. I went to South box and the signalman (who kindly provided sufficient sustenance to pass for my tea) confirmed that it would return with a ballast train for Guide Bridge. The day was looking up. Two weeks running now we'd been blessed there with the rare opportunity in 1968 of Saturday evening steam freight without a surfeit of enthusiasts in the neighbourhood.

Shortly after 6.15, 48115 came plodding up the bank, stopped at South box and restarted a little more energetically. Two recordings were obtained as the train halted at Peak Forest North too, though I had to run to clinch the second, initially walking alongside the 8F on the road. A single car hummed by as the 2-8-0 faded from earshot, reminding me of an identical feature on one of Peter Handford's recordings in Scotland from the L.P. 'Rhythms of Steam'. The guard had spotted my activity and blew his whistle too as the train receded. Noticeable at the low speed I'd heard it working at, 48115 sported a split fourth exhaust beat after a louder third, which produced a novel sound that made one feel for the locomotive on account of its apparent condition, though in purely mechanical terms the defect may not have been debilitating. Those audible characteristics and the general state of 48115 appealed to a ready sympathy I always had for engines that might have seemed more 'poorly' than they actually were. This, plus surprisingly frequent sightings of the 8F in the coming weeks, quickly established it in my mind as a symbol of the decay and deterioration that the surviving south Manchester steam stud struggled against, but as a 'hero' too, all the more for overcoming the odds. This sentiment spread willingly through my close friends, aided by the apparent aptitude that the 2-8-0 had in attaching itself to more than one exceptional event.

With a satisfaction rightly or wrongly boosted by being the only enthusiast on hand to have caught 48115 in such a desirable setting, I strolled contentedly back to Dove Holes station. A pleasant engaging aspect of the 18.51 to Piccadilly (the same train as last Saturday) was that it steadily filled with young girls off to Stockport or Manchester for the nightlife. Around Furness Vale as the view across to the Midland line near Gowhole opened out I could see the ballast train again quite clearly, despite the advancing dusk. That prospect to the right and the girls in their glad rags entraining on the left did create a conscious conflict of interests, one actively engaged in and the other not. The approaching end of B.R. steam brought about no reactionary swing to the surviving attraction. Things took their own time.

The first two coaches of the down 'Belfast Boat Express' were by this time getting to resemble a mobile club and I have already introduced certain individuals perhaps later than I ought in relation to their becoming friends or 'members'. Others met through the common interest at indeterminable times during early 1968 are probably overdue too: Alan, always known as 'Tosh', a van driver from Rochdale; his friend Jim from Whitworth, whose dad was a signalman; Ian from Fallowfield; Frank, from a farm in Hattersley; Dave, domiciled in Derby in the early stages of his railway career, but a Boltonian; as was Harvey, whose years on the scene had curiously not brought us together much before this time. I know that there were others who travelled, many in fact, but the above, plus those introduced briefly earlier and one or two still to be so, became what was termed, at yet another indeterminable point during the spring, 'The 20.55 Club'. Beyond its name it was completely informal, but as the year wore on those that were 'Club' knew that they were. If this seems to imply elitism of any kind, may I set the record straight by stating that there never was any such thing.

No. 45025's lengthy domination of the 'Boat' diagram ended after 23 February, giving the loco a brief break from the job. No. 45134 (10A) had taken over for now. Working 1P02 on the 24th, it was driven so sparingly to Bolton that the times were actually slower between Salford and Moses Gate than the fitted freight with which I'd ridden twenty-one hours earlier! More than twenty minutes were spent in motion, unchecked, and after a low maximum of 44mph, speed was kept between 38 and 40. The train had been only two minutes late from Victoria though and in such cases the Bolton station allowance could absorb the squanderings of most tardy runs. Now on time therefore, the following two sections saw some improvement with maxima of 65 at Adlington and 62 after Leyland. Not for the first time had 1P02 left Chorley before time and this largely contributed to the early arrival at Preston. The Ivatt 4 that was to outlive all others (by a margin unimaginable then), 43106 (10D), was in use as the pilot at the time of this brief visit.

Sunday, 25 February to Friday, 1 March

Apparently no worse off for the harsh treatment imparted to it on the Friday night, 44802 benefitted from a cleaning session on the cold Sunday of the 25th, along with 73069. Word came across next day that 9K would receive some redundant power from two of the three mpds due for closure one week hence, i.e. Buxton and Trafford Park. Perhaps linked to these expectations, Bolton sustained another two casualties during what I otherwise saw as an uneventful week locally. Both 45294 and 48740, contrasting greatly in length of service at 9K, were effectively out of the running by 1 March, though the 8F officially went during the week ending the 9th. Newton Heath-based for several years at least until September 1962, 48740 then spent nearly two years allocated to Northwich until transferred to Bolton. The workshops took possession at that juncture, however, and the resultant, rather delayed acceptance to Crewe and the work done there held up its arrival at Bolton mpd until 12 December 1964. It had since then been a regular worker (forgive this sounding like a school report) and was never in store. No. 45294, by comparison, we were barely on nodding terms with. Its real stability, at Patricroft, ended in June 1963 with a brief move to Kingmoor, after which it spent periods of five to six months each at Agecroft and Carnforth. Barrow-based thereafter, March 1965 to December 1966, it moved to Workington until reaching Bolton on 4 January 1968 for what transpired to be just two months of service. The subject of withdrawals will be returned to very soon!

Joining the two aforementioned depots that were set to finish with steam from 4 March was Northwich. Collectively, this first wave of depot closures in 1968 eroded yet again the southern edge of steam operation in any density. The C.L.C. east of Hartford Jc. certainly continued to see a few such workings powered by surviving south Manchester and Liverpool mpds, and one working from Tunstead using Heaton Mersey power prevented the Midland north of Buxton from becoming 100% diesel, though otherwise decimated by the demise of 9L-allocated steam.

A lot of enthusiasts had doubtless formed some plan or other during the preceding day or two on which of the last workings to cover on Saturday the 2nd, as we had at Bolton. Certainly my brief love affair with Peak Forest in a lineside capacity put me fully in favour of concentrating on Midland metals, the near deprivation of steam over which constituted the greatest loss personally. I'd felt quite ill on Friday with a sudden humdinger of a cold but also went to the dentist. Dentists, it seems, were much less sensitive to seeing patients so afflicted than they've become, but further diary statements that included a surfeit of exclamation marks concerned the facts that I yet again did not attend orchestra rehearsal and that 'I am still going tomorrow!!!' I suspect that my continued absence in the clarinet section had more to do with last-minute preparation and news regarding THE TRIP than not being up to it. Buxton mpd had been contacted by phone to give us an idea of the most fruitful location to head for initially and Chinley North Jc. seemed to fit the bill.

Saturday, 2 and Sunday, 3 March

Against considerable parental disapproval I duly joined Paul, Keith and Harvey for a 'Boat Train' start, and what a start it was! After four days, 45134 had given way to fellow 10A machine 45025 again. Closely resembling the superb effort of 45017 (10A) a month previously, Bolton saw the train off ten minutes late and today we were a bit slower out to Moses Gate, but then the speed just kept rising until a full 75mph was reached before Clifton, where the curve brought about an easing to 62. Another burst took 1J05 over Agecroft Jc. at 73, though it seemed even faster and a clear road into Salford permitted a start to stop time of slightly over eleven and a half minutes for the 9.91 miles, and a few seconds under a quarter of an hour to Victoria. We'd recovered a fraction over three minutes in that short sprint plus the brief continuation

A very successful start to the day on 2 March 1968 near Chinley North Jc. is represented by this image a couple of months before of Buxton's 48744 tackling the 1 in 90 grade with empties for Peak Forest on 3 January 1968. *I.C. Simpson*

into the larger of the two cities served.

Joined now by Pete, utilising the day's first St Pancras express, 08.40 from Piccadilly, we were quickly out with D133 to its initial stop at Chinley. Walking to the vicinity of North Jc. it became clear that we weren't alone in choosing this spot to begin the day. After a considerable flurry of diesel-worked goods, three of the six double-headed, 48319 (9F) forged up the 1 in 90 with forty-five empties for Buxton. This appeared to be the prime objective of most photographers, a minority of whom were not averse to shouting near abusive instructions to people 'in the way', as they had largely dispersed when twenty minutes later (11.10) 48775 (9L) reappeared (it had dropped down to Gowhole on freight nearly two hours earlier) on a twenty-nine-van special for Grindleford. Both of these made fine recordings. We now realised that the then slightly enigmatic reference to 'Grindles' in our phone call to 9L had alluded to this, as suspected. Grindleford seemed an odd destination, unless the train was to continue beyond that point after a change to diesel; but that didn't matter because we'd

secured it and now it was time to move on.

Somehow my colleagues were nowhere to be found and I recall some surprise and annoyance that they'd gone without me. Whatever explanation, it's gone in the mists of time.

Walking the couple of miles to Chapel-en-le-Frith South station for the next Buxton-bound unit, I reached Peak Forest at around 12.45. Fair weather for the season prevailed, suiting I expect the many photographers that abounded here. For four months from the end of February I didn't use a camera at all, my growing preference for sound recording as the medium in which to capture the essence of steam's last days having taken over completely. It was a step I've never regretted.

Buxton's 48744 headed LE for home at 13.21 and soon after, 48493 (8E) pulled up to South box hauling the 12.00 Tunstead–Runcorn and uncoupled to pick up four more wagons in the yard, labouring oddly with this tiny load. Getting on for two hours late today, this train had no allowance in the schedule for a traffic stop here. With the full formation made up, 48493 departed with a frantic-sounding

The final act for Buxton mpd under the old order. After a busy day in the district 48775 (9J) pounds up through Wye Dale past Topley Pike box with a ballast train on 2 March 1968. The sizeable group on hand to witness and capture this historic moment were anything but disappointed. *F.J. Gradwell*

whistle to the banker and safety valves lifting until the generous use of steam silenced them again. Approaching 3pm and representing Newton Heath, 44890 clanked steadily up the bank on a twenty-three-wagon northbound ballast train. These steam-worked freights were interspersed with the usurping motive power that accounted for exactly half of the actual traffic seen, including, later, one of the Port Talbot limestone block trains. This 50/50 sharing of the traffic between steam and diesel refers to goods only as for some reason I failed to note down the St Pancras workings that day, except for the ones used to get to and from Chinley.

The activity so far would normally, during the last few months of steam operation in the area, have been considered good already for a Saturday, but there was more to come, some of it artificially induced by the clearing out of traffic from Buxton Sidings to Peak Forest North as the former closed that weekend, too. Fast becoming engine of the day, 48775 (9L) completed this task in two sizeable trips up to 17.15. These were interrupted in time by another ballast towards Manchester taken by 48327 (9L), which had gone EBV in the Tunstead direction earlier. It was the third train of its kind to head north that afternoon for Sunday permanent way operations elsewhere. It is less likely that 48327 would have returned to Buxton mpd afterwards as Patricroft took charge from the 4th. When 48775 was transferred away from Agecroft in October 1966, the published movement to Patricroft (9H) was erroneous and never corrected. After the imminent Buxton closure it did indeed become 9H-based.

By this stage in the afternoon, if not before, I'd been reunited with my friends, or some of them, as we obtained a lift to Great Rocks in expectation of another trip from 48775, but the engine availed itself of the turntable there to face south in preparation for a Tunstead–Buxton ballast. Back in the car, driven by Frank, I was in the hands now of those better acquainted with the district away from Peak Forest itself and we headed for an eminently suitable vantage point called Topley Pike, the first block post up Wye Dale, just off the main line. What a name, I thought, as we inspected the little cabin, closed at this time on a Saturday. The occasion also marked, if I'm not mistaken, the first time I made the acquaintance of Ambrose, a friend of Frank's and another member of what was the embryonic '20.55 Club', made up of increasingly familiar, if not quite regular 'Belfast Boat Express' patrons. However, today that was still some hours away after we'd captured and experienced the final minutes of 9L depot's steam duties.

Mostly positioned on the catwalk, we'd not long to wait for what categorically was Buxton's farewell steam job. No. 48775's energetic exhaust quickened as the fifteen-wagon train entered the dale before the driver eased just slightly, having got up to about 25mph on the 1 in 100. We can only guess at the thoughts going through his mind as the 2-8-0 pounded by towards Pic Tor tunnel and on to Buxton in a fitting climax to the day, the

As one on an independent trip on 2 March, Peter Barber spent time at various Chinley spots and a very snowy Hindlow, whilst managing to also catch busy engine of the day 48775 (9L) at its roofless home depot. *P. Barber*

occasion and the far longer reign of steam there.

Those of us who'd come by train via Chinley that morning were kindly dropped off there by our more mobile friend, Frank. He didn't get out with us often during the daytime due to commitments on the farm, but today had been special. Since the steam age, stations other than Chinley have followed similar paths from complexity of layout to insulting simplicity, to an extent that closure would seem the kinder option. A simple verbal request saw us into one of the two signal boxes then controlling that layout while we awaited the 19.51 to Manchester. Chinley Station South Jc. box was not far beyond the Peak end platforms.

The 'bobby' unsentimentally remembered that the expresses went into Piccadilly now as he explained the basics of accepting a train on the instruments and sending it on, to a particularly resonant series of block bells. Directing this intelligence chiefly at myself, knowing smiles passed between the others in recognition still of my undisclosed time at Bolton East Jc. Well up to time, as might it well be with twin 'Peaks' D133 and D80 at the head, the 19.51 whisked enthusiasts to the city, happy with the day, but acutely aware that another landmark step had been reached in steam's decline in the North-west.

No. 45025 (10A) today had an extra coach on the evening Heysham 'Boat', making eight plus the van, and we experienced one of the least inspiring runs made with steam on 1P02. Five minutes late from Victoria, the 'Black 5' made an atrocious start out to Salford, taking nearly another five, after which the top speed of 45mph steadily dwindled to 37 by Moses Gate! Just a couple of seconds short of twenty-two minutes were expended to the first stop and the same old reliance on Bolton's generous station allowance alone accounted for the 'illicit' gain of sixty seconds upon leaving. By Lostock Jc. the express had not crossed the 40 mark, then near Horwich Fork Jc. came a lengthy PWS slowing to 25mph and in the remaining miles to Chorley exactly 60 was attained. Signals approaching Euxton Jc. were not entirely in our favour, causing the prescribed 25mph limit to be drawn out, after which the 'B.B.E.' took the Slow line, not as booked, and slow we went. Another PWS soon after Leyland prevented any recovery there might have been here, though a better entry into Preston, considering the low approach speed, was facilitated as the points were set, most unusually for this train, for No. 5 platform, the Down Main, instead of the more devious route into No. 1, as they were numbered then. Arrival here, nearly five late, gave little more than time to check the station pilot, worked by 43019 (10D), before returning to Bolton.

Evidence of the cold I'd endured that day survives in the very nasal and 'bunged up' commentary on my tape

From its early 1968 stud of Ivatt 4MTs, Lostock Hall has selected 43019 to fulfil Preston station pilot during the first weekend of March. Photographed here on the Friday night into Saturday on 2 March, it was also thus engaged when the author and friends arrived on the Saturday evening 'Boat Train'. *I.C. Simpson*

recordings, but I don't remember it being much of a nuisance. Nevertheless, I wasn't up until midday on Sunday, which I allowed to pass steamlessly. Grandpa, in his penultimate year, came to tea and I was OK for the evening service.

The weekend's shed closures had left thirty-five steam locos high and dry. Buxton mpd continued to operate with diesel locos, but the direct jobs of Trafford Park and Northwich, which closed completely, must have been covered by more remotely based rearrangements, the likes of which were rarely explained in the railway press and we didn't care enough about to try to find out. Buxton's final steam allocation of seven 8Fs was all transferred elsewhere with the exception of 48442, which was condemned at 9L. It will soon be seen that in some cases there was little to choose between each method of disposal. Two locos went to Patricroft, one to Heaton Mersey and three to Bolton. Of the nine remaining 8Fs at Northwich, five were scrapped, two went to Rose Grove, whilst Edge Hill and Speke Jc. each acquired one. The last rites at Trafford Park saw seven machines, class 5s and 8s, withdrawn and the remainder distributed as follows: Newton Heath (two class 5s), Stockport Edgeley (two class 5s), Bolton (two class 5s), Rose Grove (one 8F), Heaton Mersey (three 8Fs) and Lostock Hall (two 8Fs).

2

After the First Contraction

No. 73156 Shopping Proposal.

4 March to 5 May 5

Up to the Stockport, Heaton Mersey and Edge Hill depot closures

If nothing else, steam shed closures through 1968 were evenly spaced in time, except for the shorter interval after the end of June, but none of this was known for sure at the time of the first wave just described, as regards the order and dates. General opinion considered that more depots would be operating up to the end in August than the three that actually did. Evidence of the uncertainty will appear in due course and I am certain that many professional railwaymen knew little or no more than the enthusiasts.

Monday, 4 to Friday, 8 March

On the increasingly windy evening of 4 March, which brought no end yet to the lengthy spell of dry weather, I noticed that 9K had already taken delivery of the two 'Black 5s' from Trafford Park and 48532 from Buxton. No. 44929 served at its new depot until closure, but 44965 saw barely a month of usage. The fact that I have 48532 in my notebook as 'withdrawn' so soon after arrival strongly suggests that the established procedures for reaching such a conclusion had changed with the pointlessness now of the Shopping Proposal system in its literal sense. Amongst the internal B.R. documentation I have for Bolton engines, the one to survive longest happens to be 73156. No wording on the Shopping Proposal form had been changed to reflect the fact that steam locomotive overhauls in any category had ceased with the much-publicised shopping of 70013 in early February 1967. The latest submission for work to be done to 73156 nearly ten months after that still contains the printed wording 'I RECOMMEND THAT THIS ENGINE SHOULD BE CONSIDERED FOR SHOPS FOR THE FOLLOWING REASONS:' followed by a blank space for the depot to type in the defects.

The likelihood is that depots were simply using up stocks of the Proposal forms knowing full well that no shopping would take place and that the outcome would be 'Submit for Cutting Up' with the infamous rubber stamp. So the explanation of how we learned so quickly about the condemnation of 48532 lies in the fact that the depot by this stage knew the outcome of any Shopping Proposal the moment it was typed up and, hardly needing to await the official reply, sometimes passed on the news to ourselves. That way we found out about the ex Buxton 8F a full two weeks before the official date. I mentioned 73156 just now. That engine was stated to be 'stopped' on 22 November 1967, the Shopping Proposal was dated the 23rd and the 'Submit for Cutting Up' stamp clearly shows the 24th! Now that I cannot explain!

Bolton had no use for the ex Buxton 8Fs and though active on the last day of the spa town's depot, powering the final steam working to Hindlow, 48744 undertook no 9K work and was condemned by 16 March. Here it is seen at Bolton on the 17th. *P. Barber*

It went on from 48532 in grand style that week with resident 48111 written off on the 6th with a blown off cylinder head and the other two ex Buxton 8Fs, 48465 and 48744 (the latter in use on 2 March) withdrawn virtually upon arrival. This was certain by the 7th, yet both had only reached 9K on the 5th, 48465 in the evening and in steam. The fitters wasted no time at all on whatever appraisal the 2-8-0s were granted and word got to us almost immediately.

The train that 48465 arrived on was a Willesden–Bolton van special routed unusually via Clifton Jc. Shortly before 9pm the station pilot, 73040, took over and drew the vans at Burnden Jc. straight into 'A' Sidings. A rumour was abroad the next evening, the 6th, that 9K might be getting 44709 and 44894 (both 10A), but this proved groundless and I quote it only as an example of the kind of oddity that could surface! We'd had rain at last and the winds remained for now as our station visit was punctuated by a train of old track off the Blackburn line hauled by 48335 (10D) and a jaunt into 'A' Side on 73040. The 'Boat', still with 45025 (10A) was reaching Bolton well to time midweek.

As Bolton engines for the briefest imaginable time, the three from Buxton are eligible to a sort of obituary by allocation upon their demise. No. 48532 had enjoyed years of stability on the N.E.R. at Royston up to the end of July 1962, Twelve months at Edge Hill followed, then Lancaster Green Ayre became host to the loco for nine months up to June 1964. Barely two months each at Patricroft and Newton Heath transpired before it had close on a year allocated to Bury. From late October 1965 it settled at Buxton until disturbed by recently related events there. No. 48744 moved the short distance from Longsight to Stockport Edgeley in November 1960, where it remained for four and a half years. Remaining within Manchester, it shifted to Newton Heath in June 1965 for the rest of that year, then moved to Buxton. No. 48465 made an identical transfer to the former loco in 1960, but left Edgeley very soon after, in January 1961, for Buxton. This 2-8-0 easily therefore became the longest stationed there of the three.

Nearly eighteen months before the ill-fated ex Buxton batch darkened 9K's door, a similarly ill-starred group of refugees from Agecroft knocked upon it and, having gained admittance, reeled straight away to an almost identical blow as that imparted to the Buxton three. The common thread in this little tale is 48111, the only convincing survivor of the Agecroft group of 8Fs, which happened to meet its end on virtually the same day as the Buxton unfortunates. Rather mysteriously it had a cylinder end blown off while coasting LE past Bolton shed. Briefly at Agecroft up to that depot's closure on 16 October 1966, it had previously been a long-standing resident of Nuneaton mpd and had managed almost eighteen months based at 9K.

Away from Bolton, most of the passenger trains still steam-hauled were portions of diesel-hauled expresses from Glasgow or London Euston, detached at Preston for Manchester, Liverpool or Blackpool South. One portion (already mentioned) was the 05.45 Wigan N.W.–Manchester Exchange and there was a nocturnal Leeds via Halifax to Manchester Vic. still hanging on to traditional motive power. Having the 'Boat' on our doorstep influenced the urgency, or lack of it, with which we sought out these other workings. The 'Boat' remained rock solid with steam until the end in early May, whereas some depots providing power for the other passenger jobs still generally considered steam-worked, had irregular and fluctuating access to diesels that could be and were rostered inconsistently, as and when conditions permitted. A good example was 1J42, the 12.17 Preston–Manchester, now reliably diesel on Saturdays and decreasingly dependent on steam during the week. The same naturally applied to the diagram's other workings, i.e. the 09.00 Liverpool Exchange–Preston and 21.23 Preston–Liverpool.

Saturday, 9 March

Whether the local and therefore cheaper trip that transpired on Saturday the 9th was a direct reaction to the theft of my wallet at work earlier in the week I can't say now, but it also proved an unobjectionable idea to my friends at the night before's meeting. Local Saturday trips, as we found at intervals through the spring, could be very successful and rewarding in the new constricted sphere of things, but in view of the blank morning to come it does surprise me to see that that day earned itself an 'OK' rating at the time.

Of the newer, non-Bolton friends, it was Peter who joined us far more often than any other during the day. Not always did the Bolton four of Paul, Keith, Vernon and myself concur on the Saturday plan to a man, but we remained closely knit generally, the whole or part sometimes being augmented by Harvey.

Somehow we found out on the 9th before leaving the Bolton station meeting point that the first intended objective, 9K's Bamfurlong trip, was cancelled. It must have been realised that the second choice, the 05.25 Brewery–Burnley, 4P50, despite being known to run several hours late, was a real gamble. More than an hour's wait at Bromley Cross (from 09.55!) reconciled us to the conclusion that it had gone, or maybe not run either. Third on the 'programme' was 7N55, the 12.35 Halliwell–Healey Mills. With this the day started to look up as 45290 passed Bradley Fold in fine style on thirty-seven coal empties, and only a few minutes late.

Shifting again, as one had to do, much further up the bank to Waltons Sidings, beyond Entwistle and summit of the Bolton–Blackburn line, the next objective was the 13.25 Colne–Red Bank parcels vans. This train too was an unpredictable timekeeper, but we were in time to record the working topping the 1 in 69 out of Sough tunnel, three-quarters of an hour late. No. 45350 (10F) brought 3J83 rather hesitantly at first into the daylight, then more strongly with a slightly uneven exhaust and accompanying wheeze. Only the Down line was in use through the tunnel due to long-term repair work and at Waltons crossing over to the Up again necessitated some reduction in speed, unless the ascent was slow enough to begin with. At Spring Vale, the other end of single-line working, the operational movements caused by this were taken advantage of in more ways than one during several future visits.

News from the signalman at Waltons, probably the eccentric Mr Carroll, was bad. Bradshawgate box, just out of Bolton, had recently closed (without obvious visible signs yet) and Entwistle cabin was due for the same treatment at the end of March. The authorities also had similar intentions towards Turton, but these did not materialise for some years because of the crossing gates. With Entwistle's demise would go the Fast lines between there and Waltons, so even the latter would be a less active box.

The curiously Bolton-worked 18.45 Heysham–Ardwick SO duty had been retimed to a 16.50 start, the same as the SX Heysham–Moston. Though I do not recollect this discovery, proof that we knew lay in the fact that around 18.00 on the 9th I waited, alone now, at Bolton shed in anticipation of the train about two hours earlier than formerly. Running Shed Foreman Arthur Hulton and one of the Hesketh brothers who'd attended the same school as me, representing the greatest disparity in grades or seniority to be found at 9K, were in the yard as 45110 hurried past on Heysham–Ardwick with fifteen container wagons. Four minutes earlier, at 18.25, 45290 arrived on the ashpit from Healey Mills from the working we'd seen six hours previous. Also on shed of note by 1968 standards was 48335 (10D), seen on the track special on the 6th.

To finish off this 'local Saturday' I soon after headed for Manchester for a curtailed 'Boat Train' run. Two Patricroft BR 5s handled pilot work on Exchange-related traffic and the 'usual' quota of four 9D 'Black 5s' were on hand at Victoria, 44851 being fresh to Newton Heath from Trafford Park. Every feature of the 'Boat's' run to

Above: Representing an upturn in the fortunes of our 9 March trip, 45290 puts up a decent show at Bradley Fold West working Halliwell–Healey Mills on that day. *V.A. Sidlow*

Bolton that evening was normal for a Saturday, from the lateness ex Victoria onwards. No. 45025 (10A) made times and speeds that were neither excessively slow nor fast, calculated not to maintain schedule to the 'usual' sort of degree.

Running shed Foreman Arthur Hulton we have to thank, amongst many others, for tolerating our presence on Bolton shed on such a frequent basis during those closing years. Here, he make a gesticulatory request or instruction to the driver on 48392 as the loco comes off the 9K ashpit. *P. Kirkham*

British Railways Steam 1968

Above: Volunteer cleaner Paul Salveson, with a replenished bucket of oil, is part-way through a session at Bolton shed in this semi-elevated 1968 view of Stanier engines.
P. Kirkham

By the spring of that last year, 44802 was looking very presentable, reposing in steam on 9K.
P. Salveson

Sunday, 10 to Friday, 15 March

Sunday the 10th saw us in very clement weather for early March, maintaining the shine on locos 44802 and 48773. The local evening observation periods often presented a still bustling scene around East Jc. Notable features from the following list for Monday, 11 March were a Rose Grove loco on the early Burnley–Moston in lieu of the usual 9D class 5, an unusually heavy load on Heysham–Moston and the brief toppling of Carnforth dominance on the 'Boat'.

youngest 'bobby' I worked with at East, still able to impart his remarkable knowledge in the current year of 2018. No. 45017 (10A) 'sneaked' onto the Heysham on the 13th before 45025 (10A) was back again. I missed the Friday night meeting that week by going to watch *The Ghost Train*, courtesy of the St Simon & Jude affiliated New Players, a universally enjoyed performance that incorporated some of my own recordings.

D5138	18.05 Manchester Vic.–Blackpool N. parcels SX 3P05	18.34
48257 (10F)	16.40 Burnley–Moston SX 5J13 (20)	19.11
D5255	Parcels stock to Manchester 3T39 (unidentified)	19.16
44894 (10A)	20.20 Bolton–Bedford parcels engine SX	arr. 19.38
45424 (10A)	16.50 Heysham–Moston SX 7J32 (54=58)	dep. 19.40
D5202	20.05 Bolton–Wigan parcels SX 3F17	dep. 19.43
45290 (9K)	Up side pilot	–
44942 (10D)	20.55 Manchester Vic.–Heysham ('Boat') 1P02	arr. 21.16
45318 (9K)	17.45 Colne–Ashton Moss parcels SX 3J20	dep. 21.36
D5209	21.05 Oldham Clegg St–Blackburn parcels SX 3P03	arr. 21.46
D1618	17.25 Glasgow–Manchester 1M40	arr. 21.50
48451 (10F)	19.05 Burnley–Moston SX 5J10 (29)	21.58
45110 (9K)	Station pilot	
48335 (10D)	Still at Bolton mpd	

With nearly half of through traffic, i.e. pilots excepted, still steam-hauled, the evening was rated as 'pretty good', fair assessment, whilst the same journal entry acknowledged that conversely (and perversely?) my mood lacked its usual cheer for reasons unrecorded and probably unknown.

No steam-hauled enthusiast special had run on B.R. since 25 November 1967 due to a ban imposed a month before, but it had recently been lifted and the quite well-remembered William Deacons Bank tour from Stockport to Morecambe, deferred to 17 March, soon had to be duplicated to cater for the reactionary demand. By Wednesday of the week in question we'd discovered that 45110 and 45290 were earmarked to pilot the trains north of Bolton. Though two of our best 'Black 5s', they couldn't hope, of course, to spend all their last days on top-class work, or anything like it. No. 45110 had stood in for 73040 on station pilot during that evening of the 11th, but now with grander things in prospect. On the 12th, 73040 had resumed and, having bought a new cassette tape, I used up the old one on the pilot and 45424 (10A) working Bedford parcels. This illustrated too that when things were normal the Heysham–Moston engine worked Bedford the day after. Although the fairly frequent and welcome invitations to revisit my old box at East Jc. lay in the not too distant future, I did converse with relief signalman Maurice Blackburn from the footbridge that evening, too. He was a superb signalman, meticulous in every way, knowing many boxes intimately, and as the

Saturday, 16 March

I nevertheless knew of the planned Woodlands Road and Clayton Bridge trip for Saturday the 16th and joined the 'Boat Train' start of it. On time leaving, 45025 ran very smartly to Manchester with a top speed of 70mph at Kearsley, slackening to 60 through Clifton Jc. and another high of 67 over Agecroft Jc. Producing a time of 12'-06" to Salford (now Salford Central), impossible in the twenty-first century, the train reached Victoria two minutes early.

Despite clearly having grounds for expecting to catch the Bolton-worked Patricroft–Crumpsall coal train on the bank at Woodlands Road, nothing turned up. It seemed we were too late. However, come compensation appeared in a glimpse of the industrial scene as the diminutive 1898 Hunslet-built *Lady Armaghdale* was engaged in gently shunting wagons between the I.C.I. works and B.R. siding. The Clayton Bridge part of the trip was abandoned in favour of returning to 9K, where four hours were occupied in cleaning the two class 5s selected for Sunday's aforementioned specials.

The Down 'Boat' on Saturday night plumbed new depths in terms of timekeeping and running quality. Departing from Vic. a full twenty minutes late, no noticeable effort was made to regain time. Only 46mph was reached by Agecroft Jc. and the rate fell to a dreary 39–41mph through to Bolton. Now seventeen minutes late away, the start out to Lostock Jc. was average, but a 10mph slowing before Horwich Fork Jc. was responded to by weak acceleration and a low max of 60 prior to Chorley, reached 20 late again. Even by keeping to booked times beyond, a negative 'connection' into the last train back from Preston loomed. Many enthusiasts therefore, not all that regrettably, left 1P02 at this point. There was no need to wait for the 22.27 as the 17.25 Glasgow–Manchester, itself a good half an hour in arrears, stopped out of course at Chorley on this occasion to have the driver and guard advised that due to the very recent derailment of 3J40, the 17.36 Carlisle–Red Bank at Bolton, we'd be taking the Horwich Fork Jc. to Dobbs Brow Jc. link, thence via Atherton to Manchester. Passengers such as myself then had to change again in order to get home. Despite the dull performance from 45025, the frustration of being 'forced' to miss part of the intended journey, and now the delay and detour, these irritations were tempered by traversal, albeit in darkness, of the by then little-used line through Hilton House, which (embarrassingly) I'd never done before. 'Big Noise', aka 'The Wellington Mouth', was amongst the 'Boat' people bound for Preston that night too and recent events provided him with plenty of material for raillery on a railway theme as we headed south. Regaining Bolton shortly before 23.00, I don't recall seeing anything of the derailment.

Sunday, 17 March

By way of a change from the upper reaches of 'our' long and still (nationally) little-known bank to the north out of Bolton, we opted for Turton Towers to witness the passage of both outward bound specials on Sunday morning, 17 March. The tours, 1L30 and 1L31, reached Bolton from Stockport behind two engines seen only on such work now, in 1968. These were 4472 *Flying Scotsman* and 70013 *Oliver Cromwell*. Both trains picked up passengers and assisting engines at Bolton, and some shunting was necessary as the pilots were marshalled inside the Pacifics, becoming in effect the train engines. This was to suit the rather complicated arrangements later on at Accrington caused by routing via Colne and Skipton instead of the far more straightforward Clitheroe route to Morecambe. Six locos were involved altogether, Rose Grove's 45447 and 44899 piloting the Bolton 5s from Accrington to Skipton where the Pacifics resumed after turning and the trains' reversal.

'The March wind doth blow', they say, and it blew that day alright, but I was becoming quite good at finding pockets of relatively still air to aid successful tape

First up the bank with the two Sunday enthusiast specials on 17 March 1968 was 4472 *Flying Scotsman* piloting 45290, seen here at Turton with 1L30. 9K men Fred Sharrock and Harry Smith were on the 'Black 5'. Harry recalls to this day how it didn't steam well for him. *V.A. Sidlow*

'Cromwell's' train followed twenty-three minutes later at 11.23 on the second of the identically routed railtours. No. 70013 (10A) and 45110 blast uphill close to Turton Towers with 1L31. The coat of arms borne by the Pacific relates to William Deacon's Bank, the organiser. *Not known*

Survivors No. 1 – The author's original cassette tape recorder, a Philips model 3301, purchased on 19 November 1966 and which lasted, with various early repairs, through the remainder of the B.R. steam era and just beyond in working order.

Closed for almost two years, the unvandalised signal box at Entwistle, seen here on 14 February 1970, stands sentinel-like above the station. All is as it was, except for the removed signals and the Fast lines that ran under the gantry. With no northbound evening steam there in 1968, Waltons Sidings, 1,453 yards further on, became the focus for such trips, on foot from Entwistle, along with Spring Vale. *S.A. Leyland*

recording and did so in the cutting (not that all was calm there) just north of the castellated bridge. First up was *Scotsman* with 45290. Being at the front, the Pacifics dominated each recording and live event alike there, exhausts rising and falling on the wind, particularly the exciting whip-crack punchiness of *Cromwell*, which, with 45110 showed the cleaner pair of heels of the two at near to 40mph. The load on each was eleven bogies.

Combinations of Bolton engine/Pacific switched over the same section for the return runs. Both trains were quite late reaching Bolton. We'd tucked ourselves down at rail level, out of the wind below the old Down side cattle dock at O.B. The 'Brit's' pilot, 45290, uncoupled, repaired to 9K and 70013 left at 21.23 shortly after 45025 (10A) ran in with the Sunday 'Boat', which was not a boat train on that day of the week, but Morecambe, same as the specials! Some good sound blew back towards us after the first tour's passage. *Scotsman*'s train didn't arrive until 22.51! The pilot detaching this time involved 45110 throwing half its fire out in a lightning dash to Burnden, this action being Bert 'Colonel Cut-Off' Welsby's farewell to the proceedings. Badly dragging brakes on the A3's train contributed to the twenty-one minutes it spent in the station and caused two false starts and ferocious roaring wheelslips that seemed to reverberate around the quiet town. All was eventually well and the Pacific left for Stockport sounding in good shape. All in all it had been a great spectacle and all the better for local locomotive involvement, too.

Monday, 18 to Friday, 22 March

Several related aspects of the tours came our way the night after. No 45110 was on Up side pilot and Bert related animatedly how the loco had pretty well dragged the A3 and its train away, up the gradient from the Spring Vale restart due to the L.N.E.R. engine's instability – a restart necessary after reversal onto the Down line due to the continuing engineering work in Sough Tunnel. The 'Colonel' was probably exaggerating to a degree, but I've no doubt it was quite a show, and we knew how late the train was into Bolton. Purely through coincidence, one of the two Rose Grove 'Black 5s' involved with 1L30 and 1L31, 45447 (10F) started its week off on the 17.45 Colne–Ashton Moss parcels, which worked forward from Bolton on the 20.57 Guide Bridge, 3J28, and so was part of our evening observations on the 18th. Finally, 70013 (10A) had come onto 9K about 22.30, en route back home, but it stayed the night and much of Tuesday.

The original railtour that the above locos had hauled had been initially advertised to run on 16 September 1967, but it fell foul first of a guards' work to rule, then the steam tour ban. The latter, it is generally believed, was lifted following the resignation of Sir Stanley Raymond as Chairman of B.R. In his place at the beginning of 1968 came Mr H. C. Johnson. Described as the first long-serving railwayman to be appointed to the post since nationalisation, it's understandable if he was more tolerant to steam, at least as far as permitting it to be celebrated in the most appropriate way when so little time remained to do so. It is probably the same H. C. Johnson who appeared in the British Railways Year book of twenty years earlier in the position of Operating Superintendent (Western Section), Eastern Region. At any rate, the floodgates were open for such steam excursions now alright and from April to August barely a weekend went by without one or more gracing lines in the North-west. By special arrangement, as they by definition had to be, the railtours were still an integral feature of that last year of steam that it would be historically negligent to disregard.

One of those single-day absences of 45025 (10A) on the 'Boat', probably necessitated by a boiler washout, occurred on the 19th when 45342 (10A) stood in, but it was the night after when, undaunted by several known dismal efforts of late, I chose to ride the first leg of 1P02. It proved to a good choice to say the least. No. 45025 had an eight-coach load and made a sure-footed start, a prelude to a very sprightly run that demonstrated what could be done without thrashing the engine.

The sound departure at booked time, plus a minute, gained a good thirty seconds on an average effort to Salford. A top speed of 53mph by Agecroft Jc. wasn't exceptional, but after a characteristic drop through Clifton to 51, the rate increased to 55 by Kearsley and was all but held to Moses Gate. A checked run-in past 9K proved not too damaging, but notwithstanding this and the extra coach our skilful driver had knocked half a minute off the seventeen-minute booking that so many failed to keep.

Saturday, 23 March

The initial impact on my morale at being told I had to work the coming Saturday morning is not something I can convey outside the context of those times. I saw an anticipated, but as yet unplanned, day with the steam crumble before me, and that was dispiriting in the extreme. The shock wore off somewhat though, as Friday wore on. Besides, that evening no cohesive plan of action lay with my friends and the next day I managed to get a commuted 'sentence' of only three hours, up to 09.00. Straight from work therefore I decided to sample Skelton Jc., now without contributions from Northwich, Trafford Park and Buxton depots, of course.

Recreationally, the author permitted only pre-existing musical outlets to 'interfere' pleasantly with railway pursuits in 1968. The programme extract shown here is an example from 23 March.

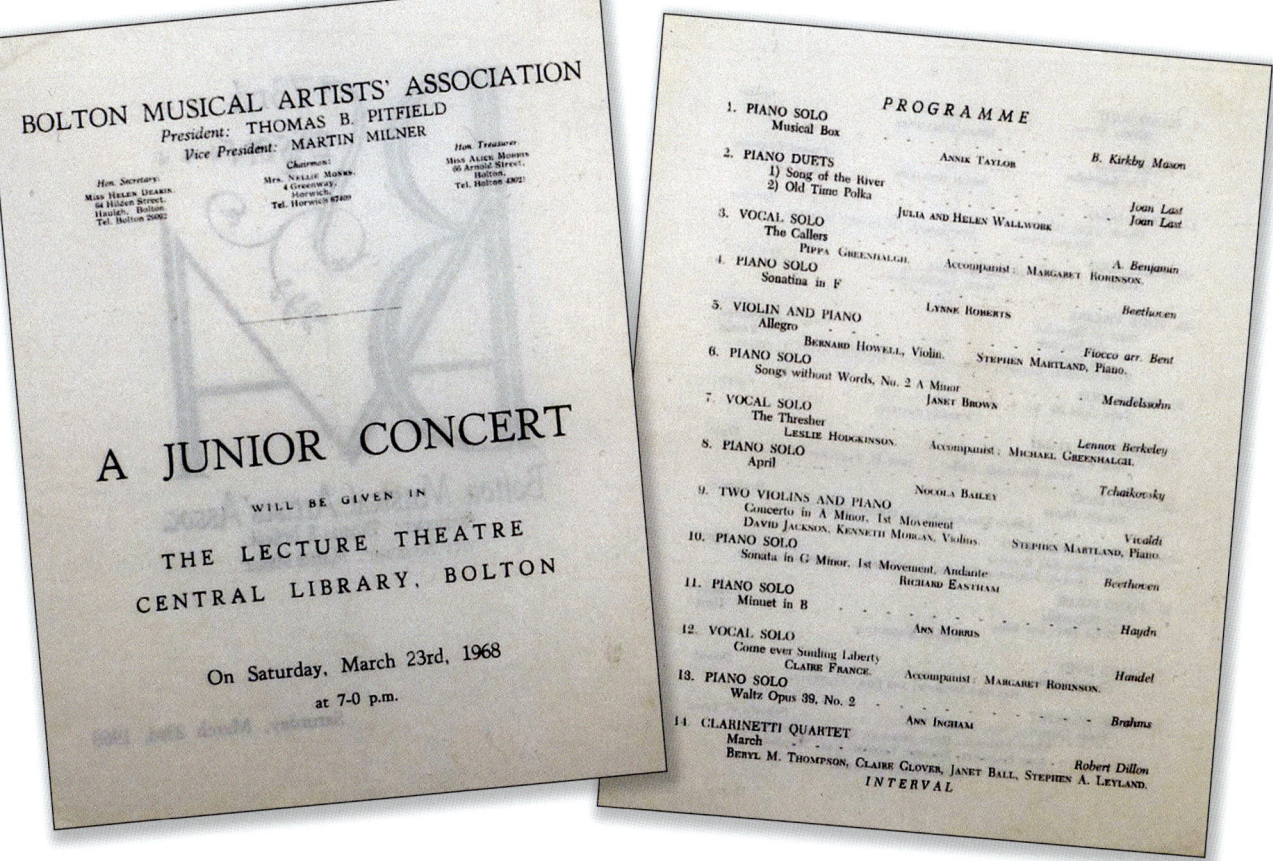

Hopeful of a 9F 2-10-0, there wasn't any Speke Jc. representation at all, but plenty of 9F shed plates as in the hours 10.45 to 15.00 a Heaton Mersey monopoly was broken only by a solitary light Edge Hill 2-8-0. Of the eighteen freights of all classes observed, just seven had steam in charge. 48720 (9F, as are all the following 8Fs) sounded markedly out of beat on a substantial mixed goods towards Arpley and soon after, 48252 took coal onto the Northwich line. No.48471 had the swiftest initial run at the 'hump' on coal for Glazebrook, but I didn't record all on tape. A two-hour gap separated 48684's Arpley run from 48546, which made a determined restart to Deansgate Jc. on Tunstead–Runcorn, 8F56, only twenty-five minutes late at 14.15, though the interval was well-filled with diesel-worked goods and some LE 2-8-0s, mostly off, or for, trains that were seen.

Two more Arpley-bound coal hauls with steam, including the redoubtable 48115 (sounding tolerably good today) finished off the time I could freely spend at this south Manchester junction, which I never got to visit again. 8F56 was the solitary identified freight with its distinctive load of 'covhops', except for the I.C.I, block stone runs. The other reporting number-toting diesels didn't match up satisfactorily with the current W.T.T.! The uneven beat of 48720 could be borne in mind when, seven weeks hence, a further encounter with the 2-8-0 would feature the defect rather more spectacularly.

Between that trip and meeting the 'Boat' at Trinity Street I had an appointment playing with three girls – a clarinet quartet for the Bolton Musical Artists' Association – item 14, just before the interval. After the concert I only just made it to the 1P02 rendezvous with 45025, unless 21.24 was the time that it pulled in, rather than the moment I flew down the steps! Amongst the chat afterwards there emerged a piece of intelligence from depot level and probably communicated by Paul, which at the time held a significance beyond its direct meaning. This was that 9K would be getting five BR 5s from Patricroft when the latter shut. The information proved to be absolutely false, but it serves to illustrate that Bolton was expected to outlive Patricroft and that the depots still didn't all know where they stood in what I might flatteringly term the closure 'programme', even at that late stage. Only two weeks after the above item of news, it was almost turned on its head by the loss of Bolton's last two Standard 5s to 9H! As is well known, both mpds ended up closing simultaneously in late June.

Sunday, 24 to Friday, 29 March

The distinctly wet Sunday of 24 March followed the usual pattern, but was void of any after dinner cleaning activity at 9K, by myself at least, and I took no content details. Ahead lay an activity-filled week though, starting with a Monday decision to sample the evening 'Boat'. This coincided with another break in 45025's (10A) dominance as 45435 (10A) trundled through Victoria at 20.03 (from Patricroft) to pick up the stock. Between then and 1P02's ECS reaching platform 12 twenty-nine minutes later, two freights descended Miles Platting bank hauled by 48327 (9H) and our own 48773 on loads of thirty-nine and forty-four respectively. The usual pilot movements completed the scene.

If not actually aware of the date set for dieselisation of the 'Boat' diagram, an increasing suspicion that it couldn't be far off led to a furtherance of the train's popularity with the enthusiast fraternity, as suggested earlier. My own endeavours in that respect, as well meant as any, were, however, about to be diluted somewhat by an irresistible attraction elsewhere on the railway, but tonight I was on the spot. No. 45435 (10A) put in a very average kind of run to Bolton in a time of eighteen and a quarter minutes after a punctual start, speed falling to a steady 43mph from 52 over Agecroft Jc. with the seven coaches and a van.

The next evening, the 26th, it was 'Hey Lads Hey' in 'A' Side with a Brush Type 4 off the road and attended by two cranes (Newton Heath and a bit later Longsight's), 'about twenty fitters and all the inspectors'. Taking this into account, observations that night stand as fairly representative of the period at O.B. and were as follows, in rather more detail than those shown for 11 March, net of regular pilot movements and showing my original notes converted into time order to better illustrate traffic progression. Dmu traffic, as always in these listings, is omitted.

D1808	Derailed light engine in 'A' Sidings	18.30 (by)
48612 (9D)	Newton Heath steam crane in attendance	
45104 (9K)	Bolton Station pilot	
44929 (9K)	'B' Sidings pilot	
45420 (9D)	16.40 Burnley–Moston (27) SX (via Victoria)	19.06
Type 2	Longsight crane arrives 'A' Siding	19.13
44963 (10A)	Loco for 20.20 Bedford pcls. SX ex shed arr. station	19.33
D5207	Loco for 20.05 Wigan pcls. SX ex 8F arr. 'A' Sidings	19.53
D5207	20.05 Bolton–Wigan pcls. SX dep. 'A' Sidings	20.04
45394 (10A)	16.50 Heysham–Moston (35) SX dep. 'B' Sidings	20.12
44963 (10A)	20.20 Bolton–Bedford pcls. dep. station	20.16
D7502	3T38 Special pcls, vans towards Manchester	20.45

73069 (9K)	Loco for 17.45 Colne–Ashton Moss pcls. SX ex shed arr. stn	20.49
44947 (9K)	Up side station pilot to shed	20.52
44690 (10F)	20.57 Bolton–Guide Bridge pcls. SX dep. station	20.56
45212 (10D)	20.55 Manchester–Heysham arr. station	21.13
48323 (10F)	19.05 Burnley–Moston SX arrives	21.13
48323 (10F)	19.05 Burnley–Moston SX departs	21.20
D5207	Loco for 23.00 Bolton–Wigan pcls. SX arr. 'A' Sidings	21.21
D5254	21.05 Oldham Clegg St.–Blackburn pcls. SX arr. station	21.23

The 'Boat Train's' departure could not be seen from Orlando bridge. 'B' Sidings pilot had been ordinarily diesel shunter-worked since the very early 1960s and 44929 tonight was merely a stopgap for an unknown reason. Traffic normally routed via Castleton Curve was running as booked again for some time now (see page 22) and the reason for the 16.40 Burnley–Moston's passage via Vic. that night is not known. No. 45212's involvement on the 'Boat' lasted for four days.

Had it not been for the signal box's close proximity to the re-railing exercise and likelihood of inspectors coming in, I could have had an evening in East Jc. Cabin, according to Bob Middlebrook, with whom I'd spoken from the bridge. The next evening I set out with the intention of another Heysham Boat Train run, but a repeated invitation to visit the scene of happy times in 1967 proved too great a temptation and instead of travelling on 1P02 I got to the station for its arrival after a couple of hours in the box. Since I'd left, the old telephone console had been replaced by a brand new one that sported the deluxe feature of light indicators for each of the circuits, a tremendous aid to anyone having to 'learn the phones', but, I suspect, providing a level of satisfaction at mastering it far removed from that of its antiquated predecessor, which doubtless had been unceremoniously broken up.

I booked for an hour and a half, in my element, the enjoyment heightened by the novelty of doing so again after weeks away. Whether I replaced the lad or one of the three men who were perhaps acting as booker that late turn, I can't recall. With Bob were John Winward, introduced earlier, and Arthur Plant. Arthur had been an occasional trainee on the block since well back in 1967. He came from Hindley with an accent to match and a peculiar habit of frequently interrupting his own speech with the word 'there', out of context with its meaning and often at a pause. Maybe it was a form of stammer and the utterance of that word freed him up to continue. I never knew him well enough to ask! The evening traffic yielded nothing beyond the norm, or what has been mentioned; nor did the one after when I was down before and after choir practice, visiting East again to copy out the substantial special trains being run for Saturday's Grand National plus a batch of Liverpool Exchange–Leicester football extras. That Thursday, the 28th, the season of spring burst upon us, bringing exceptional warmth and sunshine and although the agreeable weather persisted in lesser degrees for several days, one of those all too common reversals so early on lay just around the corner.

Reasons why the trip of 30 March that centred initially on Liverpool was broadly fixed a whole week beforehand are not immediately clear in retrospect, unless a certain train of coal empties that redeemed it (or more generally the 9Fs of Speke Jc. mpd) was the focal point all along.

Saturday, 30 and Sunday, 31 March

None of the Grand National specials reached Aintree before 11.59 (ex Coventry) and the last 13.15 (ex Euston). There were three other Eustons, and single trains from Newcastle, Watford, Swansea and Grimsby, but none were seen with any hope of steam haulage, even nearer to Merseyside. The seven football extras, however, were in our programme, but as Vern, Harvey, Keith, Pete and myself set out on the 07.26, optimism towards them was far from high, a vague chance of steam as far as Manchester being all that could be hoped for. Observing the first two powered by D343 and D323 as we approached the city, those hopes faded, but we did slip out to Sandhills to watch the passage of 45397 (10F) with the 09.00 Liverpool–Preston (Glasgow portion), 1P08, which must have been unspectacular at that point in the absence of any tape recording. We then quit the north end of the city for the drab environs of Speke and Garston.

Depot visits were not a priority at that stage and the incompletely recorded contents of Speke Jc. mid-morning testify to the main purpose of our finding the depot. This was to ascertain the motive power for 7E81, the 12.25 coal empties from Runcorn Folly Lane to Spink Hill SO. Spink Hill was near Killamarsh, G.C. Having done that, we were off, because the news was good and there was little to gain and a great deal to lose by loitering among the other locos, interesting though they were. At that time 8C was a collecting point for condemned engines from elsewhere. 'Black 5s', 8Fs, 9Fs, plus one 'Britannia', 70024 (ex 12A), some being out of service since well back into the autumn of 1967, stood in the open, but going concerns there were too, including one of the few in steam, 92218 (8C). This would be leaving shed shortly to take up the duty sought and we rushed back to Allerton station for the train to Runcorn and new ground.

One of the difficulties I encountered in the preparation of this book (and which the same would benefit from containing) is that of determining the precise point at which certain things became known to us and the way in

The snow of 2 April caught south Liverpool too, and probably earlier than Bolton, as evidenced by this general view of Speke Jc. shed on that date. Only one loco for sure in camera is warm enough to stop the 'white stuff' from settling on it. *Wallace Sutherland/M.L.S. collection*

which that knowledge reached us. The train that all minds were now focussed upon had more than likely come to our notice by other means than just emerging from the pages of the freight W.T.T., in which tome the starting point of 7E81 was given as 'Runcorn F.L.' and Folly Lane was not named on the O.S. map. We continued with confidence, however, spirits lifted during the short journey to Runcorn by the prospect of double chimney 9F action, and I remember calculating the gradient from what could only be Folly Lane to the main line junction based on 1in O.S. map contours. Another half hour would reveal the conclusion of 1 in 80 that I'd come up with to look about right. Certainly we'd long enough to gaze at it and wonder!

Inexplicably, no engine arrived and we soon realised how unnecessary had been our haste in forsaking Speke Jc. shed, including the last unpreserved 'Brit' I ever saw in one piece as well as the unrecorded engines. Of course, we had to assume that 7E81 would leave on time or even early. Without the sound and unambiguous information regarding our chosen working, it's doubtful we'd have persevered so long, but the success of this venture was very important. Pinning one of these engines down to such a favourable location was not easily done and the trip desperately needed a shot in the arm. For an hour or so, suggestions as to what might have gone wrong fuelled the main topic of conversation and after two hours they had long been exhausted! More than once hopes soared, only to be dashed again as distantly, but with a bewildering clarity, side rods were heard clanking or a whistle was perceived, but nothing came of them. We had an uninterrupted view of the line (most of it on an embankment) across common land, a prospect that has since been obliterated by something called the Runcorn Expressway. The weather at least that day was sympathetic to those subjected to lengthy waits in the open.

Finally, after three hours, amidst appropriate and unrestrained rejoicing, the sounds we had evidently imagined before actually materialised into the 9F reversing LE down to the sidings. Shortly after, two and a half hours past its booked time, the 2-10-0 drew its thirty-six high-capacity coal wagons steadily up the bank, the characteristically 'hollow' exhaust beat gratifyingly clear. A wonderfully eloquent, rather 'pleading' whistle from 92218 as it approached the main line to complete its 140 degree turn to the south-east crowned the long-awaited event. We'd split up latterly to preferred positions as the engine arrived and the whistle was, I think, a response to Vern and his tape recorder being seen by the fireman, nearer to the track than I.

Clear of Runcorn's Folly Lane Sidings, bright hope of the day 92218 (8C) finally fulfils all expectations working the empties to Spink Hill on 30 March 1968. This train, routed via the Woodhead line was, of course, steam-hauled to Godley Jc. only. *V.A. Sidlow*

What we'd eventually witnessed that day was like an oasis of purest water in a pretty barren desert and its sustaining qualities needed to last longer than expected! We really were trying to single them out, partly as there was little option at that time of day on a Saturday, and being so far west. So, now came the turn of 8F56, the 12.00 Tunstead–Runcorn SO, the location selected being a bridge near to Sutton Weaver, about 3 miles' walk away.

The earlier experience turned 'Folly Lane' into a catchword among ourselves in the months ahead, subsequent long waits eliciting the question, 'Is this going to be another 'Folly Lane'?' and other such banter. Had the 9F turned up and departed as quickly as expected, Sutton Weaver may have been adopted instead, for a wait of similar proportions ensued into the bright and sunny evening, only to end in the discovery that Heaton Mersey had provided a diesel locomotive for the job in D237!

Along the way, or right from the start, 8F56 had lost nearly three hours, passing our spot at 18.55. We were too far from any open station at that hour to make a bid for the 'Boat' at Manchester or Bolton in a last-ditch attempt to salvage the lion's share of the day from failure and it ended as much of it had passed – steamlessly. Words such as 'grim' and 'hopeless' sum up the time either side of 7E81, and contrast with the three minutes of action with 92218 in my late-night assessment of 30 March. I must stress that those negatives apply to the paucity of steam action in relation to the efforts made to achieve it, and not to the many hours amongst friends in that quest. We often saw the funny side of things, whilst banter and humour styles reflected the individuals we were. The solitary disagreement I can recall when any offence was taken concerned Keith and me when a Test match commentary on his transistor radio was ruining the silence and tranquillity under Ribblehead viaduct one August afternoon the year before! By the standards of many we were long-term friends already through the common interest, but not of cricket, and the seeds were sown on good ground to ensure it became lifelong. This was a war that steam lost, though battles were won within it. My father, in a real war, never lost touch with his closest comrades from a similar span to our end of steam chase. Our parents' ages during the conflict were not much senior to ours now, and so runs the theme. Maybe their release to peacetime equates to our progression to preservation?

Maybe too the 09.00 Liverpool–Preston had been unfairly evaluated on the day just related, but this of course is retrospective judgment with knowledge of how the rest of the day panned out. In order to take that Saturday off I'd worked until late on Friday evening and for much of Sunday on a stock take!

Monday, 1 to Friday, 5 April

The B.T.E.G. Bulletin for the coming month dropped through the letterbox on 1 April. Its editorial 'barometer' continued to climb out of the deep low into which it had plunged with the January edition, buoyantly predicting that membership, long buffeted by reaction to an increasingly dieselised system and far fewer depots, was starting to stabilise. However, having as much as said that its future prosperity depended on members that embraced the new way of things, in the next breath the Guild's truer colours surfaced in a thinly veiled gloating and sarcasm over some 'stop press' news about the withdrawal of several early 'hydraulics' and other Western diesels 'built as long ago as 1965'. Why shouldn't they gloat? And it did demonstrate the smaller society's ability to get news out more quickly than the national periodicals. The 'stop press' and plenty of other transactions were correct to 18 March.

The simultaneously published 'Steam Allocation List' was proclaimed as the last that the Guild would produce as the end was so near. Stated 'correct' to 24 February 1968, it was in fact rather incorrect in incorporating a number of small errors and one or two large ones, such as the omission of all ten of Newton Heath's 8Fs! After reconciling the others too, the steam total given of 299 locos (at thirteen depots) was ten fewer than the true figure.

It would be another two months before the June issue of the same publication brought confirmation of 44965's demise – Bolton's latest casualty, officially withdrawn in the week ending 30 March – and July editions of *Railway World* and *Railway Magazine* carried the news under the period ending 20 April. No. 44965's eighteen months at Trafford Park prior to reaching Bolton on 4 March 1968, and more so its eleven months based at Oxley before that, were but fleeting when set against its many years spent as a Saltley machine up to September 1965.

The current week marked the end of 48090, another very short-term 9K loco. Like so many, years of steadily working from the same depot (Northampton in this case) were arrested by the turmoil of the mid-1960s. This loco, however, anticipated the 'Great Migration North' by a fair margin, reacting instead to the 'big freeze' of early 1963 in a January move to the lesser extremes of Mold Jc. mpd. It next joined the mass exodus to Chester's 'passenger' shed upon the closure of 6B in April 1966. March 1967 brought it to Newton Heath, from whence it reached Bolton on 8 February 1968.

About this time, late March or early April, 48702 went into disuse at 9K, though official withdrawal wasn't until the week ending 4 May. Diesel locos of Type 2 or 4 started to become common in ones and twos on Bolton shed at the weekend, but their origin and usage wasn't investigated. In those days they were just ignored as much as possible, details of their integration never being recognised as information that would have a future use.

The fault with my 9K documentation in 1968 was not restricted to omitting infiltrating diesels, but a deplorable lack of general contents/status of locos altogether. Thoroughness in that respect had gradually degenerated from a daily event in October 1966 to the proverbial 'once in a blue moon'. Apathy cannot have been the reason as it manifested itself in no other way. Diminishing variety in the general goings on at the shed and the much smaller allocation are more likely to have brought about the unsatisfactory state of affairs that I now see it as. I am therefore occasionally forced to plumb alternative sources.

What appeared loosely to be replacements for the recently described losses at 9K arrived a few days later on 2 April. They were 48340 from Rose Grove and 48392 ex Lostock Hall, the only two locos in 1968 to find a new home at Bolton from points north, that is after January's '12' Division receipts. No. 48392 almost reached the end of Bolton shed's existence and the other 8F survived it to continue, back at 10F. The day of their arrival saw well over two hours of blizzards over teatime, ending with clear skies when it froze hard and decisively 'at 19.20', leaving plenty of crunchy snow where it had fallen. In these conditions I watched 73040 continuing to execute its station pilot duties, unaware that this was its last week on 9K work of any kind. Other traffic at O.B. on that evening conformed with the current norm too.

In the thirty-one months that Carnforth depot had been responsible for the 'Boat Train' diagram I can find no case, other than that of 45212 (10D), where any foreign engine had lasted more than four consecutive days on the job. No. 45212 handed it back to 45025 (10A) for an uninterrupted fortnight from 30 March. In the five weeks remaining to it with steam, the precedent set by the Lostock Hall loco was not threatened. On the evening of a cold and dry 3 April I sampled the Down train's first 10¾ miles to Bolton. Conveying a load of eight bogies plus the van, 1P02 left a minute late. Despite a multitude of minor wheelslips over the west end curves, the 'Black 5' made a better start than average to Salford due to sound acceleration past Exchange station, though the driver soon eased again. Speed worked up to 54mph over Agecroft Jc., evening out to 47/48 thereon. The time to Bolton was 17'-51" unchecked, a bit over schedule, but better than many.

A very small number of steam locomotives were cut up at the depot where they were condemned, due perhaps exclusively to being immobilised somehow. The cracked wheel rim of 48469, withdrawn at Bolton in December 1967, brought the 8F into that category as it was deemed not safe to move. A start was made on breaking up the 2-8-0 early in April. By the 3rd the boiler had been cut up completely and four days later only the tender remained. I am grateful to Vern for this report.

More snow later in the week, chiefly overnight and into Thursday, was short-lived on the ground locally and excellent weather at the weekend restored the season to what is hoped of it. As it was known that the two remaining Liverpool sheds would be caught up in the next wave of closures, Saturday's venture was planned again with the intention of seeing working steam in that direction. We could no longer be certain that pre-planned arrangements would be adhered to because of the unpredictability and increasing scarcity of Saturday steam workings, except at a few 'safe' locations up to 14.00 or so. Contingency plans to minimise failure such as phoning the depot responsible beforehand and turning up earlier than should have been necessary in the case of single objectives often meant poor utilisation of time, though those single objectives in a way could be the most rewarding when things worked out.

Saturday, 6 April

Saturday, 6 April began with the 'Boat', 1J05, Keith, Vern and myself participating today. The train was unusually strengthened to eleven bogies on this run a week before Easter. Overtime in the platform contributed to the nine minutes' lateness out of Bolton. No. 45025 (10A) ran moderately well to Salford in 13'-22", 63mph through Clifton Jc. rising marginally to 64 soon after. The approach to Victoria was unhindered and nearly one minute had been pulled back. It was a pity we couldn't wait for this much heavier formation going up to Queens Road. No. 73142 (9H) took the Glasgow stock out at 08.22, but the half past unit from Exchange beckoned.

Our first goal today was the climb out of Warrington Arpley to the Manchester Ship Canal bridge, 'Latchford bank' as we called it. En route, both old and new forms of motive power shared several westbound freights seen from the train out to Newton-le-Willows, but no Patricroft steam. The site of Dallam shed as we passed a few minutes late contained at least one Type 2 diesel and an unidentified 8F, the latter almost certainly condemned. Once at Latchford, on foot, the diesels were outnumbered 6:1 on actual goods workings in the two and a half hours after 10.00. Heaton Mersey 2-8-0s ruled the roost again and most ascended the 1 in 135 from either direction with little audible fuss, to a degree that I retained only one recording.

This was 48322 on fifty-three eastbound empties. Very soon after, at 10.03, D231 *Sylvania* went west on loaded coal. Just a light engine occupied the next fifty minutes. From our vantage point near Latchford signal box, any train leaving Arpley towards Manchester was visible for some time before it reached the bridge. The fireman's exertions at raising steam in 48115 prior to departure resulted in an immense pall of black smoke that drifted over south-east Warrington, as if an oil tanker negotiating the canal had caught fire! No. 48115 had made its mark again. Providing less in the way of individual spectacles, four goods in succession, all westbound in the next eighty-five minutes were powered by 48417 (coal), 48329 on mixed, 48720 (I.C.I, wagons and vans), and 48191 (coal). I'd enjoyed the tidy period spent there up to dinner. It ended with 45305 (8C) ascending the canal bridge, five minutes late but with steam to spare, hauling 'The Lancastrian' railtour, 1T85, from Lime Street on an anticlockwise route via Manchester and Southport, ending up at Liverpool Riverside by teatime. The L.C.G.B. were the organisers.

The intensive stoking up of 48115, seen from afar on 6 April, is still quite evident as the 2-8-0 tackles the eastbound ascent to the canal bridge at Latchford with a thirty-wagon load at 10.52. *V.A. Sidlow*

British Railways Steam 1968

Running extremely late, 48546 (9F) starts the climb south of Northwich with the 12.00 Tunstead–Runcorn covhops at 17.40 on 6 April, more than five hours after the previous steam observation, but in intention and anticipation holding the trip together. *V.A. Sidlow*

Following that event we left the area. Based on the previous Saturday's experience with Runcorn Folly Lane–Spink Hill, it was decided to gamble on another late departure of the train, but a tedious bus journey and walk to the spot proved fruitless. Though we didn't hang around for anything like last time, the conclusion was that it had gone. Catching 7E81 had been a gamble indeed, fired by the recent memory. A move far less risky of the outcome discovered would have been that of heading straight from Warrington to a spot between Northwich and Knutsford, but a lack of suitable buses or knowledge of eastbound gradients on the C.L.C. line, or both, overruled that.

It being not yet long after 14.00, the possibility of succeeding this Saturday where we had failed last, in seeing 8F56, Tunstead–Runcorn behind steam was reckoned worth a try, not at Sutton Weaver, but somewhere more conducive to getting a bit of a show from the engine. Northwich itself we knew and to Northwich we flew, faster in our minds than the bus could match and not therefore without some tension. Remoteness from the railway spelt danger and fostered a feeling of vulnerability as the train we sought might just be on, or close to, time. It had been known. In spite of this preoccupation, manifested in a scanning of whichever horizon seemed appropriate, I did during the journey experience briefly some truly nostalgic twinges as the route reunited me with a small part of our family's time-honoured and oh so familiar way to Abergele after a three-year absence from those childhood holidays and day trips. Even into middle age I salute the place I first saw 45686 *St Vincent* at Sutton Weaver, but to 1968 we must return, as the approaching outskirts of Northwich ensured I did that spring afternoon.

We were able to leave the bus on the west side of town and soon after reached Hartford East Jc. signal box, about an hour after 8F56 had been due. Even by ringing back (as the signalman kindly did for us) towards Knutsford, the train's whereabouts could not be discovered. Especially with a generous forty-three minutes allowance at Northwich for water and relief, there was clearly no cause to panic in finding a suitable position for a photo, or, in my case, tape recording. It had kept clear and sunny, but with a fair breeze and some shelter from the wind was available amongst trees on the less taxing

Pleased enough to secure an 8F in steam so late in the day that same Saturday evening, this view of another 2-8-0 on coal taking the route under the W.C.M.L. shows well the whole layout there. The date and engine number are not known. *Peter Reeves/M.L.S. collection*

gradient after the viaduct. However, fearful of a reduction in power output from the engine there, I decided, after considerable deliberation, to go for the more exposed 1 in 100 nearer the station. It turned out that the move was doubly wrong and a good example of being over gradient-conscious, for, at 17.40, two and a half hours late, 48546 (9F) departed with nineteen cov-hops on the train that had become familiarly known as 'Tunny – Runny', its 2-8-0 not opening out fully until the less steeply graded track we'd forsaken! Wind in the microphone too provided the only instance I can recall from the era when an otherwise good recording had to be scrapped for that reason. Despite this personal setback I regarded the afternoon a success. At the now steamless mpd, D5001 and four other diesels were present.

Wending our way rather deviously back to Manchester, by bus again to start with, in order to use the return half of rail tickets held, afforded a lucky meeting with 48723 (9F) as we dallied around Arpley for a few minutes. It was on its way home (LE) as late as 19.30. The comfortable loco-hauled Holyhead–Manchester, with buffet, got us nicely back for a 'Boat Train' finish. It duly departed ten minutes late, now with a ten-coach load and 45025 (10A) still in charge, but no extra effort was made to counter the additional train weight or lateness. Speeds were poor, i.e. 47 max. at Agecroft Jc. tailing off to the low 40s and 36 by Moses Gate. Nearly twenty-one minutes were expended in motion to Bolton and there I alighted.

Sunday, 7 to Thursday, 11 April

Cold nights and beautiful days continued into the new week. On Sunday, 7 April, I markedly improved the appearance of 45104, revealing its RH cabside lining by scratching off the poor latter-day Crewe paint. There was nothing new about this trick, but plenty we hadn't got round to yet! Coincidental rather than ominous was the omission of both 73040 and 73069 from Bolton's allocation in the recently published B.T.E.G. listing dated 24 February, but the week ending 13 April these engines did, to our annoyance and surprise, become transferred to Patricroft. Their physical disappearance from 9K by late on the 9th was quite a shock in fact, and not only because we'd lost two of our cleaner engines. The rumour of 23 March, or belief in it,

Still bearing signs of its last cleaning at 9K, 73069 has been at Patricroft less than a fortnight, yet its numberplate, newly cast at Crewe eighteen months earlier, has already disappeared. Inexplicably too, enlargement of the photo reveals a 9D (Newton Heath) shed plate! As last of the class, as it would become, the loco nevertheless took on 'celebrity' status. This image is dated 21/4/68. *Peter Reeves/M.L.S. collection*

crumbled somewhat in the light of this. On the plus side and discovered that same Tuesday night was the receipt of 45073 from Stockport mpd. I still thought instantly of the caning it got on a certain trans-Pennine relief the previous Christmas, but the 'Black 5' outlived 9K, not that that was saying a lot! Before learning of the latest gain and losses, I'd gone straight after tea to Bradley Fold West for the early evening traffic, up to and including Bedford parcels; five trains in two and a half hours. Regular motive power and average action including a rather out of beat 45095 (10A) on Bedford is the summary. I came back with three recordings, though I can't think why 48380 hauling 42 on the 18.05 Bolton–Moston wasn't one of them.

So, Bolton had finally sunk, with the loss of our BR 5s, to the level of a two-class shed (from five a year earlier). Only Speke Jc., Carnforth and Lostock Hall could boast more now with three each. I'm fairly certain that 45381 didn't run again until its withdrawal a month hence and 48702 was already dead in effect, so eighteen engines constituted the stud that did the work and for now most of them were needed. With the latest changes, the allocation was as follows:

Pre-empting the closure of Stockport Edgeley shed, 45073 moved to Bolton in early April and was first seen there on the 9th. In company with 48773, the 4-6-0 stands inside the repairs section of 9K, which consisted of roads 1, 2 and 4. Road 3 ended in buffers outside the building.
Bart van der Leeuw

44664/802/29/929/47/5073/104/10/260/90/318/81, 48026/340/80/92/504/652/702/73.

Keeping track of the Horwich Works diesel shunters status into 1968 has not been possible as the 9K internal paperwork on that subject in my possession expired during 1966. In all published listings they were shown allocated to 9D with no secondary designation. What is now known, however, is that four of the old batch, presumed still at the Works, were condemned during April 1968.

Despite the huge advancement of dieselisation's march upon the North-west during the past twelve months and its crippling effect on the overall scene, the approaching Easter weekend even then instilled flutters of excitement regarding additional traffic and the possibility, but no longer the promise, of steam involvement. Hope sprang eternal in the breast of the enthusiast of 1968. It had to! Maundy Thursday was always a big day in the past, catering for those able to make the earliest start. Relief trains abounded, chiefly on the W.C.M.L., trans-Pennine via Standedge and North Wales routes. This year I didn't have access to information on the former, but the latter two were seen to be slightly down on 1967 intensity when I'd taken a very late opportunity to get to Llandudno with a Caprotti 5. Because the 1968 offerings would stand so little chance of employing steam and due to my working normally on that day, I made no effort to find anything out for the rest of the weekend until after tea, when I telephoned Patricroft shed on Eccles 1533. This enquiry revealed no steam booked for any Standedge route reliefs. North Wales I didn't see any point in asking about.

That Thursday our church choir would normally have been practising the anthem for Easter Sunday, but this year an aria and recitative were being performed instead, so I was excused rehearsal. Setting off therefore with a free evening and firm intention of sampling the 'Boat', I got another offer to go into East Jc. and my original resolve crumbled! The booker on duty was Charlie, who came in late 1967. Signalmen Alan Hofton and Geoff Dewberry liaised with each other over parcels train and pilot shunts as they came to be made with the customary purpose of harmonious movements. 'I'll not get this one over, Alan' (before yours) and 'Top end o' one with Guide Bridge' being examples of randomly recorded comment. Whilst there I copied from the N2 notice details of more specials on the back of a vacancy list, mostly Monday's Blackpool and Belle Vue extras. Of these, hopes were entertained for a few. There being no other realistic choice, 'Black 5s' were treading in 73040's footsteps on station pilot, 45104 being employed tonight. The 350hp diesels started to creep in later in April. Up side pilot (44947) and the steam-hauled line workings conformed with the norm prevalent at the time.

Friday, 12 April

Good Friday's timetable was structured on that of a Sunday, as usual, with no freight. I'd no reliefs of any interest noted, if indeed there were any. A weekday train that had been marked to run, however, was the 08.25 Glasgow–Liverpool and its Manchester portion, the 12.17 ex Preston, 1J42. This then was my daytime objective and just one of several reminders of how condensed had become the scope when compared directly with the festival of only twelve months ago.

A Manchester–Blackpool special parcels running via Clifton Jc. and booked to precede my dmu to Preston was

Hit and miss with steam by late March was the 12.17 Preston–Manchester. Seen here approaching Bolton through Deane Clough, this is at an earlier date and with preferable power to that of the author's Good Friday attempt! *H. J. Scowcroft*

Complying with the Sunday timetable of Good Friday, 45025 (10A) awaits departure from platform 11 Middle, which connected Manchester Victoria and Exchange stations, with the 20.55 to Morecambe. This train did not have Belfast boat connections at Heysham on Sundays away from mid-summer. A very poor run to Bolton ensued on this occasion, 12 April 1968. *P. Barber*

hauled by D5053, which, I happened to notice bore a 34G (Finsbury Park) shed plate! At eighteen months out of date, this was far more extreme than any steam engine I've known bearing an old code, except one. The Type 2 moved to Eastfield and no recorded movement prior to that spring morning can be found! The 11.24 'cart' I boarded was 'packed solid' with trippers responding to their day off and the superb weather that blessed it. At Preston it was bad news as a Type 4 was waiting to work the 12.17. The 12.44 Preston–Blackpool engine would have been about then, but no mention of it or the train in my notes suggests that it was not laid on additionally and I returned, somewhat disconsolately, behind D267. The rest of the afternoon I spent cleaning 45110 with Paul at 9K. Four 'Black 5s' and two 8Fs were fired for the brief resumption of at least some normal working on Saturday, though as with 1967, a proportion of Bolton's jobs seemed to be cancelled for the day.

Whether there was any connection that night between the appalling run experienced with 45025 (10A) on the evening 'Boat Train' and the engine being replaced on the diagram next morning, I don't know. Certainly 45025 had been in continuous use for two weeks and may have been due for a washout. Though not actually producing the slowest overall journey time known to Bolton (that was soon to come!), the running was dire indeed, the current catchword for such lacklustre efforts being 'chronic'. As the Sunday arrangements applied, departure was from platform 11 Middle – easier than from the curved No. 12, but the route via Pendleton Broad Street and the 30mph restriction over Agecroft Jc. Having negotiated this, with hardly need to slow at all, the eight-coach train accelerated only marginally to 36 by Clifton Jc. and at that figure it steadfastly remained to Moses Gate! The time taken to Bolton was 22'-22", after a punctual start from Vic.

Saturday, 13 April

Though devoid of any Bank Holiday Weekend 'feel' or flavour, Saturday's (13 April) local trip turned out to be the most rewarding, successful and enjoyable of its kind in 1968. Luckily I had plenty of recording tape. Anything less than the twenty-three minutes I used up would have led to regrets and this is indicative of what a fulfilling day lay ahead. I think all the Bolton group took part and we first went to meet Pete at Manchester on the 'Boat' (of all trains!). The change mentioned earlier was to 44894 (10A), an engine that had not had involvement on the

A justified sense of purpose can be detected in the group's step as permission is given to ride in the front brake van to Halliwell behind 48026 following its traffic stop here at Westhoughton on 13 April 1968.
P. Barber

diagram since mid-January. The eight-coach set remained in use that day and 1J05 pulled into Bolton two minutes early. A decent run to Manchester transpired, speeds fluctuating in the range of 62/66/61 between Kearsley and Pendleton Old. Salford received the train in 12'-29" from Trinity Street and a minute was gained to Victoria.

We'd hoped to get up to the thoroughfare known as Red Bank where the curved 1 in 59 ended for the two empty stock workings around that hour, but the first, the Glasgow portion, 05.45 ex Wigan NW, 1C50, left at 08.11 behind 73133 (9H) before we'd even got off the station. I was sorry to have missed the Caprotti on that tough initial stretch out of Vic. At least it proved timely in the future. No. 44894 at least obliged by waiting until we were ready, making several initial slips, but a strong, blasting and by no means slow climb on its way with the 'Boat Train' stock to Queens Road C.S.

It had been collectively agreed to next try for better fortune with Bamfurlong–Halliwell, which we knew to be running, and this occasioned my only journey straight back to Bolton off the Up 'Boat', on to Hindley, too. In fact, we were too late to intercept the train there, for approaching Crow Nest Jc. in the dmu, the rather disturbing sight of 48026 going the other way caused the timetable to be brought out again. The dire nature of this line's local service on a Saturday morning had been encountered before (on 10 February), and so for the second week in succession public road transport saved the day. On this occasion it got us back to Westhoughton before 48026's train had completed shunting in the Metal Box Co. siding. The last movements of this we watched from nearby, noticing the friendly driver, Wilf Faulkner, who was well known to us. Wilf's fireman at this time was Jim Markland, whom I knew less well then than many

No. 48026 takes a 'breather' at Halliwell on 13 April after safely depositing its sidings and train in the sidings and its unofficial passengers likewise.
P. Barber

Another view of 48026 at Halliwell on 13 April with tape recorders in the foreground, whilst driver Wilf Faulkner, halfway down the steps of the old cabin, and fireman Jim Markland descend with fresh brews. *V.A. Sidlow*

years later during the preparation and writing of his well-known 'Bolton Engineman' series.

Trip 87 (as it certainly was known from early May, if not now), as previously mentioned conveyed a brake van at each end and as the goods prepared to leave we were fortunate in securing a ride to Halliwell in the vehicle not occupied by the guard since the reversal. Without Wilf's kind, accommodating nature we would not have found ourselves in such a privileged position, four or five feet from the smokebox door as today the loco was tender-first from Hindley. The day was turning into one of joining trains at unusual and unauthorised places.

At 10.06, hauling twenty-three loaded coal wagons (16-tonners) and the two brakes, 48026 was rightaway Halliwell with three microphones held towards that smokebox door. Only Keith never did any taping. Wilf launched into a very rousing restart up the brief remaining adverse grade before coasting down to Lostock Junction.

For much of the level or near level track over Deane Clough and the site of the water troughs the metallic 'clinkety clink' of our 8F's anti-vacuum valves overrode other sounds. Having slowed in order to negotiate Johnson Street Fork and Bradshawgate tunnel, the 8F was not opened out as expected upon emerging from the latter, and in fact coasted or near coasted so far up the 1 in 78, gradually losing speed that it became plain that the driver had something in mind for his unexpected 'passengers'.

Much later than the Astley Bridge Jc. Signalman would have expected, the regulator was thrust open, fully it seemed, and the terrific blast remained rock steady with the speed at around 10mph until a few yards before the cabin when 48026 lost its grip, probably on pointwork. Ten seconds is a long time to listen to an engine slipping with steam still on and the engine wanting to grip. That's how long Wilf left it before shutting off and we forfeited a lot of momentum. The next few minutes were taken up with a struggle to clear the junction, punctuated by much more skidding and momentary adhesion. The train practically stalled at one point and maybe even Wilf wondered if he'd misjudged the show, but in the end we didn't need the quarter of an hour it wanted before the Blackburn dmu would need a road and 48026 stopped in Halliwell yard at 10.30.

Although the display of raw and even unrestrained power (harnessed or otherwise) from the 8F had been largely for our benefit (without the deliberate slowing on the bank no difficulty would have arisen), any artificiality was suppressed by the exhilaration of such an event that, had there been a dearth of worthwhile action elsewhere on 13 April, would have carried the day alone. Three-quarters of an hour later, after shunting and the replenishment of brew cans, three vans and two brake vans were conveyed to Burnden with ourselves back on board to alight after a rough shunt or two at that point. No. 48026 then retired to shed.

Next for 48026, a featherweight load bound for Burnden and the end of that day's duty, approaching Astley Bridge Jc. *P. Barber*

The long-obliterated Johnson Street fork that the trip with 48026 negotiated, granting direct access between the Lostock Jc. and Bromley Cross lines, receives scant attention in this book. It completed the second of two triangles within the Bolton complex. Unlike the Burnden Jc.–Rose Hill Jc. fork it was a passenger line, but was mostly used by goods trains. Here, home engines 45381 and 45260 double-head a working probably for Halliwell in March 1968. *Tom Morris*

At the other end of this short avoiding line, 48313 approaches Bradshawgate tunnel – only 88 yards long, but twisty – and has the distant signal from the box of that name in its favour. This view is from June 1967. *V.A. Sidlow*

Not only had B.R. lifted its ban on railtours behind steam, but the day's next objective had been organised BY the Scottish Region. The Up line through Sough Tunnel was still closed whilst extensive maintenance was carried out inside the bore. As mentioned earlier, this meant that all southbound trains on the Blackburn–Bolton route had to set back at Springs Vale onto the Down line and restart on a gradient of 1 in 74½, an arrangement that was not ideal operationally because of difficulties sometimes encountered in getting heavy trains on the move again. This was the very reason that Spring Vale was our next port of call on 13 April, firstly to intercept the enthusiasts' special hauled by 70013 (10A). The tour, 1Z36, Edinburgh to Stafford (but not wholly steam) arrived more or less to time, but minutes were lost after reversal as the Pacific's efforts to regain motion came to no avail. The first ten attempts resulted in nasty wheelslips with no ground covered, but after blowing out some packing from the RH piston gland, the 'Brit' kept its feet and ponderously moved off towards the tunnel mouth. The load was one of eleven coaches. After its passage we weren't alone in waiting for 3J83, the 13.25 Colne–Red Bank vans SO, to make the same manoeuvre. Running more than an hour late today (and not held up by the special), 48519 (10F) had no problems restarting from the stop with a train equal to about ten coaches in length and it romped past us at 15.34.

Southbound dmus, after reversing for the single-line section, stopped in the remains of Spring Vale station platform (closed 5 August 1958) whilst the points were reset and the pilotman embarked. On this occasion we took advantage of the unofficial halt, as far as the public was concerned, to catch the train home, thereby avoiding the lengthier walk to Darwen. It's a minor joy in the retelling so long after to repeatedly come across activities that would be utterly forbidden in the present day, and a reminder of how free and easy things often were. On the way back we examined several late nineteenth century L & Y telegrams discovered in the course of rummaging around a recently demolished building on Spring Vale station.

Opportunities for steam naturally thinned out by late Saturday afternoon and our group sometimes followed suit during local trips in 1968, partly disbanding around teatime until the later evening steam run. Just Pete and I stayed the course today, chancing a jaunt to Chorley for the 18.45 Heysham–Ardwick SO, 5J44. Quite unheeded, we just walked down the track, possibly having spoken to the signalman – I can't recall – with a good sense of timing. No. 44947 scurried up the 1 in 134 at a good pace hauling nineteen container wagons. I'd actually recorded it as Heysham–Brewery, acknowledging the last change to its finishing point, doubtless brought about by more late Saturday Manchester yard opening hours being curtailed.

No. 70013 (10A) draws up at Spring Vale before setting back onto wrong line working with 1Z36, the Edinburgh–Stafford railtour. The drama began with the attempted restart upgrade. After the Colne–Red Bank vans a couple of hours later, the best excitement of 13 April was behind us. *V.A. Sidlow*

A sure-footed restart is made by 48519 (10F) from Spring Vale hauling the late-running 13.25 Colne–Red Bank empty vans SO train on 13 April 1968. *P. Barber*

At the end of an undeniably worthwhile day came the only rather disappointing aspect of it after we'd regrouped at Victoria in the performance of the 'Belfast Boat Express'. This, its full title, did not sound particularly out of place amongst those of greater fame such as 'The Royal Scot' or 'The Elizabethan', which, by their slightly loftier status seemed contemptuous of the need to contain a reminder that they were indeed 'expresses'. Whilst the same might equally have happened to one of the above named elite passenger trains, the demeaning nature of an incident on the 'Boat' that night somehow dashed any comparisons with the 'mighty', especially in the minds of those who had seen so much mediocre running over the past few months. To those regulars, the loss of the fireman's shovel shortly after Clifton Jc. symbolised the lowest ebb that the train had reached in terms of performance and prestige under the control of man.

Ten minutes late to start with, 1P02, headed by 44894 (10A) made a slow start, achieved 47mph at Agecroft Jc., then gradually fell to 35 by Farnworth. Obviously, as the shovel was now lying by the track somewhere, steam pressure had to be conserved until another implement became available. Bolton shed supplied the same during a brief stop opposite the depot office, so nearly twenty-four minutes were taken for this first part of the run. I'd covered almost 100 miles by rail in nearly fourteen hours without straying more than 11½ miles from home and didn't feel inclined to add to this with a late evening extension.

Sunday, 14 and Monday, 15 April

Afternoon activity on Easter Sunday took the form of painting the lining out on 45110 where gaps existed still. This was the first of two sessions and something I hadn't indulged in for quite some time. A meeting at the station after evensong (for me) in order to discuss the Bank Holiday Monday and decide on a plan was 'most unsatisfactory' due to a complete lack of specials that we could target with any sort of confidence. After noting that the 'Boat' had changed locos to 45134 (10A), the gathering dispersed inconclusively. Somehow, we knew that the single Southport and Blackpool extras from Manchester were booked for diesel power, so must have done some phoning to find out.

It's possible and probable that my excursion 'master' list for Monday was leaner than that of 1967 for three reasons, i.e. not having seen an N1 notice, some being ruled out for steam and therefore not transcribed, and simply because fewer were running. I'd say that the middle reason was the least likely because of my broader interest in the excursion scene evidenced by plenty of 'no hopers' to Blackpool and Belle Vue transcribed from the N2 document onto my own paper. Adexes to those two destinations were, I'm sure, comprehensively listed, revealing them to be 25% and 50% down respectively on the previous year's levels. Because of this and the anticipated dearth of steam, Easter Monday 1968 was

The lining out exercise on 14 April must have been concentrated on the LH side of 45110 as the loco appears complete in that respect in this 3 April view on the fireman's side as it reverses up Bolton shed yard. *V.A. Sidlow*

1P58, the 12.44 Preston–Blackpool South, played an important part in the Easter 1968 search for steam on passenger work. Just over a month earlier, 44713 (10D) begins its journey under the famous signal gantry towards No. 5 box on 8 March 1968 with that same train. *I.C. Simpson*

Inside looking out, at Blackpool North mpd, one of the few sheds to display a regionally coloured enamel sign at the entrance to, or in this case, within the premises, proclaiming which engine shed it was. Can you spot it? Blackpool North depot had originally closed on 10 February 1964, even before the main Rigby Road establishment. When Fleetwood mpd shut too in February 1966, the Fylde had no steam servicing facilities, essential especially in summer, and so the modestly dimensioned North depot was revived, though without allocated locos of its own. *S.A. Leyland*

clearly going to be a different kettle of fish. The big question was: 'Could Blackpool, which had done so much to seasonally enrich the steam-hauled passenger scene during its long decline, pull it off one final time?' There was little cause for optimism based on what we knew. However, following a natural inclination to make for the Fylde, where lay, I reckoned, the best chance of something unexpected turning up, I found, not surprisingly, that others with the same hopes had the same idea.

A mid-morning arrival at Preston found Harvey and Alan ('Tosh') of my acquaintance. Still normally steam-worked Monday to Friday was the 12.44 Preston–Blackpool South, 1P58, a portion of the 09.05 Euston–Windermere, but this being a Bank Holiday, engine diagramming wasn't necessarily the same. Expectations were rewarded, however, by the arrival in Preston station of 45149 (10D) a good hour and a half prior to the train's departure. One or two specials had already gone to the coast, but now, with spirits lifted, the modest flow of the rest could be observed more light heartedly for what it was. Modern power had done nothing to change traditional points of origin – pleasant reminders of steamier and busier times. Through not spending much time on the main line in 1968 so far, the new D400 Type 4s were still a detached novelty. About fifteen had entered service by mid-April, slowly releasing older diesels onto other work with the inevitable effect. As D411 (only the second one I'd seen) took out the 08.20 Birmingham–Perth at 10.43, D228 passed through Preston on the Blythe Bridge–Blackpool North, 1L36. The others were as follows:

I was thoroughly enjoying the run and credit to the crew must be given for pushing this worn old '5' with the slick timings in mind. We'd dropped a little on schedule to threading the Kirkham junctions at a bit less than the 40mph permitted before climbing the short rise after North Jc. Speeds downhill through Wrea Green were strangely less impressive than on the level (63 max.), but we reached Lytham, the first stop, only half a minute slower than the Limited Load timings demanded. The remaining 6¼ miles included booked halts at Ansdell & Fairhaven and St Annes-on-the-Sea, but not Squires Gate. The rate rose to about 50mph on each occasion, whilst platform allowances of a minute each were cut smartly, so arrival at South station came at 13.21 instead of the scheduled twenty past. We'd experienced a good effort from a machine that sounded rough to Kirkham. Ex Llandudno Jc. and Shrewsbury in recent years, it hung on to usefulness until the early summer.

Of the two routes to Blackpool South, I never made any differentiation in earlier spotting notes, even though recording the engines that hauled the trains I travelled on. To this day I can't actually prove that I went, or came back, via Marton, though it is as likely, if not more so as the coast route. Today's run at least eradicated any ignorance left over regarding the surviving alternative to North via Poulton-le-Fylde. This latter route had been much more favoured by steam passenger duties since Central station and shed closed in 1964 and I knew it well. Even in April 1968 it was impossible to predict developments that enabled the coast line behind steam, with its sprints through the rural Fylde, then engine exhausts bouncing a tattoo off the residential

D395	09.08	Bradford–Blackpool N.	1M72	
D7595	10.10	Manchester–Blackpool N.	1L03	11.07
D307		Walsall–Blackpool N.	1L35	11.22
D356	09.02	Castleford–Blackpool N.	1Z51	11.26
D1541		Chesterfield–Blackpool N.	1Z39	11.30
D214	09.27	Dewsbury–Blackpool N.	1Z43	11.41
D7570	09.54	Leeds–Blackpool N.	1Z45	11.57
D216		Warrington–Blackpool N.	1L02	12.12

The Euston–Windermere we awaited was punctual enough coming in and left its rear six-coach portion to 45149 and the 12.44 to Blackpool South. Three minutes late away, our 4-6-0 was taken fairly easily up to No. 5 box and over Maudlands viaduct, but once onto the former racing stretch the regulator was yanked open and 45149 got into its stride. One wouldn't expect to hear a 'Black 5' on level track with this load at more than 50mph or so, but this was an exception. Acceleration in this range wasn't brilliant considering that the loco was being moderately thrashed along, but speed eventually built up to 68mph in the vicinity of Salwick. Clearly audible throughout, a raw-sounding choppy exhaust combined without clattering progress over pointwork of the still frequent signal boxes to give an impression of even higher velocity.

brickwork, to become so well-known, too. This it did, however, becoming a major feature in our story through the approaching late spring and summer.

Joining the throngs along the 'prom' and reaching Blackpool North mpd – both essentials of the day, and not unlinked – were accomplished in the same movement, one leading to the other. The latter objective was to weigh up the loco situation for the evening reliefs as they offered our only chance of a steam run back. The fulfilment of this goal now was all important. Far beyond just a preference or wish, upon it hung the principle of upholding Blackpool's holiday railway image in our eyes, powerless though any of us were to influence whatever the outcome would be.

North shed housed four steam engines; nothing else, plus 45149, which came on soon after we arrived. The

The regular (non-excursion) part of Blackpool North station as it was in late steam days and from where the 'life-saving' Easter Monday Accrington relief with 45268 (9D) departed on 15 April. *S.A. Leyland*

others were 45268 (9D), 44690 (10F), 48212 (9H) and 45444 (10D). No. 45268 left, hauling a parcels to Preston at 15.01, and 45149 with empty stock to Blackpool South twenty minutes later, then things went quiet. Two of the other locos, though not yet fired, were to be seen working the next day, partly in an unexpected capacity. North shed had closed as early as 10 February 1964, even before the much larger Rigby Road mpd. When that went, soon after, the authorities realised that Fleetwood was the only Fylde depot left to service steam and reinstated the Blackpool North facilities for visiting engines. When Fleetwood closed (February 1966), and with the swing to North station for excursion work, its renaissance was complete. North station still had its six regular platforms and another ten for seasonal extras.

From the chalked notice boards along the sloped entrance to Preston's main platforms some relief train details not in the N2 notice had been copied down that morning. Just one, a late evening Blackpool N–Heysham, was found to have no loco available for it. This was taking the diesels into account too, of course. Those that had worked in earlier occupied the extensive carriage sidings nearby. Despite this, there remained several hours for something to turn up for the Heysham, although we'd no reason to believe that anything would be other than diesel-powered out of Blackpool whilst we remained.

Towards teatime, 45268 returned, and even this rather inconclusive development raised the hopes of those still present, loitering in the shed yard. Spirits though, were by no means low. It had been a warm, pleasant afternoon with morale sustained by the recent efforts of 45149 and no knowledge of better steam activity elsewhere. Soon after 45268 had got back on shed, it began to look as if the day was not doomed to be the first steamless Easter Monday at Blackpool on excursion work after all as the loco was now booked to stand by for a possible unscheduled relief to Accrington, providing sufficient passengers accumulated in between the hourly dmu service trains and two reliefs already laid on. I think these were from South station. Talking to the crew of 45268 revealed that they didn't want to go to Accrington, whilst we did, though not as bona fide returning trippers. Who was going to win? Unchallenged for much of the afternoon on North mpd, we were at least at the cutting edge of any decisions made.

Eventually, it transpired that the queue forming at the barriers, though not of fantastic proportions, was considered large enough to warrant running the special! This didn't cheer up the crew, but it was marvellous news to the few enthusiasts who had waited; a fairy tale ending I'd even say, in view of the prospect earlier on and for the period. Blackpool, which had given us so much pleasure from steam passenger work in the closing years, had come up trumps once again. It was a happy band then that returned not to the excursion platforms, but the regular station. As the stock was propelled in, the low capacity of the six-coach scratch set, which comprised largely of brake seconds, became apparent, but even this didn't become crowded.

Departure came at 18.48 and with no set times to keep, the driver couldn't really be blamed for running at his own pace. Having been given a job they professedly didn't want, the crew now seemed intent on making it last. Progress to Preston was leisurely with a top speed of 50mph at Lea Road and four signal checks at various points, including a near three-minute stand waiting to join the main line. I'm less convinced that the news had travelled fast enough to attract more enthusiasts to Preston than by the thought that the not inconsiderable number that boarded now had already been there, waiting around in the slender hope of the unexpected and probably with even less cause for optimism than ourselves. I was valid to Preston on the return half of my morning ticket, but had no desire to risk rebooking during the stop and in fact we were on the move again less than a minute later.

Running out via the long-obliterated East Lanes, lines towards Todd Lane Jc., the special made an unexpected passenger stop at Bamber Bridge. To a classic 'Rightaway driver' from the man on the platform there, 45268 pulled away strongly towards the only hard work that would be demanded of it as the start developed into a good slog all the way up Hoghton bank, speed rising to 38mph towards the summit. Our 'Black 5' had been out-shopped at Crewe just over two years before and was well out of condition again. The exhaust, urgent, rather raw and loud, ought, with only a light load on the 1 in 100, to have produced more power in its earlier passage through the cylinders, but it delighted those listening to what only a few hours ago seemed such a remote prospect. The special encountered several signal checks and a P.W. slowing between Pleasington and Blackburn, but it mattered little as this was one run that gained atmosphere in its unhurried, casual nature that resumed with the easier grades.

After a three-minute halt at Blackburn we were next stop Accrington and the relief (in the truest sense of the word) sauntered on at under 40mph, arriving in the sharply curved platform at 20.12. Some uncertainty here as to whether the train should terminate led to the enthusiasts reboarding. Possibly a few normal passengers had been told they were alright for certain points beyond, but it was the bulk of people travelling purely for the steam haulage and who were largely without tickets that swayed the decision in favour of extending the train! From our point of view the day had already been won, but this surprise continuation only strengthened the assertion as 45268, after a halt of just over seven minutes, proceeded northwards at an easy pace. Having called at Burnley Central and Nelson, the last ever direct steam run connecting Blackpool with Colne rolled over the viaduct to terminate at 20.49. As the 'Black 5' drew out the empty stock into the advanced dusk, few, if any, thought the town would see steam on any passenger train again, beyond enthusiasts tours, but who would have put money on it? Those of us for Bolton caught the penultimate through unit home, well contented with how the day had turned out.

Tuesday, 16 April

Plenty of people seemed to have Tuesday the 16th off as well. Regular non-passenger traffic had apparently reverted to normal, but nothing amongst the sparse excursion scene was even contemplated as a target for steam. Keith and I opted to try a morning at Clayton Bridge for any Ashton Moss-bound goods workings that came along. Starting on the 'Boat', 44894 (10A) was making a brief return. Nearly to time from Bolton, no high

Another view of the 12.44 Preston–Blackpool as it passes through Kirkham behind Carnforth loco 44667, an image borrowed from 1967, entirely representative of the train in its last year with steam. *V.A. Sidlow*

The 13.50 Blackpool N.– Manchester parcels SX was part of the 'Belfast Boat Express' diagram. It is seen here passing Burnden Jc. behind the year's prominent engine on that duty, 45025 (10A), on an unknown date within it. The Bolton shed outlet road is on the left.
Photographer unknown

speeds were needed and running at close to 60mph towards Salford recouped more than the minor arrears. By watching 73050 (9H) head out with the Glasgow stock at 08.17 we missed the 08.18 to Clayton Bridge and went via Dean Lane instead, then on foot – not the extended walk it sounds! However, this jaunt seemed misguided and we retreated after not much more than an hour with sights set on the 12.44 Preston–Blackpool again. There had been (and still was) a fair amount of steam around Victoria and at sundry points through train windows, both LE and on jobs, but none of it on specifically identified work. Several locos were encountered twice at different locations, but not helpfully enough for trip identification.

The engine that had powered the 12.44 yesterday, 45149 (10D), we observed on much less prestigious work, shunting ballast wagons at Adlington. Conversely, 45444 (10D), seen at Blackpool N. shed with the chalked inscription on its cabside 'Ballast 15.00 Tues' had been considerably elevated as this machine was waiting to take over 1P58 as we arrived at Preston! The main train from London came in a little late, so the Blackpool portion, again of six coaches, didn't leave until 12.50, six minutes late. Adverse signals immediately after starting and a stand at No. 5 box made the train eight and a half minutes late at that point and thus impeded the run into speed down slightly favourable grades towards Lea Road (1 in 360). No. 45444 proved much less sprightly here and on the near level straight, reaching only a brief 61mph at Salwick then tailing off to the Kirkham approaches, by which point, at 36mph, we'd lapsed to eleven minutes late. The gravity-assisted mile at 1 in 119 after Wrea Green and gentler drop to sea level produced 64mph and from the Lytham start (which was all I tape recorded) today's run almost equalled that of 45149, both sharing 52mph through Squires Gate. South station saw us terminate now only eight minutes behind time. En route we'd overtaken a westbound coal train at Maudlands (the cause of the early checks), hauled by 48727 (10F) and 48212 (9H) shunting at Kirkham.

The irregular and often unfixed travels of a single day sometimes created an imbalance in tickets held and the impracticability of rebooking could compound the problem too, unless one came completely 'clean' at journey's end. For example, on 16 April, alighting to rebook at Bolton would have defeated the need to do so by causing us to miss the 12.44 at Preston. Having no 'validity' then to go through the barriers there, it was less trouble to carry on to Blackpool. There being no reason to go off the station at South, the temptation to try and return FOC as well loomed large, and in this instance Keith and I succumbed to that temptation. Ticket Collectors on trains were very sparse in those days and this bred the form of fare evasion suited to the system. The barrier was absolute, meant to be just that, the all-controlling point, entering or leaving a station. On the 16th we fell fowl of a Travelling Ticket Inspector (T.T.I.) south of Preston and were 'gripped', following whatever excuse was proffered, receiving in turn an 'excess' ticket back to Bolton. Looking back, it surprises me to see that I was using the word 'gripped' then. It was an extension of 'clipped' (as in ticket) and meant a ticket check of any kind, quite irrespective of one's validity or otherwise. This was the enthusiasts' term in vogue and part of a much larger vocabulary, much of which was not known to me until later.

The concept and art of fare evasion amongst steam enthusiasts had its origins on any kind of large and deliberate scale in the mid-1960s and was chiefly a Southern thing, brought north when the Southern scene ended. The self-styled 'Do All Availables' (D.A.As.) embraced fare evasion as an essential as they couldn't afford all of the steam haulage they 'had' to get in in an addictive way. Free travel therefore became an 'entitlement' as the only way to carry on and was not entered into or looked upon as a criminal act by those who habitually indulged in it, despite what the law said. Except for those who had to travel to reach the North-west in 1968 for steam, it had largely fizzled out as there wasn't the choice or frequency of steam any more to keep people on the go all the time.

We dallied unnecessarily at Preston an hour on the way back to see what was about and usefully saw 44894 (10A) on the 13.50 Blackpool N–Manchester parcels. This train had brief booked stops at Poulton-le-Fylde and Kirkham. I only noted its punctual 14.25 arrival at Preston, where fifteen minutes were allowed for loading and unloading. With five minutes at Chorley before the Bolton stop (15.22/36) it would normally have well preceded our 15.12 dmu from Preston. We'd no further thoughts of the train, 3J06, or recorded sighting of it on the way home, nor during a late afternoon linger at Bolton station whilst 44929 and particularly 44802 provided local trip activity in the one and a half hours up to teatime. Yet we must have overtaken the parcels because when something made me return to O.B. very soon after tea, 3J06 pulled out at 18.40, four hours late, behind 44942 (10D). This suggested the failure of 44894 nearer to Preston, hence the Lostock Hall replacement, but why had there been so much delay?

At the later evening gathering, further 'fun and games' were revealed. The Type 2 on the 12.17 Preston–Manchester (Glasgow portion) that day, which we'd crossed en route to Preston, had failed nearer to Bolton and 45290, as the nearest engine to hand, or most readily available on shed, had hauled the train tender-first to Manchester. I think it was Paul who had seen it, but can't be sure. No. 44942 had not enjoyed a long turn-round time in Manchester, but it duly stuck to the diagram, bringing the 'Boat Train' slightly early into Bolton at 21.11. Starting the next day, 45025 (10A) began a session that turned out to be its last of any duration before the diesels took over in early May.

Wednesday, 17 to 19 April

The next three days passed uneventfully on the local scene, except for two enjoyable part evenings I spent in East Jc. box. Relief men on duty were Winward, whom we've met before, and Tommy Shepherd. 'Shep' was youngish with a voice not at all unlike that of Eric Idle. A smashing bloke to get on with, he used to pronounce my abbreviated name 'Stey' with a hard 'e'. I seem to remember him always wearing pumps in the box. His little passion was the horses, but with cash available for bets strictly regulated by what was in his tobacco tin 'float', which (presumably) never ran out. Much later, but before the main cabins at Manchester Victoria closed, he was more or less in charge there and I reintroduced myself to a not surprisingly rather more serious-minded 'Shep' about twenty years after the end of steam at the start of an official evening group visit that he conducted around Victoria East and West boxes.

That April 1968 visit to Bolton East enabled me to copy out detailed timings of one of the year's best-remembered railtours and its six associated light engine movements. This particular special was advertised in *Railway Magazine* as a 'Steam Railtour from Birmingham', but without a real title and organised jointly by the Manchester Rail Travel Society and Severn Valley Railway Society. If a little more grandiose than most, it was nevertheless typical of so many from that period that wandered all over parts of Lancashire and West Yorkshire, sometimes touching Derbyshire and Cheshire, too.

The lineside potential of 1Z77, as it is best referred to and known, was such that early in the month we'd contemplated hiring a vehicle to follow it about, largely at the expense of whatever normal service steam could be tracked down instead. In the end, the trip took on no less of a pioneering nature when Pete engaged the services of one of his non-railway minded colleagues to drive us around to various locations where the train could be observed in conditions that suited us.

Saturday, 20 April

Our rendezvous with the car was in Manchester so this involved the Bolton contingent (minus Paul, who had something else in mind) catching the Up 'Boat' into the city. Easter had left me devoid of spare tape by the end of Monday, but a Thursday purchase saw me flush with the commodity. It is this fact that leaves me simply aghast in retrospect at not recording the really dynamic start from Bolton by 45025 (10A) that carried 1J05 through Moses Gate at 56mph in two and three-quarter minutes! Whilst 1968 did, in a general sense, see a far more liberal tape usage by myself than earlier periods of cassette machine ownership, contradictory examples such as the above appear, when looked back upon with present day values, to have been the product of unthinkable restraint! The odd style of driving exhibited that morning became apparent after Moses Gate as speed increased only marginally to 61mph by Clifton Jc., but the earlier vigour held the key to a two-minute early arrival at Victoria. Maybe an unnecessarily heavy fire at Bolton needed to be livened up and partially thrown out?

B.R. were in no hurry that morning to get the ECS out of Vic. and we comfortably witnessed both that from which we'd alighted and the Glasgow sleeper stock blasting uphill at our Red Bank location, a quarter of an hour apart, before having to join the 'chase' car. Today the Glasgow was first up with 73010 (9H). Both were sure-footed, but slow enough round the 'S' bend to produce individual exhaust beat echoes.

In those days, tour organisers could request and/or choose specific locomotives to haul railtours. 1Z77 today had come main line via Crewe to Stockport, where reversal and the change to steam took place. Although the home shed, 9B, currently had a dozen 'Black 5s' allocated, few of which would be needed on a Saturday, the pair chosen to start 1Z77 off were from elsewhere and I can't help

The steeply graded 'S' bend out of Manchester Victoria, and scene of our first location on 20 April, is well illustrated by this view dated two days later of a prominent Bolton shed duty. Known generally as Patricroft–Crumpsall, it had lots of north Manchester yards involvement, but the more simplistic MO version seen here found itself three hours after leaving 9K at 05.10 departing Patricroft with Astley Green-mined coal for Crumpsall. At Victoria another engine direct from Bolton (MO) was booked to bank the train to its destination, then assist with shunts including the I.C.I. siding. The banker later performed Bury–Heap Bridge trips and if necessary banked the afternoon Horwich–Moston up to Broadfield. No. 48026 heads the Monday train here, banked by 45290. The double wonder is that the job did not involve a Patricroft loco and that the Target number 239 had remained unaltered since at least March 1967. *E. Bobrowski*

Bolton's 'star' 'Black 5' of the period, 45110, does most of the work in keeping the 1Z77 railtour moving at a respectable rate up the long climb through Chapel-en-le-Frith on 20 April 1968. The train engine is 44949 (9D). *V.A. Sidlow*

wondering if anyone associated with Edgeley depot took this as a slight. It's not as if 9B had nothing good enough for passenger work, as proof will soon be seen, but today, Bolton's 45110 and Newton Heath's 44949 headed LE to Stockport to take over the tour's first leg, which was the L.N.W.R. route to Buxton.

Our first port of call, therefore, was just after Chapel-en-le-Frith on the lengthy 1 in 58 climb, which dictated two 'Black 5s' for the ten-coach train, seven bogies being the limit for a single '5', as I'd discovered on the footplate of a railtour the previous November when another Bolton engine officiated. Despite the provision of a double-header, punctually at 11.00 the strong and perfectly even exhaust of one engine interrupted the silence and tranquillity of that beautiful spring morning as the special pounded uphill at just over 20mph. No. 44949 (9D), the train engine, seemed to be barely pulling its own weight and was inaudible, but 45110 leading and adorned simply with '1Z77' continued unfalteringly to hold the same rate for several minutes after, until the sound died away. Unless the lining painting exercise on 45110 a week before had been with this tour in mind, I hadn't had a hand in the external preparation of the loco that had left 9K at 09.00 with Paul on the footplate. Two hours later he was still there!

Our second chosen location lay less than 3 miles away as the tour, after negotiating the Buxton junctions, emerged on Midland lines, providing me at least with an 'excuse' to revisit Peak Forest station. Here it was then that thirty-two minutes later the pair came stamping up the 1 in 90 at just under 40mph, clearly now with 44949 contributing, too. The recording there briefly bears my first ever experience in nearly fifty years of taping of a member of the public vocally wondering what was happening! Exactly the same interval elapsed again before, on account of its booked ten-minute water stop at Chinley, we successfully chased the tour to Strines.

Having travelled via Woodley Jc. and Guide Bridge East to North Jcs, 1Z77 changed power at Stalybridge to 73069 and 73134, both Patricroft locos and the latter a Caprotti. News of 73069's transfer from Bolton mustn't have yet caught up with those who prepared the LE paths as it was scheduled to leave 9K at 11.10. In reality they no doubt

With the rest of the ascent to Waltons Sidings ahead of them, 73069 and 73134 (both 9H) have reached Spring Vale on 20 April with 1Z77. The two 4-6-0s ensured a sure-footed restart. Peter Barber, photographic contributor to this book, is adjacent to MP 19¼, the distance from Manchester Vic. *V.A. Sidlow*

came coupled from Patricroft. Despite only ten minutes being allowed for the switch to BR engines, the train was next observed passing Saddleworth thirteen minutes early at 12.34! Those two Standards continued via Diggle, Huddersfield, Bradley Wood Jc. and Hebden Bridge to Hall Royd Jc., where the line over Copy Pit Summit was taken. Selectivity in my recordings prevailed throughout the day and that at Copy Pit, where ample power precluded any trouble on the grade, was only my third of the tour. Beyond Gannow Jc. the train had a lengthy halt booked at Rose Grove where another (single) light engine was due to arrive from Lostock Hall at 14.10. Whether or not it did, no change took place as our next sighting proved.

At Spring Vale we first observed 1Z77 running more than five minutes late. Restarting here after reversing for the single-line working, the two Standards made a sure-footed pull away, some twenty minutes in arrears, the twin exhausts almost coordinated. At Bolton the double-header gave way to 48773, which had come straight off

9K for the purpose. This formation was seen by our little party at Bradley Fold nearly half an hour late as the tour turned east again, and at Rochdale East Jc., where it took the Oldham loop to Thorpes Bridge Jc. Further meanderings saw the train traverse 'India Rubber Jc.', the universal nickname for Miles Platting chord, then turn right at Droylsden Station Jc. and on to Stockport for the last engine change at Edgeley No. 2 Jc. This brought 92160 (8C) out from Speke Jc. mpd to take over for the last leg behind steam, to Liverpool Lime St via Arpley and Ditton Jc. We had somewhat cautiously missed most of this by going to Thelwall viaduct for a final sighting of 1Z77. The unkempt 2-10-0 stood out as the only machine not cleaned for the occasion, though it wasn't responsible for the arrears having reached forty-five minutes or so.

The day had worked out 'pretty well', though nothing impressed us more than the Chapel experience. It turned out to be one of only two days I spent that way up to the end of steam, other tours being taken in with what we could find working normally. Most would probably agree that the ordinary steam-worked duties on B.R. were more important than the 'arranged' attractions, to which I was nevertheless warming. There's no doubt too that railtours were more of an integral part of the 1968 scene than in the past, more perhaps than we realised at the time. Travelling by them, however, was not something that took my fancy during that final year (except for one exceptional case) and I do wonder if we considered railtours in 1968 to be for the latecomers who'd not had the chance to do much with regular steam passenger services. At any rate, the R.C.T.S's 'Lancastrian No.2' steered clear of the one we'd followed.

Remaining faithful to the 'Boat' brought no rewards that night though, a 'typical poor run' on top of a late start producing a speed drop from 50 to 38mph on this occasion. No. 45025 (10A) on seven coaches and the van took almost twenty minutes to Bolton. I hadn't been to Preston with the train for seven weeks! Crew apathy during these turbulent times for the railway in general was nothing new and doubtless made its mark on the overall standard of running, more so now than ever, but not to a man! Those that shone through, such as Bolton's Jack Hartley on 45110 with 1Z77 on a by now very rare opportunity of its kind and certain keen crews still on regular class 1 work, might be thinner on the ground now, but they hadn't gone. In the majority seemed to be those rendered less keen (or never were) by general conditions surrounding motive power in these transitory times.

Sunday, 21 to Friday, 26 April

The presence of Edge Hill's 48467 on 9K the next afternoon was close to the extent of potential foreigner rarity these days, just as the engine was close to the extent of its home shed's existence, there being just two weeks to the next round of closures. My not engaging in engine cleaning that afternoon was through no influence of the Small Faces' new single 'Lazy Sunday' just starting its successful run up the charts!

It was another 8A loco that contributed to a dead engine movement scheduled for the 22nd, one movement amongst many still, but official notice of them seemed sporadic. Whilst I worked at East Jc. box I saw none for the dispersals from 9K. Engines just turned up under orders to remove certain items from the scrap line, but here were details of an operation that didn't affect Bolton in any way. It was, however, incorporated in a notice for something that did, hence my copying it down during one of my recent visits to the box. Three locos were booked to be dragged from Speke Jc. mpd, leaving at 07.30, to Albert Draper's scrapyard in Hull. Mr Draper was a household name amongst steam enthusiasts as so many machines had already been cut up at his infamous premises. The engines due to head there that morning were 92151 (ex 8H), 48119 (ex 8A) and 45493, withdrawn as a Kingmoor loco. Two of them we'd seen during our late March visit to 8C. The 2-10-0 had been out of service for a year, the others considerably less. The cavalcade was scheduled to attach 48609 at its own shed of Patricroft and pass through Manchester Vic. at 10.11.

At Bolton station that wet Monday night of the 22nd, we were witness to some cumulative delay that contained elements of sardonic humour in our eyes, as always when 'carts' were in trouble. Tonight the 20.20 Manchester–Colne put several other trains in disarray. It arrived fourteen minutes late with brake trouble, spent a further twenty minutes in the platform and left with fitters on board. During most of its stop the 20.40 Manchester–Blackpool was stuck behind it, being 'done' twenty-two minutes. Meanwhile, the 19.05 Burnley–Moston (28) had gone by unaffected on the Up, behind 48727 (10F). The Blackpool moved up to platform 3 West briefly before leaving at 21.21 to allow the 'Boat' in at 21.20, hauled by 45025 (10A). The 'Boat' was then held up by the 20.30 Rochdale–Bolton, which came round it on the Down Through and into the now vacant 3 West via the scissors crossover at 21.25, twenty-nine minutes late. No. 45025 didn't get away until 21.32, also (and normally) via the scissors. Four minutes later, the 21.25 Bolton–Wigan (the same dmu as from Rochdale that used to be advertised as a through Rochdale–Wigan) signified the end of the mess by its own departure.

Hardly had the grass under foot along the stone wall at Spring Vale recovered from our tread than Paul and I were back again on the 23rd and able to alight at the old station. Soon after, 44899 (10F) appeared on the fourteen-vehicle Colne–Ashton Moss parcels, restarting strongly and a little out of beat, at 20.31. Almost straight behind came a lightly loaded 19.05 Burnley–Moston (15) hauled by 48410 (10F). One could hardly go wrong at Spring Vale, especially while the reversals were on for single-line working. Initial wheelslips from the 8F preceded another punchy start into the mild spring evening, its own sounds accompanied by distant strains of children at play and blackbirds in song. I wonder if any of those youngsters of 1968 have since had cause to tell their own children that they did remember steam, but only just, recalling those half-discerned bigger trains between the diesel units, which, in the cutting there were probably not heard at all.

The parcels train we'd seen was only ten days away from dieselisation itself as far as Bolton where, as before, it switched to Bolton–Guide Bridge parcels, but with both Burnley–Moston goods (if one got there early enough) and an elusive, but interesting, oil train to Darwen that we soon got to know about still steam-worked after May 6th, evening trips up there retained enough magnetism right up to the end, though Spring Vale itself had seen the last of me for normal service steam.

On Wednesday we were all at the shed, scraping the grime from 44802, the motion I expect, and from 48652, which I'd never touched before. Now there was a purpose in selecting the 8F as it had been picked to take part in a repeat of the justifiably popular 1Z77 railtour on the section previously covered by 48773. No. 48652 may have been stopped the night we worked on it (I didn't make a note) as some firebars were reported missing from the middle of the box after its turn of duty on 20 April. Surviving internal paperwork from Bolton shed in my possession is practically non-existent for 1968, but that snippet and other similar reports are an exception. Later on, as 48730 (10F) threaded the Bolton junctions on the second Burnley–Moston, the fact that its load amounted to about twice that of our Spring Vale trip and the night before too did not go unremarked upon!

The arrival on the 25th of former L & Y 0-6-0ST No. 11456 at Bolton shed seemed totally out of place in 1968. Though much of it was painted a ghostly white, the loco was real enough, en route from Parsonage colliery, Leigh, to a new temporary home at Heap Bridge paper works, Bury, following private purchase from long-term industrial use. A spell of lovely weather looked set to bless the weekend, but although pleasant enough I don't recall Saturday the 27th as particularly sunny.

The proportion of it devoted to the 1Z77 railtour rerun was, in fact, less than first intended due to the 'Woodley latest' revealed at Friday night's meeting, which switched the focus to that location as the main objective and consigned the otherwise steamless Middlewood Lower to an undefined point in the future. In fact, I finally got round to recording a tour there in the year 2000! The 'Woodley latest' probably took the form of general knowledge from our Manchester colleagues; Frank knew that area very well, though he couldn't come on the trip.

Saturday, 27 April

An 'eleventh hour' one-day stand-in by lower-profiled Carnforth engine 45394 on the 'Boat' opened a more varied final week (if one is permitted to count two weekends) in that respect than may be thought, based on the recent consistency of 45025 (10A). Though appropriately allocated since Green Ayre mpd took over the work in September 1965 and commonly seen at Bolton otherwise, 45394 never made more than very occasional appearances on the 'Heysham', the last before this being just over twelve months before, according to comprehensive information held. Certainly three, and possibly four, days in mid-March 1966 stood way above anything else on the chart. This large cabside-numeralled 'Black 5' left Bolton five minutes late on 27 April and was quite noisy out to Green Lane bridge in the first mile and a bit, but later marginally exceeded 61mph only to Salford, maybe due to riding qualities. Despite this and a check to 27mph approaching Agecroft Jc., 1J05 picked up one minute to Victoria.

We Bolton four were now joined by Pete for the day. No. 73010 (9H) had the Glasgow stock again, but we didn't make anything of this, getting over to Piccadilly for the Woodley train, which got us there for 09.02. Other than my late afternoon visit in darkness nearly three months earlier, I didn't know the place, but we quickly sussed the layout and gradients during a fairly frantic first hour or so. Every freight seen, as it turned out, had at least some uphill work to contend with, within walking distance of the station and irrespective of direction of travel. What a place!

Such a busy introduction to the spot ensured that we were rarely motionless in a successful effort to catch each train on the upgrade, walking quite a distance cumulatively and largely along the track. A reference map of Woodley and nearby Apethorne Jc. with gradients and distances appears in Appendix V.

On the 27th, between 09.10 and 15.30, eleven freights were hauled by steam and eight by diesels, though taking into account LE running too, the scales were evenly balanced at fourteen each. This was hardly surprising as the next shed closures only a week away saw Edge Hill, Speke Jc., Heaton Mersey and Stockport Edgeley all finish with the old power. Some of the 8Fs seen were into their final working week. Engine changes

After working east on empties as our inaugural Woodley sighting on 27 April 1968, Speke Jc. loco, 48206, devoid of its numberplate, works back at 10.27 with Warsop–Edge Hill as Vernon Sidlow and the author behind him check their recording levels. This engine did not survive the fast-approaching demise of its home depot.
P. Barber

British Railways Steam 1968

The commodity of a Scunthorpe–Warrington goods train may well be guessed at as steel and in this case it would be correct as 48723 (9F) pauses at Woodley station on its return working that same day, 27 April. *P. Barber*

Godley Jc. and yards, as the change-over point to/from steam and electric for many years is a prominent feature of the traffic list for 27 April. This view incorporates the all-important turntable for steam locos working back westward. No. 48115 (9F) is using this facility after coming in with an Arpley–Tinsley goods, whilst fellow Heaton Mersey machine 48684 is setting out with a train for Partington on 6 April 1968. *I.C. Simpson*

to or from electric traction at Godley Jc. had a direct bearing on the amount of light engine running seen and also the incidence of return loco workings. I have therefore decided to set down observations for 27 April in table form to include as much information as possible and minimise tedium in the narrative. In this table the time observed is on the right, whereas the figure in parenthesis on the left indicates, where applicable, engines seen more than once during the session.

the 1 in 61 or vice versa when a policeman hailed an enquiry from the main road bridge as to what we were doing on the tracks. My honest reply 'Tape recording steam engines' appeared to placate or satisfy him. Away he went and we heard no more. How things have changed! Here are the day's observations:

(1)	48206 (8C)	?	Garston–Godley Jc. coal empties (54)	09.10
	48493 (8C)		LE Heaton Mersey	09.21
	92091 (8C)	?	Dewsnap–Northwich, mainly covhops (34)	09.27
(2)	48252 (9F)		Garston–Godley Jc. coal empties (53)	09.40
	48373 (9D)	08.10	Dewsnap–Gowhole, 7H38	09.47
(3)	48723 (9F)	?	Garston–Godley Jc. coal empties (49)	09.59
	48191 (9F)	?	Seymour (Barrow Hill)–Northwich (34)	10.03
(4)	D205	?	Coal empties to Godley Jc. (37)	10.09
(1)	48206 (8C)	05.04	Warsop–Edge Hill, 8M21	10.27
	D7513	LE	Dewsnap	10.33
(5)	D5252+D5261	LEs	Heaton Mersey–Mottram	10.38
(2)	48252 (9F)	08.20	Rotherwood–Garston MX, 8M56, coal (31)	11.23
(3)	48723 (9F)	05.21	Scunthorpe–Warrington Monks Sdgs, 8M67	11.41/43
	D7651	?	Dewsnap–Portwood (28)	11.50
	{44781 (9B)} {45046 (9B)}	10.37	Railtour ex Stockport 1Z77	12.07
(4)	D205	?	Coke empties for Shotwick (35)	12.10
	45411 (9D)	LE	Newton Heath	12.10
(5)	{D5252} {D5261}	10.27	Mottram–Partington, 8H63 (31)	12.24
(6)	D5153	?	Arpley–Tinsley (33)	12.39
	48365 (9F)	LE	Heaton Mersey	13.03
	D312	LE	Dewsnap or Godley Jc.	13.07
	D375	?	'7L63' (Unidentified)	13.18
(6)	D5153	LE	Heaton Mersey	13.35
(7)	48115 (9F)		Coal empties to Godley Jc. (50)	13.55
(8)	D215	12.45	Buxton–Sproughton Sdgs SO, 5E00 (32)	14.20
(9)	D5205	12.25	Runcorn–Spink Hill, 7E81, SO (36)	14.44
(8)	D215	LE	Romiley direction.	14.50
(9)	D5205	LE	Bredbury?	15.17
(7)	48115 (9F)	12.47	Wath–Garston, 8M70, coal, (29)	15.29

A questionable wrong had been righted with regard to the railtour 1Z77, running again today with different engines than on the 20th, insomuch as the Stockport start with steam had been given to that home shed, as seen in the table, and in the process eliminated two light engine movements needed for version one of the train.

A word about our complete freedom of movement around the Woodley environs might not be out of place. I am reminded of an incident during one of several pedestrian transfers from around Apethorne Jc. back to

We'd enjoyed a terrific start with the six consecutive steam-hauled freights or empties. Although the three eastbound empties in that batch were reckoned by the signalman to be specials, all the engines returned on regular workings. Interspersed between them and keeping us on the hop, 92091 (8C) made quite laborious progress up the not too long a grade from Hyde. It wasn't working very hard, but the distinctive 9F sound was there alright. No. 48373 (9D), twenty minutes behind it and checked by the second special to Godley, showed how it could be done, forging towards the station from a dead stand with little, if anything, in reserve. The 2-8-0's front end could be clearly seen shifting from side to side, jerking laterally with the mighty thrusting forces at play – something rarely seen from the lineside. Trains from Godley had a 25mph restriction over Apethorne Jc. (where there wasn't a signal box any longer), and were in a dip at the junction itself, so locos were opened up properly from the point, often discerned, when the train weight began to drag momentum down and the couplings tight again. The Seymour–Northwich was the only steam-hauled rake that I didn't obtain a worthwhile recording of, maybe through being out of position. We were back at the station for 1Z77, which clattered through three minutes early off the Romiley line, both engines opened up impressively on the faintly rising grade, at about 45mph.

Naturally, as the afternoon wore on, its tendency to fewer steam workings and reduced freight frequency became more pronounced. Sometime after the tour's passage but before 48l15's eastbound movement we visited the box at Woodley Jc. The train register there and my own W.T.T. provided most of the traffic's identity and detail that is transcribed into the above listing. It wasn't then until 13.55 that the old soldier 48115 (9F) fought its way up the 1 in 61 (over a mile of this inclination after mostly 1 in 80 from Tiviot Dale tunnel) with the fifty empties. This was the only one for which we'd got well below the junction. A slog in single figures mph was fairly normal here, future experience would reveal. In any case, 10mph applied over Woodley Jc. from that direction.

In isolation, the appearance of a Type 2 on Runcorn–Spink Hill would have dealt the kind of blow we'd already felt on Saturday afternoons past, but having enjoyed such considerable action already on the 27th softened it considerably. As I commented at the time, 48115 compensated for the other. There was nothing to lose by waiting for that 8F (which sounded fit enough now) to reappear and again it didn't disappoint

After Wath–Garston we moved off by dmu to catch up with 1Z77 near the top of the climb from Droylsden Station Jc. to Ashton Moss Jc. Alighting at the salubrious Fairfield (for Droylsden) and walking back brought us close to the canal bridge, where our own 48652 made a fine ascent at around 25mph of that short and useful cut-off line that didn't remain open too much longer and which climbed at a gradient of 1 in 88. Saturday evening high hope, the 9K-worked Heysham–Ardwick goods, was awaited near Miles Platting with expectation, but it disappointed our group to find that the shed had got hold of a Type 2 for the duty. At least the load was a light one of eleven wagons. Even at this late stage it proved not to be regularly diesel, but it was another sign that couldn't be ignored.

Pilot work at Victoria that night at least remained unchanged for a Saturday with four 'Black 5s' in use. Five at times were noted, but not today, whilst 73128 (9H) ran about on vans for Exchange and 48652 heading back light to Bolton mpd at 20.20 was the last trace of 1Z77 having delivered the railtour to Stockport. The 'Boat' arrived behind

Nearby, having just passed Brookfold signal box, 48765 forsakes Godley Jc. with a run of coal on 25 April 1968. *P. Barber*

45394 (10A) fifteen minutes prior to departure time. Some of the train's more recent patrons (and numbers were still increasing), lured by the final days of its steam haulage, may have been surprised at the lack of urgency in reuniting the engine with its stock (see 27 January), but the twelve-minute late start was all too familiar to us.

No. 45394 made a good effort, or enabled its driver to do so, to Preston at least. Reaching 48mph by Pendleton was well above average, but 1P02 had to slow (to 32mph) for P.W. work just after Agecroft Jc., a slack that dogged some determined attempts over the next few days. However, our loco tonight got back to 44mph and virtually maintained it to the Bolton approach with intermittent bursts of quite strong exhaust noise. The time taken was 19'-34". The platform staff were sharp tonight and a stop of well under two minutes saw us off again, coinciding with the slightly late 21.25 Bolton–Wigan. A 'race' out through the Moor Lane tunnels and towards Bullfield enlivened our own start as the loco and our coach paced the unit initially. Although the crew of 45394 didn't persist in the contest, quite a creditable run to Chorley ensued with 60 through Blackrod and 66 beyond. In 15'-16" we'd pulled back nearly a minute.

Maybe this lesser-known 'Black 5' needed to be a little more pressed to 'deliver the goods'. Certainly this tactic added to our enjoyment as after just one minute at Chorley an energetic start and crackling exhaust down the bank produced 57mph before the old R.O.F. station. No. 45394 was particularly lively piling it on through Leyland, Fast line as booked, and though 64mph by Farington Curve Jc. was unexceptional itself, it was good to have been entertained more or less throughout. A slight check, almost inevitably, saw us into Preston in fourteen minutes from Chorley and only three after schedule from a worst of fourteen and a half into Bolton. Cooperation from all works wonders! Unlikely to have escaped our attention, however, was the fact that nearly everything we'd seen and done that day would be gone in a week! On Preston station pilot I never subsequently saw an Ivatt 4 – just 'Black 5s', though spring withdrawals to date left 43019/27 with maybe a week or two left and 43106 (all 10D) a few more. These were the last of the class. No. 44816 (10D) acted as pilot tonight.

Sunday, 28 to Tuesday, 30 April

Oliver Cromwell took to the rails again next day, Sunday the 28th, working another Stockport-based special, a 'Circular Tour of Lancashire'. I got a lift to Bromley Cross with my parents as the station was closed on Sundays. No. 70013 (10A) had things comfortably in hand with the eight- or nine-coach train, holding around 30mph on the 1 in 73.

Diesels had certainly had the upper hand on the 12.17 Preston–Manchester since March and the last-known interruption to this current and future trend occurred on

Time had almost run out for steam on 1J42, the 12.17 Preston–Manchester, by late spring. Seen from Bolton West footbridge, 44831 (8F) runs in during the earlier era of Springs Branch power on this working. *V.A. Sidlow*

During the last interruption in 1968 to regular 'Boat Train' motive power, 45435 (10A) arrives at Manchester Vic. on Sunday morning, 28 April, complete with the first headboard made to mark the end of steam on the train a week hence. The 'Belfast Boat Express' was one of the very few titled trains of B.R. not to have an official headboard. Fifty years later there is no train that will deposit one in the centre of Salford, or Manchester from Bolton as quickly and in great comfort as a smart run with steam, and until the line limit is raised from 75mph this will not happen. Electrification alone may rectify this, but the very patient must wait till then. *P. Barber*

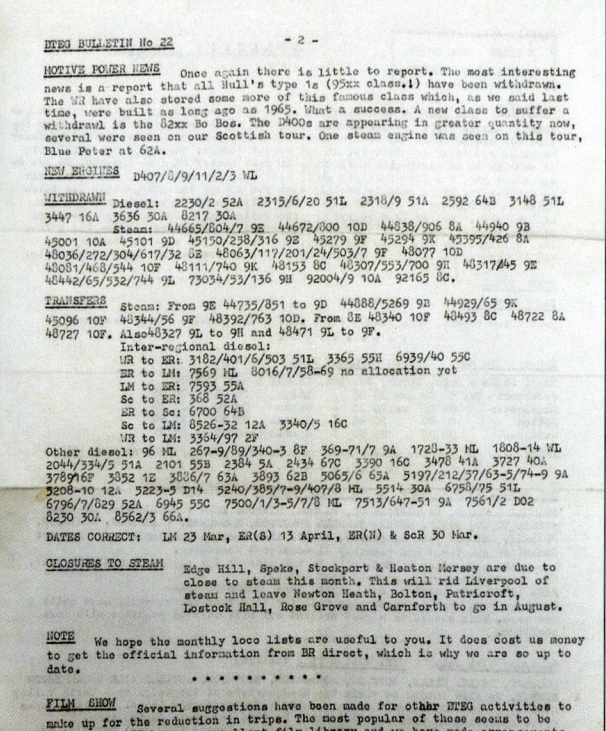

Motive power news from the B.T.E.G. was always 'hotter' off the press than the national railway magazines. This extract from the May bulletin, posted on 29 April 1968, though doubtless giving the latest on shed closure dates in good faith, still shows Bolton, Newton Heath and Patricroft as continuing until August, whereas they succumbed at the end of June instead. Upon receiving this bulletin I have no recollection whatsoever of knowing or suspecting that the prediction for 9K, 9D and 9H was incorrect. Very late in 2017, after this book was written, the equilibrium of its author received a severe jolting when an illustrated *Bolton Evening News* article on Bolton shed dated 7 March 1968 came to light. Well down the column it stated the closure date of 1 July, which did come to pass. As a paper that in those days practically the whole town took, I can only conclude that our family didn't, which seems as odd as the news not being passed on verbally, either by friends or the depot staff.

No. 45435 (10A) had had several spells on the 'Boat' in 1967, but virtually none since New Year, until coming in with a three-and-a-half day run to open the last week of steam traction from the 28th. On this, the only consistently 'Black 5'-hauled class 1 passenger in recent times, a palpable sense of occasion ran through the fairly large crowd at Victoria, even on Monday night.

Spoken thoughts and hopes of record times being attempted by the drivers during this final fling were bandied about, and the unprecedented sight of the fireman hand-sanding the rails ahead of the engine as it awaited departure seemed to augur well. During the course of this I overheard someone who actually thought that oil was being laid down! The exit from platform 12 was one place where engines needed no extra encouragement to slip; and what a very perverse notion I'd heard in the first place!

Monday the 29th when 45268 (9D) officiated. This observation, by Vern, could well have been the last of its kind. In various May publications, the railway press advised that in line with 'slight' changes to surviving steam-hauled passenger diagrams from 4 March, the '12.17' would be steam MO. As 'slightly' was the operative word and because few, if any, diagrams were by now strictly adhered to due to random diesel availability, I have not listed these supposed changes. By the time the May 'glossies' reached the public we were on the verge of B.R.'s final steam passenger ban anyway. Like all the others, it failed in its intention to be absolute, but ravaged the little that existed up to its implementation.

Photographed at around the time it was laid aside as a working unit, on 7 April 1968, 48702 proved to be the only Bolton engine I can recall that was condemned, then reinstated for a period up to the above date. Its true demise is related in coverage of the month end, along with that of 45381. *Peter Reeves/M.L.S. collection*

No. 45435's own sanding gear may or may not have been operative, but by hand it was more effective. With such an abrasive rail surface an unquestionably better than average start transpired, one minute late, producing 33mph through Salford. However, our loco tonight was undoubtedly sluggish. Having reached 49mph by Agecroft Jc., steam was shut off for the P.W.S. to 25 before Clifton Jc. Recovery from this to 43/44mph took some time and the journey to Bolton occupied nineteen and a quarter minutes. I left the train at that point. Despite this largely forgettable performance and what I said about 45435, I can only think it was the night after that so impressed a friend of mine, met some ten years later, which induced him to purchase, many years later again, from me, the engine's numberplate.

A 350hp diesel became a common, though not yet exclusive, sight on Bolton station pilot from 29 April. Two older ex L.M.S. shunters were currently in 'B' Side, withdrawn from Springs Branch. One was later dismantled by torch on 9K. The Guild's May bulletin arrived early in the current week, still asserting August as the closure for all remaining steam sheds, and at this stage I'm sure we too believed that Bolton would last until then. Inexcusably, there is no 'realisation point' in my notes to reflect first knowledge of the end of June closures that were able to be made. The probable reason that three were brought forward to that time will be aired in due course.

There can be few connections indeed between the steam age in Britain and decimal currency, but the Guild, sharp as ever, advertised its 12 May Crewe Works trip quoting the visit fee as 6 old pennies (or 2½ new ones) – tongue in cheek, but prophetic and a reminder of how early that upheaval was in the air.

The current week marked the official withdrawal of two 9K machines that we'd considered out of the running for a few weeks already. They were 48702 and 45381. The 8F was unique in my experience at Bolton in being condemned unofficially in late 1967, then reinstated soon after. It came from the N.E.R. to Edge Hill in late August 1962, moving to Speke Jc. a year later, but only for three months, when Heaton Mersey took over its welfare. Barely a month in south Manchester transpired and 48702 settled at Northwich for the year of 1964 until August brought about its transfer to 9K, where it arrived on the 22nd. No. 45381 had been an established Willesden engine until Edge Hill took on the 4-6-0 in October 1960. Only ten weeks later it moved on again, to Dallam, where it remained based until June 1964. Newton Heath then acquired the loco for five months and in November of that year it went to experience the last months of Bury mpd. Upon closure of that establishment it reached Bolton on 11 April 1965 along with many other engines from 9M that weekend. These two latest casualties lay dumped at 9K until well after its own closure. The inscription 'FLOWER POWER' in large letters along the 5's boiler, though only 'written' with a rag in the dirt, was, I think, still legible from that previous summer. On 30 April we learned that '48026 is doomed shortly', and in fact this was another put away soon after, though not officially written off before mid-June.

Swelling the ranks on the 'Boat Train' during its last days with steam were not only the younger, newer enthusiasts, but those at the other extreme, men considerably senior to ourselves who'd seen, through the good fortune of being born earlier, so much more, and had 'retired' latterly from normal service steam, having in full railway consciousness experienced a greater spectrum of decline than we had. They now viewed what remained, or should I say responded to it, very differently to my contemporaries and I. They were the 'founder member' types; sports jacket, cords and one enamel badge, for whom the bleak scene of 1968 had really gone rather too far, though they kept in touch with it and not just via the main society mags. The end of the 'Boat' was worth turning out for as an 'occasion'. We might have inadvertently looked down our noses at some of them, but those I knew from Bolton and environs were so pleasant and unassuming, good friends in a few cases even, that any such notion would have been absurd. Bert Mather and Dave Hampson were met off 1P02 on the Tuesday of that last week.

Wednesday, 1 and Thursday, 2 May

On this May Day, 1968, a distress call of no mean import in railway circles, short of an actual accident, must have rung out mid-evening because the engine due to work the 'Boat', 45435 (10A) failed, and at the last minute I would say. The loco that replaced it, possibly without any preparation, was 44899 (10F), which not much earlier (though I didn't see it) had passed Bolton on the 16.40 Burnley–Moston usually between 18.30 and 19.15. 1P02 reached Trinity Street nineteen minutes late. Nor was I on the train, but several were the comments on 44899's considerable difficulty in recovering from the Agecroft P.W. check.

No. 44899 probably just did the single northbound run as 45342 (10A) had resumed the duty by the following evening. There had been considerable speculation as to what would be selected for use over the last weekend and I doubt that anyone was disappointed in the choice of locos made. Adding to the sense of occasion was a predominance of drivers who had extracted the best performances from their machines on certain 'Belfast Boat Express' runs during the year so far. Hero status in the eyes of some, spread in direct proportion to the liveliest journeys. I don't think anything special happened in that respect on the Thursday night, the 2nd, but it was the time I bought my ticket to Heysham for the last ever opportunity (on Friday) to make a full return trip to the port with steam haulage. This was to be a mass overnight for the throngs that travelled throughout.

Friday, 3 May

All of my steam recordings of the 1960s and for long afterwards contain a brief spoken introduction or conclusion that often reflects my mood at the time. That at Victoria prior to departure was not a joyous one, for that weekend saw the last steam runs I ever expected to make to, or through, my home town. The large crowd assembled there, however, was not sombre to a man and the presence of so many friends inevitably distracted and lightened the mind from dwelling on the straightforward outcome of what was being commemorated too heavily.

Carnforth 5MTs in evidence amongst the normal traffic were, as we set off, 45209 on Bedford parcels, 44874 coupled light to our own 48504 heading through Victoria for 9K and between those, 45342, engine of the moment, threading the station layout to collect its stock for the 'Boat'. This was drawn into platform 12 earlier than I'd ever known it, at 20.22, enabling much discussion between enthusiasts and the crew. How widely known amongst the former was the identity of tonight's driver, one Jack Sullivan, who had made his mark earlier in the year I cannot recall, but his contribution to the power-packed run that lay ahead only enhanced his status. To time at 20.55, and hauling the regular seven coaches plus a long wheel-based van, 45342 (10A) moved out with 1P02 round the curves towards Deal Street, slipping only twice. Once clear of those curves the regulator was thrust further open and the loco bit into the straight track. Rapid acceleration produced 39mph through Salford, my fastest through there since an ill-fated footplate ride more than a year before. Our rate quickly increased with the noisy offbeat exhaust, laterally characteristic of 45342, to 52mph by Pendleton and probably a little more prior to the P.W. check after Agecroft Jc. caused him to ease to 32. Recovery, though good, was not brilliant, culminating in 53mph by Moses Gate. Despite that setback and a badly impeded approach to Bolton – 8mph past the depot – the express stopped in 17'-41".

Another dynamic departure ensued, the 60mph mark being crossed soon after Lostock Jc. and this gradually increased to 74 on the easier road through Adlington, giving an excellent time to Chorley of a second over thirteen and a half minutes for the 11.6 miles. Not surprisingly the train was early here, but not held to time and the premature departure proved far more restrained to Euxton Jc. Beyond it, however, receiving no adverse signals, Sullivan ripped into more fast and gravity-assisted acceleration, early audio effects of which prompted such comments as 'all out!' and 'slaughter!' in my notebook, but with more exclamation marks. No. 45342 sped northwards, touching 76mph, I made it, by Farington Jc., though this may be slightly high. Either way it had been a remarkably similar effort to that of 45017 (10A) on 17 February, but judging from the resultant tape recording, less noisy at speed. 1P02 tonight ran into Preston unhindered, despite being five minutes early From Chorley, 8.56 miles had been run off in 11'-35", despite the Euxton Jc. restriction to around 35mph and earlier sedate progress down Chorley bank.

Our engine therefore gained a seventeen-minute 'breather' before leaving Preston a minute late with a fresh crew at the controls. Very tight for class 5 steam was the Limited Load booking of twenty-two minutes to Lancaster

(21 miles). An uninspiring start and P.W.S. to 35mph at Barton & Broughton put the schedule hopelessly out of reach, even though the driver's tactics did undergo a transformation following the slack. Though five and a half minutes late passing Garstang, we were blasting along in the upper 60s and 45342 put another 10mph on this, still audible too around Bay Horse. Steam was shut off soon after for Lancaster, where 1P02 halted in 26'-14".

With four minutes in arrears, the start out to Morecambe South Jc. proved comparatively restrained, though once onto what was for me 'new' steam track, the loco received another moderate 'caning' through Bare Lane, many glowing cinders landing in South Road alongside, and a little more time was pulled back. At Morecambe Promenade station 45342 ran round its stock for the final section to Heysham Harbour. Even this 4½ miles of tender-first running included a maximum of 57mph and a volcano-like eruption from the chimney! So ended an epic run and our four-minute late arrival testified to the sharpness of the 'BBE' schedule north of Preston. The train had terminated at 23.01.

Acting station pilot that night was 45095 (10A), never common on the 'Boat'. Doubtless more enthusiasts than ever before had travelled through to Heysham on one service train and for many, like myself, it would be the first and only time with steam. All those with no intention of sailing to Belfast had the night at their disposal – not a prospect to be overly savoured – and either individually, or in groups, plans and decisions were variously made. I remained with the bulk of what was openly now known as the '20.55 Club'. It may have been christened prior to this most pertinent of occasions, but 3 May is the earliest date that I have it in writing. We walked to a railway bridge not far from the station where, in the still and quite cold air, delightful motion sounds from the approaching light engine, 45342, changed as it passed beneath to a snappy offbeat exhaust as the 4-6-0 rapidly gained momentum en route to Carnforth shed as Morecambe Bay's most unlikely taxi, its footplate crammed with enthusiasts lucky enough to have obtained transportation to a place where the nocturnal public abroad might be viewed with less suspicion. Unexpectedly, as it turned out, we fared, in that respect, better than they did.

Saturday, 4 May

Having ascertained that no other form of transport was available in that direction (or any other landward), the 'Club', anxious to avoid any police patrols considered likely in dockland, ended up packed into a brake van that looked like remaining stationary for the night. I for one wasn't in the least comfortable and my level of involvement through those hours of ribald jokes, stale heat and sleeplessness, though not recalled with any clarity so long after, would doubtless have been well down on the ringleaders such as 'Tosh'.

Thankfully it wasn't a long night and at 03.55 we emerged to a clear and frosty morning – unusual for the season I'd say, proximity to the sea and mild reputation of Morecambe Bay. Considering numbers and the element of surprise, we were very well received by the man in charge of Harbour signal box, who provided tea.

The end of an overnight that has since (among those whose friendship it seemed to cement, as well as those already longstanding) become legendary, came with the empty stock arrival of 1J05. Probably the least remembered engine from that weekend's 'Boat Train' activity is 44963 (10A), which started the train on its way,

Overnighters congregate around 45342 (10A) as it awaits departure from Morecambe Promenade on 4 May at 06.30. This was the last weekend of steam on the 'Belfast Boat Express' and the forthcoming run rewarded those who had stayed in the Heysham area in one capacity or another.
P. Barber

just to Morecambe on the Saturday morning. The most memorable part of this first leg came when, adjacent to Heysham Moss Sidings this undistinguished 4-6-0's cut-off and regulator were rammed (it appeared) into full forward and fully open, better known as 'flat out' for a half-minute burst that, even in the rear coach, was more effective than any alarm clock at 06.20 for those who may still have needed one!

Now, at Promenade station, 45342 coupled up to the train's rear. In charge was Ted Fothergill, another man with a reputation that suited those that had unofficially worked to improve the external appearance of his loco and those who would not have turned down the opportunity. Considering the less than ideal conditions, including the volunteer force being broken up, it transpired, by B.T. Police, a fair result had been achieved for the one special occasion. Nothing exceptional transpired on the run to Lancaster, which included a passenger stop at Bare Lane. Our earlier reversal had left me, as intended, at the front of the train, but on the non-milepost side, and it has never been clear to me since why I appeared to be content not to record our hoped for high speed in the most reliable way.

A forceful departure (still a minute early I made it) from Lancaster Castle station ensued up the mile-long 1 in 98, resulting in seven wheelslips on the lower slopes of the bank and another halfway up, by which time the express was nevertheless accelerating well. No. 1 box marked the commencement of near level track and the seven-coach train passed this point at 29mph. No. 45342 surged ahead rapidly now, and in the vicinity of Garstang reached 82½mph, this being the figure sustained for a couple of miles and generally agreed amongst timers on the train. The same P.W. check encountered the night before slowed the express to 27mph at Barton & Broughton, but a powerful recovery enabled a mile a minute to be attained soon after Oxheys, prior to the Preston stop.

The vigorous driving and five minutes' recovery time from the Lancaster start brought about an arrival at 07.05½, six early, having in effect wiped out the P.W. slack and dispensed with the recovery time too, in a journey of 24'-37". As 45342 stood bathed in sunlight at the south end of platform 6, many enthusiasts took advantage of the longer stop to photograph the loco, which carried an unofficial but traditionally shaped and pleasing headboard that had been specially made for the last weekend with steam.

Punctually, at 07.14, the B.B.E. moved into action again and in no uncertain terms! The rip-roaring start enabled speed to reach 61mph on the rising grades through Leyland – only the second time I'd done this rate with steam going south. More than a minute had been gained to Euxton Jc., just 5 miles out. A maximum of 50mph was

Survivors No. 2 – The numberplate from 45342 (10A), a less prolific engine than 45025 (10A) on the 'Boat Train' in 1968, but well remembered for its latter day exploits.

sustained up the top part of Chorley bank (1 in 130) and 1J05 came to a halt in 11'-49" from the start, two and a quarter minutes early and close to the optimum journey time that could be achieved. Unexpectedly, the section to Bolton resembled a more conventional run, though the maximum of 70mph after Blackrod was good, bringing us into Trinity Street still two minutes before time.

We were held until one minute late and again experienced a start that did not unduly stand out from many recent runs, until around Green Lane that is, when the opposite came into play and Kearsley flashed past at 72mph. We didn't, however, get above that and 1J05 came down to 15mph for the P.W. check at Agecroft Jc. Without any further fireworks, we still reached Manchester Victoria a minute early.

It wasn't all over yet. Mindful of our next appointment with the 'Boat' twelve hours hence, we refrained from lingering too long around the engine at Victoria, for another very special event, or series of events, were already under way – the last day of steam freight workings from Edge Hill, Speke Jc., Stockport and Heaton Mersey depots. So, from a wholly passenger train happening, it fell to goods work to monopolise the next nine hours. There'd been no dilemma over where to absorb what amounted to the last rites of those four sheds. With the overwhelming success of Woodley a week earlier fresh in our minds it would have been virtual folly to have risked a probably less productive alternative for the sake of change. The strategic location of Woodley proved a unanimous choice by, I am quite certain, the Bolton four and Pete. We naturally knew there'd be some variation on the rich pickings of 27 April and three unpredicted aspects of the traffic and motive power further prevented the day from simply being a repeat performance. Traffic flows, density and steam percentage themselves were very similar overall, but only four specific freights were common to both trips. Identification was again good, thanks to the signalman.

In a way I derived more satisfaction from pursuing freight workings with steam in 1968 than participation in following the final passenger jobs, mainly because of the less than natural atmosphere generated by large crowds on the class 1 duties. Today, for example, we seemed to have Woodley to ourselves! Feelings too that anything

Opposite: 9F 2-10-0s appeared at intervals during our lengthy vigil at Woodley on 4 May. This was another big 'farewell' weekend, not only to the class 9s in that area. No. 92160 (8C) made an early impression on the proceedings with its lengthy rake on the steepest approach to the junction. *V.A. Sidlow*

Returning nearly two hours later, 92160 (8C) brings coal westwards through Woodley station. This engine is widely regarded as the last active 9F in the early summer at its new home of Carnforth. *P. Barber*

special on the performance front was motivated to a degree by the occasion itself and not representative of what would have been done under normal conditions went a little against my preferred way of things.

From the 08.30 Piccadilly–Macclesfield dmu both steam and diesel activity appeared en route. Amongst the locos that would be 9K-bound after the weekend's upheaval was 45046 (9B), seen at Guide Bridge coupled to 70013 (10A), probably just LE, though I didn't note it. In this account of Woodley I leave the reader to imagine diesel power integrated with the stuff that interested us along the guidelines mentioned above. Twenty goods trains (eleven of them steam) and thirteen light engine movements altogether made up the total for the hours 09.05 to 18.15 – I had to be selective over recording tape usage, fading out all the featured freights before they had fully passed. One very welcome feature, however, was an increase on the previous week's 9F involvement.

The pedestrian progress of Speke Jc. Loco 92160 (as low as 6mph) up the 1 in 61 (see map for 27 April) had regulatory origins to prevent the fifty-four empties in tow from being halted by signals at Woodley Jc., but the crucial Home came off just in time, to an immediate and appropriate sharpening of the 2-10-0's exhaust. This engine returned on thirty-one coal for Garston more than two hours later. 'Black 5s' were well represented this time too and Newton Heath's 45203 appeared on the 08.10 Dewsnap–Gowhole (34). It was this that had caused the 9F's check, barring its route across Apethorne Jc. Follow-up work for the 4-6-0 that day proved to be one of Victoria's pilots, probably the 18.10 SO to 23.00 SuO turn.

No. 45386 (8C), not long out of store, it was thought, had to work quite hard to avoid losing momentum up to Woodley station on thirty-three of coal for Garston at 10.25. A quarter of an hour later, a close anagram of the 'Black 5's' number, in the shape of 48356 (9F), one of the

We found Edge Hill engines were very much in the minority on both Woodley trips (and completely absent on 27 April). Representing the depot on 4 May, however, 45282 was destined for withdrawal and almost certainly on the last run of its thirty-two-year career, Working west here at 11.22, with a Dewsnap–Peak Forest goods, it had had, unlike the 9Fs finishing too, a lifespan much closer to what was intended when built. *P. Barber*

day's busiest locos, brought forty-seven empties up Brinnington bank for Godley, its own exhaust battling for supremacy over that of a low-flying jet plane.

After the 9F's return on more coal to Garston at 11.15, as soon as it had cleared in fact, 7H57, the 08.29 Dewsnap–Buxton (curtailed since 4 March to Peak Forest) came on the block. This produced 45282 (8A) after its earlier passage LE to Dewsnap for the job and the only machine seen that day of many officially withdrawn immediately after the weekend. Heaton Mersey's 'pride and joy', 48115 was next, off the 1 in 61 just before midday and taking the Godley route with fifty empties, closely followed by a train of identical consist headed most surprisingly by Carnforth's 92118 on a swifter than usual ascent at 15mph or so. A slight inflection in my voice on the tape after this train's passage suggests an increasing emotion over the morning's procession of steam,

enhanced or affected by the occasion itself and the railway's intention to end all we were witnessing at a stroke. Straight after the 9F came Mottram–Partington (31), diesel on 27 April, but a return path for 48356 today, though it provided the slowest plod we saw upgrade from Apethorne Jc. at 12.14.

I wonder if any local churches took the opportunity to emblazon their 'wayside pulpit' boards with the advice 'TAKE THE GODLEY ROUTE'? Probably not, and neither did any other steam-hauled freights heed it literally for several hours to come, for after 48356 there commenced a very long interval with nothing but diesel-hauled goods plus LEs of both power types, during which time our numbers dwindled to two. The brake van 'overnight' was beginning to tell! So, just Pete and I were left, dozing on the banking at times no doubt. Conspicuous by its absence so far was 7E81, Runcorn–Spink Hill. There seemed a chance of

Speke Jc. doing a 9F swansong on this and it wouldn't be good to miss it! Eventually the dearth of steam under load was broken by a train of prefabricated track on concrete sleepers from Dewsnap taking the Bredbury route for Sunday relaying somewhere and hauled by 48720 (9F). Clanking most prominently, it had gone light specially to work the job, reappearing at 15.57.

Later, near the top of Brinnington bank, I began recording on a two-minute snatch of tape (reclaimed from something earlier) what was from afar mistakenly thought to be 7E81. Instead, what took shape proved to be an engine transfer movement from Heaton Mersey powered by 48356 for Newton Heath, hauling 92118 (10A), now without a fire, and 48319 dead and ultimately bound for Bolton mpd. All day there had been nothing to indicate that the engines in use were partaking in a 'last day', except for the nature of the working just mentioned. Rectification of this was given to the reappearance of 48115 working the long awaited Runcorn–Spink Hill. The 8F slogged up the bank with thirty-six on, two and a half hours late at 17.36, sporting a decidedly lacklustre decoration of oily balloons and what I took for a wreath festooning the smokebox of this grimy 2-8-0 as it took the Godley route for the last time ever.

7E81 was normally a Speke Jc. duty with relief by 9F men only at Heaton Mersey East Jc., so the presence of 48115 (9F) strongly suggested a loco change on this occasion too, arranged by the depot and/or enthusiasts to commemorate the last day. Adding further conjecture, there'd just about been time for the 2-8-0 to have been sent to Runcorn since we last saw it, in time for it to reappear now, but it seemed very unlikely and unnecessary. Also in our minds was the possibility of a 9F starting the train off, but having been detached at Heaton Mersey. These questions remained unanswered for forty-six years until I struck up a correspondence with one Ian Simpson, who happened to be on the footplate of 48115 from Heaton Mersey and the returning LE afterwards. My latter-day friend explains, 'I was certainly not responsible for the balloons. I absolutely hated that sort of "last day" adornment. In a roundabout way I

After it was all over in the early evening at Heaton Mersey shed, Ian Simpson was on hand to capture the disposal of 48170 (9B) by driver Jack Lewis, while 48115 (9F) stands opposite. Both engines would live on for a while. With smokebox contents proportionate to the hard work done that day, only the longest rake from ground level enabled the disposer to keep reasonably clean! *I.C. Simpson*

At more or less the same moment as the previous photograph was taken, the opposite view in the adorned smokebox door of 48115, three-quarter rear angle of 48170 and the driver still brandishing the long rake, was captured. *T. Heavyside*

benefitted from the balloons as their presence deterred me from going up the bank for a photo and led me to requesting a cab ride instead. Incidentally, it was not a wreath on the smokebox door, but a coat of arms, presumably for the town of Stockport.' We needn't have feared missing a 9F 2-10-0 as far as Heaton Mersey as 7E81 was worked by 48493 (8C) to that point. My brief recording of 48115 running back LE to 9F features the distant cheering of an enlarged band of enthusiasts in the cab as the loco was forced into several wheelslips for effect. The additional 'passengers' were photographers picked up at Godley Jc. The Woodley 'Farewell' had certainly fulfilled every expectation and provided a memorable end to another phase in steam's elimination from North-west England.

Doubtless there had been other locomotive transfers effected during Saturday beyond what we'd seen. As the evening shifted towards 'Boat' time, 48319 (9F) made further progress through Victoria station, now hauled by 45046 (9B), both being reallocated to 9K. More than ever boarded 1J05 tonight as this was reckoned to be the very last with steam. Preston men were in charge of 45342 (10A) and departure came six minutes late with the usual load conveyed. Even with any spare tape left it's doubtful I'd have recorded much of this special occasion on account of its largely anticlimactic action. In the absence of any audio reminder in the twenty-first century, the log still speaks. No special effort to Bolton took place at all, practically proving that some enginemen were impervious to the emotion of the times, of which they could hardly be ignorant. Even in a run amongst thousands ten years earlier there should have been some evidence of attempted time recovery! We had a brief signal stop on top of the P.W. check at Agecroft, but sluggish progress onward transpired with speed in the mid-30s at best!

The Bolton start was much more lively, even reflecting in a good 50mph by Lostock Jc., but nothing over 63½mph was attempted on to Chorley, the driver seemingly content to remain about three minutes late. From Euxton Jc. we were turned Slow Line and never exceeded 53. This disappointing run was felt by the majority that alighted at Preston. North thereof, it later transpired, matters if anything deteriorated with a new Carnforth crew, and there for me it hung. I'd finished, whether the train on Sunday produced steam or not. Coming home from Preston with established Bolton enthusiast Bob Maxwell, our conversation would be interesting to recall now; thoughts and expectations of the next few months.

Sunday, 5 May

Busy with Sermons Sunday services and the church procession on the 5th, I didn't make contact with the railway until a 'curiosity' evening visit to Trinity Street that revealed 45025 (10A) had been turned out for the Up morning run from Morecambe. Apparently, quite a good performance as far as Preston partly rewarded any hardy double overnighters, and the evening train had run into Bolton after a superb display recovering from the Agecroft Jc. slack to reach 57mph by Farnworth. That steam was not certain on this probably influenced my decision to let it go, but no further uncertainty over motive power on the 'Belfast Boat Express' clouded the issue. From D1617 on 6 May another chapter had firmly ended.

Not the 'Boat' (it didn't get a mention), but Carnforth mpd 'Graveyard of Steam', found its way journalistically gracing the centrefold of an unlikely and rather highbrow publication in *Lancashire Life*'s current edition (May). A gushingly sentimental opener ('The last mournful whistle has shrilled out for them across the land' and …'those buttermilk summer days watching the coal black giants rip by on shimmering rails …') runs into a partially accurate summary of eleventh-hour Carnforth mpd as the implied last bastion of steam. There are references to 'Block 5 engines' and 70013, 'named after a famous historical character, built in 1931', but the photographs are good and representative; 45342 no less, portraying the still working locos; the stored and the scrap, 9Fs down to 4MTs; the preserved, *Cromwell* and 6441; the new diesels and an inset of the Station Manager. Outside the railway fraternity this was probably the first widely distributed piece on the imminent disappearance of the steam locomotive, preceding as it did several cringeworthy sensationalist summer offerings in some national papers, nearer to the end than ever and encompassing the still-to-be-announced '15 Guinea Special'.

Seven minutes before that first regularly diesel-hauled 'Boat Train' was due to leave Victoria, the last of Bolton's ten acquisitions from the now closed steam sheds of 8A, 8C, 9B and 9F arrived on the 9K ashpit. It was 48720. Also occupying space at the shed by now (not that space was a problem, as it had been three years earlier when Bury mpd closed) were six diesel shunters, including four of the Horwich Works batch, D2224/6/7/34. Depending how one construes the withdrawals of steam during the week ending 11 May, Bolton's allocation had fallen to eighteen or sixteen (it's seventeen the way I've described events herein), so ten 'new' machines together at this stage was a big boost by comparison and the biggest single-date transfer to 9K since the dozen BR 5s two years back (though their actual arrival was well staggered). The new arrivals at Bolton from 6 May 1968 were as follows:

From Stockport 44781/871/88/5046/269/312

From Heaton Mersey 48168/319/720

From Edge Hill 48692

Out of service at some point since mid-April, 44829 was officially condemned the week ending 11 May, partly at least due to some defect that prevented it from being conveyed to the scrapyard that purchased the 4-6-0. It was cut up on site by Drapers in late July.

We'd only had the engine since New Year when it came from Workington. Years at Bushbury ended for this loco in June 1963 when a move to Holyhead sparked off several such medium- or short-term transfers in the closing years. After four months at 6J it returned to the Midlands (Saltley) for twenty months until being reallocated in June 1965 to Crewe South. It remained there for nearly two years, Workington taking charge in April 1967 until its closure brought about the transfer to 9K.

Returning to what passed for the national scene during that weekend of 5 May 1968, from the four depot closures, no fewer than seventy eight locos were redundant. Well over half (forty-five) became transferred elsewhere, meaning a reprieve lasting a few days for some and up to twelve weeks for the more 'fortunate'. One or two gained a distinction in enthusiasts' eyes that without their little reprieve would have been wanting, and in three other cases their brief stay of execution perhaps meant the difference between being saved for preservation or not.

Only Heaton Mersey had (marginally) more locos withdrawn at the end than reallocated. Eleven were condemned from its final quota of twenty-one. Three class 8Fs went each to 9K, 10D and 10F, whilst 9D received one. Edgeley mpd had seventeen to dispose of and seven of these went for scrap. It despatched six 'Black 5s' to 9K (see above), one to 9D and three 8Fs to Patricroft. Edge Hill had nine taken out of service and no fewer than sixteen transferred, starting with five 'Black 5s' to 9H. The remainder were 2-8-0s. Four went to 9D, two to 10D, two to 10F and one to 9K. Most (five) of the Speke Jc. 9Fs became withdrawn as well as two 'Black 5s'. Two 9Fs escaped to Carnforth, however, as did two 4-6-0s. Four more of the latter moved on to Lostock Hall and Rose Grove acquired one 8F. Such a huge influx to the remaining depots represented more than 20% of what was still left in service, the total gain to each mpd being as follows: Newton Heath, six; Patricroft, ten; Bolton, ten; Carnforth, four; Lostock Hall, nine; and Rose Grove, six. More than anything it gave the above sheds a very late opportunity to replace the poorest engines with a unit in better shape, the transfers having presumably been selected on condition.

A final trio of 'Boat Train' images from Sunday, 5 May, a day that was uncertain for steam, but turned out to be successful. At Preston in brilliant sunshine, 45025 (10A) is admired and photographed by many. In clearest conditions too about half an hour later, 1J05 pulls into Bolton under clear signals, and lastly, the same engine standing at platform 11 Middle with the evening run to Morecambe.
P. Barber (1 & 3),
V.A. Sidlow (2)

3
Pastures New and Pastures Old

6 May to 30 June
Up to the Bolton, Newton Heath and Patricroft closures.

Monday, 6 and Tuesday, 7 May

Although I am at a multiple disadvantage in being able to state authoritatively whether or not 9K picked up some work from Newton Heath that same weekend for the few weeks it remained open, various sources of evidence as well as personal observation strongly suggest this to be the case. Those ten incoming transfers, the first officially based turns listing I'd seen in a long time, which became available in May and a by now all too rare 9K engine status listing I made up for 21 May comprise the main evidence in favour. The absence of a turns listing for any period earlier in 1968 provides the only element of doubt or means of the increased workload being proven.

The new turns listing, clearly based on official B.R. documentation, was admirably compiled by one Stephen Dent and sold as an aid to enthusiasts via the Stockport (Bahamas) Locomotive Society. It purported to encompass 'all remaining steam workings of freight, empty stock, parcels and passenger trains'. In other words, only such as station and yard pilots that did not venture beyond very fixed limits with a train and 'as required' work was excluded, as well as light engines to work specific jobs. The publication was entitled *The Final Hours* and any necessary future references to it herein will simply be known as 'Dent'.

In converting the above work to depot order instead of train starting point, to ascertain post-6 May work levels, especially of Bolton mpd, I ended up with something more akin to the B.R. 'Shunting Engine and Local Trip Notice' format. A clear enough picture has emerged from that conversion. Bolton now worked Target numbers 83 to 95 inclusive, Monday to Friday, though the MO and MX version of each differed in some cases. Some of the old familiar turns are still recognisable from their content and some are not. Judging by the operating times of the thirteen targets, each one required a separate, dedicated locomotive off shed, i.e. none were back early enough to cover a second, later target/turn. Enough of them, however, had returned to shed in time to be serviced and rostered for the afternoon and evening jobs that, following the trend of earlier periods in 9K's latter-day history, were all full line workings outside the trip structure. Therefore, the number of locos required daily (SX) simply equalled the number of morning departure targets, i.e. thirteen. To be added to this are Bolton station pilot, still not fully dieselised after 6 May, Castleton pilot and Special Trips, if indeed the latter still ran by May 1968. Bolton Ballast (SX) is marked down for a 2-8-0 loco, but with the depot of origin left blank. I would tend to think that this was wrong and that the duty was still covered by the visiting Carnforth 5MT off the previous evening's Heysham–Moston goods.

The preceding evidence indicates that fourteen or fifteen engines were required daily (SX) for regular work, but this assumes that the locos from two much later duties, 8M05 and 1P97 (see further tables), were back in time to be reutilised the same morning. If not, it increased the total needed by two, to sixteen just for regular work. With the immediate pre-6 May allocation it would have been virtually impossible to cover the soon to be described duties known to apply straight after that date. Also, the work does tend to lean more heavily towards south of Agecroft, Windsor Bridge, Moston, Brewery, Ashton Moss and Dewsnap than at any other time known to the author, and this too more than suggests a partial handover from Newton Heath.

Some of those thirteen targets covered a lot of common ground at various times and the majority operated south of Bolton in a still labyrinthine 'tangle' of short runs between such yards as Rose Hill, Kearsley, Pepper Hill, Agecroft, Brindle Heath, Windsor Bridge, Tank Yard, Moston, Brewery, Ashton Moss, Dewsnap and Hartford Sdgs (between Oldham Mumps and Royton Jc.). 'Kearsley Pilot &

Trips', a twenty-two-hour job in total, worked amongst some of the foregoing yards, spending seven and a half of those hours at Kearsley as the pilot itself.

Longer, supposedly non-stop (traffic-wise) trips worked Rose Hill–Moston, Horwich–Moston, Agecroft–Dewsnap, Kearsley–Dewsnap, Brindle Heath–Horwich, Brewery–Horwich, Hartford–Dewsnap and Astley Green–Kearsley. In the same district there was still Patricroft–Crumpsall with its associated workings and assistings. The lion's share of eight targets were involved with the foregoing, whilst on other routes out of Bolton we still had Castleton pilot (which started its day with an early morning Brewery–Castleton), Heap Bridge Trips, Rawtenstall pilot (with trips to Bury), Bolton–Bamfurlong, also 'Continuous pilot', not forgetting Trinity Street pilot and Bolton Ballast (10A loco?). Odds and ends such as the evening Up side (Bolton) pilot were covered within the target structure.

The seven targets that ran Saturdays too were, except for Castleton pilot and Bamfurlong, all in the north Manchester area again, mostly performing cut-down versions of their SX schedule and a fair proportion of it was in the early hours, so only four locos left 9K 'after breakfast'. The non-target work is set out below, made up of some familiar duties from earlier times, and some not, all booked for 9K power, unless otherwise stated.

probably conveyed that commodity in its consist to supply Bolton mpd. 5N12 was now shown with a Halliwell start, rather than the long-standing Burnden departure. 8J38 I would also categorise with the first three goods' listed as being covered by a 9K engine already in the field. The 6th also marks the point at which our SO Heysham–Ardwick East Yard was redirected to Brewery Sidings. Ashton Moss parcels, 3J20, now ran via Castleton curve, Moston and 'India Rubber Jc.' (Miles Platting) with no booked stops and was Newton Heath crewed.

One Bolton job that vanished through discontinuation was the 18.16 Rawtenstall–Rochdale parcels (worked to Bury by 9K). Two other parcels trains via Bolton were dieselised that same weekend as the 'Boat', but not affecting 9K. They were the 17.45 Colne–Ashton Moss, 3J20, as far as Bolton, the engine of which still went forward on the 20.55 Bolton–Guide Bridge, 3H28, via Clifton. 3J20 continued to be re-engined off 9K at Trinity Street.

Collectively these changes and the diversion of 3J20 after Bolton considerably altered the complexion of local evening steam-hauled traffic even further, particularly that which passed the mpd, leading us to more frequently forsake our home town after tea for other potentially more rewarding locations that weren't too far flung,

Freight		
00.36	Ashton Moss–Agecroft	8J32 MX
05.17	Ashton Moss–Agecroft	8J24 MSX (04.30 ex Mottram)
13.35	Ashton Moss–Agecroft	8J33 MO (also runs MX, dep 14.04)
05.25	Ardwick–Moses Gate	5J16 MSX
11.20	Abram–Bolton	8J50 SX
12.35	Halliwell–Healey Mills	7N55 SO (to 25 May only)
14.40	Halliwell–Healey Mills	7N95 SX
[22.16	Halliwell–Healey Mills	5N12 SX
03.25]	Healey Mills–Bolton	8M05 MX (formerly 03.05 dep)
22.52	Mottram–Philips Park	8J38 SX
16.50	Heysham–Brewery	5J44 SO

Parcels and Empty Stock		
[21.45	Bolton–Ashton Moss	3J20 SX (17.45 ex Colne, now diesel to Bolton)
03.05	Red Bank–Manchester Vic.	3P97 MX (worked by Newton Heath MO)
03.45]	Manchester Vic.–Colne News	1P97 MX (worked by Newton Heath MO)

My own square brackets indicate which jobs were worked by the same engine. Two trains powered by a Carnforth loco, but worked by Bolton men were the 20.20 Bolton–Bedford parcels, 3M13 (to Rochdale only) and the 22.30 Ancoats–Heysham, 5P05, both by the same loco, unchanged from the early 1968 table. It is my considered opinion that the first three freights listed took their power from the target structure after completing that work in the Ashton Moss area. Another train never seen, 5J16, though not suggestive of a coal carrier,

hence Broadfield bank becoming a favourite in the coming weeks. Light evenings spent on the cutting slopes west of the station, rarely meeting anyone else there for the same purpose combined with the (even then) diesel-free haven (on regular loco-hauled work) that Bolton–Castleton still was in the hours after 6pm to create a spot well worth revisiting.

Bolton's 45252 has just passed Heap Bridge Jc. (for Y.D. Papers) signal box during the ascent of Broadfield bank. In a slightly earlier era than that of 1968, it nevertheless represents evening trips we made to the locality during the closing months of steam. *Ray Farrell*

Wednesday, 8 to Friday, 10 May

An unextended visit to 9K on Tuesday, 7 May, saw Paul and I arrange Broadfield for the 8th. Making the best of it entailed going almost straight from work on the 17.45 train to be in position for the 18.05 Bolton–Moston. It's hard to understand why such an ideal location so late on wasn't more popular – semi-rural then and with most of the traffic heading east against the 1 in 82 grade. Our 'newish' loco, 48392, sounded spot on hauling twenty-seven wagons on the aforementioned Moston at a sedate pace. There didn't seem to be anything for the 17.15 Castleton–Bolton (Castleton pilot's SX finishing trip) as 45104 ran LE towards Bolton somewhat after the expected time. No. 45269, however, trundled past with a good load of thirty-seven at 19.00 on the 18.33 Brewery–Bolton, and this was Trip 95's final movement of the day. As this receded, 5J13, the 16.40 Burnley–Moston (thirty-two on) came into earshot behind a rather rough-sounding 44910 (9D), which nevertheless made a confident ascent.

A cold and searching wind for early May kept us company that evening, whistling at times through the telephone wires and putting paid to any ideas of complete relaxation in unsheltered parts of the lineside. Heysham–Moston (thirty-two on) was next after a near half-hour interval, its engine, 45394 (10A); but by far the most impressive, audibly, that night was the 20.20 Bolton–Bedford parcels, 3M13, 44874 (10A) in the hands of driver Horrocks, his steed obviously (and typically) well notched up throughout the climb, producing a healthy even blast and a cheery whistle for ourselves. No. 48773, light to 9K, had broken up the otherwise lengthy wait for Bedford. Finally, running earlier than usual, at 21.00, came the second Burnley–Moston (twenty-five on), 5J10, powered by 48519 of Rose Grove. He'd have been home and dry an hour before time at least. I'd coped well with the wind until changing position for this last of the procession, but even then it more adversely affected our comfort than the practicalities of tape recording, and with everything possible 'in the bag' we returned to Bolton.

A project to properly catalogue all recordings I'd compiled since the cassette innovation in November 1966 partly kept me off the railway on the 9th. Orchestra rehearsal the next night was again sacrificed for steam, but not much of the latter through being late down. Both were heading irrevocably to their own end, the former for myself only, because for some time my seniority in this musical organisation for 'youth' had caused me to wonder if the proper thing would be to stand down. Maybe these thoughts seemed to condone, if not justify, a pretty dire attendance record since shortly after my alternate railway turns had ceased to provide an incontestable reason for being elsewhere. At the station we fixed the early part of a local trip for Saturday before Pete, from Gorton, easily obtained a ride to within 3 miles of home on Ashton Moss parcels. His unplanned footplate run on the train's aforementioned new route was with loco 45260, its 'very friendly Newton Heath driver' making it all possible. The point at which Bolton men relinquished this working may have been as recent as the 6 May changes. 9K was in full command at least until later 1967.

Saturday, 11 May

Westhoughton seemed (in the light of recent experience) to offer a greater chance of success with the 08.58 Bamfurlong–Halliwell than Hindley had. So, on Saturday the 11th we were ready and waiting on the platform end by 09.25. Not for a further fifty minutes, however, did there come, rising and falling on the fresh westerly, an urgent staccato exhaust, immediately impressive. At first the wind proved rather troublesome with a recording I couldn't afford to mess up, but a subtle movement or two found some still air. In the more advanced stages of 44802's dynamic approach it became clear that today it had been diverted away from its normal traffic to take over a van special.

The 4-6-0 thundered past, having accelerated slightly during earshot to 26/27mph up the 1 in 97 on a load of fifty, plus the two brake vans; 415 tons or so. This was comparable to a contemporary twelve-coach express's weight, but with 104 axles instead of forty-eight and on goods wagon bearings too! No. 44802, hauling what we identified as a Mold Jc. van special, was considered one of the many outstanding lineside experiences of 1968. If any diesel banker had dropped off, it had done so early and the discernible acceleration against the grade was certainly accomplished without any such assistance.

We'd plenty of time to savour the spectacle after as B.R.'s new timetable hadn't done anything to release Westhoughton folk from the grip it held on any perhaps desirous of travelling east on a Saturday morning. When the 11.42 finally broke the three-and a half-hour dearth of stopping dmus, some of its passengers noticed 44802 again, at Bullfield, LE this time. In contrast to the recent

The last of very many van specials to Bolton that I saw, steam-worked or not, has 44802 putting on a terrific show on 11 May climbing the bank on the approach to Westhoughton station. *P. Barber*

A tangible reward for keeping the 11 May trip together, apart from time spent in the signal box, was steam on the 16.50 Heysham–Brewery SO, photographed from the top steps to East Jc. box and hauled by 45260. *P. Barber*

haulage feat of this obsolete form of motive power, at Bradley Fold (our next objective) soon after midday along came two Type 2s, D7550 and D5285 on a featherweight Brewery–Carlisle (fourteen on), a new train and never steam. The working we'd gone to see, Halliwell–Healey Mills (twenty-six on) was diesel today, too (D7589). Luckily we'd not troubled to go far for it, the disappointment felt being mellowed by the still fresh memory of what had started our day.

It was now time to gamble on the SO 13.25 Colne–Red Bank empty vans not running too early. Hastening via a decent connection at Bolton to Entwistle, then on the sleeper ends to Waltons Sidings, we were in comfortable enough time to keep Mr Carroll in the box company before and after the train. At 14.48, 44899's (10F) exertions as it topped the long climb from Blackburn (see 9 March) were rated amongst the best there so far (and were to be) with 3J83. I have a recollection of not understanding a great deal of what Mr Carroll said on the subject of politics, but that was my fault, no doubt, this subject and the one that brought us to his door representing the two extremes that engaged me least and most. Nevertheless, we were grateful for the 'waiting room' ¾ mile from Entwistle station. Its own signal box

had been closed for six weeks now, rendering the quadruple track between the two points double only, i.e. the Slow lines as they served the platform.

Back at Bolton for 16.22, the prospect of 5J44, Heysham–Brewery was not sufficient to hold our group's interest collectively. Maybe the possibility of another diesel did it. Pete and I again remained on the scene until evening, not in some windy cutting, but pleasurably for three hours in Bolton East Jc. box on Bob Middlewood's turn. Certain recreational activities at quieter times, facilitated by the cabin's generous length, were found to be still in vogue, no doubt to Pete's bemusement, as to mine when first beheld, though I'd heard of the custom first from my brother when he worked there before I did in 1966. Today we joined in a sort of golf game and I think it was a way of welcoming Peter, who'd not been in before. His footplate engine of just the previous evening, 45260, worked Heysham–Brewery as the only steam sighting of our visit, as expected. It had to be stopped to allow a passenger train to clear, then pulled out with seventeen containers behind the tender at 18.37.

There's no doubt that whilst the 'Boat' became increasingly popular with enthusiasts during its last weeks behind steam, two other identically hauled passenger duties in the North-west had their own devotees, dictated jointly by choice, and, I think, the ability of those enthusiasts to get home in the late evening. Those two trains were the 21.25 from Preston to Liverpool Exchange, 1F51, a portion of the 17.26 Glasgow–Manchester, 1M40, and the 20.50 Preston–Blackpool South, 1P58, itself a portion of the 17.05 Euston–Carlisle, 1P79. From 11 May the enthusiast contingent on these trains was swelled by the Heysham exiles making a natural progression. Just as a host of unfamiliar faces appeared on 'our' West Coast Main Line steam-hauled expresses with the fall of Southern steam in July 1967, so we 'exiles' from the 'Belfast Boat Express' further populated these two portions ten months later.

My own reasons for always choosing the '20.50', as it was best known, were varied. It offered fast running (as did the 21.25) to Lytham, beyond which point the schedule demanded smart accelerations. In recent years Blackpool South had been in the shadows where steam passengers were concerned, with most excursion traffic being attracted to the far more capacious North. Here, therefore, was a chance to repeatedly experience the Coast road following our Easter 1968 'taster' and earlier occasional runs. Add to the above my unshakeable fondness for Blackpool and the lines leading to the resort, plus a more adaptable 'bale out' service back to Bolton in the event of significant late running, to explain my loyalty to 1P58 during that late spring and summer.

Swelling the ranks of however many habitually supported the 20.50 Preston–Blackpool before 5 May were most of those recently deprived of steam on the 'Boat Train'. Seen here long before that 'transfer' date, and therefore after dark at journey's start, is 45212 (10D) waiting to leave with that duty on 23 March 1968. The impressive No. 4 signal box beyond the bridge appears well illuminated, but in reality they were often not. No. 45212 appeared on two more occasions known to the author. *T. Heavyside*

Other than the Ansdell stop which it omitted, 1P58 was comparable with the 12.44, which seemed to have only briefly survived the 6 May changes under steam with its new time of 12.50. Both trains were now in D450 timings, indicating the maximum tonnage on a given schedule for a Type 4 diesel. Such a diesel timings designation in the W.T.T. was a danger sign for steam enthusiasts, without meaning categorically that a train really was diesel-hauled. Scaled down for the 20.50, its six- or seven-coach portion for Blackpool at 200/230 tons with a 'Black 5' was equally realistic and, as will be seen, taxing. For 1P58, however, I wasn't at Preston every Saturday evening for sundry reasons, one being that steam couldn't be guaranteed, so phoning beforehand became a common necessity. Despite this, Preston station's number 5 platform did adopt the same 'focal point' atmosphere at day's end that Victoria's number 12 had recently lost.

The average lateness of 1P58 away from Preston on the nine journeys I made was eight and a half minutes, a figure dragged down badly by a single exceptional case. On 11 May a punctual departure ensued with 44816 (10D) hauling six coaches. The 5MT made a better than average start up the 1 in 101 to No. 5 box. Speed rose then on gently falling grades and level track to 66mph at Spen Lane cabin, where steam was shut off. The driver applied the brakes to 30mph for pointwork through Kirkham & Wesham, then followed the mile or so, mainly uphill to just before Wrea Green and the 2-mile descent to Moss Side, though the maximum of 67mph came beyond this on the level again.

Just over a minute had been lost to Lytham, but we were right time away because 1P58 needed less than half its allowance at both of its Fylde coast stops. No. 44816 nevertheless left Lytham in very lively fashion and I made us slightly early leaving St Annes. Intermediate speeds of

51 and 49 would have provided a punctual arrival at South, but signals halted our approach, making the train nearly four late in. For a six-coach load, tonight's performance could, in the light of subsequent runs, be classed as good. Without being able to economise on stops the coastal timings were really too tight, but rarely in my experience was the train held for the full two minutes at Lytham or St Annes. The dmu 'connection' back to Bolton at 21.35 (thirteen minutes officially) was made with ease that evening. Some tense approaches to Blackpool South on 1P58 were saved for future occasions. A summer Saturday train much later from North station hadn't started its run yet, but was eventually resorted to twice.

Sunday, 12 to Friday, 17 May

There were still some gaps in the lining out of 45110, all on the tender I think, so another session aimed at completing this occupied Sunday afternoon, the 12th. Another engine put at one side during the previous week (an action probably facilitated by 9K's recently boosted allocation) was 48380. Its official withdrawal took place later in May. I enjoyed a film on TV that night called *Storm Warning*, but its portentous title was shrugged off by the dawning of a beautiful warm spring day on Monday. I'd likely have been on the mill's south-facing fire escape at dinnertime and was definitely on the alternative ironwork of Orlando footbridge for three evening hours later. Relegated now from its remarkable availability on the 1968 'Boat', 45025 (10A) was first to appear working Heysham–Moston as it increased its load to thirty-six wagons during the forty-two minutes the train spent in 'B' Sidings. Other loco-hauled traffic ran normally too with 50% steam excluding Up side pilot (44802) and the second Burnley–Moston being on the late side and not seen.

The good weather didn't last into Tuesday, 14 May, when my Dad gave Paul and I a lift to Darwen. We'd picked a wet evening for attempt number one to clinch an oil train that had recently come to our notice, but which we were still (it transpired) under-informed about. The train and its corresponding empties working did not appear in Dent. After heading for Hoddlesden Jc. box, the signalman, to our great disappointment declared that our objective, 4P20, the 16.12 Heysham Harbour Jc.–Darwen, to give it its full title, ran MWFO. The train must have fallen into this pattern for the W.T.T., as we subsequently discovered, gave it as SX and 'Q', i.e. any day except Saturday, if required. The duty was understood to be booked for a Carnforth 9F, wherein lay the main attraction, and the sidings at Hoddlesden Jc. seemed to be on the same gradient as the main line at that point, i.e. 1 in 79. We'd been too late for the first Burnley–Moston and the next snippet of news imparted by the 'bobby', as if of no importance whatsoever, revealed that the second Moston was breaking up at Blackburn that night! So, with the trip in tatters, but a resolve to try again the next evening we went home on the 22.04.

We duly returned on the 15th, by train this time. Stage one went well, Darwen being reached, as hoped, before the first Moston goods. Eighteen minutes later, 44899 (10F), not the usual 9D loco, hauling an exacting load of thirty wagons pounded past, maintaining l4mph or so on the 1 in 71, its exhaust reverberating from the still substantial station buildings.

This, however, proved to be the only steam action we were destined to see for our mile walk to Hoddlesden Jc. revealed almost the same news from the same signalman – both 4P20 and the later Moston were being held at Blackburn, probably until morning! The reason was not forthcoming and all it did was provide an inkling into why the second Moston goods, when thought to be 'late', was held as described. This second trip failure did my temperament no good at all, but it wasn't long before we did succeed along the lines attempted, but not with the hoped for power.

Thursday and Friday evening that followed were more musically orientated than railway, up to the 'summit' meeting to discuss Saturday. On the meeting's attendance I can't be more specific than 'Everyone was there'. Beyond the Bolton four and Pete (the next day's participants) there were more, as we'll soon see, so Trinity Street remained a focal point on Friday nights even with a steamless 'Boat'. The 20.55 Club had survived the demise of its adopted train's traditional motive power and it was set to endure beyond the need to pool ideas for the next day's trip; and the rest!

Saturday, 18 May

Whether the plan was already formulated on this occasion or Paul and Vern's action was a result of it is not recalled. Bolton mpd was taking part in a push of special coal trains from West Yorkshire the next morning and 45104 and 44947 were cleaned in readiness overnight into Saturday. The reasons for such an operation in mid-May were less obvious than for the last known event of its kind in the early winter of 1967/68, which was on an enormous scale.

We intended to observe the aforementioned special traffic round about Todmorden. Most of the steam activity noted en route, via Manchester, was employed on various pilot duties it seemed, ten engines in total as far as Rochdale and excluding the few numbers grabbed while passing Newton Heath. Recent Speke Jc. casualty 92054 was visible, dumped here, and not the only ex 8C 2-10-0 to end up at the wrong place. Evidence too, en route, was of the additional coal movement, but diesel-hauled so far. Rose Grove still had the responsibility of supplying Copy Pit banking engines and when we arrived, 48519 and 48191 (both 10F) were simmering at Stansfield Hall, awaiting their next jobs and suggesting that nothing had gone up the bank recently. Those next jobs weren't imminent and only a rake of empties with an eastbound Type 3, D6829, punctuated our first hour and a quarter there. Matters improved after 10.00 though; two diesel-hauled coal runs that required banking and appeared to be special judging from their reporting numbers. It was novel indeed to be

A smoky 48410 (10F) is understandably being readied for the big climb as it prepared to take the Copy Pit line at Hall Royd Jc. as the first steam action we encountered there on 18 May. It would be banked by 48519 (10F) shortly before noon.
P. Barber

taping both steam and the 'opposition' on the same train, the growling D6953 audible as well as 48519 at the rear of 7Z24. Even the Type 4, D394 on 7Z48 didn't spurn the assistance of 48191. The bankers returned separately as these trains were twenty-eight minutes apart.

Having unpredictable coal traffic on both lines west of Todmorden kept us on our toes to avoid the risk of missing something on one or the other as the best audio effects were obtained away from Hall Royd Jc. itself. We found that the best policy (though it meant a lot of fast walking at the least on a very warm day) was to return to Hall Royd after most workings, ascertain the destination of the next and take appropriate action. We didn't stay together all morning by any means, partly as I was taping only, as was usual now. The signalman certainly cooperated after the two diesel/steam combinations. No sooner had he spoken than I heard a freight approach, necessitating not the only four-minute ¾ mile that morning into Lydgate woods, just short of the tunnel. For this, the third one over Copy Pit, we were rewarded by steam at both ends as 48410 (10F) slogged up the 1 in 65 hauling thirty-two loaded, banked by 48519. Its exhaust died away at 11.35. Luckily, I'd sat down to consume the day's first sandwiches (while they retained their original shape!) when another item of special traffic appeared – a wandering ten-coach Warwickshire Railway Society railtour, 1L66, hauled presently by 73069 (9H) and 44949 (9D). The pair, which we'd not seen the last of, were already taking the climb comfortably in their stride. We'd seen the BR 5 on Newton Heath when passing earlier. Probably both were there.

As the excursion cleared and 48519 ran back LE I saw that a westbound coal train had been held on the main line, presumably to allow the 11.05 dmu ex Leeds to take preference, and this bit of regulating fortuitously enabled me to reach the station in time for 45104's contribution to the day. It moved off, cautiously at first, then with a strong exhaust up the 1 in 182 towards Walsden, hauling thirty coal bound for Brewery Sidings. This wasn't an easy start for a Class 5 and it seemed odd that 9K hadn't marked 8Fs to the work. Very soon after a 2-8-0 ran onto the Burnley line from the east with more coal, but its passage to Stansfield Hall and subsequent departure, assisted by both of the bankers, was viewed, not by choice, from a fair distance. At last I'd been run out by the intervals and frequency of the diverging traffic.

Fast becoming railtour favourites in the spring of 1968 were 73069 (9H) and 44949 (9D). Working the 1L66 railtour, as described, the 'Black 5' leads the B.R. engine (unseen) as they fork left at Todmorden to take the Burnley line after 48410 (10F) had cleared the summit. *P. Barber*

The double banking of this goods occurred purely because it coincided with the end of their turn of duty and not through any exceptional train weight. It also served as a pretty clear indication that westbound goods work over Copy Pit had finished for the day. We hadn't, however, seen the second Bolton engine. After walking back to the station again, meeting Paul in the main street, it quickly became apparent that 44947 had been close behind the previous goods, its twenty-seven of coal for Brewery being brought through at 12.35, albeit not too energetically. So ended a fairly hectic, but rewarding morning – the planned part of the day.

In the course of our return to Lancashire, 44947 was seen standing in the loop at Smithy Bridge, LE, having evidently left its train there for whatever operational reason. Probably before we'd left Todmorden it was discovered by phone that prominent 9K Saturday jobs Halliwell–Healey Mills and Heysham–Brewery were either not running or earmarked for a diesel. So, it was decided to meet up with the railtour again, then look at the situation on Lostock Hall depot, particularly with motive power for that night's 20.50 in mind.

With two smart changes of train and travelling via Bury this time, we reached Preston before 2.30pm. Through the windows of the 14.48 unit out to Bamber Bridge appeared a new working to us – the empty tanks returning from Darwen to Heysham to balance 4P20, unsuccessfully sought out during the week, as the reader may recall. The loco for this far more gravitationally favourable run was 45382 (10F) today. Since we'd last encountered it, the railtour, 1L66, had been to Blackpool North via Bolton's Johnson Street fork and it now headed via Blackburn and Hellifield to Morecambe. No. 70013 had taken over at some point and for the Pacific we walked east nearly a mile from Bamber Bridge to Hospital Crossing, onto the 1 in 99, and were rewarded by the 7MT's sharp exhaust as it impressively got stuck into the lower slopes of Hoghton bank at around 35mph on this very fair afternoon.

Nearly eighteen months had elapsed since I'd trodden the familiar cinder path into Lostock Hall mpd (26 December 1966) and the contents then bore no resemblance to today in class variety or serviceable steam strength. The allocation of 10D now stood at twenty-five

Opposite top: Copy Pit signal box on 11 June with one of the day's banking engines, 48519 (10F) pausing there prior to running back light to Stansfield Hall for its next duty of that nature. *I.C. Simpson*

Bottom: Bankers on 18/5, 48519 and 48191 (both of 10F) take a rest at Stansfield Hall between duties. At 12.28 both would return to their home depot at the rear of the day's last coal train that needed assistance. *P. Barber*

131

The first of the two closely spaced Bolton worked specials, behind 45104, makes its elevated way through the centre of Todmorden, heading for Brewery Sidings on 18 May. *V.A. Sidlow*

of just three classes, not that this was exceptional in 1968. A solitary foreigner (from 9D) was present. Of the forty steam on the premises in total, eight still had a noticeable pressure in their boilers and not all were cooling down. Seven I identified as withdrawn, based on their physical state. They were indeed, but so were seven more that had not yet featured in the listings to the public. Recently condemned machines were not readily distinguishable from unused or spare locomotives. It was difficult to tell which category the surviving Ivatt 4, 43106 fell into, but as we now know it certainly was in stock at that time. The time of day was about 17.30.

Rose Grove's 48247 coasts downhill at Hoghton with 4P21, the 18.40 Darwen–Heysham empty tanks, on Friday, 21 June. It was the much earlier 13.35 SO train that we intercepted just outside Preston on 18 May. *R. Weisham*

With just one engine apparently in steam, this view of Lostock Hall mpd paints an outwardly bleak picture. Taken on a Saturday at the end of February 1968, certainly the left-hand row of locos have run their last and maybe the next row too, but plenty more would be out of sight, serviceable. *Peter Reeves/M.L.S. collection*

By mid-May the reign of Ivatt 4MTs on Preston Station Pilot was probably over with one surviving only. Forlorn companions 43027 and 43019 were not the only ones of the class dumped at 10D on 18 May. *P. Barber*

Light retention in the western sky enables 44950 (10D) to be silhouetted as it leaves Preston at 21.30 on 18 May. We witnessed a gentle enough departure that held no foretaste of the sensational run to come on the 21.25 to Liverpool.
P. Barber

Lostock Hall was not by now without a main line diesel element, seven being present, though only shunters were actually allocated. One recently withdrawn resident 8F, 48763, had come north from Colwick via Trafford Park, the last move to 10D being made in early spring 1968. Until that teatime moment on 18 May I had never seen it before and this forlorn 2-8-0 served as my last ever steam 'cop' in the traditional sense. Reminded I am while briefly on the topic of train spotting of the soft spot I long held for 44950 (10D), (one of those fired that afternoon of 18 May), ever since seeing it pass eight times in two consecutive days at Leyland in August 1963. Though on nothing grander than Manchester–Blackpool runs, the impression once created in even more impressionable times always remained. Continued prominence to a Boltonian (until the demise of Blackpool Central mpd) ended when the 4-6-0 was 'secreted away' at Speke Jc. depot until recent events stirred up that nest for the last time and released 44950 to a wider public again.

We'd ascertained sadly that the 20.50 would not be steam-hauled that night, and though 44950 was to take the 21.25 Liverpool, 1F51, chose an alternative option to travelling behind my fondly remembered 'Mickey', which I have subsequently much regretted. The day's railtour, 1L66, still had plenty of wind in its sails and there was nothing wrong with the idea of a leisurely wait for it to reappear at Skew Bridge (which it did at 19.08), back in the hands of 73069 and 44949. It would leave the W.C.M.L. at Hartford Jc. to relinquish steam at Stockport via the C.L.C. route. Two hours before, 44950 had looked very dilapidated on 10D, a state always heightened by the lack of a numberplate (unusual too on an L.M.S. loco before that last summer itself). It was this, the cost of additional train fares on top of the day's so far and the late finish (23.18 into Trinity Street) that turned us in favour of watching the 21.25 depart. This we did from Avenham Park, just south of the Ribble.

The unhurried nature of that spring evening permitted a reminder of how motive power developments beyond steam were taking place, too. The engines that a few years earlier were ousting the bigger L.M.S. types from top-class work (E.E. Type 4 D200s) had themselves been largely relegated, first by the Brush Type 4s and now, hints of their heyday coming to an end were evidenced by the new D400 series, from English Electric again. The following list from our two vantage points more economically illustrates the above statement:

D5061	16.30 Manchester Vic.–Blackpool N. Parcels SO, 3P05	17.58
D1952	17.45 Liverpool Ex–Glasgow Cen., 1S76	18.14
D367	17.45 Manchester Vic.–Preston (portion of above) 1P33	18.26
D371	? Special freight 4Z10 (direction not noted)	18.41
Brush 4	15.15 Kings Norton–Bathgate freightliner TThSO, 3S49	18.56
D1859	18.15 Blackpool South–Euston, 1A80	19.05
D400	16.05 Euston–Glasgow Cen. 1S83	19.11
D417	17.05 Euston–Carlisle & Blackpool South, 1P79	
D1955	18.40 Euston–Heysham 'The Ulster Express' 1P44	
D5212	20.55 Manchester–Heysham 'Belfast Boat Express' 1P02	

Near the end of that list would come 44950 (10D) on the 21.25 portion ex Glasgow to Liverpool Ex., 1F51. The 'Black 5's' unspectacular departure over the river, on time, held no hint of what I many years later learned had turned into a scorching run with no less than 86mph achieved! Appearances could still be deceptive. Several logs, almost dominated by 44950 and 44816, and an excellent accompanying article appeared in *Railway World* for March 1974. No. 44816, incidentally, last week's (11 May) 20.50 engine, had come off 10D since our afternoon visit, to work Preston station pilot. Mr Berry, the article's writer, agrees with my impressions of this loco, but even the best had to come down to earth now and then!

Sunday, 19 to Friday, 24 May

I made a late start to Sunday the 19th and even abstained from 9K in the afternoon, but Broadfield was on again for Monday evening. Paul again and Barrie, a much less frequent companion from Crumpsall, made up the 'team', so it was probably an all tape recording night. All the traffic that could be expected, i.e. six goods and a parcels (and listed with the 8 May trip), were observed within four hours, though the first and last were viewed from the train to and from Broadfield. The out of beat 48168 held 15mph at best on the 18.05 Bolton–Moston on a load of thirty-two. Conveying slightly fewer vehicles on the first Burnley–Moston, 45076 (9D) made the climb at around 25mph. A quizzical glance from each of the crew may well have met across the cab as the loco slipped momentarily on a small deposit of oil laid down experimentally by Paul for that purpose. In the prevailing conditions loss of adhesion would have been the last thing on the driver's mind. We never did that again for steam!

No. 45435 (10A) heading the 16.50 Heysham–Moston (forty-six on) put up the best performance of the evening,

period it hung on to steam haulage on this, its new route, was not seen at Broadfield and neither that night was the second Burnley–Moston. With customary power, it crossed us at Radcliffe Black Lane. Still, a 'very good' comment awarded to the trip obviates the need to guess so long afterwards the level of enjoyment it provided.

This book does not extend to 1 December 1968 for obvious reasons, but that evening Broadfield trip from then on would not have been possible by train because B.R. discontinued the day's first morning service each way and the last three or four at night, clearly with a view to running down the line to eventual closure, a process that took until 5 October 1970.

The recorded contents of Bolton mpd for the evening after, 21 May, at 20.15 are those that influenced comment on the workload of 9K in relation to what it was prior to the 6 May changes, by virtue of the number of engines in steam. The premises that had supplied us with such a wealth of memories over the years presented that night a situation certainly not indicative of a depot heading for closure in just under six weeks' time. We now knew that an end of June date was set for Bolton, Newton Heath and Patricroft. I did note at the time of that visit that the active steam presence seemed higher than perhaps expected; but now I am inclined to think not. Why?

Because of our increased evening activity of late, away from the shed in search of steam, the 21 May visit to 9K was only my third since the early May changes. One of these was on a Monday – never representative – so the more than implied surge in requirements for Bolton shed may not have been as noticeable until now. Short-lived though it was, the following inexcusably last detailed contents list of 9K that I compiled, shows the place in its best light so near to the end, listed in original order, reading down the columns:

48652 Stopped	D2226 Withdrawn	45269 In Steam	45381 Withdrawn
45110 Stopped	D2234 Withdrawn	48340 In Steam	48090 Withdrawn
44929 Stopped	D2227 Withdrawn	48392 In Steam	44965 Withdrawn
48773 In Steam	45073 In Steam	44871 In Steam	48380 Withdrawn
45046 In Steam	44781 New Fire	44802 In Steam	48692 In Steam
44888 In Steam	44947 In Steam	48702 Withdrawn	45104 In Steam
45290 In Steam	44664 Withdrawn	48465 Withdrawn	12012 Withdrawn
45312 In Steam	48111 Withdrawn	48532 Withdrawn	12023 Withdrawn
48026 Withdrawn	45318 Stopped	44829 Withdrawn	48720 Arr. Ashpit 20.20
D2224 Withdrawn	48319 In Steam	48744 Withdrawn	48168 Arr. Ashpit 21.05

maintaining the upper teens mph with that considerable load, whilst not being thrashed. We were expecting 44709 (10A) to appear on Bedford parcels, but 45290, blowing off on the climb instead, worked 3M13 at about its usual time, indicating a re-rostering for whatever reason. In preferring to catch the 21.37 dmu back instead of the last one an hour later, Ashton Moss parcels during the short

The status regarding withdrawn locomotives (diesels were either ex Horwich Works shunters or had been sent in from Springs Branch) is as we understood it at the time, based on information imparted and physical condition. No. 48026 was officially still in stock, but in effect permanently retired, and 48380 had actually been condemned during the current week. The 'Carnforth engine' had already left shed to work Bedford parcels and

135

44888 was about to follow suit for Ashton Moss parcels, but not before 48720 arrived, so the total in steam at that point was sixteen, plus 44781 newly fired. Two 9K locos, 45260 and 48504 were absent, presumed out in traffic (plus 48168, which arrived later, as shown) and this ties in well with the Dent compilation, but only if our station pilot was diesel that evening, as was very common from now at that time of day. It was on the 22nd and at least by the month end there was a separate 350hp (from 'B' Side pilot) on hand for the job.

Kettering mpd had been the long-standing domicile of 48380 (Bolton's recently withdrawn 8F) up to September 1964, when it moved to Coalville until early November 1965. It hadn't time to settle there as the 2-8-0 took part in the Midlandisation of Colwick at the year end, remaining at the newly renumbered 16B for most of 1966. The 8F's next move brought it to Bolton, where it arrived on 1 November 1966 for service lasting until the depot's last weeks.

The evening after the above shed statistics were compiled, 22 May, I went purposely to the west end of platform 2 in the hope of capturing on tape a struggle out of Bradshawgate tunnel with the first Burnley–Moston, but 48132 (9D) had no trouble on a thirty-wagon load. I knew from experience that it could go either way here and two nights together, for example, a longer and seemingly heavier train could 'walk it' out of the short but tightly curved tunnel, then upgrade a short while into the end (No. 1) platform, in contrast to a right old battle for adhesion or simply to keep moving. Results could not be predicted. At O.B. later, what turned out to be my last sighting of Ashton Moss parcels in the hands of steam featured 45269. The train probably saw the week out under the old order when Type 2s took over. I may have gone for the wrong Burnley–Moston that night as Vern told me later that the second train had delayed the 21.02 unit ex Darwen by a full half hour! He'd been up at Spring Vale. The engine was 48167 (10F) and its load thirty-four wagons.

Participants in that Friday evening's station gathering were threatened by an inspector for 'loitering'! Extreme indecision also pervaded the meeting, which ended only in a resolve to phone Rose Grove mpd (Burnley 28260) early the next morning to ascertain some dependable 'gen', particularly I recall with a view to activity on the freight-only Grassington branch. Rose Grove had the loan of a 10A-based BR 4MT for this work, which comprised the distribution of ballast from Spencer's Swinden Lime Works. Dent quotes the work as daily and Carnforth as the solitary destination, but I have good reason to believe that much more flexibility existed. Oddly, I always thought, the 4MT had to pay periodic visits back to 10A for washout and other maintenance, then vice versa, when allocating an engine to Rose Grove would have made more sense.

At the north end of a not very well thought out trip on 25 May, the Grassington branch loco, 75027 (10A), has already completed its work and waits in a short siding at Skipton to return light engine to Rose Grove. How we expected to access the branch by public transport is no more easily answered now as then: The 89B shed plate borne by the engine probably originated with enthusiasts. It was the early 1960s' code for Croes Newydd and of no sensible use in North Yorkshire. *V.A. Sidlow*

Saturday, 25 May

The above activity was selected as Saturday's first objective. Maybe we paid for not taking the first service to Skipton, but the second at 07.55, also with a quick change of train at Blackburn, but we did have to phone Rose Grove first. Of interest en route was 44888 heading light for 9K at Accrington after working the 03.45 Manchester–Colne papers, 1P97.

The LE was the tail end of the diagram that began the night before on the 17.45 Colne–Ashton Moss parcels (from Bolton), as recently related. This proved that the latter (and therefore the diagram) had been steamworked on 24 May, probably for the last time. Legion and (in time) legendary were Bolton drivers' tales of their exploits on 1P97, largely claiming journey times that were as implausibly fast as the schedule was leisurely for a train as light as the 'papers'. With a late start, however, the scope was wide open for what the men wanted to do, and even allowing for a degree of exaggeration there must have been more than a few reckless nocturnal dashes. Ten minutes to Darwen (from Bolton) I heard more than once. No. 44888 was more than an hour and a half late returning light that morning, so maybe the train itself was less punctual than its class 1 status would suggest. But there (to the best of my knowledge) was another lost to modern power from now on. Perhaps the exploits continued with Type 2s? But who would be as avid a listener to their relating?

Freight movement in the vicinity of Rose Grove behind both forms of motive power provided a strong temptation to alight there. It was resisted and later regretted. All stations to Skipton took more than an hour and a half, even with the efficient change at Blackburn, but we should still have been able to do something with the 4MT, despite an 09.32 arrival and no car thereafter. However, as we pulled in, 75027 (10A) stood in the little bay platform, having completed its duties and soon after returned to 10F for the weekend, or maybe Carnforth. Either way, it had finished earlier than we'd been led to expect. Booked times had the engine at Spencer's Sidings until 09.55. Targeted much by photographers around this time, pictures of the Grassington branch featured quite frequently in the magazines of summer 1968.

We weren't sharp enough to get the 09.47 back, maybe waiting until the engine had moved off, and so were left with two hours to kill. This interval was occupied as unexpectedly as it was profitably, and in a very different way to original intentions by an inspection of the closed mpd at Skipton. Though resident engine operations had ceased just over a year before, the depot appeared not to have been abandoned completely until more recently. We found nearly everything intact and a large store of shed records, heavily loco-orientated, dating mostly from the 1940s was discovered in the loft. Wartime paper economies abounded as many sheets were of poor quality and typed on both sides with a different subject on each. What was to us fascinating material would certainly be burned at a later date, so we had no qualms about leaving the premises with bulging duffle bags! I also unscrewed a small framed paper listing local internal telephone circuit ringing codes, dated October 1933 and with only one alteration made to it subsequently. Even 'Keighley Loco', closed in mid-1962 had not been deleted, its code a short and two longs.

Having made a fairly atrocious start to the day steamwise, our attempts to rectify this began with a return to Blackburn – nothing was noted around Rose Grove well after midday on a Saturday – then by bus out to Hoddlesden Jc., even though heavy rain had set in for the

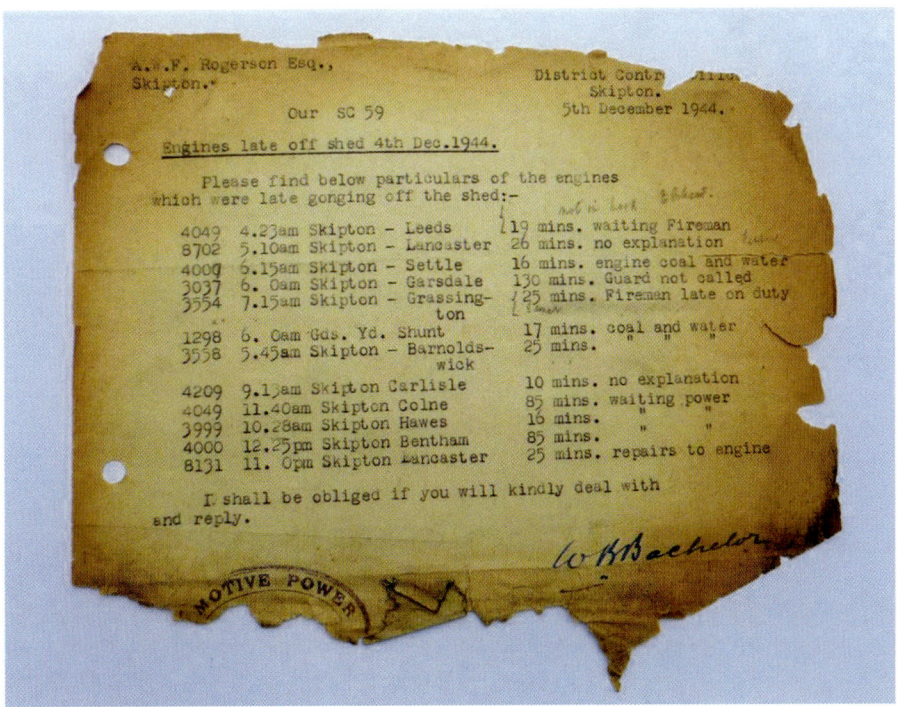

Survivors No. 3 – An intriguing item from the store of old paperwork rescued from Skipton mpd on 25 May 1968.

afternoon. Quite a wait ensued through the diesel-hauled Brewery–Carlisle, until 45382 (10F) made a rather plodding climb towards Sough tunnel with the SO Colne–Red Bank. Coming off the 1 in 101 onto steeper grades immediately and noticeably retarded the train's already inconsiderable velocity to that more akin to a goods working at the same location. Only by keeping still could sanctuary be found from the rain and it was a very damp and disconsolate group that waited for an engine to arrive to take the Darwen–Heysham tanks. No. 48493 (10F) duly did, but this event actually marked the day's low spot as a combination of desperation and effrontery in asking to ride with the guard was rejected. After the Blackburn reversal, of our fortunes too, we hoped, he would have been in the other brake and we at the front of the train. The idea of the guard accepting responsibility for our illicit presence on his train through a sensitive complex such as Preston was quite daft, aside from the question of how far we'd go and where to alight. In the end, the mid-afternoon departure of 48493, tender-first downhill in the sloshing wet, didn't cause any of us to run out of film or tape!

The ascertaining, after the bus ride back to Blackburn, that the 20.50 would be steam somehow reset all evaluations of the day so far to nought. There lay a good goal ahead, but it still left ample time to examine the divided spoils of Skipton shed and while away the steamless early evening at Preston until 45353 (10D) ended it with a 19.29 arrival to take up pilot duties. This may be misleading and readers with notions of the 4-6-0 actively shunting this, that and the other, ought instead to picture it simmering on sleeping cars at the north end. These would be attached to the 20.45 Barrow–Euston. Those berths, meanwhile, received steam heat from 45353.

The little blackboard discreetly displayed part way down platform 5 bore no bad tidings of the 17.05 ex Euston tonight and this in turn meant that 44816 (10D) left Preston punctually on its seven-coach portion. It made, too, a clean start up to No. 5 box with only minimal wheelslip. Acceleration after Maudlands Viaduct was brisk. Our engine was whipped through the 50s, crossed the 60mph mark at Constable Lane and reached 67 before the Kirkham crossovers. Having negotiated these and topping the rise beyond, 44816 ran up to 70mph on the descent to Lytham, stopping there in 18'-31" (for 14.01 miles), but still half a minute outside the allowance.

The starts were solid, with appropriate echoes, but 1P58 slowed to 10mph through Ansdell & Fairhaven for no apparent reason. The remaining section in from St Annes, however, was brisk enough, producing 53mph through Squires Gate (consistent with the better runs) and we were spot on time in South – a model run. As implied earlier, this very lively effort largely influenced the contemporary assessment of 25 May as 'a good day'. Most Saturdays in 1968 were rated as successful to one degree or another, but this, prior to the late evening boost, had been easily the most dismal for weather and action since 10 February. Pieces of good news in the midst of such were therefore all the more sustaining.

The 20.50 employed steam on more occasions than the 21.25 Liverpool from then, but this provides me with no excuse for not noting the Mersey-bound working's motive power. I can scarcely give credence to this and must fall on the likelihood that its engine used to reach Preston station with a far slimmer margin to departure than that of the Fylde run. If so, we'd already be heading west on the other train by the time it appeared.

Sunday, 26 and Monday, 27 May

South Lancashire's weather, at least, promptly changed the following day into that more readily associated with early summer, heralding in fact three weeks blessed with more hot and sunny days than not; days of the kind that in hazy recollection bestow their pleasant nature on the whole season, banishing the indifferent or worse. That's how the memory seems to work with such reveries, though mine of 1968 between spring and autumn is an exception, even discounting simple written reminders of how it really was, whilst that of 1967, though still documented in the same way, does retain its 'endless summer' illusion. Anyway, the best of 1968's was now upon us, but how many Lancashire summers since, loved or otherwise for whatever reasons, have practically spent themselves by mid-June?

On that very warm afternoon of the first Sunday after Ascension I smartened up the lining on 45104 again at 9K, but didn't see an S.L.S. eight-coach railtour, 1L36, steam-hauled north of Stockport via Hellifield to Ravenglass, even though its outwards time at Bolton didn't clash with church. The start of the climatic improvement coincided perfectly with a short holiday spent by my parents at Borth-y-Gest, close to Portmadoc, still much-loved after several years as a family haunt and a place I'll always associate with certain experiences of a puberal nature, intensely personal, but which all go through, etched in memory alongside those of fading Western presence on nearby Cambrian lines, and much more; unlikely partners in the mind, but no less indelibly stamped there for it.

Before picking up the thread at local railway haunts, a reminder of what was happening at some not long abandoned ones. During the three days commencing Monday the 27th, a batch of four special trains was organised to convey eleven withdrawn steam locos to the Midlands and South Wales for cutting up by private firms. 8L80 left Heaton Mersey, dragging 48063, 48201, 48503 and 48507 to Coton Hill, but these 2-8-0s, last allocated to 9F, were ultimately for Buttigieg's yard in Newport (Monmouthshire). Also on Monday, 73034 and 73136 were taken from their home depot, Patricroft, to the same stopping off point on train 8L82, but bound for the other big Newport yard, Cashmores. Scheduled for Tuesday and Wednesday were two departures from Northwich mpd to the firm of G. Cohen of Kettering, 8Z57 taking 48036 and 48304 (ex 8E). The other three, 48272, 48617 and 48632, were booked off 8E at midday as 8Z55. They too

Hoddlesden Jc., scene of several visits during 1968, looking north with the signal box out of sight on the left and the truncated Hoddlesden branch leading off right. Though from several years earlier, this shot shows the basically unchanged layout, including access to the sidings behind the photographer. *H.L. Holland*

had last been in use at the depot of origin, which closed in early March. This local 'window' on what was happening too elsewhere on B.R. wherever ranks of the condemned were still congregated, was copied from notices at Bolton East Jc. box later in the current week.

In this narrow period of 1968 we were frequently drawn back to Darwen and Hoddlesden Jc. Monday's trip for me primarily targeted 4P20, the Heysham–Darwen tanks, hoping it would be third time lucky! With a flurry of early evening steam workings at Bolton just prior to the 18.45 dmu that Vern and I utilised there wasn't much else of interest we could expect up there. However, the second Burnley–Moston was well up to time, 48191 (10F) hauling twenty-six and passing at 20.35. Being positioned on the 1 in 101/79 gradient change was interesting when receding exhausts were audible too, as with the slightly slowed train just seen (and heard). The lengthier second portion of the climb to Waltons Sidings, including Sough tunnel, though variable, was all tougher than the first section from Blackburn Bolton Jc.

4P20, due off Blackburn at 21.00, didn't come into earshot until 22.15 and the first noticeable thing was the absence of a 2-10-0. It was originally thought that the oil conveyed was for the nearby Crown Paint factory, but in fact a small power station built in 1965 to supply various local industries, created the traffic. The eleven loaded oil tanks plus two brake vans that 4P20 conveyed weighed approximately 600 tons. The driver tonight of 48546 (10D), very conscious of the load and the road, shut off intermittently to lose as little momentum as possible in crossing over the Down line and again into the lengthy Down Sidings, whilst also slowing enough to negotiate the lateral move safely. Once 'inside', the 8F plugged away at around a fast walking pace prior to setting back. The guard, however, seemingly mistook the set of points that the train had to clear, necessitating a laboured restart, not without several severe wheelslips both then and during a subsequent shunt. Vern and I got our money's worth and despite a late finish on the 23.02 dmu home, a considerable satisfaction was felt in at last pinning down this elusive train. Six other (diesel-hauled) goods or parcels trains, partially identified, had made use of the Bolton–Blackburn line during our time on the scene, emphasising a since forgotten importance.

Tuesday, 28 May

In the most clement conditions imaginable, the cooling off of a hot day, I spent a by now quite rare full evening at Orlando bridge on 28 May. Several friends came and went in their own time and plenty of activity at rail level ensured an enjoyable spell, even if steam was thin on the ground in the last hour or so. One month before the closure of 9K, the findings are set out below, as per the 26 March listing, but with additional detail such as arrivals and departures (on separate lines).

powerful start hauling thirty-nine vehicles at 18.59. I would place this in my 'top five' energetic departures from Trinity Street on the Up. Of course, I had no tape recorder with me! For both trains I was better positioned for such appreciation on the footbridge, prior to obtaining the 'OK' to join my signalman friends. It was hot in the box, 82°F

45110 (9K)	Shunting at Burnden	18.30
45025 (10A)	16.50 Heysham–Moston (45) SX arrives	18.41
45017 (10A)	Loco for 20.20 Bolton–Bedford parcels SX arrives station ex 9K	18.43
45025 (10A)	16.50 Heysham–Moston (45) SX departs	18.59
D5238	Carlisle–Ashburys vans (60) arrives	19.00
44802 (9K)	Moston–Bolton (2) arrives on passenger loop.	19.11
D5238	Carlisle–Ashburys vans (60) departs (via Clifton)	19.12
D3860	Orlando Bridge–Burnden (34) departs	19.13
D7634	Loco for 20.05 Bolton–Wigan parcels arrives 'A' Side ex 8F	19.14
44809 (9D)	16.40 Burnley–Moston (33) SX arrives	19.15
44802 (9K)	2 wagon shunt–Passenger loop to Branch loop	19.19
44809 (9D)	16.40 Burnley–Moston (33) SX departs	19.21
44802 (9K)	Light engine to 9K	19.32
D7634	20.05 Bolton–Wigan parcels SX departs 'A' Side	20.04
D3844	Bolton station pilot	–
48720 (9K)	Light engine from Bury line onto Fork (and to shed?)	20.15
45017 (10A)	20;20 Bolton–Bedford parcels SX departs	20.17
D7677	20.55 Bolton–Guide Bridge parcels SX departs	20.48
D224	Southbound parcels or empty vans (3J40 Carlisle–Red Bank?)	20.56
D206	21.05 Oldham–Blackburn parcels SX arrives	21.09
D7589	Loco for 17.45 Colne–Ashton Moss parcels SX arrives ex 9K	21.11
48257 (10F)	19.05 Burnley–Moston (29) SX passes	21.12
D303	? Ancoats–Carlisle goods SX	21.15
D5198	20.55 Manchester Vic.–Heysham 'Belfast Boat Express'	21.23

Since the 6 May revisions the engine for Bedford parcels had begun to arrive at the station much earlier than before, perhaps now 18.35 off shed and possibly to replace Up side pilot, which I never noted again, unless, in the above listing D3860 was thus engaged. Only one passenger train is featured, by way of its loco haulage, but integrated in the above movements were, of course, all the evening dmu workings,

Wednesday, 29 to Friday, 31 May

The next two evenings I spent largely in East Jc. box on Bob Middlebrook's turn, as were all my subsequent visits up to the end of steam. For reasons not recorded, on 29 May the 18.05 Bolton–Moston (28) and the 16.50 Heysham–Moston were routed via Clifton. 48392, well over half an hour late away on the former, was an imminent casualty and had barely a week to run. No. 45435 (10A) on the second train, after a nine-minute halt on the through line to let a Blackpool unit clear, made an exceptionally

from the day's constant sunshine, a bit less on the 30th.

The familiar 48115 (10F) worked the later Burnley–Moston on both of those evenings. Its return duty was 6P69, the 23.28 Brewery–Blackburn SX, which I only saw once. That second night in the cabin, made possible due to there being no choir practice (dad, the organist and choirmaster still being on holiday), we only got D5714 and another Metrovic LE to Reddish for repair beyond the regular traffic plus another Type 2 light to Guide Bridge. I was amused to see one prominent enthusiast, rather out of keeping with the image he perhaps subconsciously radiated, running up the track into 'B' Side in the hope (I presumed) of obtaining a footplate on 45231 (10A), which made a lengthy stop there tonight on Heysham–Moston and left with thirty-five on. I didn't see him come back, so his persuasive ways must have done the trick, unless, of course, he'd had some prior communication with the driver and was trying to keep an 'appointment'. Outwardly it seemed a most audacious act. It was one thing to ask for a footplate ride standing opposite the cab at a station platform and quite another to rush through a maze of lines up to an unsuspecting crew. I'd hoped that the S.T.Ns. for the Whit weekend would have reached the box by that Thursday evening, but not so. Paul had heard that there would be a lot running on the Monday, but I knew I had to work!

For the district next to become most devoid of steam (at the end of June) we had need to look only to our own back yard, so to speak, for although Bolton did see the occasional regular passage on through workings beyond then, the demise at 9K and Newton Heath virtually eliminated that which we could still enjoy home-based. An area neglected by our attempted coverage of what was most immediately threatened was that west of Patricroft because 9H's very few forays towards Liverpool and Chester were all nocturnal or SX. Locally we were making the most of it on weekday evenings and despite the odd temptation elsewhere over those last remaining weekends, trips did concentrate on that which was next set to go in a big way.

The last month in the existence of 9K as a going concern was punctuated by the withdrawal of fifteen steam locomotives within the last two weeks. These were the official dates, but in practice, as has already been seen, engines could be laid aside before then, examples being 48392 and 48504 about the beginning of June.

Saturday, 1 June

Brewery Sidings and environs were selected on Friday night as the focus for Saturday's trip, 1 June. An early start was conducive to success and 07.00 saw our usual group, minus Vern, at the location. Local goods workings and associated LE movement prevailed over other loco-hauled traffic, proving quite plentiful until early afternoon. Steam outnumbered its rival 2:1, and Bolton engines were singularly prominent, almost as if they'd turned out in a deliberate show of strength to snub the 9D stud on its very doorstep. It was, however, further evidence of the extra work in north Manchester taken on latterly by 9K. No fewer than seven from that stable (five seen on trains) busied themselves on the railway between Brewery and Moston up to midday, compared with only three Newton Heath machines. Only a small number of trips matched up with traffic shown in Dent, but that was down to the erratic nature of such work, rather than anything else. I have confidence in the few that WERE identified and that these were not founded on assumption.

In Brewery Sidings as we passed on the train were 48356, 45206 and 48373 (all 9D) and soon after the latter, banked by the 5MT, left for Royton Jc. (Hartford Sdgs) on a goods that did match 9D's planned work. Various duties of this nature to and from Moston followed through the morning with 44929, 48392, 48340 (all 9K)

Looking out from the shed building at Newton Heath towards the coaling plant and ash facilities on 1 June 68. *P. Barber*

What goes up (hill) must come down and for the serious-minded tape recordist engines and trains running under gravity rarely became subject matter. This is here demonstrated on 1 June as your expressionless author observes 48392 as it coasts past Newton Heath mpd with a goods from Moston. *P. Barber*

and some diesel interspersion. No. 48392 we'd observed in 'B' Side (Bolton) at 06.10, waiting to work to Moston. This engine stood on the brink of withdrawal, as mentioned previously.

We broke up the morning with an inspection of Newton Heath depot, which I'd last 'done' on 28 August 1967. Today at 09.45 the shed contained thirty-three steam locos and a Type 2. Of the former, only seven were clearly withdrawn (including 92054, ex 8C) and sixteen were either fired or cooling down, having been in use earlier. Low in pressure, 48356's injector provided a delicious, hollow gurgling accompaniment to our saunter between the rows of grimy 'Black 5s' and 8s while these statistics were being compiled. Only a solitary visitor, 73069 (9H), was present. Of the current steam allocation of thirty-three, there were three we didn't see that day, one way or another.

Had we loitered too long in the building, the day's premier lineside display, heard before being seen, would not have been fully experienced. At first it seemed that a freight was approaching Thorpes Bridge Jc. at an exceptionally slow rate, but the marked sharpness of its engine's exhaust was not characteristic of a machine virtually at stalling point.

As the 8F came into view, however, we could tell that it was wildly out of beat and travelling at four times the speed its erratic blast suggested until the three very subdued beats became audible. The rather explosive fourth was all we'd discerned at first, doing its best to tear holes in the fire. Described at the time as 'quite loud', 48720 struggled up the 1 in 155 at less than 10mph hauling a Brewery–Middleton Jc. train of thirty-three loaded coal. Very modest acceleration took place as the goods passed and receded, then, after I'd stopped recording, approaching Moston yard the driver submitted his crippled-sounding 2-8-0 to a gruelling session with the controls obviously 'flat out' (a 'Froth-de-Luxe' in terminology of the day), proving audibly what had been in reserve earlier. It was very rare for any Bolton loco to sound so bad, even as late as 1968, and I'd like to think the valves

Shed outlet view of Newton Heath's access road featuring 48368 (9D), D345 and a short tripper. Newton Heath Jc. box is in the near distance. 31 June 1968. *P. Barber*

had gone wayward in the last few hours. Once and once only, other than that, have I been fooled over the speed of an approaching engine for the same reason, and this of all things was *Flying Scotsman* leaving Rhyl in 1991.

Shortly after 48392 had made a late morning trip from Moston, probably for Dewsnap, we repaired to Miles Platting and Brewery for a while. No. 70013 (10A) worked the Scottish Region-organised 'Grand Railtour No. 5' to Guide Bridge and the 7MT was subsequently seen three more times nearby. En route to 9D for servicing, it followed 44818 (9D) onto Miles Platting curve after the latter had made a pleasingly lively restart from the chord line with a Gowhole–Brewery (nineteen on). Sundry other movements of 9K and 9D power in the vicinity meant we'd seen 48773 three times with long intervals in between. In totting up the steam off shed up to mid-afternoon and counting multiple sightings it was still 11:6 in favour of Bolton motive power.

No. 70013 had returned to Guide Bridge to pick up its tour, which had meanwhile been electrically hauled over Woodhead, and the returning Pacific-powered train later ran through Victoria, comfortably ahead of the 15.40 Blackpool dmu. Our low-profile observation of the tour that day emphasises the priority given to normal service steam as we were actually in its path by chance and thinking of Colne–Red Bank as *Cromwell* threaded Victoria to head north. Instead of appearing any moment (it was already late), the Red Bank vans kept us waiting a fair portion of that still 'sweltering' afternoon, lolling on a wall opposite the initial steep bit out of Victoria. Eventually, nearly two hours overdue, 3J83 appeared behind 48257 (10F), fortunately putting on a decent show after a check on that critical 1 in 59.

Not to my knowledge had I ever before been through Kearsley at 73mph on the Down, but the 17.45 seven-coach Glasgow portion's 'Brush 4' whisked us homeward with that highlight, having accelerated from a most regardful 55 at Clifton Jc. We'd had to cross over from Slow to Fast line at Windsor Bridge and missed Burnden's distant at Green Lane, but not East's at Weston Street, so the time ended up being two seconds longer than the best-known steam-hauled 'Boat'.

Aware that I had yet to secure details of the weekend's excursions and that Bob was still on at East, Pete and I visited the box in the interim; a steamless period when Heysham–Brewery was either diesel or not seen and certainly not noted on paper. I wrote down the specials on the back of a 'Message from the Chairman', H.C. Johnson. To all employees, it spoke of how essential the modern railway was to the 'wellbeing of this country', of 'one of the most challenging periods any industry can be called upon to face', and ended with a plea, mindful of the individual's own choice 'to join a Trade Union which is party to the machinery of negotiation'. How relevantly those words ring truly appropriate today, after forty-nine steamless years of enormous changes to the railway and when present day concepts of 'modernity' have, in many people's eyes, still not been sufficiently realised.

Probably every one of those excursions I noted down at the box would reflect that 'modern railway' in their motive power at least, but I extracted them from the notices just the same, the 'dead certs' for diesel as well as the wholly-within-Lancashire extras that maybe had a remote chance of being steam-hauled. That overall scene still had an appeal hard to resist, but I'll leave the detail for now to continue with coverage of 1 June.

On the customary 20.00 dmu we now more collectively headed for Preston and the 20.50, 1P58 for Blackpool. The main train was close enough to time and our seven-coach portion left four minutes late behind 45212 (10D). The engine was in fine form, once warmed up. That warming up came over as sluggish acceleration out towards Ashton and in fact the driver's laudable sensitivity towards a fairly 'cold' loco was an indulgence that the schedule did not permit. We dropped two and a half minutes to Kirkham on the already tight booking of eleven minutes to pass, despite reaching 67mph immediately before braking for South Jc. and we came down to 30 through Kirkham itself.

Hard and noisily went 45212 up the rise that follows, and though we secured a '70' on the sprint southwards to Lytham another half-minute had been lost to arriving.

Easily the highlight of our visit on 1 June was 48720 noisily plugging away past 9D with coal for Middleton Jc. The badly uneven exhaust is not reflected visually. Across the main line, Lightbowne C.S. contains nothing in this dmu age. *P. Barber*

Much later in the day, 48257 (10F) heads the SO Colne–Red Bank vans up the stiff curve out of Manchester Vic., a mere stone's throw from its destination. *K.F. Pendlebury*

Little economies in station time there and at St Annes preceded starts that were hardly less than blasting and 1P58 reached maxima of 52 and 53mph intermediately to terminate six minutes late, having clawed one back. Once over the slow start, 45212 and crew had provided dynamics that night which were beyond criticism.

Sunday, 2 to Wednesday, 5 June

In the still very warm, but less sunny afternoon of Whit Sunday, I waited at 9K for 70013 (10A) to return from Carnforth with yet another railtour, 1T80. Due at 16.46 to Manchester Vic., we subsequently found that the 7MT had run hot on the outward journey and been replaced by 44874 (10A), but I'd gone home before it appeared locally. Earlier, the diverted Up 'Royal Scot' had been through behind D1838.

None of the nine Blackpool specials I'd noted for Sunday were expected to have any steam involvement, and they hadn't. Only an Accrington, 1L02, had any chance. The others were all Midlands and Yorkshire originators. Paul called mid-evening with details of more for Monday than I'd listed (probably from the N1 notice that the shed got, but the box didn't), but with news too that Lostock Hall weren't intending to use any steam on passenger duties.

Monday's excursions consisted of at least thirteen Blackpool adexes from the usual quarters (including three ex Accrington), a couple of Manchester–Southports and a Darlington–Manchester relief, as well as several evening reliefs from various Lancashire coastal points to Preston or Manchester. What hopes were entertained for steam were pinned on the latter or maybe an Accrington adex.

I repeated my move of exactly two years earlier (when I'd also had to work the bank holiday) when catching the teatime Glasgow portion to Preston had such a spectacularly different outcome. There by 18.30, I found not surprisingly that several others, some known and including 'Wellington', had the same idea. The procession of returning diesels, quite steady after 7pm, held an interest of sorts, but higher aspirations kept its potential to please at bay, so we remained unrewarded, even though a few unexpected reliefs turned up from 'promising' points of origin. The only steam engine seen that evening proved to be 44816 (10D) as the Preston sleeping car heater. Earlier in the day, a Preston–Windermere and return, normally dmu, had been made loco and stock, but even this had failed to bring out the desired motive power, as Lostock Hall had already said.

145

Seen by the author from East Jc. box and photographed on 30 May, the same evening, 45420 (9D) passes the clear distant signal at Heap Bridge Jc., Broadfield bank, with a thirty-one-wagon load on the 16.40 Burnley–Moston, 5J13. *V.A. Sidlow*

By 21.00 I gave up hope and returned on a Blackpool South–Manchester relief, 1J40, its Type 2 emulating the most pedestrian of steam runs! So ended the first ever steamless Bank Holiday. On the Saturday night just gone, I'd had added to the bottom of my excursion listing what was Tuesday's (4 June) bright hope – an evening Morecambe–Bradford relief, first stop Keighley, actually reckoned to be a Carnforth 'Black 5', but the depot later denied this when I rang up to find out. The train's start time was outside my scope for reaching Morecambe after work anyway. Instead I frequented Orlando bridge and 9K. The depot sported, in contrast to the ongoing clutch of withdrawn diesel shunters and those partly cut up, two Type 2s even on a weekday evening, symbols of what was just around the corner. I didn't note the active steam on shed that time.

The skylark's sustained and exuberant song could still be heard over Broadfield bank during that last summer of steam; sustained until disturbed that is, something that 48257 (10F) managed to do on Wednesday the 5th as it made a sprightly climb on the early Burnley–Moston (twenty-eight on). The loadings on this train fell off rather suspiciously a few weeks hence. Before it that evening we'd crossed Castleton Bolton (45073) in Bury en route, but were in position for the 18.05 Bolton– Moston, unusually double-headed by 48692 and 48652 on a huge sixty-five wagon load, but this proved less of a sound spectacle than might be imagined. Only by fading the recording soon after the two 8Fs had passed did I succeed in fitting four trains onto little more than five minutes of tape! Heysham–Moston (thirty-five on) with 45231 (10A) was conventional in every way and it again fell to Ronnie Horrocks on Bedford parcels to take the honours for his lively handling of 45390 (10A).

Thursday, 6 and Friday, 7 June

High on the list of 'star' trains for me while I'd been at East Jc. in 1967 had been the very lengthy Carlisle–Red Bank empty parcels vans, 3J41 with its almost guaranteed 'Britannia'. It had gone diesel, of course, with the demise of 12A and since the May changes was booked through Bolton about six hours earlier at 06.08. Another, 3J40, which had lost its steam haulage even earlier, was still a late evening runner locally and for some reason that Wednesday took its SO routing via Broadfield behind D332.

Either prior knowledge of Ronnie on 3M13 had prompted the Broadfield trip or realisation from the lineside that it was he prompted me to look for him at 9K early the next evening to consider my request for a footplate ride on Friday, but he wasn't there. '8392 has had it' I noted at the shed, but didn't follow up the other as choir practice loomed pleasantly, electing instead to go straight to Trinity Street on the 7th shortly before departure time. Persuading Mr Horrocks to let me go wasn't easy this time, but to my relief he eventually agreed.

Tonight we had 45134 (10A), seventeen on to Bury and a start ninety seconds early. Since the new Working Timetables, commencing 6 May, all parcels trains tabulated between the covers of the quite huge 209-page 'Section N' and the 188-page 'Section L', which incorporated the whole steam operating area and more, were given 'blanket' D700 (or 'E' for electric) timings rating on the same basis as outlined in the entry for 11 May. It didn't mean they were any faster. In many cases schedules themselves were unchanged. Most trains never even approached the tonnage quoted and a small percentage of those designated D700 were still booked for steam, entirely or for part of the journey. The reason for the diesel (or electric) timings system encompassing all class 3 parcels workings was that long before the timetable's expiry date those employing steam would cease to do so.

Bolton–Bedford parcels was still (since 4 September 1967) supposed to depart at 20.20 from the station, propelling to Burnden and leaving for Bury via the fork, but it had been setting off direct from Trinity Street certainly for several months, so our marginally early departure on 7 June 1968 suddenly became much more so upon passing Rose Hill Jc. In fact, I have no recollection of anything different to this while I was at the box, post-4 September 1967. 3M13 showed a disregard for the W.T.T. in another way, too. Since 6 May 1968, if not earlier, the engine for Monday's train was shown as coming light from Newton Heath via Castleton (19.12, ex 9D). From two Monday observations since 6 May, we knew it to still be the Carnforth engine that had worked Friday evening's Heysham–Moston that otherwise repaired to 9K, not 9D. In fact, it didn't go to the Manchester depot on Friday either. Our Broadfield trip of 20 May provides one good refutation of the book, insomuch as we were expecting 44709 (10A), doubtless through it being seen locally earlier. By pooling my own resources and those of Vern's, observations from several weekends in May and June prove the point conclusively.

To the trip in hand once more then. Compared with my 23 February run, the time to Bury was marginally slower and minus the checks experienced then. The driving style tonight did not match that which was expected of Mr Horrocks. Half regulator and 25% cut off had for the most part sufficed on this section. Of course, we were very early and this seemed to be the key. Shunting at Knowsley Street, where the load was increased to twenty-six mostly 12-ton (10in wheelbase) vans, took slightly longer than the seventeen minutes allowed. I didn't note the method of working up Broadfield bank because of tape recording, but initially Ronnie was slower than on the occasion of my own effort of 23 February! Again with half regulator and 25% after the summit, the run to Rochdale took a minute over schedule, though we accelerated quickly enough into the dip at Castleton North Jc.

Two other 'Black 5s' were facing Manchester via Moston in Rochdale station. No. 45268 (9D), which would continue with our train to Gowhole, had left Newton Heath at 20.40 for the job. No. 45203 (9D), I suspect was working the 21.43 Rochdale–Stockport parcels, 3H16. On SO it was extended to Crewe (but not beyond Stockport with steam) as 3K20. Before either of these departed, we did, with 45134, LE to Ancoats in thirty-two minutes.

Tucked away at Ancoats by 21.49, I was left to keep an eye on the engine as the crew sought liquid refreshment in one of the district's plush bars. I'm sure they'd have gone anyway. Legion are enginemen's stories of capitalising on inactive periods in such a way in the days of steam and often with a humorous or even hilarious outcome. This did not apply to tonight, however, and there was no need to touch anything on 45134 during the men's thirty-five minutes or so absence. Possibly as a reward for minimising any apprehension they might have felt, but still surprisingly, in view of the initial reluctance to take me along, I was invited to drive all the way home! I leaped at the opportunity, putting away my book and tape recorder to concentrate on the business in hand. Our train, the 22.30 to Heysham reversed out of the yard with the untaxing load of fourteen container wagons plus brake. I intended to let it rip up the bank to Philips Park and so activated the sanders as we changed direction, but Ronnie cautioned me at that point as he didn't want to finish too early. Perhaps it was just as well for our loco had a bad blow on the left and at low speed the escaping steam impaired visibility.

With no written or audio record of the late-night journey through Manchester to Burnden beyond an overall time of fifty-one and a half minutes to arriving three minutes early at 23.29 I have little to add. Anything more than sedate and uneventful progress I hope would have stood the mental test of time or have been put into an account at the time, however briefly.

Saturday, 8 to Tuesday, 11 June

On the 8th, a Saturday with a difference, I had ample opportunity to set down anything I wished to prevent fading from memories of my drive on Ancoats–Heysham beyond the basic details recounted earlier, but I didn't. To have participated next day in the annual church choir outing at such an advanced stage in the rundown of steam throws up questions of commitment to the Cause, etc., but what was done was done and I didn't regret it, probably feeling, if anything, that the Friday night compensated at least partly for a Saturday of unguaranteed success on the railway. In fact, a lovely day was had, the best features of high summer returning after a less memorable week in that respect. Keswick station was investigated, then more conventionally, Derwent Water by rowing boat. After tea and a walk towards Easdale Tarn, with thoughts not wholly devoted to the surroundings, I telephoned Lostock Hall (OPR2 35320), curious to know how the 20.50's prospects lay that fairest of evenings. All seemed well with 44971 (10D), the booked loco, but of course I could only 'enjoy' it in the most detached way imaginable! I later learned that four minutes had been lost in running and 66mph had been the top speed, at Moss Side. Vern at least, from 'our lot', had travelled. It was a different story on the 15th.

The heat of Trinity Sunday afternoon softened the accumulation of grease and dirt scraped from 48773's motion at 9K as I assisted some of the five others that had assembled there and were engaged in similar work.

A busy week of evening trips lay ahead. On Monday, the 10th, I dozed off unintentionally after tea, trying to get rid of a headache and 'surfaced' too late to catch the planned 18.45 To Darwen. My brother, Martin, who'd pretty well let his railway interest drop by now, gave me a lift in his Ford Anglia and I caught up with Vern and Paul as they approached Hoddlesden Jc. on foot. The second Burnley–Moston with 48348 (10F) was not retained on tape, probably due to the light load of only fourteen

wagons that night. The main objective, 4P20, the Heysham–Darwen tanks, came in good time, the driver of 48278 (10F) making a clean sweep of it from main line across to siding with the apparently standard eleven tanks.

Tuesday turned cloudy, but still very warm and I headed straight from work for Walton's Sidings to catch both Burnley–Moston goods. I did so comfortably and 45350 (10F) accelerated swiftly over the see-saw summit with its nineteen vehicles before shutting off for the long drift down. Carlisle–Ashburys (sixty on) was next on the Up with D341 and over an hour later, but before time, D5212 passed on the 17.45 Colne–Ashton Moss parcels. Paul had arrived on his bike by this time, well before the second Moston, 5J10, burst from within Sough's dank and gloomy bore into the warm evening, 48493 (10F) providing the liveliest sound of the two steam engines on its moderate haul of twenty-one wagons. My friend had picked up news of a certain special oil train and this dictated the flavour of next weekend's trip. Thus ended my penultimate Walton's visit during steam days.

Wednesday, 12 June

From contemporary comment, Broadfield saved the best to the last, as an overall appraisal of the evening, for the lineside session of Wednesday the 12th proved to be my last there. It yielded a 'full house' of eastbound steam freights and parcels trains, plus Castleton–Bolton trip, seen with 45110 before we (the Bolton four) arrived. It was so fortunate that all the evening traffic via Bolton in which we still, at this advanced stage in the 'game', had an interest in, should be channelled into a comparatively narrow time span in one direction on a line that afforded such a good vantage point, and at a time that coincided with the leisure hours of those who worked during the day. The 'one direction' claim did not include the above mentioned trip. At the current train fare a Broadfield evening worked out at a shilling an hour. A short-lived experimental ticket on light card on that line at least measured no less than 6in × 2½in and to us brought up on the standard Edmondson card they were enormous!

No. 48692 scampered uphill hauling Bolton–Moston (22=26 in length) shortly after we'd reached the position, shutting off steam briefly on its approach to generate smoke by special request, no doubt! Tonight's skylark proved less easily distracted from his lofty song by the passage of that train. No. 45350 (10F), rostered for a second day (at least) to the first Burnley–Moston, was working hard on its seventeen-wagon formation at 19.06. In complete contrast, such slow progress was being made by 45394 (10A) on Heysham–Moston (thirty-five on) that words such as 'plodding' and 'ponderous' seem over-complimentary.

Opposite: No. 48278 (10F), the same engine that the author saw working the Heysham–Darwen tanks on 10 June arriving at Hoddlesden Jc., also hauled the train ten days later, as seen here at Hoghton straining against identical uphill grades. *I.C. Simpson*

With only three wagons more than it had on our 8 May trip, its passage took up more than four times as much recording tape, barely bettering a fast walking pace! I'd tend to think that deliberate slow running, rather than shortage of steam, was behind such an exceptional display, though then it was the latter that was suspected. No very obvious evidence of struggling with the fire is recalled.

Two unexpected (not in the sense that steam was expected) diesel workings filled in the next hour. A retired employees' reunion of the interestingly named company, Steel, Peach and Tozer, returned from Blackpool on 1Z47 behind D1575 to Rotherham. Then followed the long-dieselised later Carlisle–Red Bank, 3J40, tonight running about two hours early behind D294 and again diverted via Bury for some reason. Ten minutes behind this at 21.14 appeared Bedford parcels with 45209 (10A) at the head, making a steady ascent, but no more. The second Burnley–Moston with 48400 (10F) turned up two minutes after our usual train home at 21.40. The absence of a recorded load in my book, or a tape recording, suggests that we caught the 21.38 back.

Thursday, 13 to Saturday, 15 June

The cloudier midweek gave way to five perfect days from Thursday the 13th, when, in the evening at 9K, Saturday's trip was broadly arranged. Before that weekend and after it, a number of dead engine movements, including removals from Bolton shed, took place. On 14 June, a 9K class 5 with Bolton crew and 'rider' (also known as 'caretaker' – the man who rode on the condemned loco(s)) was booked to drag 44965 via Castleton as far as Newton Heath, where the condemned 44851 would be attached. The assemblage, 8Z58, then continued with a 'spare' Type 4 diesel, Newton Heath crew and riders to Gowhole for a scheduled liaison with 8L09, which had arrived eight minutes earlier ex Heaton Mersey and consisted of 44903 and 45253, Type 2 hauled. Thirty-two minutes were allowed for remarshalling before the cortege of four 'Black 5s' ground its way up the 1 in 90 behind the larger diesel, bound ultimately for Kettering via Dore and the scrapyard of G. Cohen. All steam engines were ex residents of the depot they departed from that day.

We needed to get to Carnforth earlier on Saturday the 15th than a conventional 06.38 start permitted. I don't think any of us had seen a 9F since the few that escaped from Speke Jc. had gone to 10A and our main objective lay in a special 06.50 Heysham–Ecclesfield West oil tank train, 4Z57, booked for a 2-10-0 and 5MT double-headed. An overnight journey via Manchester provided the answer and also stretched to the limit the validity of a Day Excursion ticket to Carnforth, costing 18/- (90p). To capitalise on anything worthwhile en route clearly made sense, so on the 22.25 unit from Bolton thoughts were first focussed on the 22.16 Bolton–Healey Mills climbing out of Manchester Vic. Before we took up position for that, however, the 22.30 Ancoats–Heysham passed through behind 44897 (10A).

Whilst 9K engines were going for scrap, the final allocation remained active enough, as evidenced in these two photos unrelated to the direct text. A panoramic view over the Calder valley on 11 June 1968 features 44802 near Todmorden with a mixed eastbound goods, described as Halliwell–Healey Mills. If so, this is the later SX working. The much longer-established lunchtime departure was always coal empties only. Nearer to home, 44871 crosses Brooksbottom viaduct, Summerseat, with Rawtenstall shunt and trip on 13 June. *I.C. Simpson*

Possibly through uncertainty over which route the Healey Mills train took to Thorpes Bridge Jc., we headed for the known spot not far from Victoria out towards Red Bank where anything ascending via Miles Platting instead would not go unnoticed. This is what happened in fact, as at 23.21 a 'Black 5' stoically blasted unaided up the 1 in 59. Even at this time of year it was too dark to see anything of the train itself and to this day it is not known whether this was Bolton–Healey Mills or something a bit later. I do think though, that we should have caught a train earlier to be sure. Either way, the sound came across impressively from the middle distance, rising and falling in accordance with sundry obstructions and the light breeze. The brief taped commentary to it was the last I sounded at all enthusiastic about in the next twenty-two hours, not that much came our way to be judged good or bad in the first place, and although the trip's theory was quite sound, we may well have questioned at times the wisdom of spending a valuable Saturday in the way to be described.

Patricroft pilots (three engines) plied about, but 73133 was on ECS only and no longer eligible power to take 1F30, the 01.00 Glasgow sleeper from Exchange. This portion, combining with the Liverpool Lime Street half (1S21) at Wigan NW, seemed to be the preserve of a Type 2 (D5207 tonight) now. At least steam was not expected. Our intended connection at Preston, the 23.45 Euston–Barrow, the once time-honoured 'Barrow Kippers', thus dubbed by Southern enthusiasts as favourite transportation for a steamy weekend in the North with the promise too of a 'good kip', was running well behind time. Rather less frequented now by our sub-Watford compatriots (its heyday had been mid-late summer 1967) the Barrow train's tardy progress prolonged our steamless wait to a seemingly interminable two and a half hours. In contrast to the current spate of lovely summer weather, with matching temperatures, it felt damn cold on those North Union platforms. We eventually left well after first light, seventy minutes late at 05.00, but the delay itself was of no other consequence to the trip.

In early bright sunshine my first tour around Carnforth mpd in more than a year dictated the tone of at least the part of the day that mattered most. The general content was a far cry from even that April 1967 visit and the steam total of thirty-five gives a very false impression. All the 9Fs present were, according to visual inspection, withdrawn, except for 92160 (10A) and this lay cold. There were no more in existence and a nearby Type 2 diesel more than ominously displayed 4Z57, the reporting number of the special oil tank train we'd specifically come to see!

The allocation for 10A currently stood at twenty-four steam locos. Seven were absent at 06.30 that morning and nine engines, all resident, were in steam, including 70013 prior to working part of the following day's R.C.T.S. 'Dalesman No. 2' railtour. Curiously, there was no trace of

This to us all too familiar view from the entrance to Bolton mpd would soon be devoid of our reason for ignoring those twin trespass notices literally thousands of times. Back Dobie Street was merely the gap between two rows of terraced houses on Crescent Road. The eye is led to Stanier front and rear ends in this June 1968 early evening view, which may well have been taken during the 'five perfect days' from the 13th. *Lee Johnson*

44897 (10A) all day; nor did it figure on the working board, yet we'd seen it on Ancoats–Heysham late the previous evening, as herein recorded. Excluding the Pacific, all three allocated classes, 'Black 5s', 75XXX and 9Fs were represented, plus 48393 (10F), the solitary foreigner. My assessment of which locos were condemned proved almost correct. Other than the 9Fs mentioned above, only 75034 and 48124 (ex 8A) fell into this category. I'd done 75020 (10A) a disfavour by presuming it withdrawn, based on appearance. Four preserved steam locos and a considerable diesel presence of four Type 1s, seven Type 2s and two Type 4s made up the total.

Of those engines in steam, some were due to leave shed soon, according to the working board. Either it was incomplete or my notes from it were, but the following information was provided:

   07.25 Heysham 44963
   09.15 Windermere 45025
   08.00 Carnforth Ballast
   08.25 Grange 45017
   06.00 Special Trips 44758
   07.25 Assist 44758
   03.45 LE Heysham 44709

No. 44963, meanwhile, on the first listed job, had drawn into sidings opposite the station with a long raft of tanks, presumably empty, while D206 'whistled' and moved about nearby. In view of the much-diminished appeal of 4Z57, the Heysham–Ecclesfield tank special (we had at least learned that the Type 2 would be double-headed with a 5MT), attempting to reach an outlying location didn't seem worthwhile and so Carnforth East Jc. sufficed well enough. Coupled inside D5147 (now displaying 4Z55) was 45394 (10A), which certainly did its share in getting the twenty or so loaded tanks round the curving climb and under way from the stop at the junction at 08.15, but it still wasn't what we'd gone for.

Pick of the working board at 10A, such as it was, seemed to be 45025 (10A) on the 'Windermere' trip (on SO it ran only to Kendal) and on the strength of that we headed for Oxenholme on the 08.59, where, until early May, there had still been a regular steam banker. In perfect weather a most fulfilling morning might have been had, had we not seemingly been there for the wrong reasons. After a freightliner, a thirteen-wagon ballast taxing D5712 to the limit and the Newton-le-Willows–Stirling Motorail (WThSO, unadvertised) had all gone north my record of main line traffic is unquestionably incomplete, but no steam appeared until 45025 just trundled through with a brake van from Kendal, having finished for the day at 11.20. Doubtless we wondered if the Grange tripper would have been a better option.

By then we perhaps wondered if anything today would come up trumps. A midday return to Carnforth and change of train there saw us next homing in on a known job not apparently listed at the shed, i.e. 45342 overseeing the Lancaster Green Ayre track lifting operation – not something oozing potential on either the recording or photographic front, as doubtless acknowledged at the time. Called to mind too perhaps were the staggeringly contrasting steam activities being enacted and enjoyed on that same main line exactly twelve months before. A 'Black 5' on track lifting would have hardly turned a head then. Now we were reduced to actively seeking it out, but in vain because that working too was over for the day and 45342 with its train of redundant materials crossed our dmu at Hest Bank! We therefore remained on the unit to Preston with a view to taking in Darwen–Heysham tanks, but this was found to be cancelled. Classic signs of lethargy and drowsiness on a hot afternoon following our sleepless overnight played

Carnforth was the base for the last surviving active 'Britannia', 70013 *Oliver Cromwell*. With booked action the following day, the 7MT stands in the open at 10A just as we reached the shed at 05.50 on 15 June. *V.A. Sidlow*

There was no need to include this Type 2 (D7624) front end, but Peter Barber seemed to like taking old and new juxtapositions, though the contrast in that respect between the diesel and several condemned 9Fs (92004/77/118) is not very great. *P. Barber*

Although 92160 (10A) alone seemed physically capable of working the special tank train we'd primarily gone to Carnforth for on 15 June, it was the far less attractive combination described in the text that actually appeared, seen here at Carnforth East Jc. just after the tightly curved and uphill start. *P. Barber*

further havoc with my notes, and I can only guess that a phone call brought the unwelcome news of a diesel on 9K's Heysham–Brewery SO job, rather than us having identified the loco heading light through Preston.

One by one the options were collapsing around us and at that point we temporarily forsook B.R. for industrial steam at Preston Docks. Nothing was working except for a two-day-old Rolls-Royce diesel, but a surprisingly warm welcome included a tour of various lines on the engine and two of the half dozen steam locos pulled out of the shed for my friends to photograph. *Energy* was the one I remembered often seeing from the family car as we skirted the docks in previous years en route to Blackpool or Cleveleys.

By early evening, thoughts turned towards the 20.50 Preston–Blackpool and the Lostock Hall visit (reached by bus this time) that would reveal the motive power for it. Things had not appreciably altered in the month since I'd been on the premises. Scrap removals had reduced the ranks there somewhat and not quite as much lay in steam. New knowledge, however now, of 44971 (10D) rostered for the 20.50 and not one of the four apparently available diesels, kept the day alive as I repeatedly, but momentarily, nodded off on a wall while waiting for the bus back, before opting for the train instead. Loss of balance or poise always jolted one back to sentience, only for the process to start again. I couldn't take my overnights as well then as in later life, oddly.

At Preston station the 17.05 ex Euston was chalked up as about forty-five minutes late. I forget exactly what it said on the board. As the latest in a long line of setbacks, the import of this particular blow may well have been softened somewhat by a now more resigned attitude to such news. By the time 44971 was ready for the 'off' with its seven-coach portion off the Euston, the 'connection' back from Blackpool South had shrunk to about minus three minutes, even at Lytham and even assuming the best possible run to that first booked stop. A seasonal train starting that very day, the 22.45 Blackpool N–Manchester provided a later unit back home in the event of steam arrivals at South in excess of thirteen minutes late and this was clearly what I had in mind as we set off under Preston's overall roof, forty-three minutes behind time, even after the 21.25 Liverpool, but this, apart from isolated cases, was diesel-powered of late.

Together all night and day with Paul, Vern, Keith and Pete, I think only myself from our group travelled on 1P58 that night, but there were others who, in all probability, were not pushing their trip duration even further over the twenty-four-hour threshold through a reluctance to risk

The noon arrival of 45025 (10A) at Oxenholme at the end of its morning's work more than suggests there was no traffic to take back from Kendal. Except for the glorious weather, not much was working in our favour so far and our fortunes were hardly to change at all that day, 15 June 1968! *P. Barber*

A general view of the attractive station layout at Oxenholme featuring 44709 (10A) bringing a goods off the Windermere line on 2 August 1968. *Peter Reeves/M.L.S. collection*

passing up the chance of a fast run, given all the incentive of our lateness. Within ninety seconds of leaving, that 'fast run' potential was evaporating more rapidly than the exhaust steam at our chimney top, for 44971 had begun to prime, losing half a minute on an average start, even by No. 5 box. By that point the 'taps' ought to have been open to clear it, but they weren't. Nor do I recall them coming on at all, for in an appalling exhibition of engineman-ship we primed our way across the Fylde, the whole way to Kirkham! After 36mph at Ashton matters deteriorated even further until a brief 'rallying' to 38 by Treales. Then, unexpectedly, we stopped at Kirkham & Wesham in the unprecedentedly bad time of 19'-02".

The train back from Blackpool North was still within reach if 44971 ran normally on to South, but by alighting now I would get home sooner and avoid paying for the dire display just witnessed; and, of course, there were no guarantees that matters on the footplate would improve markedly. It was time to cut my losses. Another lad who seemed to share this view asked the crew what had been wrong with the engine and as the 5MT pulled out its fireman's shouted reply ran 'Primin'; running on water instead of steam', as if it had been entirely outside their control! Sure enough, as if to rub salt into the wound, the exhaust had regained its characteristic sharpness and clear 'stack talk' (as the Americans would say) receded towards North Jc. as my dmu (from South) fast approached from the west. Of course, I wished I'd stayed on! The stop we'd made had been for passenger purposes and from that date on most of the 20.50 runs I made did stop at Kirkham, but not all, creating something of a curiosity.

Sunday, 16 June

A compensatory 'lie-in' on Sunday the 16th, in spite of the weather, preceded the customary 9K visit, which transpired to be my last ever at that distinctive time of the week while things were 'normal'. To my eternal shame I took no notes at all. No matter how delinquent this appears in retrospect, it proves that at the time I had neither the will nor inclination to do so and I can't explain the reasons without owning up to some degree of apathy. Emotions concerning the shed in these last few days were not purely led by that tendency, however, as will be seen.

From Bolton East Jc. box I did, however, save the special notices that detailed the conveyance of nine more condemned locos from North-west mpds on Monday, 17 June. Train 8L85 was due off Springs Branch at 02.40, a Type 4 hauling 48510 and 48637 (ex 10D), plus 48061 (ex 10F) and 45226 (ex 10D), bound for Shrewsbury and manned by a Springs Branch crew and riders.

The first three engines were ultimately heading for Buttigieg's yard and the last Cashmore's, both at Newport (Mon.). From Speke Jc. depot another four left at 07.55

British Railways Steam 1968

Not the 15 guinea special, as might be thought by the crowds, but the R.T.C.S. 'Dalesman No. 2' railtour on 16 June 1968 part-way through a photo opportunity at Clapham. Unrestricted wandering on the tracks by enthusiasts was in those days and earlier not confined to fairly rural locations such as this. The loco is 70013 (10A). *T. Heavyside*

with Garston men on 8L86. Nos 45426 and 48450 (ex 8A) with 92008 (ex 8B) were for Buttigieg's again and 45395 (ex 8A) Cashmore's. Engines making up the third convoy, 8L80, were not specified in the notice. It left Rose Grove at 06.47 for Lostock Hall, where it combined with 8L79 from Bolton (dep. 07.20). Both were crewed and powered from the starting point. A process of elimination using 9K contents listings compiled by more diligent enthusiasts than I reveals 48090 to have been the withdrawn Bolton loco involved and subsequent research 48441 (ex 10F) and 48335 (ex 10D) the others on this fourth cavalcade, with an ultimate destination of Cashmore's, Great Bridge.

Monday, 17 to Friday, 21 June

Preston Docks again was the perhaps less than predictable initial objective on Monday evening for Vern, Keith and myself. Of the three of us, only I would become immersed in industrial steam to any depth from the late summer. Paul would be too, but the extent of that development was not yet anticipated. Relative to the current intensity of our presence on the B.R. scene, that coming immersion never became (or was able to become) more than partial. It had the dual attraction of being able to be taken seriously whilst allowing plenty of time for the other things in life. We fared a little better in the Ribble town than on Saturday, though the shunting (with two steam locos this time) ended after half an hour there.

Finding ourselves unlucky with buses and trains to reach some part of Hoghton bank in realistic time for the Heysham–Darwen tanks, we hung around a not entirely steamless Preston station until D1622 on the 21.19 (ex Glasgow), 1M40, provided a more comfortable ride home than the average 'cart'. No. 48727 (10F), seen light at Ribble Sdgs, proved to be the evening's last sighting. My diary mentions a recently discovered train as being in the running for Hoghton (if we'd managed to get there), i.e. the 18.40 Preston–Healey Mills, 7N99 if it had run late. Later experience would reveal this tendency.

The signalmen at East on Tuesday's late turn were Bob Middlebrook and Arthur Plant. It had been very warm again, but without the recent sustained sun. 'We were playing cricket most of the time', the actually recorded words, seem so at odds with the legitimate level of activity still necessary at this busy box on a weekday evening, but it was all managed without compromising safety, and in fact nothing new! A Rose Grove engine, 45350, had got onto Heysham–Moston, which spent more than three-quarters of an hour at Bolton, mainly making its train up in 'B' Side from twenty-two to a substantial forty-three wagons. Earlier that day, what was probably the last ever steam-hauled rake of ex Works electric ECS left Horwich as 8X62 for Altrincham, though I don't know which 9K locomotive was used.

Heysham–Moston the next night had regained 10A power in 44877 and it too left 'B' Side on a big load of 41=48 in length. No. 45350 had stayed on the night before's diagram, now working Bedford parcels, and the second Burnley–Moston more than doubled its paltry load of ten by picking up in 'B' Side with 48348 (10F). I was in the box again for these few steam duties, which were well in the minority now (one quarter of tonight's locomotive activity). D5209 on Carlisle–Ashburys terminated today with its forty-nine vans in 'A' Side and in doing so delayed the 19.28 Rochdale–Bolton dmu by about six minutes. The blame went on rather hapless Clarence, a shunter, known for his propensity to mismanage things. For a European he had extraordinarily flat-faced features. A downpour of summer rain came on just as the above moves were being enacted and Bob gave me a lift home later, which meant I stayed long enough to end my notes with the rarely seen 20.50 Blackpool North–Normanton parcels, 3N29 SX, with D5251 and not steam-worked for a long time now.

Photographed earlier in its journey south than my Bolton East Jc. observation of the train on 18 June, 45350 (10F) hurries past Farington with the 16.50 Heysham–Moston. *R. Weisham*

July's *Railway Magazine* arrived on Thursday, 20 June. I was currently taking this periodical on subscription. Spanning, as ever, as many different aspects of the interest as seemed possible, only a fraction of its contents touched on the North-west drama being enacted and much of that was unavoidably out of date; April loco notes, photographs of April tours stretching to the early May 'Belfast Boat Express' dieselisation, the end of Oxenholme's banker and *Flying Scotsman*'s much-publicised NON-STOP commemorative runs. Despite undeniably having a drama of their own, I saw them distortedly then as a contrived event, far removed from the realities of North-west steam's last gasp; the northbound special's repeated flirts with immobility as mere proof that 'B.R. '68' was not in the same league as anything predating it. Yet the rereading of O.S. Nock's journey description as I prepared the first version of this volume, thirty-four years after the event, brought tears to my eyes, just as the elemental forces and sound of 4472 itself would first have an identical effect on me only weeks after the end of true steam operation.

As far as 9K was concerned there were 'only nine days to go'. The summery weather had broken and there loomed industrial unrest on B.R. that threatened to even further curtail what little steam activity would commemorate not only the fall of Bolton mpd, but Newton Heath and Patricroft, too. But through the darkly gathering clouds of full dieselisation and dispute, the last vestiges of ever-receding blue still found the strength to shine through.

I was lucky, after the last orchestra rehearsal prior to the holiday break, to intercept the second Burnley–Moston during our station meeting on that Friday, 21 June. No. 48348 (10F) crawled into the Up loop with thirty-one on – fifteen of coke, one cement and the rest vans. The 2-8-0 made a terrific row and a single violent slip punctuated its laborious progress up past Byng Street into the platform; a most impressive show with the regulator handle up near the seated driver's head as I watched the 8F forge slowly by, clarinet case in hand, but no tape recorder!

Saturday, 22 June

A near repeat of 1 June's Brewery trip was decided for the 22nd, starting early again, but alighting at Miles Platting first. Neither the proportion of 9D to 9K locos seen in traffic, nor the intensity of that traffic bore much resemblance to the earlier experience in the vicinity, further illustrating the unpredictable nature of trip work and the near impossibility of identifying what was seen with specific turns when more than two or three were engaged in the same area on multiple movements. Our own train identification on the day seems too informed to have been assumed; neither was it based on Dent as the steam workings seen didn't match up with anything in that document. Nevertheless, I perpetuate them here with confidence, despite the inability to quote an information source. This was one place where we didn't walk in and out of signal boxes!

It proved to be less busy on diesel- and steam-worked trips and freight than on 1 June, and Newton Heath machines were in the ascendant this time, 44884 (9D) being the earliest and most frequently observed, first running LE to Newton Heath at 07.15. It reappeared at 09.00 with a freight to Philips Park. Soon after, the 09.00 Manchester–Filey Camp SO train crested Miles Platting bank behind consecutively numbered Type 2s, D5205 and D5206. Next, and well out of its path, at 09.14 appeared the 08.30 to Scarborough, 1N73, with half that power at the front end (D5238) and therefore banked, by 44910 (9D). This train's thirty-nine-minute lateness may have been due to one of its Type 2s having failed. In the same D385 timings as the Filey, both would normally be ten-coach sets, though I failed to verify this on paper. Adding to an already bad start, the Scarborough passengers would have been further dejected by their holiday weather so far. Six minutes after 1N73 had gone by I received a thorough wetting whilst recording 48665 (9D), tender first, I recall, as it unsteadily dragged a load of thirty coal off the curve at 'Platting, hauling a Philips Park–Chadderton. By immediately boarding a dmu for Dean Lane, we again secured the 2-8-0 slogging sure-footedly now, still upgrade, past Newton Heath shed.

An hour later and the morning's decent action was over with the near crossing of two 9K machines. No. 48319 on forty-nine vans from Brewery was banked out by a 'Black 5', which dropped off prior to reaching my spot, and 45318 coasted by with a Moston–Ordsall Lane (thirty-one on) – Hardly surprisingly, the findings on Newton Heath shed, one week before the end there, closely resembled those of our 1 June visit. The single scrap engine removal (44851, see 13-15 June) had been countered by three obvious additions, but to the eighteen in steam should be credited five known working locally. Five were dead and three were not seen at all to make up the current and possibly final allocation of thirty steam (one more with the only foreigner present, 45394 of 10A). Four Type 2s were also on the premises.

Up to our 13.05 abandonment of the area, only one more steam working appeared – 44884 again, with flats off 'Platting curve ('India Rubber Jc') as per 48665 earlier. On this Saturday even I didn't attempt to keep the trip's continuity going right through. What was doubtless a hastily written diary entry – 'After dinner we went home to the shed for 3J83, then to our houses' – perhaps gets closer to how we'd come to think than any carefully thought-out passage intended to express the same; or was it just careless sentence construction? 3J83 (Colne–Bed Bank) passed 9K twelve minutes late behind a less familiar 45096 (10F).

We'd plans for that same evening and Sunday too, hence the more willing surrender of a Saturday afternoon that, after 45096, would have been very lean at best and, in all probability, barren. Besides, I had another project to get on with, that of manufacturing a suitable headboard

The Colne–Red Bank empty parcels working could produce either 5MT or 8F power from Rose Grove. In the first photo here, 45096 (10F) brings the train past Bolton shed on 22 June at 14.50 as the last observation before the day's trip fragmented. An earlier shot from 3 April has 48423 (10F) at the same location with a weekday extra run between the same points. *P. Barber, V. A. Sidlow*

for whatever would be the last steam loco to leave 9K a week hence on the last operational day. I'd found an old bed head that roughly conformed to the 'right' shape. As I couldn't saw curves in those days the bottom edge stayed straight. On a white-painted background, plain but neat black letters and numerals would proclaim to the uninformed exactly what was taking place that day.

A record run to Lytham on the 20.50 looked on the cards that night of 22 June, only to be ruined by signals. Our nine-minute late start and lightning dash across the eastern Fylde brought us into conflict with other traffic, though the first offender, the 21.05 Kirkham–Fleetwood local, should have been out of the way. We had the ex Speke Jc. (and suspected ex store) 45388 (10D) on seven coaches. Quite vigorous driving from Preston itself preceded quieter acceleration to 72½mph by Spen Lane and the 7.13 miles to passing Treales box took only 9'-25". 1P58, however, was quickly brought to a brief stand at Kirkham South Jc. We made no station stop and went hard after North Jc, but unaccountably Moss Side's distant proved stubborn enough to knock us down to a mere 10mph there, further eroding the already tight 21.35 'connection' back from Blackpool South. The driver hadn't given up though and slamming echoes of our exhaust provided a memorable feature of the starts, from St Annes particularly. These developed into maxima of 55 and 54mph intermediately, and we'd undoubtedly have gained time tonight without the checks, but they left us with a three-minute loss.

1P58 came to a stand forty-five seconds before the adjacent dmu's departure time and the arriving train disgorged about sixty enthusiasts who, in a single lunging movement, poured into the 21.35, to the consternation of passengers already seated and perhaps, even more so, the platform staff at South! A yet more dramatic transfer, not easy to imagine, lay in store, unbeknown to us then, of course. I'd like to think now that one or more resisted that surge of youth, if only not to deprive 45388's crew entirely of the praise that was rightly theirs. Such a mass obsession with the 21.35 had its origins in fraudulent travel. It enabled the vast majority of travelling enthusiasts who were ticketless, certainly west of Preston, to return without passing through a barrier and therefore F.O.C. Platform tickets would have been plentiful, likewise the excuses proffered, had some unexpected challenge by authority come along. Some, myself included, were properly 'valid' on most of these runs and it rather surprises me now to be reminded that the possible midsummer return on the 22.45 Blackpool N–Manchester seemed to be considered such a poor option, but it all boiled down to wanting to get home as soon as possible and in the company of my friends, both close and less intimate. The boisterous 'takeover' on that 21.35 from South proved an altogether alternative form of entertainment on more than one occasion, to which the 20.55 Club contributed significantly.

Swelling the enthusiast presence on the 20.50 Preston–Blackpool South from 11 May had been refugees from the 'Belfast Boat Express' seeking steam haulage elsewhere. Saturdays that ended that way for those particular patrons coincided with the lightest evenings of the summer. This view from the train never varied in its principal features, i.e. the big signal gantry, St Walburge's church spire and Preston No. 5 box. Date and loco not known. *David A.J. Shirres*

On 22 June 1968, the day before our second 1968 trip to the Copy Pit line, 48410 assisted by 48400 (both 10F) climb through Portsmouth with a westbound coal working. *R. Weisham*

Sunday, 23 June

A 52-year-old Farnworth man stepped in front of the Up 'Belfast Boat Express' the next morning, close to what was, up to the moment of impact, his home station. Keith and I were on the train with its new (11 May) Sunday time of 08.28 ex Bolton. It's an indication of how things have changed that despite the fatality we were in Victoria by 9am. Now joined by Pete, this trip, to Todmorden, was designed to capitalise on B.R.'s. provisional measures to combat anticipated traffic disruption during the coming week. The guards' complex productivity dispute had flared up again and we understood that a work to rule would start on Monday the 24th, perfectly timed for the last week of steam from 9K, 9D and 9H! A series of additional coal runs (the vital commodity) were therefore being laid on over the Copy Pit line with some steam involvement beyond just banking. Such a scheme relied on the cooperation of the same body of men whose imminent protest was the cause of that scheme, but the men had their case and time and three-quarters was rarely turned down!

The information source for these coal specials is long forgotten; it may even have been myself. At any rate, it was sound. Carnforth's 45394, seen on Newton Heath the day before, presided over pilot work at Victoria as we left slightly late on the 09.05 train. More than an hour after our Todmorden arrival on a fine morning, 48423 and 48730 (both 10F) rattled past our position, back to Stansfield Hall from banking earlier trains. Before long the latter 8F assisted D392 on 7Z75 at 10.58 on a load of thirty-three. After that it was all Type 3s on the diesel side, leading the next two steam-banked trains westwards, returning east light from earlier specials and with one rake of empties in a like direction.

Towards dinner, the combination we'd hoped for, an 8F at each end, materialised in initially distant and laboured exhaust beats, distinct through the bird song in Kitson Wood. Firstly, engine 48247 hauling thirty-three loaded, then just over an hour later 48278 (load thirty-one), both banked by 48423 (all 10F locos), plugged away through the tree-lined approach to what we knew as Lydgate tunnel. No. 48278 wasn't putting up as much of a show as the other leading 2-8-0 and even the Type 3-hauled trains were travelling at least half as fast again as those

No. 73069 (9H) at Earlestown and at that point in charge of the L.C.G.B. 'Two Cities' Railtour, which we just missed seeing at Manchester Vic. on 23 June. *T. Heavyside*

with double 8F power, which didn't better 10mph on the 1 in 65 whilst audible to ourselves. The trains would have weighed 700 tons minimum. Still, we were well pleased, I with the two all-steam recordings in particular.

They lasted twelve minutes between them. In various forms we'd seen evidence of nine specials, but there were probably more and all on the Burnley line, eliminating the rush and uncertainty of our 18 May trip. We caught the intended 15.07 train back with only a faint hope of catching something of the L.C.G.B. 'Two Cities' railtour, due through Miles Platting at 15.12, but 73069 (9H), which had banked 1T85 out of Victoria, was seen standing at Brindle Heath Jc. as Keith and I journeyed back to Bolton.

Very near the end of Newton Heath mpd steam working, 45200 (9D) heads out of Bury on the Bolton line past West Jc. box with coal at 09.55 on 27 June. Bury 'hollow', as it was known, demanded skilful handling of the engine with loose coupled goods trains, and in fact the box here was not long afterwards partly demolished by a breakaway from a similar train to that depicted when 'snatching' resulted in a broken coupling. The back of the train then ran back down the 1 in 94 gradient. The signalman, in an apparent act of self-sacrifice, turned the wagons into his own box. As is often the case with lower-profile accidents without loss of life in those days, the stories were just handed down in the absence of any known official paperwork, leaving behind them unanswered questions such as (in this instance) why the 'bobby' reacted in that way, and what happened to the guard? *I.C. Simpson*

Monday, 24 to Friday, 28 June

During the week just gone, four more Bolton locos had been officially condemned. We knew that two, 48504 and 48392 had been out of use for some weeks. The others were 45046 and 48026. No. 48504 had been with us longest, coming from Nuneaton on 25 May 1966. It had been allocated solely to that depot since before 1960, qualifying therefore as the least itinerant of the four casualties in question. One distinctive feature of 48504, acquired during its time at 9K, was the creased down edge, through some mishap, of the rear 4 or 5ft of the LH running plate. No. 48392 followed the not unfamiliar trend of stability (at Kirkby-in-Ashfield) until a January 1963 move took it to Cricklewood, for six months only. Burton took it on from late June for a nine-month period up to its end of March 1964 transfer to Stockport Edgeley. It was able to settle there until late October 1967, when Trafford Park became its custodians for the next four months, up to the closure of 9E. For a mere two weeks Lostock Hall had the 8F before it came to Bolton on 2 April 1968.

Between the current decade opening and August 1965, 45046 had alternated from Crewe North to South mpds, until it went to Stockport Edgeley from 5B. It remained there until closure brought the 4-6-0 to Bolton on 6 May 1968 with several others. No. 48026 had been long-term Canklow-based in 1960, moving to Staveley (Barrow Hill) at the end of 1962. In April 1964 it came over to the L.M.R. at

British Railways Steam 1968

The Bolton location known as Orlando Bridge, or O.B., at the immediate east end of the station is here depicted with 45104 apparently on pilot duty. Steps from the road bridge (out of shot) gave direct access to the open-doored headquarters on the right. The massive L.M.S. warehouse overlooks the scene. The date is unknown. *Bart van der Leeuw*

Edge Hill, but fitted in two subsequent moves by October of that year, to Speke Jc. and Agecroft. Its early June 1966 transfer to Newton Heath preceded that which saw the 8F reallocated to Bolton, where it arrived on 6 February 1968.

Taking into account the above, for the last week of its existence, 9K's allocation therefore stood at twenty-one steam engines, but what would have been the final days of normal operation were already over, thanks to the guards' dispute that began on Monday, 24 June. During that first day, members of A.S.L.E.F. voted to join too and in nearly three hours at O.B. from 18.30 only two light steam locos were seen amongst the diesel-hauled traffic that did run. The latter was not noticeably affected beyond the 'Boat Train's' absence, but none of the steam-worked Mostons turned up, and though 44877 (10A) arrived from shed to power Bedford parcels at the usual time, it returned to 9K just after 20.00 and the train didn't run. On the dmu front (which doesn't really concern us motive power-wise), the 18.40 and 19.40 Manchester–Blackpools were cancelled and several Up trains were late running. From the bridge I talked to Sammy Thomasson in East Jc. box for a while. In there they doubtless had an easier evening than usual and I could empathise with them, thinking back to mid/late September 1967 when, as a booker, the eight-hour turn dragged under exactly the same circumstances.

After finishing the main painting of the farewell to 9K headboard on Tuesday evening, the 25th, I went to the shed, where there seemed to be 'little change' – little change from engines in steam with nowhere to go, being the intended meaning of this diary entry. With the contents not even representative of a normal evening and the whole show due to close at the weekend, I doubtless considered it pointless to take any further notes. Paul was cleaning and Keith had come down, too. Ronnie Horrocks was acting Running Shed Foreman and Ossie Leigh, our only known adversary there, had left the railway completely.

Opposite: Next to 'Boat Train' stalwart 45025 (10A), 45046 was the oldest surviving 'Black 5' at the time it was transferred from Stockport Edgeley to Bolton. Here on the 9K ashpit it appears ready to contribute to the already considerable accumulation therein. *Bart van der Leeuw*

Then 9K employee Bart van der Leeuw took this slightly elevated view of Bolton shed yard, chiefly featuring 45073 and 44947. The latter, 9K's second longest-serving 'Black 5', bears an authentic 'Bolton' on the buffer beam from its shopping at the Cowlairs Works in late 1965. *Bart van der Leeuw*

Off-duty enginemen were bringing their wives down for a probable first (and certainly last) look at what their men did and where they went to at such crazy times of day and night. Some even got on the locos. The operational railway I saw strictly as man's domain and even in these special circumstances the fair sex's presence inside those gates jarred on me, I well remember, in the sense that a code had been broken. The shed inviolate had fallen, so close to the end. Paul had become friendly with the girl next door but one, Hilary, and I struggled to

Occasional complaints about dirtied washing in the back yards of Crescent road resulted in a personal appearance of an irate housewife, and that is the nature of the scene set here, somewhat earlier than 1968, but no less relevant. *P. Salveson*

Into the last week of steam at Bolton shed, recently cleaned trio 44888, 48319 and 45104 reflect the evening sunlight on 26 June 1968. *V.A. Sidlow*

maintain an air of politeness with her in our group during those weeks up to August, by which time I hope my resistance was weakening. Housewives who lived on that part of Crescent Road adjacent to 9K may have noticed the fewer sources of dirty smoke endangering their washing in recent weeks. The very occasional ones who strode into the premises to complain (and it did happen!) had every right to do so. They, the one-time office lady and any wartime female labour, I would have had no mental battle with.

On Wednesday evening I cleaned the left-hand side of 45290, sweating profusely as the engine stood in steam, inside and on an obviously warm night. Somehow, advanced word came through that 73069 (9H) – not ours now, but we retained a special interest in it – would be reallocated to Carnforth after the weekend and that 'some 9D stuff has escaped'. Vern and Paul were around that evening and Keith we saw on his way down as we walked home. Our local paper expressed fears that the intended twelve Bolton Holiday specials on Friday night into Saturday would be casualties of the guards' dispute and that those who had pre-booked should get their cash back. However, a partially reassuring statement issued on the 27th read 'Most specials will run'.

I stocked up on film (my first such purchase since February), and tape during Thursday the 27th and divided my evening between the shed, cleaning the rods on 45110, and Orlando bridge. At least Bedford parcels was able to run that night, with 45390 (10A), but I only saw that, Wigan parcels (D7633) and 45231 (10A) LE to 9K in more than an hour. The latter 'Black 5' had doubtless been despatched in lieu of its cancelled train, Heysham–Moston, to provide power for the rest of the diagram.

The level of optimism, however high or low, regarding Bolton's last steam jobs' likelihood of running was done no harm by the Friday intelligence that four engines were booked off the next morning for specific regular work. This was about normal for those closing weeks on a Saturday and the Bamfurlong trip was reckoned to be the best to concentrate on. For 1968's Bolton Holidays I hadn't even made the effort to compile a list of the specials. This reflected both the revolution in motive power to be used, compared with the year before, and the uncertainty of many running. Later on Friday we saw only the regular Manchester Vic.–Paignton, 1V45, starting back from Bolton behind D1746 among other non-holiday traffic. Heysham–Moston (twenty-three on) was able to put in an appearance, albeit as late as 21.15, behind 44897 (10A), but not with the big load one might have expected in view of the train's non-appearance on the 27th. So, that 'Black 5' had the distinction of hauling the last 7J32 with steam, and (as I never saw the train again) the last ever? Had it been retimed? After 30 June the revisions must have been huge.

Saturday, 29 June

I got up more than an hour later than intended that sorry morning of Saturday the 29th, but a degree of flailing about saw me at the shed twenty minutes later at 06.35, with the headboard. 9K's last ever normal steam locomotive departure was about to take place after 45269 had turned, itself no mean historic moment. Next to 45269 stood 44897 (10A) in a curious state of limbo. After completing part of its diagram (see above), it now straddled the steam-to-diesel transition at 9K because the other part of its work on Monday belonged to the new era. So, to that engine went the distinction of being the last ever 'Carnforth engine' as we familiarly knew it after visiting Bolton daily for more than two years.

The price of oversleeping almost certainly changed the complexion of the day. I'd missed the earlier shed

The last steam working from Bolton shed was given to 45269. The loco has just turned to face south for the Agecroft–Dewsnap tripper. Boarding the 'Black 5' on 29 June 1968 are the author and Paul Salveson, and though the train itself did not run due to the guards' dispute, the occasion was nevertheless able to be commemorated with a different kind of run. *V.A. Sidlow*

departures, though the last was most important. No. 45104 had gone off with Castleton pilot, but I don't know which engine worked the intended Bamfurlong or even what the fourth duty was! No. 45269's job was Target 89, the 10.00 Agecroft– Dewsnap. The reason it left shed so early lies locked away in the cupboard of unascertained facts relating to that day. Luckily, the type of bracket and fastening on my headboard had caused no trouble and, with a small Union flag in place below it, plus Paul and I got on the footplate, courtesy of driver Tommy Sammon and fireman Malcolm Frost. Had we been offered a ride on any of the earlier jobs, the 'unmissable' last would indeed have been missed. No. 45269 negotiated the exit pointwork at 07.05, the event marked by frantic whistling and several exploding detonators, but the 'bobby' and booker at Burnden Jc. box remained unruffled by the commotion. It was, after all, not a good day for them either, as they knew.

After making swift progress to Agecroft (max 54mph), we sat there for almost two hours, waiting for a guard. No. 48652 soon trundled north LE at the end not only of its current turn of duty, but its active life, after fulfilling some nocturnal work, I imagine, in Manchester. Type 4s went by on the Up 'Boat' (D1740) and the SO Manchester Vic.–Scarborough, 1N73, (D206) starting specially from Bolton, conjuring up reminders of 73014 a year earlier.

Eventually it had to be conceded that our Agecroft–Dewsnap would not run. We'd been an unlucky casualty of the current unrest and were now detailed to return LE to 9K. Conscious of the acute disappointment over not being able to make a 'go' of the official last working, Tommy obtained permission from Control to let us make a bit of a tour and return via Manchester Vic. and Castleton curve, with no charge for the extra coal burnt! Some was too, because it took more than an hour and a half to regain 9K, inclusive of ten more stops of varying duration. Maximum exposure of the headboard came during the thirty seconds spent motionless at Victoria. Over in Exchange was 45055 (9H), another 'last', as will be seen.

Several short stops via Monsal Lane brought us to our lengthiest halt, in the loop at Middleton Jc. West for eighteen and a half minutes. Only a dmu parcels (to Bolton) was due, but interestingly as a summer Saturday partial substitute for the Manchester–Blackpool train, which did not run because of the 'Boat Train' engine's fill-in turn instead was class 1 work to Barrow and back. While we stood awaiting the road, 44735 (9D) slowly headed light for home, and in response to the inscribed bed head on our smokebox door its fireman chalked 'last day too' on their tender side as they passed – a moving moment. We wondered how Keith and Vern had got on, expecting the train we should have worked, somewhere east of Victoria. There'd been no way to inform them of the change.

No sooner had we got under way again, at 10.11, than a five-and-a-half-minute stop to chase stray cattle off the line (and possibly another reason for our being looped) was necessary. Thereafter it was fairly plain sailing with a maximum of 46mph through Radcliffe Black Lane. No. 45104, still at its post on Castleton pilot, was one of several 'Black 5s' of ours to lose its numberplate recently, but not to anyone I knew! Briefly holding us on the fork at Burnden Jc. were two Type 4s coupled LE north, but at 10.52, grateful for what we'd been able to salvage from the earlier let-down, 45269 entered 9K, greeted by about forty enthusiasts as the cameras clicked and whirred.

Half an hour later, 45104 returned from Castleton, the final 9K turn ever to arrive back on shed. Its ashes were scattered in the pit before a last move positioned it next to 48652 and another 8F, adjacent to the main line, condemned with eleven more at the end. Most of these hadn't turned a wheel on this special day and I don't think we knew which ones would live on for the rest of the summer. Two of the 'Black 5s' that did (it transpired), weren't removed from the shed for a whole week. No. 45260 had sundry inscriptions chalked on its front end by a more artistically aware 20.55 Club member than I, Jim from Whitworth. One, irrelevant to the railway, but not to the contemporary music scene, just said 'CREAM'. I didn't even understand it, having remained somehow ignorant of that first 'super-group', if indeed such a phrase had yet been

Part-way through the long wait at Agecroft Jc. on the last day of Bolton steam, 45269 simmers away while all concerned hope for a guard to appear. As related, none did, but the loco with its headboard (but no Union flag at this point) were paraded around the circular route back to 9K. *I.C. Simpson*

coined. Our Jim reminded me of his namesake in the Byrds, though in 1968 he was more of a 'Green Tambourine' man. Able to be channelled elsewhere after August 1968, a new appreciation would spring up in me of the lesser-known side of the current and exciting music scene, away from the 'charts'. The guards today had been more sympathetic to Bolton's holidaymakers than to local goods work as the Yarmouth uncomprehendingly passed by without deference to the last rites taking place so nearby.

After the last movements as described, enthusiast presence diminished. A vantage point used perhaps more that day than ever before was the coaling tower. Even a third of the way up those neglected iron ladders afforded an excellent view of the shed yard. I had been almost to the top once; an uncomfortably lofty position, unprotected by any handrails on the three open sides of the flat surface itself. I couldn't attempt it now!

Keith and Vern that morning had recognised our engine (45269) from a way off as they waited at Miles Platting and put two and two together, being back at 9K for the arrivals. Early afternoon saw us just north of Turton for any engine transfers being made to Rose Grove and we were rewarded by two movements. No. 44735 (9D) seen earlier, hauled 44809 also ex Newton Heath en route to Carnforth, and just over an hour later 45269 towed 48340 from Bolton, the 5MT being Lostock Hall-bound and the 8F for Rose Grove. Returning to 9K after this for Colne–Red Bank (not seen and probably didn't run) 44845 (9D) headed light, south, doubtless to its own depot for withdrawal. The very few usurping diesels that had been about at 9K had, like fleas abandoning a dying cat, taken off to the new Byng Street headquarters and a Sunday-like silence descended on what remained; Sunday-like, but more hushed even, and never to be broken by the familiar sounds that had for so long and with such regularity done so.

The *Bolton Evening News*, which had endeavoured to keep on top of the guards' dispute and its repercussions on the public, contained not a word about the closure of Crescent Road sheds. I'd be surprised if any such familiar installation of comparable size, prominence and distinctiveness in the town has disappeared unreported since. There were engines to see at 9K for months to come. Ironically, the last to be taken away was a foreigner and not even there at the end of June. No. 48646 (ex 10D), which had its journey to the breakers yard interrupted in August,

Looped at Middleton Jc., 45269 faces the approaching 44735 (9D) on its shed's final day too with steam. *S.A. Leyland*

was there almost until the winter. All of the active 9K engines featured in this account of the last day had been cleaned during the brief period leading up to it, so the lads had done far more than the personal jobs herein related.

Having paid our respects to Newton Heath more than once during June, a last possible opportunity to do so at Patricroft mpd provided the motivation behind that Saturday evening of the 29th, now joined by Pete and Frank. At about 18.00, 9H had an air of almost total resignation. One engine, 45156 (9H) was in steam. The other four to be granted a transfer had already gone, except for 45055 (9H), which we would return to at Exchange station. All the other twenty-nine locos on shed I marked down as condemned, except 48033 (9H), but I was wrong there. It must have looked OK in comparison to the other eighteen of that final allocation (of twenty-four) that comprised the final batch of withdrawals.

The rods were being removed from locos that had not completely cooled down! A story goes of one Patricroft R.S.F. who verged on breaking down at the waste of so

The crew of 45269 (fireman Frost on the right) pose during the Middleton Jc. check. *S.A. Leyland*

Back at its home depot, 45269 comes off the ashpit before being granted a reprieve as a Lostock Hall engine. Driver Tommy Sammon is on the left. Die-hard enthusiasts down to the mildly curious gave the shed yard the appearance of an open day by late morning. *P. Barber*

At 11.34 the less 'fortunate' 45104 arrived from its work at Castleton to have its fire dropped for the last time, an event that was enacted too at Patricroft and Newton Heath. *S.A. Leyland*

many of his young Standard 5s (ten since the end of February). The offices he'd occupied were empty now, strewn with what then passed for rubbish and not unlike the hastily abandoned headquarters of a retreating army. Most of my collection of Working Timetables was recovered from that floor, in good condition, bar the odd dirty boot print. One of them, the current Section N, perpetuated the quaint feature of a designated FO engine from Patricroft mpd (dep. 14.23) to pay wages at Astley Green signal box and then return to 9H, four minutes being allowed for the transaction and for the recipient to cross the loco over. It's my guess that the service didn't last much longer, if at all, into the diesel era.

Back at Exchange we joined the group that had congregated to mark the last steam pilot's departure to shed, an event that 45055's crew fulfilled with the usual exuberances. So, with the last rites of Patricroft commemorated, the day ended that had brought steam's demise as close to home for ourselves as any could.

Ever so young looking Messrs Shirres, Thorniley, Hoyle and Salveson are framed for posterity on the footplate of 45104 as it cools down for the last time at 9K. *Unknown*

It will be seen that most front-end tributes and comments on the locos took the form of spontaneously chalked phrases, appropriate in most cases to the occasion. This group have not quite finished with 45260 at Bolton on the last day, 29 June, but all will be washed off or wiped off later at Lostock Hall. *P. Barber*

Many braved the corroded ladders and unfenced heights of Bolton's coaling tower in those last few days for the panoramic views it afforded. Swinging round to the right from the shed yard itself, a scene strangely resembling the unwanted remains of a hen after a fox has finished feasting suggests itself. In reality the bits are what's left of diesel shunters cut up on site. Activities after closure included emptying the tenders of condemned engines – note the strategically placed wagons against 44802, 48692 and 44929 – and dispersing the reallocated locos. Turning 180 degrees (next page) to face north reveals everything from the shed outlet, Burnden Jc., Rose Hill fork and the whole layout to Bolton station, as well as town landmarks. *V.A. Sidlow/unknown*

Unavoidably, terminal-sounding words such as 'last', 'final', 'end' and 'ever', whilst never long absent from these pages by virtue of what is chronicled herein, have been, if anything, overused of late, and we haven't done yet! Of the last ever steam locomotive transfers from one B.R. depot to another for service, a much larger percentage of Bolton's final allocation (47½%) took part than either Newton Heath (26½%) or Patricroft (21%). Was this a final testimony to the superior average condition of 9K machines, even though six of the ten in question were 1968 additions to the stud? Patricroft may have been slightly disadvantaged in this respect by the authorities' decision not to impose Caprotti valve gear at such a late hour on sheds that hadn't any experience of it practically, beyond visiting engines. 9H had only four BR 5s so fitted at the end and the above theory on their being condemned rather than moved on is my supposition only. The sole remaining, and therefore distinctive, loco type taking part in these manoeuvres, suddenly alone in the world was in fact the BR 5, and it was 73069 that carried the flag for its class on from Patricroft to Carnforth.

Two engines that vacated 9K on the same last day of working steam were 45269 and 48340. Seen here at Bromley Cross, the 5MT is hauling the other, which was granted transfer to Rose Grove (from whence it came to Bolton at the end of March), whereas 45269 will become a Lostock Hall resident. *P. Barber*

Pastures New and Pastures Old

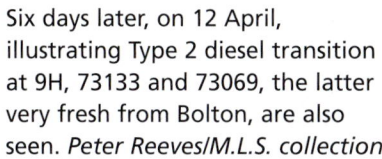

Above: Patricroft mpd as enthusiasts prefer to remember it earlier in 1968. The well-known view features 44777 (8A) arriving or about to leave on 6 April 1968. *T. Heavyside*

Six days later, on 12 April, illustrating Type 2 diesel transition at 9H, 73133 and 73069, the latter very fresh from Bolton, are also seen. *Peter Reeves/M.L.S. collection*

Closer to the building, foreigners 44971 (10D) and 45392 (9F) flank home engine 73050, which, though withdrawn upon Patricroft's closure, has survived into preservation. *T. Heavyside*

Less than traditionally, the last steam-worked Manchester Exchange station pilot was undertaken not by a BR 5, but one of Patricroft's 'Black 5s', 45055. Its work done by 20.45 on 29 June, light engine to 9H is the next move – a bicycle appears to be leaving or going back on the footplate – followed by reallocation to Lostock Hall.
P. Barber

Sunday, 30 June

Contributive proportions and classes of loco involved in those last releases from Newton Heath (eight engines), Patricroft (five) and Bolton (ten) are hardly essential reading at this advanced stage. Suffice to say little more beyond the fact that each of the closed mpds sent power to each of the survivors, Carnforth, Lostock Hall and Rose Grove, with the exception of nil transfers 9D to 10D. Gross receipts were at Carnforth, ten; Lostock Hall, eight; and Rose Grove, five. The residue left for scrap at 9D, 9H and 9K was twenty-two, nineteen and eleven respectively.

Of the engines that escaped the closure of Bolton, 44781 and 44871 went to Carnforth, 44888, 45073, 45110, 45260, 45269 and 45318 had a five-week reprieve as Lostock Hall locos and Rose Grove got 48340 and 48773. Conscious that the customary allocation history summary of all withdrawn 9K locos would (for eleven at once) clog up the flow of our 'story' somewhat, these appear below. Those condemned at the end were: 44802, 44929, 44947, 45104, 45290, 45312, 48168, 48319, 48652, 48692 and 48720. Four of them were longer-standing machines of more than three years' duration, and 45290 our first ever 'Black 5', Bolton-based since early February 1962.

It will be realised that dieselisation of the lower-class traffic, chiefly trip work and unfitted freights that nearly monopolised the duties of most steam sheds in 1968, was not done in a way that phased out the old motive power gradually and smoothly to a tidy conclusion by, say, the last week of partial steam operation. Because of the better availability of diesels, it was obvious to all that fewer units would be needed to do the same amount of work, but just how few did take over was certainly not anticipated by most enthusiasts. Most noticeable at locations one was most familiar with was the drop in activity that pervaded such areas once steam had gone. Such an unnatural quietness came over the railway surrounding these latter-day steam sheds following their respective closures that it became impossible to ignore the probability that traffic somehow had been considerably condensed when the new diagramming arrangements were calculated; 'actively discouraged' or simply 'knocked off' is a less thinly veiled way of putting it.

We know that that type of work had been in long and gradual decline, but the ousting of steam seemed to provide an excuse to accelerate the process almost overnight, transfiguring many bustling centres into something very different – but this had not happened everywhere, yet.

Post-1960 Allocation History for Final Locomotive Withdrawals at 9K, w/e 1/7/68	
44802	Holyhead to Carlisle Kingmoor, w/e 10/11/62, then to Upperby w/e/ 11/7/64. Back to Kingmoor w/e/ 7/11/64, then to Bolton w/e 6/1/68 upon closure of Kingmoor
44929	Agecroft to Trafford Park w/e 22/10/66 upon closure of Agecroft. To Bolton w/e 9/3/68 upon closure of Trafford Park
44947	Blackpool Central to Bolton w/e 19/9/64 upon closure of Blackpool
45104	Newton Heath to Aintree w/e 11/1/64, back to Newton Heath w/e 27/6/64. To Bury 4/11/64, then to Bolton w/e 10/4/65 upon closure of Bury
45290	Newton Heath to Bolton w/e 10/2/62 (first 'Black 5' allocated to Bolton)
45312	Speke Jc, to Edge Hill w/e 6/7/63. To Warrington Dallam w/e 12/2/66. To Stockport Edgeley w/e 7/10/67. To Bolton w/e 6/5/68 upon closure of Stockport
48168	Derby to Kettering w/e 4/3/61. To Annesley w/e 22/9/62. To Kirby-in-Ashfield w/e 3/7/65. To Patricroft w/e 24/7/65 and to Heaton Mersey w/e 5/2/66. Finally to Bolton w/e 6/5/68 upon closure of Heaton Mersey
48319	Toton to Nottingham w/e 2/2/63. To Fleetwood w/e 23/11/63, then to Springs Branch w/e 19/2/66. To Patricroft w/e 19/12/66. To Heaton Mersey w/e 6/1/68, then to Bolton w/e 6/5/68 upon closure of Heaton Mersey
48652	Stourton to Edge Hill w/e 1/9/62. To Bury w/e 19/10/63. To Bolton w/e 10/4/65 upon closure of Bury. To Heaton Mersey w/e 22/1/66 and back to Bolton w/e 29/1/66
48692	Crewe South to Speke Jc. w/e/ 10/6/61. To Edge Hill w/e 23/9/67. To Bolton w/e 6/5/68 upon closure of Edge Hill
48720	Newton Heath to Patricroft w/e 5/1/63. To Heaton Mersey w/e 29/1/66. To Bolton w/e 6/5/68 upon closure of Heaton Mersey.

4

Steam Survives in Small Pockets

1 July to 11 August

Up to the End of Steam and the '15 Guinea Special'.

W.W. Chamberlain, my employer, did recognise the Bolton Holiday fortnight and I therefore was completely free to follow steam for two of the five weeks left to it. The six-day L.M.R, 'Runabout Rover' I'd purchased for £2-7-6d (or £2.37½) was valid from Sunday the 30th, but I'd never counted that as an active day. The next four were all spent in the general direction of Carnforth and the Barrow or Windermere line, mostly with an arguable success rate in view of the time away from home.

Monday, 1 July

Monday, 1 July's run straight to Ulverston yielded almost no active steam en route, except a couple of lightweight ballast workings at Greenbank (Preston) and Grange-over-Sands. At Ulverston, the tripper from Carnforth, allowed more than four hours to shunt the yards there, was still thus engaged and today's engine was 75048 (10A). I obtained one or two nice sound sequences as the tranquil setting permitted several welcome subtle noises to assert themselves beyond just the exhaust; snifter valves, clanking and clanging of side rods and wagon couplings made up a pleasant recording of an under-recorded type. No. 75048 departed at 12.17 with nineteen wagons for Carnforth.

I'd primarily picked Ulverston with the 09.58 Preston–Barrow parcels in mind. Today 3P24 was running late. I felt mild surprise to see walking towards my spot, half a mile west of the station, the familiar figure of an enthusiast who I didn't associate with line-siding, but by July 1968 on B.R. it was a case of 'lineside or give up' for 99% of the time. We'd never spoken, and didn't now as he walked further up the bank. His perpetual gaunt expression and slight stoop for one of about my age exuded an impression of constant tiredness. An hour and a quarter after schedule and hauling a lighter load than I'd hoped for, equal to five or six bogies, 45200 (10A) set off smartly for Barrow at 13.25. Here was a newly transferred loco (from Newton Heath) in use the first working day at its new depot.

I'd been concerned that the lateness of 3P24 might upset my next move – that of securing the 13.50 Barrow Shipyard–Carnforth goods, 8P78 and MO, climbing the eastbound approach to Lindal Ore Sidings, at Dalton. Worse than that, however, the plan's chance of success was dealt a further blow by the 14.05 dmu to Dalton finally turning up seventy minutes late! I could have walked it faster. Was this once a week freight running at all? This was doubtless the question being asked by 15.30, but I needn't have worried, partly because the parcels engine on Mondays (it transpired) worked both jobs. No. 45200 duly emerged from Dalton tunnel at 16.00 to provide the day's best action, forging up the 1 in 100 on a thirty-two mixed wagon load as it took its place amongst the line's diesel-worked traffic.

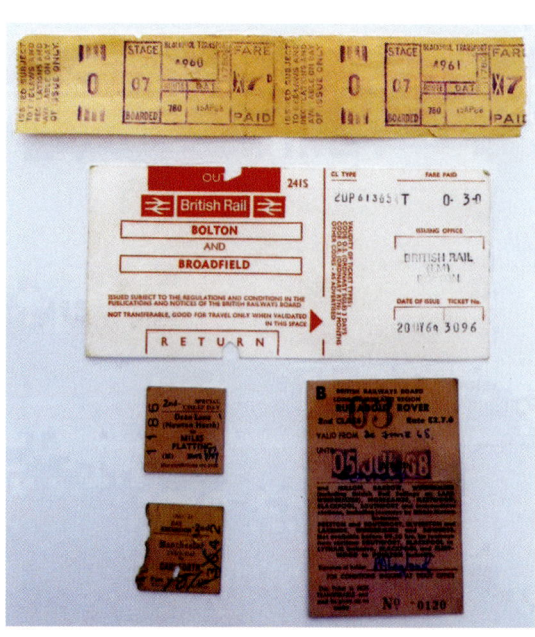

Survivors No. 4 – A small selection of tickets from 1968 including the experimental Broadfield card in proportion to the Edmondson halves.

Scene of the author's pleasant tape recording session on 1 July 68 featuring Ulverston goods yard and station signal box, and with the same engine, 75048 (10A) shunting two days later on the 3rd. *I.C. Simpson*

Three long-standing Carnforth 'Black 5s' at their home shed in morning sunshine, 44709, 45209 and 45445, all of which survived well into 1968. *K.F. Pendlebury*

Carnforth shed yard on 23 July 1968 with various diesels including Clayton Type 1s. No. 45231 (10A) is in steam, close by candidates for preservation 42085 and 61306. The 'Black 5' itself will live on in that way, too. *T. Heavyside*

Falling foul again of the Furness line 'carts' frailty that day, mine failed at Carnforth en route to Preston. I therefore went over to the Up main, a luxury soon to be taken away from that station, to pick up 1P77, the Windermere–Blackpool N. loco-hauled service. During the wait, 44897 (10A) travelled LE south, proving that 9K had returned it during the weekend when circumstances rendered it suddenly spare. Ordinarily (up to 29 June) it would have just been leaving Bolton shed to work Bedford parcels. 1P77 was twenty-eight minutes in arrears leaving Carnforth behind D5198. Three dead stands between Lancaster and Preston conspired to lose the eight-coach train over nine more minutes on the super-slack schedule of thirty-one. It was then delayed in the E.L. platform for well over twenty minutes until exactly an hour down, and that's exactly how much longer it took me to get home than it ought! From the above it can be correctly deduced that I took timing and performance notes of loco-hauled trains that, though not steam any more, came my way during travels. Never more glaring than now was the enormous disparity in comfort between locomotive-hauled stock and the detestable dmu, trailer cars possibly excepted. Logging journeys with the former was a seamless and enjoyable aspect of the railway interest for me which smoothly spanned the steam to diesel era.

No. 45017 (10A) pulls out of Carnforth on 13 July 1968 with what is almost certainly the 09.58 Preston–Barrow parcels, steam MS0 and which the author caught at Ulverston on 1 July. *T. Heavyside*

Tuesday, 2 to Thursday, 4 July

The title of this chapter is acknowledged as less of an accurate statement than a phrase borrowed from later issues of the British publication *World Steam*, which proved such a valuable source of information and reference to post-1968 enthusiasts venturing far and wide. During the magazine's heyday, the 1970s, much of the world was awash with steam as many countries phased out the old power more gradually than B.R. As the twentieth century prepared to close, steam, even worldwide, did only survive in small pockets. In England in 1968 there was only one pocket and quite a large one to start with, meaning no steam-worked area was isolated from any other. That situation ended in September 1967 when Northumberland steam on its last legs had no contact with that in the West Riding in running terms. The pocket by mid-1968 had contracted greatly, and ever more northwards.

The next four days I set off slightly later on the 09.04 from Bolton. Tuesday's trip really just comprised of largely unadventurous periods spent at Preston, Lancaster and Carnforth; unimaginative locations for observation and/or recording of course, but they in theory did combine a greater frequency of steam activity than the more isolated strategic spots and even if most of it was less sensational, the chance of something memorable turning up still remained. In short there was more going on. Of the three centres only Carnforth didn't have a significant gradient at its platform end, but its depot and yards proximity were there in compensation. At Preston, however, nearly three hours elapsed before any major steam action came along, more in the time of the 11.50 Ribble–Heysham goods. There'd been no sign of the earlier (10.05) train between those points. Anyway, 44806 (10D) made a fairly dynamic start from the station hauling forty-seven vehicles at 12.26 to, provide my sole tape recording of the day!

Moving northwards shortly afterwards, I went around Carnforth shed for the second time in less than a month, at about 14.00. The working board here provided a useful indicator of what was out and about, or going to be. Few depots made use of the working board in my experience. Bolton's, for example, was only filled in on the rare occasions that we volunteered to do it! We will return to Carnforth's later. Of the twenty-four steam locos present, excluding 70013 (10A) and the preserved machines, eight were in steam and ten condemned, though my assessment made it twelve on appearance. If one counts all the recent transfers to 10A (officially in the week ending 6 July), Carnforth's allocation stood at thirty, but it was impossible to detect which ones not yet seen had arrived and which hadn't at this point. Remember, we'd seen no reallocation lists resulting from the recent upheaval. All those quoted herein are from still-to-be-published listings later in the summer. This is why the gross figure of seventeen locos missing from that 10A visit may well have been only eight. The 9Fs were all condemned now and therefore had reached extinction. No. 48167 (10F) constituted the only foreigner, unfired today, but the table to follow will show it and another Rose Grove 2-8-0 being used. Serviceable classes amounted to 'Black 5s', 8Fs and 75XXX. Clearly I noted from the board only the jobs that still had engine numbers allocated to them, or just the ones that could be of use later. Pick of the afternoon was 5F24, the 15.05 Heysham–Warrington MSX, for which I walked from Lancaster Castle (not up the track for once) to the 1 in 98 bank's top, but to no avail. The guards' dispute we considered over for now, but no train or 44897 (10A) appeared and I got caught in some very heavy rain that dampened more than my enthusiasm!

Thoughts then turned only to returning home, but the Up trains from Lancaster had other ideas, at first. The enforced wait did reveal one interesting movement that would have otherwise evaded me when a certain pair of

As per the Carnforth mpd workings board, 73069 (10A), now with a painted front 'numberplate', works a short goods near Giggleswick with the trip working of that name. *I.C. Simpson*

'Black 5s' that would find their place in B.R. steam history five and a half weeks hence, 44871 and 44781 were getting to know one another on a somewhat contrasting occasion – that of being hauled ex 9K to Carnforth for service. It was D5153 that brought them north through Lancaster at 16.50, coupled in much lowlier status to that future event, which was, of course, B.R's. 'be-all-and-end-all' grand finale steam tour. However, not only had it yet to be advertised to the public, the motive power had not been chosen and I am premature in saying even so much early in July. So, worthwhile though it was to see evidence of how Bolton's final allocation was being distributed, that's all it was that afternoon.

The first train to appear in favour of my intention was the seventy-one-minute late 11.20 Perth–Birmingham. Still fairly sodden from Lancaster bank, I found that 1M37 did not provide a hair drying service (head held out of window at speed), but only because the slipstream just wasn't warm enough! Bolton Holiday weather was off to a not untypical start, in the north at least.

The following table shows extracts from the Carnforth mpd working board for the last three days of my repeated trips there in early July. The unbracketed train descriptions are what was literally copied from the board. My bracketed additions and notes on the right are added to aid recognition of the duties listed. All engines were 10A-based except 48167 and 48393 (10F) and 45269 (10D).

NB Not all the above jobs necessarily appeared on the working board on days when no engine is shown against them.

One or two of the above workings are not transparently clear in the place name abbreviation displayed, which was all the enginemen needed of course. 'Giggleswick', for example, which did not appear in Dent, would almost certainly have been a trip engine to that point, shunting at yards and sidings en route. At that time I'd never been to Giggleswick in my life.

My Wednesday trip had the same structure as Tuesday's and varied only in the duration spent at each place and (as with Thursday) did not include a visit to 10A beyond scrutiny of the working board. I'd switched recording tape brands on the grounds of cost to Teleton, an apparently German-manufactured cassette, but years afterwards regretted jettisoning Philips' own as the quality, whilst still well listenable, isn't quite up to that of the original type.

First at Preston on the 3rd (and contradicting the 10A board, it transpired), came 44894 (10A) on an unidentified forty-five-wagon freight heading south at 10.35. Straight after, in time, was the 10.05 Ribble–Heysham (twenty-two on) behind 48765 (10D) so with the more modest movements the day was going quite well. The Preston–Barrow parcels that I'd seen on Monday was only steam MSO. At Carnforth various shunts

	2/7/68	3/7/68	4/7/68	
00.55 (Carnforth)–Rose Grove	–	–	44894	6P77, MX
05.00 (Carnforth)–Edge Hill	–	73069	44897	5F16, Daily
05.25 Heysham	–	44709	44709	Pilot?
06.00 Special Trips	–	45231	–	
06.20 (Carnforth)–Barrow	–	–	45342	6L42, Daily
07.00 Windermere	–	45025	45025	Trip 47 SX
07.30 Heysham parcels	–	75019	–	
07.52 Ulverston	–	75048	75048	Trip 48 SX
08.00 Green Ayre Ballast	–	44877	44877	
08.00 Carnforth Ballast	–	44874	44874	
*08.20 Heysham–Lancaster pcls 3N41	–	–	75019	3N41 went to Leeds
08.25 Grange	–	44894	44963	
**12.08 Heysham–Stourton (tanks)	48393	48393	48393	4N28 Daily
12.35 Kendal	44894	44897	–	Trip 46, SX
13.05 Giggleswick	73069	45200	–	
14.25 Heysham Trip	44709	44709	–	
15.05 Heysham–Warrington	44897	73069	–	5F24, SX
18.10 Lancaster Trip	73069	45200	–	
4P20 (16.20 Heysham–Darwen)	–	48167	–	Tanks. MWFO Q
***20.28 Barrow–Huddersfield	–	45269	–	1P92 Mails/Pcls SX
Spare	75019			

* Steam-worked to Lancaster only. ** Assisted by Type 2 to Skipton.
*** Steam-worked to Preston only. 1P92 was officially 'Barrow–Preston' – then became part of 1N66,
23.15 Preston–Huddersfield parcels.

On a far more clement day than our 25 May venture to see this train, 45025 (10A) climbs past Preston No. 5 box hauling the Darwen–Heysham empty tanks on 6 July 1968. *P. Barber*

abounded over dinner time with 44963, 44758 and 75048 (all 10A). I made the same choice again of the Heysham–Warrington goods as the main objective later as 73069 was booked, but once more, at Lancaster Castle this time, 5F24 failed to materialise. Some grim late running (up to one and a half hours) proved to be another repeat feature to several long-distance trains, but less so the ones I used. Possibly we were wrong about the guards; dispute being out of the way. At Lancaster I again met the lad I'd shared Lindal bank with on the Monday. He pointed out a Carlisle–Birkenhead goods that had been diverted via Ais Gill (5F96), but with reversal at Settle Jc. passed us at 15.20 with D5250. I think this was unlikely to be linked with the expresses delay. Having 'broken the ice' with that communication, there was no shortage of subject matter to melt it further, but we didn't converse at length, even enough to prompt open recognition on any subsequent occasion. It was as likely my fault as one who then didn't mix readily when alone with enthusiasts not already known.

Partly in compensation for the absent Warrington goods, at 15.57 a lightly loaded 14.30 Heysham–Ribble (21) SX appeared behind 48765 (10D) making its return run from the morning. That, however, was my last steam of the day, despite two more hours elapsing before I left the W.C.M.L. at Euxton Jc.

Thursday's early Ribble–Heysham had the week's heaviest train, fifty-two on and 'only' a 'Black 5', but a good one – 45318, ex 9K and now at 10D. How I come to have no recording of that, but several brief ones that morning of the current Preston announcer's drawling effeminate tones and odd pronunciation is as much of a mystery as how he landed such a job! But for all his weird enunciation, the words resounded clearly enough and the whole vanished world of distinctive, if less than 'perfect', announcers was by far preferable to the ubiquitous, detached and electronically uniform 'voice' of the twenty-first century. Clearly my notes reveal that first wholly fine day of the working week, brighter too, as a welcome novelty. At Carnforth, several home engines were seen living out the working board's theory from midday to early afternoon. No. 45342 shunted around the depot, 44963 returned from Grange on ballast wagons and 44758 drew a rake of covhops off the Barrow line just before 73069 (seen at last!) arrived on freight from the south, the 11.50 Ribble–Heysham most likely, at 12.55. The Heysham–Stourton tanks with its Type 2 plus 48393 (10F), then the Ulverston tripper's return (75048) at 13.45 finished off this steamier interval than I'd hitherto enjoyed there in the current week.

It wasn't a bad thing then that the Euston–Windermere train that I next caught to Kendal didn't leave until 14.30, seventy-one minutes late, because preparing to leave as I alighted was 45025 (10A) with its twenty-four-vehicle goods from the branch terminus, Trip 47, next booked stop Milnthorpe. The driver unsuccessfully attempted to cure a drain cock stuck partly open by tugging at the lever as the train departed. Later, 45134 (10A) unexpectedly arrived at the pleasant south Lakes town, but during the rest of my stay was not overtaxed in its pilot duties, though it is noteworthy that the branch still supported two trip engines a day. No. 45134, on Trip 46, was next for Burneside, which both called at.

In the course of looking through proffered images for use in this book I was little short of stunned to find that David Shirres was fortuitously on hand to capture the surprise ECS working on 4 July. A complete rake of eleven maroon coaches was a scoop in itself by then: 48247 (10F) draws along the Down Through at Bolton to briefly await the road onto the Blackburn line and ultimately Colne C.S. If the train stopped at all it could only have been momentarily, allowing no time to set up for a departure recording. *David A.J. Shirres*

The severely delayed train I'd arrived on had sufficient turn round time at Windermere to have set the arrears at nought (which it did) when returning at 16.23 on the Up London. On timings designed to be kept with up to 450 tons, the quite new D425 had an easy task on seven coaches only, though 1A75 may have been strengthened at Preston. This latest class of diesel was commonplace now, with more than thirty in service on west coast duties. Other expresses on the Up were, however, having a third or fourth bad day in succession. This rather cheerier outing ended at 18.20 as my unit clattered over Bolton West's layout into the platform. No sooner had it done so than several electro-pneumatic point levers were thrown to permit a surprise – an eleven-coach ECS for Colne headed by 48247 (10F) – to clatter over the crossovers much more convincingly than the dmu! Though glad to have (just) seen it, that I had not done so from a better vantage point than Trinity Street station, i.e. anywhere up the bank, weighed rather heavily in terms of the lost tape recording, I have to confess. This would have been quite a scoop by that stage. Knowing as we did that Colne and district Holidays were starting the next night, such a working, if indeed anticipated, would probably have been dismissed as a candidate for a Newton Heath diesel. At this juncture of so many years I can't be certain whether we had also dismissed the second Burnley–Moston goods as a steam survivor through Bolton. I'd had chances to see it after the early evening finishes of the week's trips since Monday. Clearly it was still permissible to send steam into Manchester. I ended up at O.B. on the 4th, but did we wait long enough for the Moston?

Bolton shed was still, by sheer force of habit, maybe, a focal meeting place. Wednesday's trip had thrown up a rather specific rumour of 45156 (10F) working a Colne–Stockport holiday portion for the south, but discussions with Paul on the 4th revealed that 'all Saturday's excursions are derv'.

Friday, 5 July

Unidentified on other mornings when I'd passed through, Chorley pilot on the 5th was being covered by 45444 (10D). I used my Runabout only to Preston on its last day of validity to catch Ribble–Heysham. Somehow I'd got up to the lineside opposite No. 5 box where 45017 (10A) made an initially tentative approach on a thirty-one-wagon load, then 'went for it' to pass my spot in fine style. Paul had joined me on this trip, which now shifted to pastures new; a single location that I soon found to be self-sufficient in the same way that Woodley had been. Within a very small area several key movements, all different, provided impressive steam action and more intensively than had been found on the Western Lines I'd just abandoned, even Carnforth itself, but still with the added activity that immediate proximity to a motive power depot provided.

The reader will have guessed by now that of the limited possibilities left, the location in question could

No. 48727 (10F), not in use during the author's early July visits to Rose Grove, sets off from West Jc. towards the end of steam, taking the main line south. The Padiham (power station) branch can be seen dropping away to the right and the cooling towers of the P.S. itself are visible on the extreme right. *R. Farrell/M.L.S. collection*

only be Rose Grove! Another plus point was that, apart from shed visits in the past and passing through by train now and then, the place was quite new to me. Here indeed was a steam haven well worth the devotion of much of my remaining holiday.

Trip engines seen en route from Preston on the 10.48 at Todd Lane Jc, Whitebirk too, and on coal at Rishton, were still outnumbered by the new power on various trains, but once there a contrastingly steamy day unfolded, the best in that respect in fact of four in total up to 12 July. In just over five hours up to 18.00, 84% of all engine movements were steam. Nearly all of this preferred activity that I saw on goods work at Rose Grove then was in the immediate station area or close to West Jc.

The focal point of westbound coal traffic was the twelve-road yard opposite the station on the south side and known as the Up Grid. The strenuous efforts often required to drag loaded trains out of this yard suggest that it sloped somewhat towards the buffers. Track condition too would not have helped. Any vehicle that somehow overcame these features illicitly would have encountered a very short exit road trap that suddenly turned upwards at the sort of gradient one could almost measure with a protractor!

Loaded coal trains for Padiham Power Station would stand at Rose Grove West to have pinned down an appropriate number of wagon brakes on a less severe falling gradient than the one they would meet immediately after the junction. Engines therefore sometimes experienced difficulty getting under way until gravity took increasing effect. Rakes of returning empties from Padiham fought against this very steep mile or so back to the main line, but I won't go into detail yet. Eastbound empty coal runs from Huncoat and beyond coming out of the modest dip at Rose Grove West extracted proportionally less work from their locomotives that nevertheless contributed to the entertainment within that compact operating scene.

Paul and I inspected the depot upon arrival. I fortunately took sufficient details then and on the other visits to be able to produce the following table that can be used to ascertain an idea of engine availability at this period, a month from the end, which locos were seeing the most usage and certain other trends, such as the larger number of locos in steam during the afternoon visit, bearing out experience that mornings saw the most traffic. Featured therefore is the status of every resident loco, present on shed during the visit or otherwise, plus that of foreigners which were there. The current steam allocation of Rose Grove was thirty-two engines. The key/explanation to symbols and abbreviations used is as follows:

S	= In steam on shed at time of visit.
Dead	= Unfired on shed at time of visit.
I/T	= Known to be out in traffic at time of visit.
I/T & S	= In steam on shed at time of visit. Seen in traffic beforehand.
S & I/T	= In steam on shed at time of visit. Seen in traffic afterwards.
NF	= Newly fired on shed at time of visit.
Missing	= Not observed on shed or in traffic all that day.
Cond	= Withdrawn from service for scrap.

Some additional notes on certain locos will not be out of place here. Other sources suggest that both 44932 and 45262 were in long-term store at the old Kingmoor steam shed, and in fact I saw them in November 1968. The physical appearance of 48257 on 12 July prompted me to consider it condemned, but I didn't note down the specific reasons for gaining this impression. If actually condemned between the 8th (in steam) and 12th July it should have caught the 13 July cut-off period. It didn't, but it was listed in the *Railway Observer*'s two weeks ending 27 July report, so my 'diagnosis' was perhaps only two days premature on paper. No. 48752, the other engine not seen on any of the four days, is unlikely to have been in traffic. No. 75027 (10A) is not shown under the 12th because it was seen travelling LE home before the shed visit. Diesel locomotives on shed at the times of the visits averaged two only (Type 2s), but the number sharing traffic in and. around Rose Grove was, according to what was seen, greater than this on all but the first trip on 5 July.

EARLY JULY 1968 ROSE GROVE MOTIVE POWER DEPOT LOCO MONITOR

1. Resident 10F Engines:				
5MT 4-6-0s	Friday 5/7	Monday 8/7	Tues. 9/7	Friday 12/7
12.25 hrs	10.15 hrs	10.00 hrs	15.00 hrs	
44690	Dead	Dead	Dead	Dead
44899	I/T	I/T	I/T	I/T & S
44932	Missing	Missing	Missing	Missing
45096	I/T	Dead	Dead	Dead
45156	S & I/T	S	Missing	I/T
45262	Missing	Missing	Missing	Missing
45287	I/T	Dead	I/T	I/T & S
45350	Dead	Dead	Dead	Dead
45382	Cond	Cond	Cond	Cond
45397	Dead	Dead	Dead	Dead
45447	S	Dead	I/T	Dead
8F 2-8-0s				
48062	I/T	I/T	I/T	Missing
48115	Cond	Cond	Cond	Cond
48167	Dead	Dead	Dead	S & I/T
48191	S	I/T	S & I/T	S
48247	I/T	S & I/T	I/T	S
48257	Dead	S & I/T	Dead	Cond
48278	S	Dead	Dead	Dead
48323	Cond	Cond	Cond	Cond
48340	S & I/T	NF	S	S
48348	S & I/T	I/T	Missing	Dead
48384	Cond	Cond	Cond	Cond
48393	Missing	NF	Dead	I/T
48400	I/T	S	S	I/T & S
48410	Dead	Dead	Dead	Missing
48423	Missing	I/T	Missing	S

EARLY JULY 1968 ROSE GROVE MOTIVE POWER DEPOT LOCO MONITOR (Continued...)

48448	S	I/T	I/T	Missing
48451	Cond	Cond	Cond	Cond
48493	S	Dead	Dead	I/T
48519	S	I/T	Missing	S
48665	S	I/T	I/T	S
48666	I/T	Dead	Dead	S
48715	Dead	Dead	Dead	Dead
48727	Dead	Dead	Dead	Dead
48730	S	I/T	S & I/T	I/T
48752	Missing	Missing	Missing	Missing
48773	S	NF	S & I/T	I/T
2. Foreigners:				
44781 (10A)	–	–	S & I/T	I/T & S
44809 (10A)	Dead	Dead	S & I/T	–
44816 (10D)	Dead	Dead	Dead	–
45025 (10A)	S	–	–	–
45110 (10D)	–	–	S & I/T	–
45394 (10A)	S	S	–	–
45407 (10D)	Dead	NF	S	S
48294 (10D)	S	S	S & I/T	–
48723 (10D)	Dead	NF	–	–
48765 (10D)	–	–	–	S & I/T
75027 (10A)	Dead	Dead	Dead	–

The average motorist of today who drives along the original section of the M65 motorway does so in blissful ignorance that the road's alignment takes it exactly over the site of Rose Grove motive power depot. The narrow ribbon of steel that threads the much simplified station provides no hint of what a vast area on either side was once railway land or the activity that justified it. What follows will attempt to animate the activity implied by the mpd monitor on and around that railway land.

Today, the 5th then at 12.35, 48247 (10F) arrived under cautionary signals with empties from Whitebirk Power Station as 48062 (10F) drew out of the Up Grid on a thirty-two wagon load of coal for Padiham P.S. Too many brakes appeared to have been applied, causing several severe wheelslips and some brief false starts until the 2-8-0 overcame a reduced number of binding brake blocks to resume its short journey.

It returned quite promptly with the guards van only, just as D5238 passed through on unrecorded work. Meanwhile, 45096 (10F) had arrived on shed at 13.00. Sometimes, before complete trains could leave the Up Grid, the front portion was drawn out onto the falling gradient towards West Jc., then propelled in again. This was happening with 48247 and 48666 (both 10F) until they left on another thirty-nine of coal for Padiham at 13.30. Five minutes later, as 48348 (10F) went to pick up its train in the Up Grid, a pair of Type 2s (D7643 and D5238) passed, displaying 8F19 on half the single 8F's load. No. 48348 had hooked onto a big formation of forty-one loaded coal as the 13.40 to Ribble Sdgs, 8P32, and this 900-odd tons of dead weight was laboriously dragged out of the yard, leaving fifteen minutes after schedule. It was closely followed by 48340 (10F) on a train of similar composition, the 13.10 to Wyre Dock, 6P32. On some days only one or the other of these two SX jobs ran.

Lower Rose Grove Lane we got to know well. It led (and still does) from the rear of the shed (site) over the canal into Hollywood Lane and to a second bridge over the Padiham line and canal together. It was quiet there then and apart from occasional windborne traffic sounds from the nearby Burnley–Accrington road, an ideal spot for recording returning trains of empties. Our understanding then that the gradient was 1 in 40 or steeper is all I can certainly say. Very careful scrutiny since of O.S. map contours puts the average at 1 in 35 and experience revealed that an 8F loco would tackle a maximum of thirty wagons plus brake van. Of the two engines that had gone down, it fell to 48666, hauling the full load, to provide an unforgettable spectacle that took up almost fourteen minutes of recording tape as it slogged inexorably towards us at an average, over the 1¼ miles to the junction, of 5½mph. The length of time for

Opposite: A tender-first 8F heaves a rake of empties up the steep section of railway from Padiham Power Station in this essentially Northern view. *E. Bobrowski*

This is Rose Grove Up Grid, the yard for all points south and west. Testifying to the difficulty of moving heavy goods trains out of this location is the 350hp diesel shunter providing assistance to 45388 (10D) on a coal run to Whitebirk on 13 July 1968. More likely to need and justify help when 'only' a class 5 was provided instead of the usual 8F, it would still be down to rail conditions, the load and the driver's assessment, but at least help was always to hand. *V.A. Sidlow*

A general view of Rose Grove mpd on 13 July 1968 with only three weeks to go before closure. *P. Barber*

10F shed yard as it was much closer to the end; the last 'normal' day in fact, 3 August. Some seemingly casual visitors wander around as 45156 (10F) Keeps company with several 'Black 8s' including 48773 and 48423 (both 10F). *Allan Heyes*

which the 8F's blasting exhaust was audible is perhaps better illustrated by the fact that on the resultant soundtrack the chimes of an ice cream van are distantly heard as it made three separate calls in the vicinity! Conditions on the engine are not known, but that all-out effort proved somewhat slower than comparable ascents with several other locomotives on the full load that we witnessed over the next few days.

After that, as if in deference to what had just taken place, a quiet period followed, until teatime, some two hours hence, punctuated only by the arrival of three light engines on shed at intervals up to 17.35. At 17.50 came the arrival of 48400 (10F) with a train of thirty-eight empties from the Blackburn direction. The vast majority of such workings which continued into Yorkshire were steam-hauled to Rose Grove only now, though bankers at the east end of the Copy Pit line continued until the end of steam.

The Wednesday rumour about 45156 (10F) working a Friday evening Stockport relief from Colne to combine with a regular Newquay overnight train happily came to fruition and it was this that occupied us after the stimulating day with freight. Just prior to that rake of empties coming in with 48400, *Ayrshire Yeomanry*, as we all knew it, left Rose Grove shed to work 1T55, the three-coach additional portion. Word had got round quite widely, ensuring we were far from alone on this evening jaunt, reckoned to be the last ever steam passenger working from Colne. It was.

As we journeyed north by dmu, the industrious 48666 was observed hauling the 19.05 Burnley–Moston (nineteen on), my first sighting of the train since the last big changes and the third item of evidence that week, if one counts the relished prospect that evening, that steam was still getting to Manchester in normal service. When faced in the present day with the exposed starkness of Colne's shortened single platform it is difficult to imagine a station that could handle twelve-coach trains if need be, and in which one could almost become lost! Our train of a quarter of that length and weighing only 102 tons net was therefore comfortably accommodated. The occasion itself, rather than expectation of any hard work from 45156, had attracted perhaps as many enthusiasts as West Country-bound holidaymakers. There are, somewhere, two ladies in advanced middle age now, who may well reminisce for reasons of their own, of when, as teenage girls they went away together, maybe for the first time alone, and in a way that from Colne and a host of other places is no longer possible. Less likely to have dwelled in their memory since is how they attracted the attention, intentionally or otherwise, of a couple of my friends who would not normally have occupied a compartment voluntarily with non-enthusiasts for any steam run, let alone a specific 'last'.

BRITISH RAILWAYS STEAM 1968

Moving to the right of the previous view, a Type 2 diesel off recent parcels work and the shedmaster's bay window, also on 3 August. *Allan Heyes*

No. 48773 (10F) banked by a tender-first 45388 (10D) climbs the 1 in 97 to Burnley Barracks with 8P21, the 10.50 Burnley Central–Wyre Dock, on 29 July 1968. *I.C. Simpson*

Many of the coal trains starting from or running westwards through Rose Grove were Fylde-bound, either for export or for the industrial Wyre Dock area itself. No. 48393 (10F) heads through Kirkham for this purpose on 31 July 1968. *P. Barber*

On the evening of 5 July, 45156 (10F) draws the three coaches to form 1T55, the 19.30 Colne–Stockport holiday portion, into the station before running round the ECS to work the train into what by then was really diesel territory. *P. Barber*

For an appreciation of Colne station itself in those days, we see also 44899 (10F) prior to departure with 3P20, the evening parcels train to Preston, on 10 June 1968. *I.C. Simpson*

What those girls definitely never knew were my own thoughts, as I stood at a nearby corridor window, on how easily my friends had been distracted from the evening's original aim and purpose. Whatever proportion of their attention remained with the steam, it was their choice and so long as the transistor radio didn't interfere with my recordings, not my business. The radio, 'pirate' or otherwise, was no trouble and I had more of a job trying to suppress the 'Skelton Whine's' high-pitched and piercing tones. On a three-coach train there wasn't much escape, but I exaggerate the nuisance somewhat!

A very smart-looking 45156 set off one minute late at 19.31. We made booked calls at Nelson and Burnley Central, sporadic, but at times lively progress being made with our little train via the chain of industrial towns towards Blackburn. Five minutes were dropped to passing Accrington through signal checks. Recording of the second recovery, from Huncoat 'Brick', erased 'Lazy Sunday' by the Small Faces from my ever transitory 'collection' of current chart favourites. Continually superseded by my fast-growing sound library of the times, this particular song had just had its day as a hit anyway.

Into the dip through and beyond Church & Oswaldtwistle a very energetic burst from our 5MT whipped the featherweight formation up to 67mph through Rishton station, and this after a mile uphill at 1 in 132. Inexplicably I did not tape this sprightly rush, which helped to recoup a bit of time, despite a further signal stop approaching Blackburn. The section on to Bolton, after our unusual non-stop progress through the station, three minutes late, was completed smartly in just under twenty minutes. No. 45156 scampered up the bank through Darwen with speed in the unheard of upper 40s, still 44 by Spring Vale, but dropping 10mph on this through the tunnel. Early speeding down the other side was now inhibited by the Fast lines to Entwistle being closed, but after threading the curved Slow, our driver permitted the rate to reach 69mph by Bromley Cross and we stopped at Bolton just over three minutes before the scheduled passing time of 20.33. The few dmus that stopped only at Darwen were currently allowed three minutes longer than we'd taken, but I suspect that this praiseworthy gain may have been to facilitate a quick water stop. I didn't, however, verify this in my notes. No opportunity to take

More than halfway through its summer evening meander, 45156 (10F) calls at Bury Knowsley Street with the Colne–Stockport special portion for Newquay on 5 July 1968. *Ray Farrell/M.L.S. collection*

water existed in the schedule, but we stood on the through line for nine minutes.

Whatever the reason, further delays built up and a full recovery was put well out of reach. In and around Bury (two-minute stop booked) twelve more minutes were lost with 1T55 stationary before and after the station. Accelerating to 42mph through the summer evening upgrade to Broadfield, the relief soon negotiated Castleton curve, now twenty-three minutes in arrears. Despite running up to 72mph passing Moston, a tight allowance and brief stop at Newton Heath meant we were twenty-seven late by Thorpes Bridge Jc. Soon after, the train turned sharp left over 'India Rubber Jc' and out towards Droylsden, where we took the soon-to-be closed connection up 1 in 88 to Ashton Moss Jc. Thereafter, with not the swiftest descent I'd known (53mph max.) to Heaton Norris Jc. and a brief stop on the huge viaduct approaching Stockport, 1T55 terminated twenty-nine minutes late at 21.50. The Newquay overnight train with the three coaches added should have left nine minutes before our arrival.

Such a run as we'd had, only one month before steam finished completely, was really looked upon as something plucked out of the impossible; a real bonus. I'd enjoyed it very much, but at Stockport 'had quite a bit of trouble'. This would have been over tickets, which south of Bolton I had not held. Nobody pre-booked tickets for a journey that was not certain to take place, and that on 1T55 was not a certainty when I'd left Bolton that morning. The details are long forgotten, but as B.R. had elected, just a week earlier, to discontinue the only direct (22.13) Stockport–Bolton train of the day, I caught a similarly timed one to Piccadilly with Keith, then we 'bussed it' home, while Paul stayed at Pete's in Gorton.

Saturday, 6 July

Mysteriously unwell for much of Saturday, I didn't stir from the house until 18.00, but intentions to make an evening of the 20.50 Preston–Blackpool were thwarted by the thirty-five-minute late running of our connecting train from Bolton. The steam would need to be ten late or more from Preston or we wouldn't have made it, so doubtless with a derogatory 'This is B.R. '68' from Keith, the idea was abandoned. Another possible relevancy was that 'they are shutting down again', a morsel of information from my all too cramped diary that had to do with the guards' dispute I'm sure, and meant a late Saturday night to Monday morning complete stoppage. As we mulled these things and more over on the platform, faint indications of growing interest in, or curiosity regarding, industrial steam manifested themselves in an (unsuccessful) attempt to find the telephone number of Ifton Colliery, 'near Gobowen'. Far too late for relief to play a part, it was found that the 20.50 had been diesel-hauled that night!

Saturday's Colne Holiday specials, all diesel, as previously mentioned, were actually only one train down on 1967's four loco-hauled trains serving Blackpool, Morecambe and Llandudno (thirty coaches in total), an Earby–Liverpool dmu plus a Colne–Caernarvon with a bus connection to Butlins (Pwllheli).

Sunday, 7 and Monday, 8 July

On the quite warm fourth Sunday after Trinity but with late evening rain, the 1956 film *1984* was on TV, probably for the first time. I don't seem to have made contact with the railway, but another week's holiday lay ahead. Although the firing up on Monday the 8th at Rose Grove of three engines for later service and the lower active and 'in steam' total from the depot monitor indicates a slower build up to full freight operation locally, the much higher incidence of diesels on through workings kept the main line busy enough but knocked the steam percentage somewhat, not helped by a 'Brush 4'-hauled day excursion. Judging from the reporting numbers of those diesel-hauled freights, which did not reappear later in the week, they were assorted coal runs from Yorkshire weekend pit production, probably a reaction to the weekend 'shutting down', referred to earlier.

Accompanied today (8 July) by a younger Paul, from the church choir, whose spotting interest had revived more broadly in that final year, we began to take in the action after the 10.00 depot visit. Unlike the Friday visit, I will not relate every movement in that respect. Busy engine of the day – one always seemed to create such an impression that was obviously influenced by what was actually seen – fell to 48191 (10F), which had gone west on forty-two coal (probably to Whitebirk P.S.) and returned one and a quarter hours later with fifty-four empties. In drawing out of the Up Grid, such a load best demonstrated how the going got even tougher approaching the neck, then very suddenly much easier the moment that even a small part of the train nosed into the downgrade.

Meanwhile, just before 48191 got back, the use of two Type 2s (D7543 and D5286) on a Padiham job with forty loaded was an unexpected disappointment. The 'Brush 4'-hauled day excursion was an eight-coach Colne–Blackpool, 1L00, which ran also on Thursday of that week (and from Skipton on Tuesday and Wednesday as 1L05). Altogether, between 11.00 and 15.05, a total of eighteen freights or pools runs (empty coal) negotiated the layout at Rose Grove West, one could almost say in two rushes, as the seventy-five minutes up to 12.35 when the Padiham Type 2s left were devoid of anything but dmus. In the closing hour and a half of the second busier period, engine of the day, 48191, brought fifty-nine empties back from Padiham in two almost equal hauls. Six other 8Fs had shared the day's steam freight up to 16.27 when we left, and five other locos assorted LE movements. I'd accumulated another twelve minutes or so of recordings, all well worth retaining, even if nothing was specially outstanding, but at places such as Rose Grove 'good' became 'normal' in time and 'outstanding' all the more elusive.

I had an evening in Bolton East box to follow today's trip, with three signalmen, Bob Middlebrook, John Winnard and Sam Thomasson, but Sam was on the book. On certain occasions in 1968 when there as a visitor, they'd let the lad go home early and I'd keep the register, as of old. When given this opportunity for a short turn, the lad would estimate how many lines were needed for the traffic to come and sign off as if it were 22.00 to make it appear that all the entries were his. This sort of fiddle or agreement between regular men was as old as the system. When someone stayed on by arrangement for another who would be late, the entries were sometimes written onto a separate piece of paper, to be copied up in the 'correct' handwriting later, but I'm not citing Bolton East on that one. It was the sort of dodge that had, over the years, been exposed at more than one accident enquiry and even been instrumental in the cause. If I ever thought to ask the men at East what the inspector would say if he saw a substantial amount of entirely different handwriting (mine) that had not signed in or out, they probably pooh-poohed it as unlikely. It was a risk they took and another measure of friendliness to a past, even fleeting, employee. That evening of 8 July came as a first ever without any steam. Traffic seemed normal, except for the absence of the later Burnley–Moston, hence the realisation of this unfortunate circumstance.

Tuesday, 9 July

In the same interval as Monday (11.00-15.05), the sum of Tuesday's goods train workings at Rose Grove fell well short at 'only' ten. This almost matched that of the coming Friday, 12 July, but first we are concerned with the 9th. Machine of the day, 48448 (10J) was not the first actively seen, but rather yesterday's 'title-holder', 48191 (10F), which took twenty-four coal westward at 11.01 and didn't reappear during the slightly extended session that Paul (the elder) and I enjoyed. No. 48448 did have the day's only loaded Padiham train we saw, just before midday. The 2-8-0, restarting with some of the twenty-right wagons' brakes pinned down, would, not untypically, get under way with three or four evenly spaced exhaust beats, only for the next to be oddly suspended, held back by the variable drag of those crude brakes, with the regulator still open. Two pairs of Type 2s on eastbound pools and westbound loaded went by before 48448 reappeared on twenty-eight empty vessels (which did make the most noise) at 12.45, whistling furiously for the junction approach signal that I stood just beneath. The 'peg' came off and obviated a stand with the train still on the 1 in 35.

No. 48773 (10F) I hadn't seen move since it had forsaken the closed depot at Bolton, but that afternoon it left ON

A good twelve hours earlier in the day than any of our 1968 Hoghton trips, but representing just what we went for, 48410 (10F) comes through on 18 April 1968 with the 06.53 Farington–Healey Mills coal empties. *R. Weisham*

TIME hauling the 13.10 Rose Grove–Wyre Dock (34). As it reversed uphill into the Up Grid earlier I remember thinking how oddly drawn out its beats were, just in that LE move. With an ear never more finely tuned to the idiosyncrasies of loco exhausts, it wasn't imagination; maybe a hint of priming, but without any 'whoofliness'. After another shorter run of empties from Padiham, 48448 was off to Whitebirk with twenty-one of coal.

'Black 5s' have hardly figured in these traffic descriptions. Clearly in the great minority on Rose Grove's heaviest duties, they were (though I didn't see any thus engaged) occasionally used on coal trains nevertheless. Their availability/requirement amongst the resident 5MTs in our monitor was 33.3% compared with 53½% in the 2-8-0s, indicating less work for them in proportion to numbers allocated. These figures presume 44932, 45262 and 48752 to be out of the running, as suggested earlier. Booked work for them at this time, according to Dent was practically zero, so it would appear they relied on special and incidental work. Two or sometimes three were seen arriving on shed after dinnertime. I'd caught 45287 (10F) coupled to a Type 4 at Blackburn, LEs, and 44899 (10F) ECS in Accrington C.S. that morning and now, 16.00, 45447 (10F) arrived at the Grid on six empty ballast wagons. That concluded the active steam at Rose Grove on the 9th until we left on the 16.57.

The omission in Dent of any Padiham activity whatsoever detracted much potential from Rose Grove for the prospective visiting enthusiast assessing it from that work. From this it can be deduced that such supplies of coal were not run to any fixed times (an aspect that wouldn't necessarily be obvious in practice), so their assumed 'as required' status exempted them from inclusion, to the same effect as a holiday brochure omitting a third (or more) of a resort's attractions!

From the train to Blackburn, 48448's fifth impression on the day, i.e. its return from Whitebirk with a brake van was the last steam observed until we'd settled at what constituted a sensible diversion by bus on the way home – Hoghton. I'd not been back since a marvellous day of many football specials in late January 1967. Expectations now were much more subdued and success came with maybe only one steam-hauled ascent of the 1 in 99/100. Three evenings there and a fourth intended up to the end of steam began with this extension to 9 July. There were only two eastbound goods trains at best after tea that still held out against modern power, the 18.45 Preston–Healey Mills SX, 7N99, and what we knew as Farington–Carlton (21.45 Preston–Rose Grove SX, 7N68 in Dent), but the latter was only seen if early because of the business of being able to get home.

The usually 'Black 5'-worked Darwen–Heysham empty tanks, seen that busy weekday evening of 9 July at Hoghton, is also seen here passing Lancaster Castle behind 45435 (10A) on 20 April with the Saturday (afternoon) version. *T. Heavyside*

The frequency of general non-passenger traffic, both to and from Blackburn, impressed me on 9 July. Seven freights, two parcels and two light engines appeared in fifty-four minutes after 18.40. Considerably lengthier periods struggled to nearly equal this on subsequent occasions. 7N99 tonight was near to time, producing 48773's (10F) return, and it scampered through at a business-like rate with thirty-four on. Breaking up the run of diesel-worked goods that followed in quick succession was Darwen–Heysham tanks on one of its nights for running. No. 44809 (10A), one of the foreigners present on 10F that morning, handled the train. As this job (nor its Up working) was not incorporated in Dent, and as this was only my second sighting of the empty tanks, whether or not 10F was supposed to use a resident engine is unclear. Maybe it was one of those few 5MT turns.

An unexpected lift by car enabled on this occasion an earlier return to Blackburn, where 45110 (10D) was seen arriving punctually at 20.30 on the 19.14 Colne–Preston parcels, a daily working, 3P20; part of a Lostock Hall diagram that seems to have been the last line work for an Ivatt 4 until their late spring demise. The rest of the cycle consisted of the 02.50 Preston–Colne parcels and mails SX, 3P00 (arrive 05.05) and the 08.15 Rose Grove–Colne empty vans SX, 3P11 (arrive 08.36). The 02.50 ex Preston left from E.L., except on Mondays and in each case had provision to stop at Todd Lane Jc. to set down railway staff. On 9 July, after finishing at Colne with 3P11, 45110 had reached 10F LE at 11.01, where it rested until leaving to take up 3P20 again. This train was given nearly an hour at Blackburn for traffic purposes and we watched a shunt or two until leaving on the 20.55 unit home.

This second week of Bolton Holidays proved warmer locally, if not particularly sunny. Sunday had been the best, despite clouding later to eventual rain. The generally, if not completely, fine week to follow made for more pleasant days out on the scene, but there existed another cause to give thanks for a time without rain.

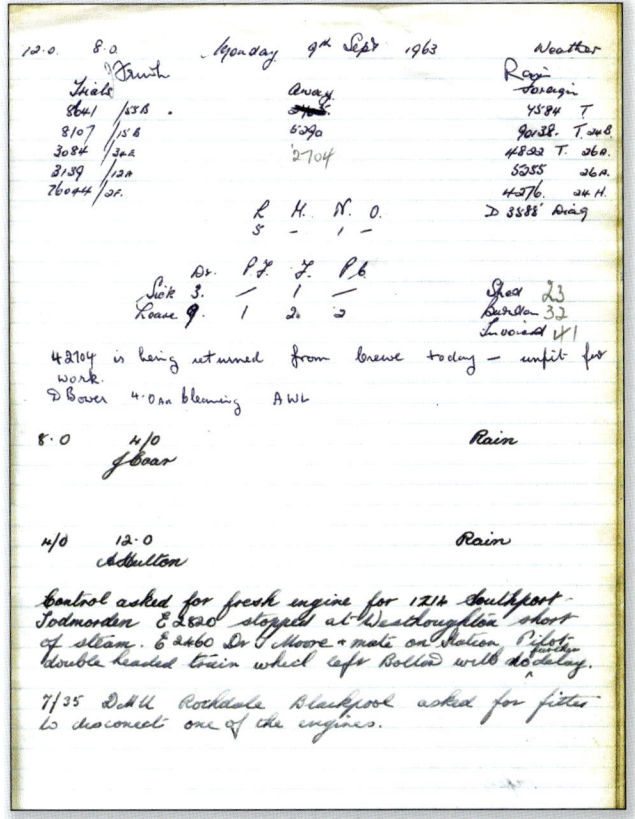

Survivors No. 5 – All of the paperwork rescued from the 9K scrap wagon predates 1968. Hard put to choose an extract from the varied documents acquired, this page from the Running Shed Foreman's logbook will suffice. Bearing the date of the big shed code revisions (9 September 1963), it records Horwich Works locos on trial ex works, home engines missing and non-Bolton visiting in traffic as well as out of course incidents, loco coal supplies and men sick or on leave.

Wednesday, 10 and Thursday, 11 July

The locomotive records from Bolton mpd were being dumped in a 16-ton coal wagon for disposal in a way that would ensure the survival of none. By Wednesday morning, 10 July, everything that was going seemed to be in there and the wagon stood isolated around the west side of the building. What's more, it hadn't got wet. Paul and I spent all that day and part of Thursday too, sifting (if that's the right word) through books and papers, cards and folders that lay feet deep therein, trying to select the most interesting and 'valuable' stuff to rescue. Either by 1968 the records had dried up or we didn't take them, everything being from 1967 and up to ten years before that – fascinating stuff!

It was purely coincidental that my parents went on holiday a few hours before I began carting it home, otherwise opposition to having it in the house may have arrived much sooner than would be the case. At the time I had no thoughts whatsoever of using the records to form the basis of or to enhance any written work. That would come later, much later in final form, but 1968, formerly known as 'Volume 4' and rewritten here on the eve of the fiftieth anniversary, does not benefit from those internal 9K records. Inevitably, a vast amount of that coal wagon's contents did go up in smoke, literally or otherwise, but that couldn't be helped.

Although I took notes during another East Jc. box evening on the 11th, it was largely a social visit, with much hilarity too, it is recorded. The later Burnley–Moston saved an otherwise steamless period, 48167 (10F) conveying 36=48 at 21.00. Substantial loadings on either train were a rarity now, and maybe I should have been out somewhere for that one, but the decent weight behind the tender, important to any such jaunt, was one thing that couldn't be found out in advance. After 10pm, the Bolton four met and conversed further into the night.

Friday, 12 July

Having noticed 48393 (10F) shunting at Whitebirk P.S. whilst Paul and I passed on the 08.56 ex Bolton, we made an unauthorised break of journey (the rule on day returns then) at the next station, marginally over Rishton's mini summit, to catch the 8F's anticipated return to Rose Grove. For heavy trains it could be quite a slog from as far back as Mill Hill (even if one discounts Hoghton bank as a separate obstacle) on an average of about 1 in 115, though the grade did ease for half a mile to the top. In the absence of a recording, and in fact any recollection of the half hour spent at Rishton, I must conclude that 48393 had had steam shut off by the time it passed through at 10.03, despite hauling a lengthy trail of fifty-seven empties. This prelude to my last Rose Grove trip (12 July) was clearly a revision in such traffic since May as Whitebirk was shown only as doing business with Bickershaw colliery. Busy engine of the day went a bit less convincingly to the one we'd just seen. In celebration of the 'steamified' six hours that followed our arrival at Rose Grove, just three weeks before the end, I set out the sum total of loco movements seen on that day (overleaf).

Positively identified for the only time, 8P21 was conveying the largest capacity 24-ton coal wagons. Omitted from my original list (and therefore above) is the return (LE no doubt) of 48393 from Padiham, probably because we'd shifted position slightly, but it was 48730's thirty empties from the same point that easily stole the show that morning. Brought almost to a stand approaching Rose Grove West Jc., the driver pulled tentatively away for a short distance, then gave his 8F the lot. Wholesome blasting echoes reverberated as every ounce of the 2-8-0's tractive effort went into that recovery as steel tyre unfalteringly gripped steel rail.

The next two 8Fs remained anonymous as we at that time were walking along the canal to Hapton for a change of view and the towpath deviated occasionally up to 400 yards or so from the line. It was at Hapton that 75027 passed Paul and I, en route LE to Carnforth. Upon

No. 45386 (10D) near Hapton, to which point we perambulated on 12 July. The train, however, is the evening Colne–Preston parcels on 13 June 1968. *I.C. Simpson*

D398	8M80–Unidentified westbound coal	10.40
48773 (10F)	10.50 Burnley–Wyre Dock (27) SX, 8P21	11.06
48730 (10F)	Coal to Padiham P.S. (30)	11.12
D6945	7M81–Unidentified westbound coal	11.13
45073 (10D)	Light engine arrive mpd	11.20
48400 (10F)	Light engine arrive mpd	11.25
48393 (10F)	Coal to Padiham P.S.	11.47
48730 (10F)	Empties from Padiham P.S. (30)	12.16
8F (unid.)	Empties from Blackburn direction	12.30
8F (unid.)	Coal westbound	12.41
75027 (10A)	LE Rose Grove to Carnforth	13.12
D7639	LE towards Blackburn	13.17
D5250	LE towards Blackburn	13.17
44781 (10A)	Empties from Blackburn direction (45)	13.31
48493 (10F)	13.10 Rose Grove–Wyre Dock (42)	13.33
D7639	LEs from Blackburn direction	14.06
D5250	LEs from Blackburn direction	14.06
48393 (10F)	13.40 Rose Grove–Ribble (34) SX, 8P32	14.35
48730 (10F)	Westbound freight/coal? (28)	14.58
45287 (10F)	Light engine arrive mpd	14.59
45156 (10F)	Unrecorded movement	
48765 (10D)	Westbound coal etc. (35)	15.44
44899 (10F)	Light engine arrive mpd	15.48
48773 (10F)	Eastbound empties (seen at Huncoat)	16.35

No. 45411 (9D) trundles through Huncoat with a goods in the Blackburn direction on 7 May 1968. Subtitled 'The Changing Face of Railway Fencing', the photo also illustrates what was adequate in that field back in steam days. The patched up example above the banking is hardly inviolate and more a polite reminder not to transgress, than the formidable uniform barriers of the present age. *T. Heavyside*

checking, I was surprised to find the route via Preston the shortest of the three options and, of course, the only one to avoid a reversal. No. 75027's repeated presence, unfired on 10F during other recent visits, could be explained by Skipton (and therefore the works at Swinden) Holidays, hence no loco for the Grassington branch being required.

Dmus to Blackburn were half-hourly at that time of day and with Hoghton in mind and the possibility of a punctual 18.45 Preston–Healey Mills there, we could probably have hung on longer at Rose Grove than the 16.27. Still, we caught that unit, but after crossing 48773 (10F) at Huncoat on eastbound empties the steam dried up and our new destination (in stark contrast to the previous one) resolutely maintained an all-diesel programme until well into the evening. Although a Friday, no 4P20 (Heysham–Darwen tanks) appeared. This was later in the railway press attributed to holidays that, for the first time ever, had turned from furthering the utilisation of steam beyond that which B.R. in latter years preferred, to perhaps impeding it overall, simply by being virtually absent from seasonal passenger work. In previous years we wouldn't have noticed the 'missing' goods work!

After the 17.20 bus to Hoghton and walking about a mile down the line towards Preston on an evening still quite busy with goods and parcels trains (eight in one and a half hours), we'd retraced our steps and were reluctantly heading for the bus stop when the eastbound pegs came off again, enticing us back. In no time, 48493 (10F) was there, asserting itself on the scene, slamming through on a mixed forty-two wagon goods, under the A675 bridge and away, impossible for even the most disinterested to ignore. For a minute or two the train had been everything; immediate, commanding; and now, as the sounds of it died away and the thick grey smokescreen slowly cleared, still exhilarated by such a spectacle out of nothing, we caught the same bus back, but with the evening now retrieved from failure. Correctly, I think, I identified that last one as Preston–Healey Mills, about an hour and a quarter late.

No. 48727 (10F) has just left the W.C.M.L. at Farington Curve Jc. to climb over it and take the Blackburn line on 1 August 1968 with a van train, which is probably the evening Preston–Healey Mills. *Peter Reeves/M.L.S. collection*

We somehow obtained a 'lift' on the 21.03 Burnley–Manchester parcels, formed (officially) of an ordinary dmu, nonstop to Bolton, and thereby gained more than half an hour on the next authorised service train, finding upon arrival the 20.55 Club meeting still in swing at Trinity Street. Burnley–Moston, seen very late at Blackburn behind 48167 (10F) on an unrecorded load, did not reappear. When the gathering dispersed I walked home with Hilary to where she turned off, adapting more by then, I hope, to her presence in a male-dominated scene. It concluded what had been considered 'a great day', but it also marked the end of my holiday as such. Problems of how to fit what we wanted to do into the limited free time during those three remaining weeks of steam would vacillate with those of there not being enough to fill the free time we did have! A mismatch between the two, at weekends particularly, was more noticeable than ever now.

Saturday, 13 July

Saturday's trip, if it can be called that, was a long drawn-out affair for few, even questionable, rewards, at least on the steam front. Starting late, and alone, I let Waltons Sidings set the scene for Colne–Red Bank vans, 3J83. Waiting for it in the signal box, I wouldn't think I'd have been much company alone for Mr Carroll, who was on late turn, without turning the conversation away from politics, but as usual it's all forgotten. No. 44781 (10A) had been in steam on Rose Grove the previous afternoon and this they'd rostered for 3J83, but when I took up position somewhere in the steep cutting, a very lacklustre exit from Sough tunnel resulted. A flat and expressionless commentary on the tape reflected the impression it made.

Whilst back at Bolton after 16.30 I saw the 'Black 5' returning LE up the bank, and D372 off an ECS train to Accrington, seen earlier, was correspondingly sent south again to (presumably) Newton Heath, as if each area had rejected the motive power type as not 'right' for it, which was partly true. With proper integration both locos could

Nearly six months after the end of steam, a large group, unchanged in character, await *Flying Scotsman* to back onto its stock at St Pancras on 22 February 1969. By then it was the only steam locomotive permitted to run on B.R. Centre stage, on the right is Mr D.T.J. Rollason engaged in conversation. *S.A. Leyland*

have been retained until a suitable job enabled them to work back more profitably, but there was nowhere for steam to stay in Manchester now. This turned out to be the last time I saw Colne–Red Bank, a familiar Saturday sight for almost two years, hauled by steam.

I discovered that my friends, out earlier than I, had been unable to alight (as intended) at Entwistle as they'd held day return tickets to some point further north, from which they were returning. This thing about day returns seems barely credible now, but instances contained herein of them being a handicap to enthusiasts who needed flexibility are just as they happened. At staffed stations – just about everywhere – there would be a challenge at least, if not excess to pay, for contravening the rules that applied to such tickets, yet Paul and I had got away with it at Rishton (though not gone off the platform) only the day before. B.R's. view was that because they were cheaper, break of journey was not permitted.

Very many, ourselves included, congregated gradually at Preston much earlier than necessary for the 20.50, as if delegates attending a sort of social convention. Large 20.55 Club representation, many smaller groups and individuals flocked and circulated like satellites around 'queen bee' of such occasions, 'Big Noise', 'The Wellington Mouth', Mr D.T.J. Rollason, who always seemed to be holding forth on some railway-related topic with an amused and enraptured audience!

The three 'Black 5s' I saw on that Saturday evening fell into as many categories of condition: No. 44761 (ex 10D) condemned and currently dumped at Farington Jc., 44816 (10D), a known good engine to heat sleeping cars, and 45305 (10D), an unknown force, personally, for the 20.50 Preston–Blackpool, which made its appearance in the station LE at 20.13. The train itself was running a little late. Three weeks without a 20.50 run seemed a long time.

Today, with six coaches only on the Blackpool portion, it departed eight minutes in arrears and never too comfortably in sight of the 21.35 train back from South station, and progressively less so the nearer we got to the coast. Had the stops not been so exceptionally brief, the outcome would have been rather different. No. 45305 left Preston solidly enough, but couldn't get up to much on the Blackpool road, a mere 55mph at Spen Lane being very poor. We observed the now debatable Kirkham call, and a cursory call it was – a quarter of a minute! Down to Moss Side not even 60mph could be claimed, but this seemed much more like driver reluctance to run. 1P58 had dropped to being thirteen minutes late away from Lytham, so our 'connection' at South was on a knife edge already.

It was no surprise to find speeds on the two remaining sections a good 10mph less than what could be achieved and at St Annes several timorous souls abandoned steam haulage to ensure catching the unit back to Preston. I don't suppose that any of the majority that stayed the course considered that those others may have had further connections to make at Preston and therefore couldn't fall back on the later train from North (if necessary). It was a familiar voice from a window in my coach that openly shamed them as 45305 pulled out, shouting 'Where's your faith in steam then?', 'Get your dmu back!' and finally 'Cowards!'. In truth we were staring a negative connection in the face because 45305 (despite the liveliest start so far) couldn't better 44 through Squires Gate, but approaching Blackpool South at 21.37, the 21.35 dmu was still in! On the incoming train there was a hand on every door handle and it looked as if we'd make it. I had the presence of mind to turn on my tape recorder to capture what looked like being a repeat of the 22 June riot in identical circumstances, but as we drew into the platform itself the unit was whistled out. 'Come on, dive off!' I ejaculated in reaction. And we did, but the 21.35 had just begun to move. A sudden and rather frightening surge of bodies across the platform's width and onto the departing 'cart' was sufficient to have it stopped and all boarded safely in the end.

The staff at South couldn't have turned it into more of a drama if they'd tried. After the 22 June 'taster' I'm surprised that a local instruction hadn't been issued to prevent a reoccurrence. If the unit's first start-up, three minutes late, wasn't just the time it happened to leave, but a panic measure by the staff upon seeing the danger signs, then it was seconds too late. The boisterous mood of all participants subsided only a little on the journey back, not as a celebration of the steam run's quality, which was nowhere near the best, but rather successfully completing it against the odds and bringing off the stunt at Blackpool South, which, it has to be confessed, was purely a bi-product of the mid-1968 steam-chasing scene.

Sunday, 14 to Tuesday, 16 July

Posted at St Asaph, Flintshire, on 31 May was the final (June) B.T.E.G. bulletin that I received. Advertised amongst others was the Guild's 'LAST STEAM TOUR' to run on 13 July, and interestingly it incorporated Bolton, Patricroft and Newton Heath depots as if they were expected to be open then. The renewal form enclosed with the bulletin I did not respond to, thereby ending just over four years' membership of a society that had provided a new dimension to my railway interest and many unique memories, too. To my shame I didn't even return the form with a negative answer. Deliberate spotting had really ended for me in 1966 and there remained no need now to keep abreast of locomotive transfers and withdrawals.

The success of that last 'steam tour' (coach tour to steam sheds) depended upon a quick response from members and there may have been a problem obtaining permits for half of the advertised depots that would, in the interim, be closed to steam or completely. On the other hand, maybe the permit issuing department would be no more aware of this than the Guild had been at the end of May, and who would be present to refuse entry to a closed shed, especially to a club whose leaders were so adept at achieving their aims when authority did challenge? I can't say whether or not the tour did materialise, but I am far from alone in holding dear the memories of days and weekends spent on B.T.E.G. trips tramping around depots in rather more fruitful times than 1968. Maybe the membership number of others too lives on in a PIN?

I was down at 9K that afternoon of the intended tour. The last two locos to leave for a brief reprieve, 44888 and 45260 (to Lostock Hall), had gone, leaving the lifeless contents to dwindle slowly as engines were purchased and despatched for cutting up.

Contrasts in the loadings on contrasting trains just then are illustrated by that Sunday's fourteen-coach Up 'Royal Scot' (diverted via Hellifield and Bolton) and a mere five wagons on the second Burnley–Moston the night after, 15 July. I saw the latter at Trinity Street only following a tip from Keith that 48423 (10F) was booked, but returned disappointed at the load and correspondingly little sound from the 2-8-0. Moaning about light loads may appear ungrateful, seeing as the train was still steam-powered, which was the important thing, after all, but loads that brought out the elemental aspects of steam locomotion more forcibly were naturally preferred.

The next night I didn't venture out, dividing my time between an examination of some of the recently acquired shed records and Hayley Mills in *Tiger Bay* on television, a film I've never seen since. I much preferred Miss Mills in a cleverly thought out film, *The Parent Trap*, when, at a similar age I nursed a considerable crush on Mr Mills' daughter that led to seeing her on two consecutive nights at a Bolton cinema in late 1961, an effect not engendered only three months earlier in the utterly captivating (for other reasons) *Whistle Down the Wind*, filmed the same year, too; but where do railways themselves come into this, beyond the geographical locale of the latter's film around Blackburn and Burnley near coinciding with where we spent time in July 1968? They don't.

Wednesday, 17 July

An after-work trip to Hoghton by the Bolton four on 17 July turned out to be the first of two evenings unintentionally spent at Blackburn instead. Tonight, approaching our intended destination came the deflating experience of

Give or take a day, there were two weeks to go and, to borrow a repeated line from David McWilliams' rather mesmerising, but wholly unsuccessful single record of the times, 'The Days of Pearly Spencer', 'The race is almost run'. Whether one thinks of this as our race around the North-west or that between the two chief motive power types that this book deals with, it is apt enough. Not for the first time on 17 July did we change direction by bus to chase a narrowly missed goods train, and be rewarded for it. In this instance, 48665 (10F) was still going about its business, as seen here at Blackburn with Preston–Healey Mills.
V.A. Sidlow

having to watch steam ascending the bank whilst we were still on the bus! We caught the next one back, still unsure of what had been so narrowly missed. Though this was just bad luck, having just one reliable steam objective there served as a reminder of how the net was closing and of how few straws there were left to clutch at. Of several clear recollections from that trip is one of Vern sharing with us the best contemporary music on his tape recorder as we waited at the bus stop; not just chart – I was currently 'sold' on Donovan's 'Hurdy Gurdy Man' – but something new to me, Blues, unaware that derivations of that and other material with less easily defined roots would become a major post-steam era interest of mine. During that early evening bus ride back into Blackburn, girls were emerging onto the streets in light summer dresses as if to deliberately tug against the primary occupation of we four, whilst resistance to the alternative was lowered by recent misfortune.

However, emerging from that setback, we were back smartly enough to find the train missed at Hoghton still going about its business and Preston–Healey Mills didn't leave until 20.23 behind 48665 (10F), hauling forty-six vehicles. Only Vern and I stayed on for the duration that evening. Colne–Preston parcels had arrived just before the goods train's departure, on time with 45388 (10D), and more than an hour later 48775 (10F) passed through hauling Farington–Carlton (forty-eight on), so something could have been salvaged from our original and preferred location and it may well have been tonight's later sighting that tempted us to hang on at Hoghton at a later date. Various diesel workings that would have been seen there, had we stayed on the 17th, were interspersed with the steam noted at Blackburn.

Another information source regarding anything special going on was, of course, other enthusiasts, met casually in the course of going after steam. Enough seeds were sown that evening at Blackburn to spark off an 'extensive'

series of phone calls to certain railway installations, but the responses to those calls regarding rumours for the 18th survive only in half-intelligible jottings and doodles in my 1968 N.U.R. diary.

Believed to be steam-worked were the 20.50 Preston–Blackpool on that weekday evening and a Morecambe–Barrow (or vice versa) out and back special – both very tantalising attractions for the period. Despite what appear to have been 'cast iron' certainties, I made no effort to cover either, but for the Barrow we seemed to be short of any timings and this was probably the deciding factor, as well as the level of faith in it actually happening. It was also a working day for me. Among those aforementioned jottings is '4874' and six exclamation marks in splendid isolation, its meaning long forgotten. Nearly forty-nine years later its exact significance and reason for it being so forcefully applied to the paper was made clear in finding a published reference to the Barrow–Morecambe special. That was the engine! A subsequent phone call had obviously revealed this and the frustration at missing it or having to miss it was worked off in those many exclamation marks. Not chancing the 20.50 from Preston either, I dutifully appeared at choir practice and afterwards helped Paul to carry the 9K working board home. As he also hadn't attempted to capitalise on the supposed extra class 1 steam work it suggests a lack of conviction.

Thursday, 18 and Friday, 19 July

More dialling on the 18th to Lostock Hall and Rose Grove confirmed an unambiguous attraction for Friday night, the 19th, which was acted upon and the much more orderly notes in that same diary applying to that date were clearly copied from the S.T.N. Much less well documented than Colne's steam-hauled holiday relief on 5 July was the one from Accrington very late on the 19th

The blame, or responsibility, for not getting to see the important special passenger working of 18 July lies with the author, though mitigating circumstances did apply: Captured by photographer Ian Simpson, and far less intentionally by the two elderly strollers, is 44874 (10A) on the outward leg, leaving Grange-over-Sands. Even today that part of the 'prom' is quieter than the length west of the station. *I.C. Simpson*

that employed the same loco in 45156 (10F), again to Stockport, but this time its train was to be attached to the overnight Euston. 1H11 didn't begin its journey until 23.35 and we went directly for it without any earlier side trip. Another (19.10) Accrington–Stockport, 1H09, I'd deleted from my list for a reason not now known, but it was never earmarked for steam. Our five-coach train did have an enthusiast following, but on a modest scale on account, I suppose, of its nocturnal nature. Reasons for the fifteen-minute late start are not recalled, but we made up all of the arrears, chiefly between Blackburn and Bolton and in the concluding stage after Denton Jc.

A sedate beginning nevertheless recovered a little time to the Blackburn stop, just after midnight, but the best work followed. On the climb to Waltons Sidings, a steady 39mph on the 1 in 101 to Hoddlesden Jc. produced a lively, crackling exhaust, though with only 170 tons net this was far from optimum 'Black 5' performance; not that we'd gone with that expectation. Over the various steeper grades thereafter, deceleration came very gradually and it looked as if the former *Ayrshire Yeomanry* wasn't going to dip below 30, but the final 1 in 69 into what would have been daylight at Sough's southern portal claimed a 29mph minimum. A speed of 64mph just after Bromley Cross preceded our stop at Trinity Street in a smart twenty-three minutes and a bit, now only six late.

I decided to stay on to the finish, despite being invalid south of Bolton, in the hope of obtaining a lift back on the footplate as no steam would be tolerated at Stockport for long after arrival. Progress on to Manchester Victoria via Pendleton Broad Street was largely pedestrian to suit the schedule between these points, then some slipping interfered with 1H11's climb to Miles Platting, but later 18mph proved a steady rate. As the hour reached one in the morning, 45156 plugged up the 1 in 88 connection to Ashton Moss Jc. in the low 30s. Then, after a sedate run down through Denton, which the driver perceptively knew would bring us in on time, it was all over and

In no less exalted position than on the footplate was friend and colleague to this day, Harvey Scowcroft who took this view from the fireman's side whilst crossing Arnside viaduct, heading towards Carnforth. Only in 2017 did I discover the reason for this ten-coach excursion – retired railwaymen having a day out in Morecambe. The circumstances of these two photographs remind the author of an occasion more than a year before when he and his parents, on totally independent trips not known to each other, came within easy shouting distance on the 'prom' at Grange and on the footplate of a different 10A 'Black 5', Carnforth-bound as it waited to depart. I leave the reader to guess who was where!
H.J. Scowcroft

thoughts returned to getting home. At 01.10 there were no trains of use, but some sort of arrangement with the crew led to nine hopeful souls waiting until the men had eaten. A small number of the waiting group were fortunate to get on the engine as it returned to 10F, but not your good scribe or the friend who'd stayed for the full run, Ian Hopkin, double bassist in the Bolton Youth Orchestra. We ended up walking most of the way to the city before obtaining a more conventional lift. It then wanted only a couple of hours actually waiting until the first (05.25) train to Bolton.

Saturday, 20 July

Preston Holidays started then too. I'd details of some affiliated specials, though not all. There transpired, in fact, one more favoured with steam involvement beyond the one we'd covered, at such a time as to force a choice, which, as is now known, favoured for some 1H11 as offering the most interest and highest mileage. The other, which narrowly missed qualification as the last ever non-enthusiast-orientated steam-hauled special passenger train, not only through Bolton, but on B.R. at all, was a six-coach 22.20 Preston–Manchester Vic., 1T55, for attaching to 1V45, the FO 23.35 Vic.–Paignton. No. 44781 (10A) worked the portion, which was due through Bolton an hour and a half before 1H11. It was later reported that twenty trains had been amended or laid on in connection with Preston and Accrington Holidays. Other Friday night departures I knew of from the former town were for Liverpool, Heysham (sailings), Yarmouth and Newquay.

It would seem that details of those trains had not been erased from blackboards lining the sloped approach to Preston's main platforms even by 16.00 on Saturday the 20th, this being the only explanation for my having belatedly noted the platform number that each had departed from. Again, like the previous Saturday, but even more pronouncedly, was my unnecessarily early arrival at Preston after resting from the overnight. A social scene had built up during 1968 in a natural and progressive way, as if to compensate for progressively fewer and more restricted attractions open to the steam enthusiast. This was never a conscious aim, but the inevitable outcome of an escalating breed of steam followers, established and novice, homing in on fewer objectives than ever. As far as compensating for what had gone forever, only the individual can judge how fulfilling for them was one against the other. The social angle that grew with the end of steam had a level of importance that varied with the individual.

Lostock Hall mpd at 17.30 sported nine engines in steam, including 70013 (10A) as the only foreigner, if the 7MT could be so termed, prior to railtour use the next day. Three locos (8Fs) were absent and seventeen other serviceable engines were cold on shed. I made (it transpired) the occasional, but customary, end-of-steam misjudgement on whether an engine was condemned or not. The true tally seemed to be fourteen, and ten main line diesels shared the premises.

The much smaller platform 5 blackboard, which I think was really for staff enlightenment on principal Down expresses, had indicated a late-running 17.05 ex Euston that evening, but not seriously so. No. 45388 (10D) had come off shed for the duty. The portion tonight consisted of six coaches and departure came just a quarter of an hour late. Progress to Kirkham proved unspectacular, not much over 60mph being attained, but after the stop (one and a half minutes) things livened up with a punchy start and the loco still audible, purring along at 68 approaching Moss Side.

The rousing starts we'd come to expect on the 20.50 did not disappoint tonight. From Lytham, eighteen and a

British Railways Steam 1968

At journey's end, steamwise, for the second of the Rose Grove-powered holiday portions for further afield. In the early hours of 20 July a group of hopefuls wait on Stockport station after arrival from Accrington for the chance of a lift back north on 45156 (10F). *I.C. Simpson*

half minutes late now (largely due to the Kirkham call), 45388 was very clean away and moderately thrashed up to 49mph. Not for the first time, I imagine, had the lively passage of this train turned the heads of evening strollers ('Do I need a cardigan?'), perambulating, albeit away from the 'front', as might be more associated with the Fylde's quieter resorts than the pulsating heart of Blackpool itself. Through Ansdell, Fairhaven and Squires Gate it was the trains (this one in particular) that did the hurrying. Our rate through the latter, 54mph, almost equalled the best yet, but we were never hopeful of catching the 21.35 back that night and terminated nearly twenty minutes late. No. 45388 had dropped two minutes net, the other three being laid at the feet of the Kirkham stop that the schedule didn't allow for.

For once, therefore, vacating South station for the 22.45 ex North presented the vast majority of invalid enthusiasts with the challenge that had loomed more than once, but up to now had been averted. North station was a hard nut to crack and at this juncture it would be folly for me to speculate on how its barriers might have been breached by methods other than the obvious, but breached they were. Frivolities of the week before were taken up on that dmu with 'Big Noise' in fine form, as he had been hours earlier at Preston. The whole scenario, actual dmu excluded, acted as a prelude for the last Saturday in July, not that we knew that of course.

Sunday, 21 to Thursday, 25 July

The Roch Valley Railway Society's untitled railtour, 1T40, on Sunday the 21st made two visits to Southport, whilst getting as far east as Todmorden and Copy Pit in between. My brother, by now only very occasionally motivated by anything on rails, granted me a lift in his car to Westhoughton (closed on Sundays) in order to witness

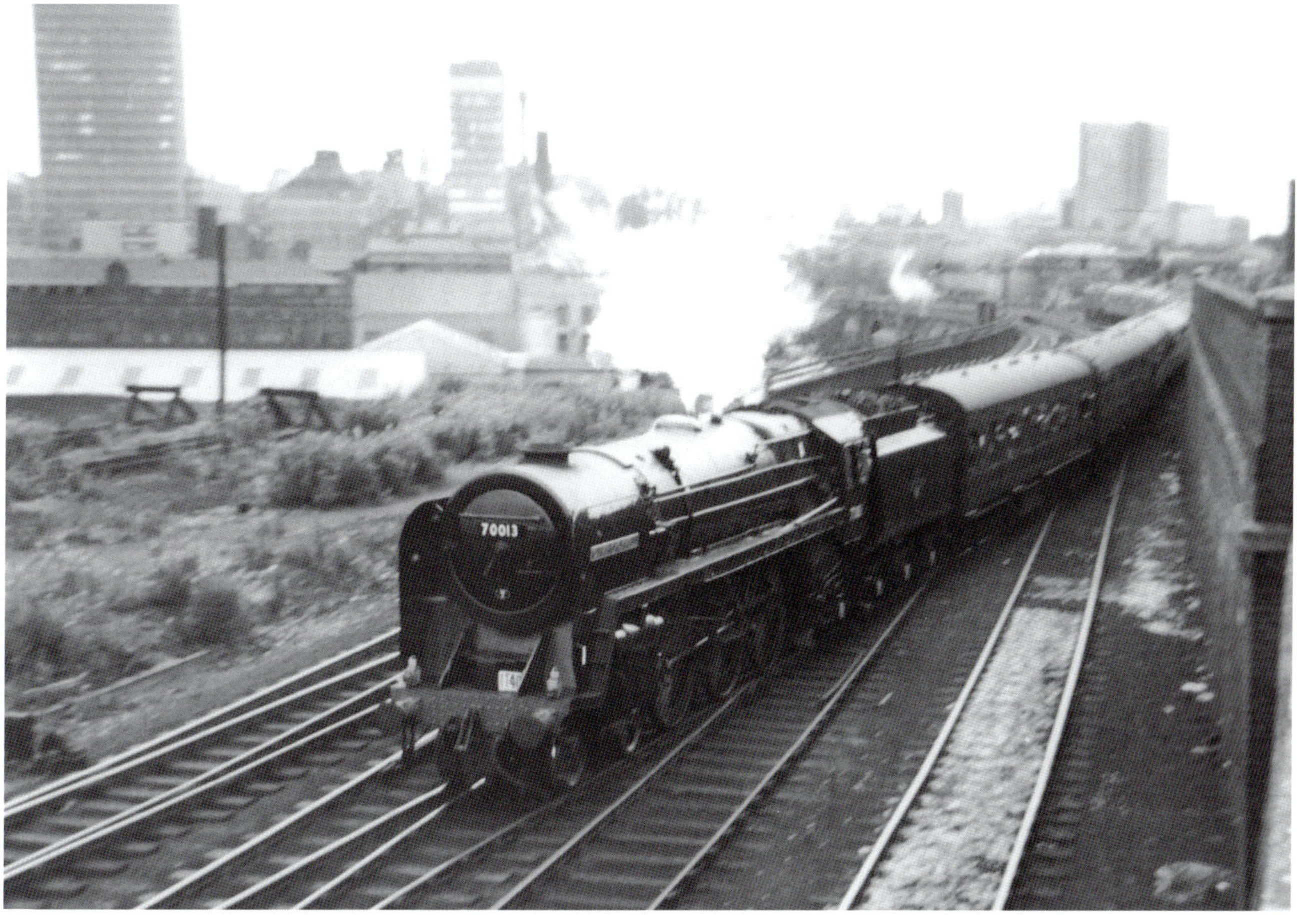

No. 70013 *Oliver Cromwell* (10A) climbs past Red Bank on 1T40, the 'Roch Valley Railway Society' tour of 21 July; one of many it undertook during the last four months or so in 1968. *P. Barber*

1T40's first return from Chapel Street behind *Cromwell*. Running fifty minutes late at that stage (due 12.48), the 7MT produced a snappy, no-nonsense ascent of the 1 in 94 for spectators and travellers alike, at around 40mph on nine or so coaches. I returned, well pleased with the recording on this, another Sunday when more summer-like weather broke through than had during the week.

Somewhat contrasting on the exertion front the night after at Bolton was the second Burnley–Moston with 48493 (10F) on a mere four wagons and halting for as many minutes. August's *Railway Magazine* arrived the next morning, its brief but all-embracing editorial summarising what events of the month would signify to many of its readers. It showed considerable restraint in commenting politely that the elimination of steam 'had been carried out rather more rapidly than originally envisaged', referring rightly to the anticipated forty-year life expectancy of the B.R. Standard designs, yet in the next breath suggesting that, sentiment apart, 'most will applaud benefits of the transformation, even if doubtful about its overall execution' (good choice of the last word there!).

British Railways London Midland Region

CWG/WS

Euston Station
London NW1
Tele. No. 01—387 9400
London Subscribers Dial 387 9400 Ext. 2419

R.L.E. Lawrence
Chairman & General Manager

S. A. Leyland Esq
44, Walker Avenue
Bolton.

y/r
o/r 55:12:03/196/PM.

24th July 1968

Dear Mr Leyland

Thank you for your letter of the 23rd July enclosing cheque for £15.15.0 . I confirm that a seat/~~seats~~ has/~~have~~ been reserved on the special train from Liverpool and Manchester to Carlisle and return on Sunday, 11th August, 1968.

I have pleasure in enclosing your ticket/~~s~~ together with detailed itinerary for the special train.

Yours sincerely,

for Passenger Marketing Manager.

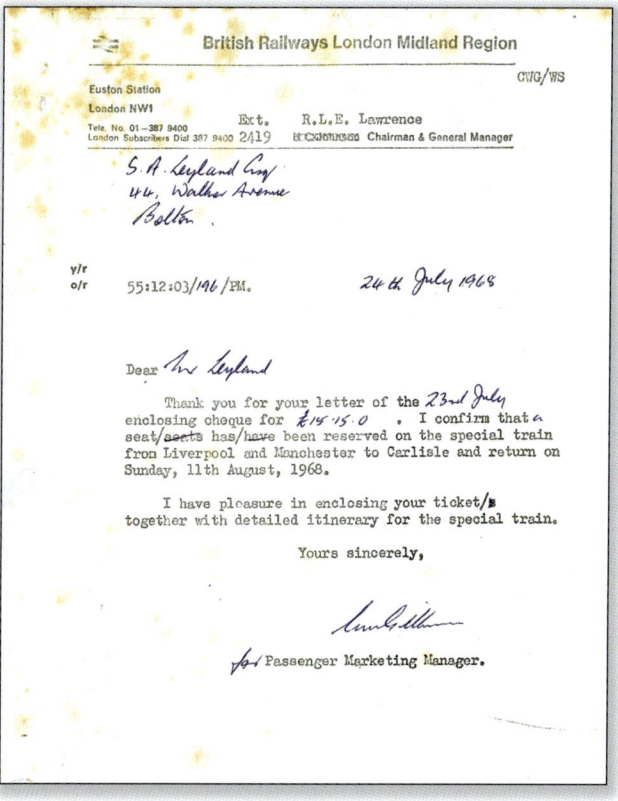

The response from B.R. regarding the 15 guinea 11 August special 'farewell' train.

It moved on to a resigned acceptance of steam's demise on B.R. as such traction 'is now rejected worldwide'. Maybe it was not envisaged that many countries would still be using it ten, twenty or even thirty years hence. The idea of global rejection in 1968 was far-fetched and a gross exaggeration for a publication that hardly ever failed to delve into some corner or other of it! True railway enthusiasts would always find fulfilment in the present and future scene, it asserted, before concluding with support for whatever 'remnants of live steam's glory' might be preserved and those that would preserve it.

The August issue still found space to encompass a wide range of railway subjects, as it has always done. Advertised under 'TOPICS', 'Going Out In Style' was British Railways' own farewell railtour to standard-gauge steam, scheduled for 11 August and instantly controversial because of the very expensive fare of 15 guineas, around five times the going rate, but with meals included. Precise times were given, which did apply on the day too, but the advertised motive power turned out to be incorrect for the 'Black 5'-worked sections. Most uncharacteristically, not having been on a tour for more than eighteen months, I booked on this one immediately.

I knew why I had booked and the reasons were no different than B.R's. assertion that it would motivate a large number of people. Everyone believed it was the end, absolutely, apart from *Scotsman* having a bit of contract running time left. Besides, what we loved best, the day-to-day nitty gritty running of normal service steam had no future whatsoever. Whatever preservation might bring, it could never be a true substitute for that. Although 11 August fell a week after normal steam cessation, it was close enough to it to still feel part of B.R., and that was important to me. The event represented a culmination of the last ten years, and especially the last few of those. My mum recognised its significance and actually encouraged me to go, despite the fearful cost. Maybe she was rather relieved it was all over and that I'd perhaps start to exhibit some conventional signs of growing up at last! Anyway, B.R. seems to have been as accurate in its predictions of heavy demand for tickets (available through other channels since 15 July) as it was sharp in despatching them, as No. 170 was in my possession two days later. The large thick green card was imprinted with an odd mixture of old-style ticket wording and practical information relevant to the day and event.

Years before, in those heady early spotting days, the pleasure of acquiring a new ABC book was tainted at first glance through by the cumulative effect of withdrawals amongst many favourite and largely intact steam classes that created new and enlarged gaps in those once uninterrupted runs. Now, at the virtual climax of all that negative activity, it was remarkable I thought that in a mere eighty or so surviving locomotives there should be any at all consecutively numbered. Yet, no fewer than three pairs remained extant. Far less surprising is that in such a confined area, supplied by only three depots, they should be seen in each other's company away from those depots. The only couple to be based at the same mpd, 48665/6 (10F), came within ten minutes of each other at Blackburn station on 24 July, during an evening unintentionally spent there as I had overlooked the fact that the 18.45 from Bolton didn't stop at Entwistle (for Waltons Sidings).

Five Type 2s and 4s occupied Byng Street Sdgs (the temporary replacement for Bolton mpd) as I passed on the 18.45 and the first Burnley–Moston (diesel since 6 May) had just gone by, with D7649 today hauling quite a decent load. Not being able to alight at the intended point, whilst a nuisance at the time, proved a blessing in disguise that night. Fortunate too was that I didn't opt for Darwen instead as the closest alternative, though the Heysham tanks just may have turned up much later. If not, all I'd have ended up with would have been little more than a light engine, so perhaps I'd been guided by an unseen hand from certain disappointment to better things. Unfortunately, those better things failed to do the trick and left me strangely underwhelmed by the evening as a whole; strangely because I'd usually have found the level of activity alone engaging, but tonight it was the 'derv all around' and near absence of a load for the second Moston that seemed to do it. I had actually booked to Blackburn and the findings are perhaps worth setting out as a traffic survey to illustrate the different levels of motive power form, if not only to marvel that Blackburn was like that once!

Though lacking in some times and train identification, the following does paint a reasonable picture and, of course, dmu workings (seven in the timespan shown) ought to be taken into account. No. 48666 was very likely en route to pick up the 21.45 Farington–Carlton, though it seemed a bit early. Pete arrived from somewhere just after 45388 had come in, so the evening wasn't without company. Neither that loco nor 48493 left before I appear to have (prematurely?) done so, without any recordings, on the 20.55 train home.

Blackburn 24 July 1968

19.16	48773 (10F)	19.05 Burnley–Moston (3) arrives
19.16	48666 (10F)	Light engine south through station
19.30	D7546	19.30 Blackburn–Wigan N.W. parcels, 3F15 departs
19.30	48665 (10F)	Northbound coal empties (32) arrives
19.32	D323	Southbound class 4 goods (45) passes
19.35	Type 4	Widnes–Long Meg empties departs

19.35	D219	Light engine south through station
19.38	D7544	17.45 Colne–Ashton Moss parcels departs
19.48	48773 (10F)	19.05 Burnley–Moston (2) departs
19.48	48493 (10F)	18.40 Preston–Healey Mills arrives
20.04	D5242	1L05 returning Adex arrives (unidentified)
20.26	45388 (10D)	19.14 Colne–Preston parcels arrives
20.26	D206	Northbound vans passes

Friday, 26 July

Prior to joining the 20.55 Club meeting on Friday the 26th, I'd particularly enjoyed all but the last fifteen minutes or so of what turned out to be my last Bolton Youth Orchestra rehearsal; the one before the summer recess. Something had happened to spoil the ending that night, but I don't think this was the occasion that Mr Holt, the assistant conductor, a young and virile music teacher, accused the clarinets en masse of sounding like seagulls during a long syncopated passage in Schubert's Unfinished symphony. I well remember, as leader of that section, taking great exception to such a derogatory and, in my opinion, unjustified remark, but mutely and in accordance with my shy nature, accepted it, only conjuring up relished images of walking out of the rehearsal in imagination afterwards! Despite this dampener (or whatever had caused it), I'd noted the September resumption date with all good intentions, but subsequently decided before then to leave on the grounds of no longer qualifying for a 'youth' organisation. September's rehearsal would have marked six years, almost to the day since I'd joined. My dad, a most accomplished church organist, who knew Mr Holt well and made those arrangements back in 1962 without first consulting me, had sparked off the most hysterical fit of protestation imaginable, to no avail. Dad was right though and years of largely pleasurable playing followed. Stifling the temptation to commit other memories to paper, I'm fully aware that affairs of the orchestra have no legitimate claim herein, except when divided loyalties with the railway demanded a decision, as they sometimes did before 1968. Hence, as it has been granted intermittent brief entries earlier, I thought the reader might persevere with this conclusion.

During the Trinity Street meeting afterwards, Burnley–Moston turned up with a respectable load for the summer of twenty-one. Most of the payload behind 48665 (10F) tonight was coke. I phoned Carnforth mpd for a specifically unrecorded purpose, but the foreman hung up on me. Depot staff were weary by now of being questioned in this way and the outcome then was no surprise. Even in 1967, certain key sheds, Holbeck for example, became intolerant of such calls, chiefly by 'Jubilee'-hungry enthusiasts.

Saturday, 27 July

The earliest (06.38) northbound start had been decided for Saturday the 27th. It turned into a sixteen-hour day, but only through embracing three aspects of railway interest, two of which were where my own enthusiasm in that direction settled from August onward into the 1970s. However, even up to four of the new aspects 'on the go' couldn't match the intensity of what was almost over now. We were very lucky at Preston with enough time after first sight of 48340 (10F) on thirty-eight of coal for Wyre Dock to get up the incline to No. 5 box for the 8F's solid pull away at 07.40. The signalman found time to shout down to us, his voice echoing strangely, about where we might have been better positioned, oblivious of the tape recorder running, or that the spot was deliberately, but hastily, chosen.

Straight after that we headed for Preston Docks and rode about on *Courageous* all morning. *Courageous* was one of the Docks' stud of Bagnall saddletanks, but this was one industrial steam installation that I never revisited. Taking place back at the station, the height of 1968's summer timetable exhibited by far the greatest motive power revolution that ever separated one northern season from the next. Double-headed Type 2s abounded late morning in particular where 'Black 5s' and 'Brits' had last been, but it still held a magnetism of a kind to keep my note-taking intact before and after Paul and I opted for a diesel-hauled run to Manchester Vic. and back. The outward run would have been considered poor, even with a worn out '5', but D369 coming back, albeit on six coaches only, was well early north of Bolton and passed Chorley in exactly 'even time' after 84 through Adlington.

Lostock Hall mpd on the occasion of my last ever visit to any such installation during the B.R. steam era had four fewer engines fired during that afternoon, two hours earlier than the Saturday before's inspection. The diesel presence was lower, too. Significant or not? It hardly mattered as the ultimate outcome was only a week away. The same number of steam locos were absent and the only department to show an increase was the scrap, both in physical appearance and when later checked with published lists that rejoiced in suitable cut-off dates.

The diesel monopoly back at Preston station ground on into early evening with several Types on more than a dozen class 1 trains and four parcels/empties stock formations up to 7.45pm. The sleeping car steam heat engine, today 44806 (10D), appeared at 19.21 and more

April seemed a long way back by the time we'd got to the last full week of steam operation, but Rose Grove's 48423 on 17 April is well representative of our encounter with that depot's 48340 on 27 July as it passes Preston No. 5 box hauling the 13.10 Rose Grove–Wyre Dock. *I.C. Simpson*

than an hour later 45388 (10D) for the 20.50 to Blackpool. Like the 'Boat' before it, enthusiasts were thicker on the ground with successive Saturday nights that drew nearer to the end, 'at least seventy' being my estimate for 27 July.

Contrary to its best-remembered features, the run that night that we had to (and did) regard as a potential 'last', was not an optimum performance. Three fairly minor points at least deprived it of this distinction. Only two minutes late away and hauling seven coaches to the six of recent weeks, 45388 lost half a minute or so with slow acceleration from Fylde Jc. to just beyond Maudlands Viaduct, but then the power was piled on to briefly offset this and we'd reached 72mph at Spen Lane, practically my fastest speed over that section. Kirkham South Jc. brought us down to 20mph. Omitting the station stop, its platforms were threaded at 26mph, prior to a solid recovery. Gravity-assisted acceleration from 50 through Wrea Green to no less than 74mph by Moss Side was especially good, but a discernibly 'slow' approach to Lytham lost maybe half a minute or maybe slightly more on what might have been.

A speed of 55mph after Ansdell bore testimony to 45388's sound form as this was accomplished without pulling out all the stops. This was saved for the St Annes restart, which proved power-packed in the extreme to give a full and unprecedented 60 through Squires Gate, barely more than 1½ miles from South!

In the mid-1980s, towards the close of my foreign steam travels, one circumstance and one circumstance alone served to duplicate that slightly odd sensation of a train hurtling ever closer, faster and more noisily towards its destination. Really close I mean. In that other instance the destination was Bloemfontein with everything but the speed on a hugely bigger scale; ten hours of a journey, thirteen- or fourteen-coach trains and a 4-8-4 blazing even more demently (difficult though that would have been to imagine in 1968) through the inner suburbs of the final town (city in truth) it served. That neither were truly termini mattered not, but 'Bloem', on curved track would have come off worst, had the regulator been closed too late! Funnily enough, the next signal box after Blackpool South was Bloomfield Road.

Not a place for exciting steam action, Preston Docks nevertheless served as a haven of sorts when all seemed dead elsewhere. It was even the focus of one deliberate evening trip. Here, on 17 June, Bagnall saddletank *Princess* goes about its business. More of a loco study than *Princess* amongst the cranes is *Courageous*, our transportation around much of the system on 27 July. *V.A. Sidlow, Anon/M.L.S. collection*

For a self-confessed Western man from the North, the valleys of South Wales provided an unexpected haven in which to live out missed opportunities of the past. Ex G.W.R. Pannier Tank 7754 rests after its day's duty outside Talywain engine shed, near Pontypool on 8 April 1969. *S.A. Leyland*

Despite the full 60mph through Squires Gate, the start to stop time from St Annes didn't sneak under the five-and-a-half-minute mark as one or two had with lower maximums, exposing the actual stop as the 'weak' bit. However, 1P58 had lost only one and a half minutes from Preston to terminate in good enough time for crew appreciation and for the ECS removal (by 45388) to be savoured and recorded as quite likely the final such experience. For that we were well prepared mentally by many other events of that ilk, all 'final' in their own way, but the word's meaning and significance were saving themselves yet.

Without necessary rush, patrons of the recent steam arrival next took up the very different '21.35 dmu experience'. The train tonight consisted of two coaches only and neither had any internal lights 'despite strong objections from the guard', who tried to fail the set on that count. The strong enthusiast presence had 'taken over' and proceedings began with a mock ticket inspection, sparked off by 'Wellington', who held centre stage during that and subsequent entertainment as we clattered across the Fylde in near darkness. A complete uproar upon realisation that the 'show' was in fact being taped (by me) after all, included repeated shoutings of the 20.55 Club key greeting 'LEADER!' (executed properly with an inoffensive single-finger salute), chiefly by Pete, its instigator, from his tongue-in-cheek admiration of Bulleid's experimental locomotive. Realisation that the tape was running seemed to spur Mr Rollason on to greater things. 'Has anyone got a loit? The motto of Wolverhampton is, 'Out of darkness commeth loit', he proclaimed. A 'loit' was produced and two hilarious items from a local Wellington paper were orated to appropriate response. A weird semi-technical piece on 'Pneumatic Frothmeters' preceded something about a police raid on a wild happening likened to a Roman orgy. 'Some of them were even eating grapes' from this became a 20.55 Club adopted phrase in the way that such things just caught on. Plenty went unrecorded or was scrapped later as a victim of my exacting censorship on what was still a 'steam tape'. Bad language of even the mildest sort played no part in the above proceedings.

There was, too, a more serious side to those rides home from Blackpool, for at that time the industrial scene looked more and more set to replace the void about to be left by B.R. steam's approaching extinction. Better-informed colleagues of mine were sowing the seeds of a future devotion to this closely related 'new' attraction that, though still plentiful in the U.K., had had little exposure to date. The imminent response from national

'There is a Land of Pure Delight' – not quite what the hymn writer Isaac Watts had in mind, but it adequately describes the author's most favourable impression of his first post-B.R. South Wales visit. Here, Barclay saddletank *Illtyd* propels empties into Blaenserchan Colliery, Talywain, East Glamorgan, on 8 April 1969. *S.A. Leyland*

Nearer to home on the N.C.B. steam scene of 1969, a three-engine (Austerity 0-6-0ST) load is heaved up the hill from Astley Green Colliery to north of Walkden, one cold and windy November Saturday. The closed Mosley Common Colliery is on the skyline. *S.A. Leyland*

magazines and other publications produced by early steam preservation bodies would soon begin to rectify this and enlighten many who were more than receptive to a fresh steam cause in their own country. Barrie Thornily, in particular, fed me with what seemed fantastic reports of G.W.R. Pannier Tanks still working in South Wales! But fantasy it wasn't. As the 'riot' died down on the 21.35 I made some detailed notes of what to find where; those wonderful misspelled names! Could it be that now, with a bit more cash and sense of liberty, I would be able to experience what had long been thought lost forever? For a Great Western man from Lancashire this was like a dream come true. It mattered little that the engines only touched upon the B.R. lines that were once theirs alone. My imagination stirred, I closed the day with a firm hope to go as early as September. In fact, August discoveries of what lay in that field practically on my own doorstep postponed South Wales until spring 1969, but that initial captivating experience ensured many returns!

Burt Lancaster got his name into July's *Railway Magazine* as top billing in *The Train*, one of nine similarly themed films presented at the Odeon, Preston, that Saturday night. Arranged by three enterprising preservation bodies that had hired the cinema, this special screening to 'Mark the End of B.R. Steam', commencing at 23.30, would have made an ideal overnight at half the price of a B&B for any enthusiasts from further afield staying up north for Sunday's railtour. Whether the half-page advert anywhere near helped to fill what was doubtless a capacious cinema I can't say, but the title 'Symphony in Steam III' does suggest this might not have been the show's first venue.

Sunday, 28 July

Sunday's tour, 28 July, was the last big individual one before the famous final series that ran on 4 August. Run jointly by the Severn Valley Railway Society and Manchester Rail Travel Society, 1L43 offered 300 miles of steam for under £4, utilising *Cromwell* and the surviving classes in service, except for lone BR '5' 73069 (10A). Rather than sporting the eight coaches marked against it in the N2 notice, the train had nearer to twelve on, if not actually twelve, meaning that the 'Black 5' sections were now double-headed. This is how it first threaded Bolton on that lovely warm day, via Johnson Street fork, but not until teatime. Whilst some friends of mine chased it all day by car, I went up to Turton Towers with my parents, expecting 70013. Instead, 45073 (10D) and 45156 (10F) were in use at that stage, making a good spectacle, despite falling to well under 30mph whilst within earshot.

Two hours later, after changing to 48773 (10F) for the easternmost points reached by the tour, 1L43 returned to my home town via Todmorden and Bury, negotiating Rose Hill fork overlooking the Wanderers' ground to face south. Checked to a stand now, almost opposite my spot at the rear of our now closed steam shed, it was as if the 8F had paused deliberately to take in the changes at what until a month before had been its home for nearly four years. Restarting without much gusto initially, the 2-8-0 began to accelerate superbly after the last coach had passed. It's wonderful quickening exhaust sound, a roar even by Moses Gate, rose and fell on the light southerly breeze to provide an eminently worthy replacement on my cassette for what I then considered the seedier, less tasteful and therefore disposable part of the night before's non-steam recordings.

After its lightning dash away from Bolton, 48773 (10F) passes Agecroft Jc. with the eleven-coach 1L43 railtour on 28 July. *H.J. Scowcroft*

Upon the disappearance of 1L43 I recognised some familiar figures down at Green Lane bridge, so walked along the track to join them and compare fortunes of the day. Hilary, entrusted with Vern's camera, had managed (it transpired) to get little more than the smokebox of 48773 on the photograph, a failing that later provided fuel for perhaps more badinage than the error deserved!

Monday, 29 July

A long but rewarding evening spent at Hoghton opened this last week of steam for Vern, Keith, Pete and myself, this being Monday the 29th. After the usual prelude of assorted diesel-hauled traffic seen en route and at the location, 48340 (10F), heading the forty-four-wagon Preston–Healey Mills, made its mark on the proceedings at 19.50 with an impressive ascent. Following it at a decent interval came a nine-coach Colne–Blackpool N. returning adex behind D5244 as a reminder of the season.

Towards Preston then, the LE for Farington–Carlton was none other than 48773 (10F) again, making it ex Bolton engines responsible for both principal freight objectives that night. So far I'd never seen this train at Hoghton, but with any uncertainty of it running dispelled, we hung on until a later hour than usual, still aware that success depended upon the train, 7N68, being early. Fortunately it was.

Unaccountably, for such a mass of swiftly moving and not unexpected metal, the 8F and its fifty-two empty wagons seemed (as I checked the tape recording again now) to burst upon us almost, 'crashing through at 21.40' and maintaining a very good rate. No. 48773 wasn't being unduly pressed either. Its passage coincided with the signalman's relief a little before the appointed time. Standing as I was, opposite the box, that everyday event conspired, by virtue of its timing and circumstance, to embellish the sound sequence, turning it into a true joy to the tape recordist, which was just as truly unique. Impossible to plan and folly to hope for, it made a perfect end to my evening. As the exhaust and train sounds died away east of the road bridge, the tail end of a conversation between the departing late turn man and the one starting 'nights' was left suspended on the top steps; and all on account of a single word, unclearly heard by the new 'bobby', not being repeated because the request to do so wasn't heeded by the other: 'Anyway, I'll get across, Vic. ****** Junction I am tomorrow'. 'Where are you tomorrow?', then no reply to this, except a rather belated 'I'll see you'. The man not called Vic was obviously a relief signalman – Hoghton Monday, ****** Junction Tuesday. On the recording it sounds like a badly pronounced 'Bolton', i.e. Blackburn Bolton Jc. Nowhere else in the area seemed to fit. What outwardly was so commonplace, two signalmen doubtless exchanging news before parting on a mild summer evening with a natural enough farewell for their profession, immediately endeared itself to me. This was the kind of railway we ourselves were expecting to say 'farewell' to, for following the steam engine, alongside it to a less noticeable degree even, other much-loved and harmonious aspects were certain to disappear, too.

Hardly any sooner had 7N68 faded from prominence than down the bank coasted an unidentified 'Black 5' working the comparatively lightweight Colne–Preston parcels, 3P20. It had secured anonymity due either to lack of light or the distance we'd already put between the line and the bus stop. Later, a fight broke out on the 22.55 dmu from Blackburn, between a man and a woman. The train had to be stopped at Spring Vale while calm was somehow restored, delaying our already late return home and preventing Pete from actually achieving this. With whom did he stay, I have to wonder?

Blackburn line-bound trains through Preston could take the Farington Curve Jc. route over the main line, or be routed via the E.L. side and Todd Lane Jc. In this instance 48730 (10F) is negotiating the latter with coal empties, but this is also a good view of the E.L. layout, which no longer exists.
P. Barber

The remains of Hoghton station (closed 12 September 1960) as 44690 (10F) passes through light, heading for Preston. Also featured is the signal box and its west end steps, from which a brief conversation, as related, was captured on tape. *Peter Fitton*

Tuesday, 30 July to Thursday, 1 August

The 19.05 Burnley–Moston became the focal point of the remaining weekday evenings I turned out. At Orlando bridge on Tuesday the 30th, certain Manchester 'Club' members who had never normally reached Bolton before 'Boat Train' time during the week joined us to witness 48773 (10F) yet again, but it conveyed a light load of fifteen only. For Wednesday's train I was on the last minute getting to Waltons Sidings, where 48423 (10F) on one wagon fewer had shut off steam passing me. Either I'd not quite made it to the summit or I'd deliberately waited just south of the crest to hopefully capture the rapid acceleration that could be a feature of that spot. On both of these evenings no more steam was seen or expected.

On the other side of a full-page advert for the new Ford Zephyr V6 De Luxe (£1,099), *Daily Mirror* reporter Donald Walker's description of his light engine footplate ride from Barrow to Carnforth on 44809 (10A) in the context of it being B.R. steam's last week brought word of what had been uppermost in our minds for so long into countless homes, where an inkling at best had hitherto filtered through. What was of concern to one held no interest for another and reaction to news of the forthcoming terminal event would have been as varied as the occupants of those countless homes. 'So what?' many may have thought. Even the views of the 37-year-old driver of 44809 were more allied to this thinking, geared as they were to dreams of cleanliness and comfort for the rest of his time on the railway. The reporter touched briefly on the spectrum of response likely from those with an interest, professionally or otherwise, but more on his solitary experience of steam on the inside. Consequently, no natural depth of feeling was possible, even had the *Mirror*'s editors been receptive to anything beyond fleeting romanticism. 'PUFF – It's the End of an Era' and the solitary subtitle 'Vibrating' provide their own clues to the article's gravity and its writer's preoccupation with creature comforts. At least the photograph of an 'also ran' 'Black 5' looked suitably imposing at journey's end.

That same day of the *Mirror* article, 1 August, I didn't even see a train. Keith rang up late with a rumour based on a supposed 100mph attempt by 70013 (10A), specially arranged to work the 20.30 Barrow–Preston parcels, due to take place on Friday the 2nd. Plenty of information, by comparison, has emerged since, but at the time there's

Almost certainly the last of countless failed dmus to be rescued by steam, here is the 09.00 Windermere–Morecambe Promenade at Kendal and relying on 44894 (10A) for motive power on 30 July 1968. It is likely that this engine was already on the branch as the daily tripper. *P. Barber*

nothing to follow it up in my notes or diary, so either some unrecorded update came along to counter the rumour or I considered the various aspects of it too uncertain to risk such an occasion (the last 'normal' weekday evening of steam) on. In fact, whilst I was otherwise engaged, something rather special was attempted, with one of Carnforth's already renowned drivers, Ted Fothergill, not with 70013, but 44781 (10A) when south of Lancaster around 87mph was attained with the train, 1P92.

Friday, 2 August

However, on that Friday evening only Vern and I chose a familiar enough haunt in Waltons Sidings, where I could bid farewell to an even more familiar working. There was another reason, for we'd resolved to stay on for the last ever freight to be steam-hauled through Bolton, and up the bank too, but Burnley–Moston it was first. Upon coming into earshot, our main hopes of a heavy load seemed to be realised as the loco approached at about a tenth of what was being attempted elsewhere. On that warm and calm August evening the midges were out in force and self-control with a handheld microphone in such quiet conditions was severely tested as the insects bit repeatedly!

Fending them off by means other than ointment or suchlike would have ruined the recording, of course. No. 48167 (10F) it was, emerging from Sough tunnel, holding close to 8mph on twenty-eight of loaded coke and the 1 in 69 retarded 5J10's progress even a little more. I think he was doing badly for steam, shutting off at the earliest possible point and with the 'jet' well on gravity was left to take over. Nevertheless, we'd witnessed as fitting an end to the train as could be expected and the sound effects were far from disappointing. The time was 20.50.

No. 48167 had one last duty to fulfil, but it wanted two and a half hours before the train even was due to leave Brewery Sidings at 23.28, to Blackburn. Answerable questions flood back in long-term retrospect. How long had the 8F and its uniform load been in section from Spring Vale? Who were the signalmen at Waltons that night? There would have been a changeover at 22.00, yet I've no recollection of whether we even sought to break up the long wait in the comfort of that lonely box. Had we considered cycling up there to avoid hours of waiting afterwards? More likely, it still being a far from uncomfortable night to be out (now that the midges had gone), we returned fairly soon to Entwistle, for my abiding memory of the nocturnal hours lies there.

British Railways Steam 1968

One is tempted to imagine the thoughts of the driver of 45318 as his steed waits in a Preston south bay platform before working the last normal timetabled steam-hauled passenger train on B.R. It's after 9pm on 3 August and the 21.25 to Liverpool Exchange narrowly held this distinction over the 20.50 to Blackpool South. *T. Heavyside*

Saturday, 3 August

At Entwistle, a wooden form faced south from the station buildings' end wall and towards the appointed hour (01.00) repeated glances back to Waltons' distant were to no avail. The last of three E.E. Type 4s (Carlisle–Ardwick) had gone by shortly after midnight. I had high hopes of 6P69 yielding a classic recording, but time went on and it got colder.

Eventually the peg came off, shortly after 02.00, and I went onto the road bridge, confident of no interference from cars. There wasn't any, but it soon became clear that 48167 was making the climb under very easy steam and only a dozen or so wagons passed beneath my spot; a let-down certainly, but at least the historic moment and movement had been witnessed and recorded, perhaps exclusively by Vern and myself – not an easy claim to make that weekend! Four hours to the first train home remained; it might have seemed warmer walking. With nothing now to set our sights on and the midge bites starting to act, unsuccessfully trying to nod off, it's small wonder I'd not bothered to note the Colne papers and parcels trains. But we got through and I spent the morning in bed.

On the eve of the biggest concentration of steam railtours ever, not only myself was keen to secure details beyond the very sketchy ones advertised. Fortunately, the week coincided with Bob on late turn at East Jc., so I turned up at 14.00, able to do them a favour in return as the lad had gone home. In between train booking for three hours I filled as many sheets of foolscap with tour and associated LE timings – everything that the N2 notice could supply. A very noticeable feature was the absence of any special booked to use the W.C.M.L. whilst steam-hauled, but that omission had been standard on Sundays through the summer due to engineering work. The alternative routes, from the scenic and gradient point of view, were rightly considered more interesting by the various organisers anyway, now that Carnforth was the northern limit. What a feast was lined up for that last day! Fourteen engines in total would work six trains, never too far from each other amidst a tracery of largely secondary Lancashire lines and incorporating several loco changes at sundry points.

Before all that excitement, however, another milestone event lay even more immediately ahead, so I took the tour details to one interested party, a more senior local enthusiast I wouldn't see later, and caught the 20.00 to Preston. In doing so I was far from alone. By the time of my comparatively late arrival the station was awash with enthusiasts faced with a choice tonight of either the 20.50 with 45212, or the 21.25 Liverpool for which 45318 (both 10D) had been turned out. There could, for the first time ever, be no doubt that neither train would ever be steam-hauled again. In memory I stood there, very torn between which to choose, for far longer than must have been the case.

Ex Bolton engine on probable fast run that would be the LAST in normal service, versus less distinguished 4-6-0 (to me) over a route lacking the freshness of the former and 'only' the penultimate steam journey, but to a destination that held so much more significance personally. Only moments I think before the 20.50 was whistled away did I opt for that, on the grounds of owing far more to Blackpool for the part it had played in prolonging steam's employment on passenger work and the enthusiasts' lot during those closing years. That's what swung it in the end. Unfortunately, 1P58 had become uncomfortably crowded during my dilemma. I'd missed the necessary dash for a window and only just managed to cram into Barrie's compartment. I could get my microphone to the top-light window, but little else.

We departed four minutes late and it's doubtful that anyone there not connected with the event was left ignorant of it. Drain cocks roared, driving wheels slipped and shouts from the train ensured this was no imperceptible slinking out. Nor was it the time for one. Steam itself had nothing to be ashamed of. All the shame was (or should have been) heaped on the way its demise had been carried out. An effect of this manifested itself in the condition of 45212 now, for despite having done very well on 1 June, traits of sluggishness were soon discerned. The rate to Kirkham turned into my second ever slowest, with nothing over 48mph recorded. The absence of anything competitive in the running, plus the overcrowded compartment, contributed to an incomplete log, I now regret, to the extent of not even noting the load. I later discovered it had been seven coaches.

Tonight we observed the Kirkham stop, fifteen and three-quarter minutes after leaving Preston. There was no shortage of 'UMPH' on the restart – hefty echoes from the Fox's biscuit factory – but it wasn't being converted into the last three letters of that expression to any impressive degree, a mere 63mph down Moss Side bank doing nothing for our already considerable time loss. On top of this a special stop order tonight for Ansdell & Fairhaven meant that we only omitted to call at Squires Gate on the whole line and speeds between the stops remained persistently and more than marginally below the norm.

Performance, however, wasn't everything. We were honouring the motive power form that had served the railways for nearly 140 years and the cheers of many voices, as one, at Blackpool South as the empty stock moved out were not diminished by the quarter of an hour or so we'd dropped from Preston. Not all of that was down to the engine anyway. The 21.35 dmu back, though late out itself, had already gone. Had this been a tight 'connection' off the steam tonight, I think most would have let it go. The clammering of enthusiasts around 45212 for autographs and photos somewhat overwhelmed the crew. I stood a little further off as the terminated 1P58 pulled out to the siding, its significance only too apparent.

Being without a ticket from Preston, due to the earlier indecision, I went over the wall at South to avoid explanations and save time paying excess. We'd obviously lingered too long to allow walking time to North for the 22.45 and, rather than risk the great likelihood at that time of year of having to queue for a tram, I shared a taxi with several others.

The journey home, to judge from my surviving notes, or recollection, saw none of the boisterous antics of certain earlier occasions. It would have been only right and proper for reflection to have occupied our thoughts, for that which had just taken place was IT. Looming for years, the event to end it all for me had happened and we lived now in a steamless land, at least in terms of where our passions in that direction had been focussed; beloved B.R., but loved and hated for the different things it had provided and taken away. British Railways was too big to be one or the other, but even it had not acted in such ways without influence from 'outside', not the least the influence of its creator, the government. How had the throngs fared who that last night of class 1 service steam had been Liverpool-bound behind 45318 (10D)? Well, it seemed, with exhilarating work over adverse grades and

78mph maximum on favourable, once the exaggerations had been ironed out, but each individual enthusiast chose the train that appealed most beforehand, for whatever reasons. It was a time for personal indulgencies and the actual merits of each proved to the very end that nothing predicted or expected was sure until it had happened.

Yes, I need no reminder of the spectacular farewell 'show' lined up for 4 August and that of the 11th too, but they were still viewed, despite my gradual warming to railtours, as outside conventional railway-run traffic, insomuch as never being generated out of genuine commercial requirements.

Sunday, 4 August

A report of there being a nocturnal shunt of sleeping cars by Preston station pilot early on the 4th appeared in the press and B.R. was at liberty to use steam for ordinary purposes that day, had it the need, but the 4th seemed to stand in limbo between one era and the next.

Recent pages within have been written with an increasing awareness that events leading up to the last day have seen progressively more coverage already in various publications at intervals since then. Usually they have been incorporated in anniversary articles commemorating the end of a much-revered time, a time that the extraordinary and then totally unpredicted preservation explosion has done nothing to devalue. It has always been correctly acknowledged that the two are quite incomparable. The railtour bonanza of 4 August has, not surprisingly, been near the top of the list in such commemorations and I will try to avoid going over old ground yet again. Its actual importance, historically, in my opinion, is low, being outside the sphere of normal operations, but both that and the 11 August event are, by virtue of their chronological proximity to the last 'normal' day (the former actually within it), inextricably linked to and seen as a natural culmination of steam's demise at the end of that summer.

The 4th did, in fact, bear no resemblance to a normal day. It would have otherwise been completely dead. Many of the tour engines used had no future beyond the day itself and there is food for thought over the selection of several on an occasion when the choice was wide open from what had survived until then. Here, in depot order, were the 'contenders', which excluded both of the previous evening's passenger engines, plus 45260 (10D), which (it transpired) had worked the 21.25 Preston–Liverpool on 2 August, and 45388, another 10D machine known to be in very good fettle:

Carnforth: 44781, 44874, 44894, 45017, 45025, 45390, 70013, 73069.
Lostock Hall 45110, 45305, 45407, 48476.
Rose Grove: 45156, 48773.

Included were several 'Black 5s' that were latterly in our eyes undistinguished, though the depots naturally knew

Negotiating Entwistle viaduct with the G. C. Enterprises railtour on 4 August is 45156 (10F), heading for Carnforth. *Anon/20.55 Club collection*

best for the selection. Maybe Carnforth had given less thought to it due to the large amount of double-heading that would halve the reliance on one unproven or indifferent loco? No. 45110, in fact, did not leave shed due to a defect and was replaced by 45305 for B.R's Manchester–Southport tour. No. 45407 therefore stepped in to cover for 45305, originally booked to pilot 73069 north of Blackburn. Very shabby it looked too on photographs, in typical condition for the period – fitting perhaps that one did. Most of those involved were concentrated at Lostock Hall by the evening before. Photographs depict and describe them as 'immaculate', but most were really just oiled over. Most tours on the 4th acquired their steam haulage at Manchester Victoria and so much of the assemblage at 10D departed that morning in relays of up to three locos to meet their respective trains. These movements were as follows:

    0T80 – 45156 depart 06.50 to Longsight (for ECS)
    0Z78 – 44894 + 44871 depart 09.39 to Manchester Vic.
    0Z79 – 44874 + 45017 depart 10.04 to Manchester Vic.
    0L50 – 48476 + 73069 depart 10.40 to Manchester Vic.
    0Z74 – 70013 + 44781 + 45305 depart 11.49 to Red Bank.
    0L50 – 45407 depart 12.50 to Blackburn to replace 48476.

All of the above travelled via Bolton, except 45156, which went via Wigan NW, Newton-le-Willows and Victoria. The three locos on 0Z74 had to turn on arrival at Manchester. The first 0L50 movement specified only one loco in the notice, but two were despatched, and needed, to get thirteen coaches anticlockwise round the Oldham loop! Another preparatory LE movement was 0Z74 from Rose Grove at 13.40 to get 48773 to Blackburn where it took over from *Cromwell*. In brief, the tours themselves were:

1T80	(G.C. Enterprises) 45156. Stockport 10.01, Carnforth, Stockport 20.53.
1Z78	(Stephenson Locomotive Society) ex Birmingham. 44894 & 44871 throughout. M/C Vic. 11.20, Diggle, Copy Pit, Blackburn, Bolton (fork), Liverpool (Sefton Jc.), Rainhill, M/C Vic. 16.41.
1Z79	(Stephenson Locomotive Society) ex Birmingham. 44874 & 45017 throughout. M/C Vic. 11.48. Same itinerary as 1Z78. M/C Vic. arrive 17.31.
1L50	(Railway Correspondence & Travel Society) ex Euston. 48476 & 73069. M/C Vic. 12.25, Oldham, Rochdale, Bolton, Blackburn (48476 off, 45407 on), Hellifield (reverse), Skipton (reverse), Blackburn, Lostock Hall (change to 70013), Burscough Jc., Liverpool (Sefton Jc.), Rainhill, M/C Vic. 18.23.
1Z74	(Locomotive Club of Great Britain) ex St Pancras. 70013 & 44781. M/C Vic. 13.30, Blackburn (70013 off, 48773 on), Hellifield, Carnforth, (change to 45390 & 45025) & ret. via Hellifield to Lostock Hall, arrive 18.18.
1T85	(B.R.) 45305 M/C Vic. 14.20, Bootle Jc., Southport S. Jc., Walkden, M/C Vic. 17.10.

Nos 70013 (10A) and 44781 (10A) have reached Waltons Sidings, summit of the line from Bolton, with the L.C.G.B. 1274 railtour on 4 August. Anon/M.L.S. collection

No. 48476 (10D) pilots 73069 (10A) arriving at Blackburn on the thirteen-coach 1L50, before the train got too hopelessly late. Allan Heyes

1Z74 had been strengthened from the nine bogies shown in the traffic notice to twelve, doubtless to cater for demand, and to the relief of any competitive L.C.G.B. members mindful of society prestige who also saw the day as one for the big clubs to have their tour(s) paraded around Lancashire. If judged on the number of coaches each could muster, the aforementioned increase still left them just in third place.

In the very different 20.55 Club there were then three-car owning or driving members, just enough to accommodate those who wanted to chase the tours around in order to see as much as possible. Who exactly was with whom and for how long matters little, but Frank shared the farm Consul and its associated internal aromas with Pete and Ian.

Late running by all the tours became the order of the day as operational delays piled up. Of the eight observations we made, the train closest to punctuality was 1Z78, only twenty-two minutes in arrears at Copy Pit, but most escalated to far worse than that and the R.C.T.S. thirteen-coach tour copped far more than its fair share of the problems to become astronomically late. The society's own report/inquest later showed hot axlebox detectors, signal failures and other checks to have put 1L50 well over an hour down before it even acquired steam haulage. Then, extended engine changes, wrong line working and pathing delays all took their toll.

We began at Turton with 45156 on the eight-coach 1T80, already thirty-six minutes late, but theoretically the most relaxed of the day, affording its passengers almost five hours at Carnforth. The engine did sport a drain cock leak that stayed with it for the day, but otherwise sounded good at around 20mph or a bit less on the long climb. The two ten-coach S.L.S. specials that kept the same 'Black 5' pairs all day were supposed to maintain the half-hour or so between them at starting, until a Blackburn scheduled stop put the second train fifty minutes behind, but by Copy Pit they were already an hour apart. 1Z78, the first one behind 44894 and 44871, pranced up at a good rate, each 4-6-0 sharing the work quite evenly.

Opposite top: After the Manchester Vic. departures of most 4 August specials, Blackburn was rightly recognised as a centre to see much more of them and not fleetingly, as in the countryside. Approaching Blackburn from the south is 1Z74 again, attracting the attention of a small semi-naked P. Way gang opposite West box and many photographers who have strayed well beyond the platforms on that warm afternoon. *Allan Heyes*

Bottom: At Blackburn, 70013 has detached from 1Z74 and now 48773 (10F) pilots 44781 (10A) for the L.C.G.B. tour's northbound continuation, whilst 45407 (10D) waits for 1L50 to turn up and make another engine change. The 8F's range of front end adornments includes the wreath brought in by *Cromwell* and a tribute to Rose Grove steam. *Allan Heyes*

A complete takeover by tour participants, photographers, well-wishers, true steam enthusiasts and maybe a few for whom this is their first awareness of the weekend's significance, has turned Blackburn station into a mass trespass. Male dominated to an extreme degree (spot the solitary sister or girlfriend), the preservation movement will start to change that, but in the meantime 73069 takes water whilst waiting for 45407 (centre) to attach, replacing 48476, which stands on the right. *Allan Heyes*

At such strategic points that drew the largest and more enthusiast-orientated crowds, copious whistling was for once not deemed unnatural by those sensitive to such things. The S.L.S. relief tour at 14.10 heralded itself initially by a distant, but harsh, roaring and black smoke down towards Portsmouth. The driver of 44874, the leading engine, had given his 4-6-0 everything, then sat back to watch the effect, an effect not lost on the multitude there! How very sad it was though, to think that in just a few hours at most, what was so vibrantly alive and all-commanding now, would be silent and growing colder towards a state from which it would never again emerge. But every one of the 20,000 steam locomotives disposed of since the war had gone through a 'last hours' thing of its own. Maybe every one of those 20,000 had affected someone in the same way because they were there, aware of the circumstances and felt it themselves.

A Blackburn engine change for 1Z74 had put 44781 with 48773 and the pair passed Gisburn an hour and a quarter in arrears. Some other and apparently unsuccessful move by ourselves would seem to have followed. Then, nearly two hours after Gisburn, having lost the thread of what was actually where (despite sheets of timings that would have been the envy of most) and heading for Bentham, I espied the returning 1Z74 stationary at Clapham far down to our right, equally late as before. Our reactionary attempt to reach a spot before the train pulled out failed, frustrating all in the car as we now paced the tour (now with 45390 and 45025) trying to find a clear enough stretch at the roadside. I began to record the engines with the windows down, picking up all the comments and modest expletives too. Then suddenly, a slamming of doors mixed with slamming twin exhausts as 1Z74 was still almost up with us. No time could be spared (the

The driver of 44874 (10A) puts on the ultimate show over the last couple of miles to Copy Pit summit. This, the second S.L.S. tour on 4 August, had 45017 (10A) as train engine for the day and is seen here at the summit. *K.F. Pendlebury*

others felt) to let me round off the tape tidily. I was outnumbered by photographers and rather bitterly regretted at the time having to surrender that fine receding exhaust noise to the chase. Nappa was next, but the locos just coasted past us on the descent from Hellifield. Since those times, the line speed has fallen in inverse proportion to road and vehicle speed so we didn't catch that one again.

Mid-evening was upon us now and Spring Vale for the returning 1T80 offered the next best prospect. Half an hour late only, *Yeomanry* that was, put in a respectable ascent until the engine was suddenly silenced by Sough tunnel. Word had got round that the R.C.T.S. tour that we'd not yet seen, 1L50, had got into such dire straits on the schedule side that a chunk of its itinerary – into Liverpool after the last engine change at Lostock Hall – was being abandoned in order to recover some time and that it would now return much more directly to Victoria via Chorley and Bolton. How fitting then, that this momentous day should be able to be concluded unexpectedly at our home station.

The waiting clientele of just myself and a few friends had changed by now, I recall. We understood 1L50 to have lost three and a half hours at worst, by Skipton, but it was nearer to four! The late route revision regained an hour, and so, in the advanced dusk at 21.08, the 7MT and thirteen coaches clattered slowly over Bolton West Jc. When clear, *Cromwell* was opened out and the 'Brit's' unmistakable crisp beat blew back pleasingly as the train got into its stride past the forlorn reminder that was 9K and on towards Moses Gate.

Monday, 5 to Saturday, 10 August

The evening after, in the course of a walk to one or two local steamless haunts with Paul, wondering if maybe it really hadn't been able to happen, we phoned Rose Grove mpd, but the stone cold fact was that they had only relieving jobs now. So it had happened. What a huge change from the bustling steam scene I'd so enjoyed there less than a month before. Relieving work. That was how most of Bolton's remaining men worked now. Occupying the summer evenings in alternative ways during those early weeks after the change came more naturally than perhaps was expected, but somehow we didn't seem to be entirely there until after 11 August. On the 6th I got booked in at a bed and breakfast for the night prior to the 15 guinea special, in Gambier Terrace, Liverpool. We had, on the 7th, a pleasant evening walk down the old line to Atherton Bag Lane, Paul, Vern and I. There was choir practice on Thursdays and the 20.55 Club Friday meetings.

Preston on the SO Barrow train was the agreed 'trip' for 10 August, but only the 'Skelton Whine' and I were on the appointed train. Lostock Hall again proved to be the base for Sunday's tour engines. We went to have a look, but after noting only 45110 and 45305 (both 10D) newly fired, were ejected in no uncertain way! There'd doubtless been many at a loose end that day, trying to get around the premises and by noon the staff were clearly fed up with it. I was once asked by a shed worker how it would feel if he walked into the factory where I worked. He had a point, there being no parallel in British industry of attempted public occupation for non-destructive purposes of an enclosed workplace. Part of that very warm August afternoon I watched the summer Saturday traffic go busily by at Preston station, then returned loco-hauled later to prepare for the 11th.

No train from Bolton on Sunday would have got me to Liverpool in time. My dad would doubtless have obliged with a lift, but it wasn't worth risking even the remote chance of delay or breakdown with so much (let alone the 15 guineas!) at stake, so I was there by train mid-Saturday evening. It was a big house, all portraits and mirrors, close by the Anglican cathedral. An enthusiast from Worcester shared the same plans and accommodation, but we didn't talk much.

Sunday, 11 August

Pictures of Lime Street showing 45110 simply adorned with its 1T57 board, the train seemingly hemmed in by countless onlookers filling every available inch of platform and more, yet kept tidily in check by a single visible policeman, are most easily brought to mind by most enthusiasts. This was easily the most famous manifestation of that reporting number but many people appear to believe it was unique to that particular train. Far from it. On consecutive January Sundays in 1963, for example, a Manchester–Ingleton walkers special, 1T57, saddled its passengers with two and a half hours of darkness leading up to departure time; and in June of that year an eleven-coach party special of Burnley dance teachers travelled to Heysham long before the reporting number acquired its fame.

My designated seat was at the train's very rear on that first leg to Manchester, so I quickly grabbed a right-hand drop window in the brake next to the engine. Some minutes before departure a TV cameraman, who'd clearly not paid to be there, attempted to 'share' this vantage point, but to my surprise I successfully defended it for sole usage on the grounds that his equipment 'whir' would interfere with my recordings!

B.R. had intended to cater for 470 passengers, but from the surprisingly varied reports that followed, 420 would seem to have been the sum of tickets sold. One minute late I made it, 45110 with its train of ten coaches, 364½ tons net, began the very difficult cold start at 09.11, paced briefly, as intended, by the electrically-hauled 09.10 to Euston. This pulled ahead quickly as 45110, after several slips, plugged away against the 1 in 93 to Edge Hill, attaining 14mph towards the top. It wasn't at all easy, but Jack Hart, the 61-year-old driver now passing close to his old shed would have known what to expect. A speed of 59mph followed a check at Edge Hill No. 4, but six minutes had been lost to Rainhill, the first commemorative halt. The cutting down of that photographic stop to eight minutes amongst a sea of freely wandering spectators and passengers was a wonder challenged only by my joining them and returning to find my all-important window still free!

On time away, 63mph preceded checks up to and a halt at Parkside to commemorate the well-known and unfortunate fatality there in steam's infancy. Though 1T57 made no inroads into the new, but slight arrears, 45110 sounded in fine form chattering across Barton Moss with such an even exhaust that it could have been a Caprotti. We were up to 63 before Patricroft, then a bad slowing after Eccles put the tour seven minutes late into Victoria. If we believe the shortlist of locos originally advised by B.R., 45110 had not been under consideration, unless, as I strongly suspect, 45310 appeared only due to a misprint. Any other misplaced digit would have thrown up a non-existent or long-withdrawn loco, thereby eliminating conjecture.

As the morning warmed up outside I walked back to claim my premier window seat for the next 125¾ miles, immediately behind the engine, on the left and facing too! The generous half-hour allowance at Victoria, again with platforms crammed to the very edge, permitted 70013 *Oliver Cromwell* to get away only a minute late, but the difficult platform 14 wasn't to the Pacific's liking. It slipped time and time again, (seventeen times on my recording), but once onto the straight, in true 'Boat Train' style leaped ahead comparatively, 44mph over Agecroft Jc. Fell to a steady 40 on to Farnworth, marginally improving before we threaded Bolton at close to the prescribed limit, having lost no further time.

Seated opposite was another tape recording enthusiast whose microphone, not unlike mine, had a curious metal cap instead of the usual foam wind muffler. I recorded the whole ascent from Bradshawgate box to Waltons Sidings. The reason that my left arm ached considerably in the closing stages was the twenty-one-minute duration of that climb, the features of which, to any 'first time Southerners' would have been handsomely exaggerated. No. 70013 started reasonably enough, but never behaved like a true class 7 anywhere in fact, and I can only presume either a persistent, but not serious, shortage of steam on the climb in question,

Unprecedented crowds were a feature at many places of congregation on 11 August to see the much-publicised '15 guinea special', 1T57. Here, during the Rainhill photo stop, passengers swell other ranks to such a degree as to defeat the object. *S.A. Leyland*

No. 45110 (10D) heads for Manchester near Parkside with 1T57. *P. Barber*

At Hellifield one could see rather more of the engine than at previous stops: *Cromwell*'s water was topped up here. *S.A. Leyland*

or a small degree of brake drag. But still the engine remained entertaining, the 'Brit's' sharp, percussive blast never deserting it. From 23mph at The Oaks we began to flag, from Bromley Cross really, experiencing a very gradual drop to 14 at worst, just before Entwistle. Waltons stopped the train briefly and mysteriously, unless the cautious descent that followed was linked to some verbal message communicated to the crew. 1T57 nevertheless pulled into Blackburn on time, thanks to the unexacting schedule so far.

Due to difficulties watering, 70013 had to come off the train for that purpose, delaying its departure by half an hour, to the delight of journalists waiting for an irregularity to pounce on. Eventually, at 12.45, after some curious playing about with the regulator in the tunnel, our driver wisely decided that a generous opening was best to produce the exciting staccato exhaust we heard so clearly on the climb to Cemetery Hill, surmounted at 36mph.

Since the first call at Waltons, just prior to midday, the stewards had experienced some problems in persuading those standing at windows to sit down for lunch, as well as clearing the tables of equipment for setting. It was good to see that taking in of the steam was uppermost in the minds of passengers other than myself. The 'trimmings' on this tour were of little importance personally and I turned down the wine offered. A couple of Southerners across the gangway, unfamiliar with the area, were amused to find two towns in particular, close together on the map they followed. 'I love this town called Salesbury near Wilpshire'. Thinking obviously of Salisbury and Wiltshire, maybe they didn't feel too far from home?

A speed of 64mph down through Langho helped a fairly swift run on to Hellifield and the 'Brit' had sustained 31mph up the 1 in 100 of Rimington bank, again with a lot of gusto. We'd kept the booking from Blackburn, but water was also deemed necessary at Hellifield, though six minutes only were needed for this. A very businesslike start to Long Preston (48mph) preceded an easing until Settle Jc. which could have been taken faster than 58.

At about this stage in the journey we were informed that the souvenir scrolls that were being given out had not been pre-inscribed with the recipient's name and would have to be self-inscribed that so-and-so had travelled on the blah, blah, blah, etc. In truth I recall this omission from what was expected rather a disappointment. Thankfully, for the few making tape recordings from the open stock, unwanted sounds were kept to a minimum. The clinking of plates and the like could hardly be objected to and it even added a degree of authentic class, as the train settled down to 32–35mph on the long climb to Blea Moor, where, if I may juxtapose separate extracts of commentary from an LP record of the event released soon after, 'Even the lonely moorland that skirts the tracks at Ribblehead was crammed to the doors'.

Things did get a bit fraught in that locale personally as I tried to cope with a tape wrap-round, log the run and have my lunch served (two hours after the first call) all at the same time. A friend later disclosed to me a 'disaster' of his own there. Whilst I'd been struggling to disentangle the twisted tape, he, by the lineside had, in the excitement, forgotten to plug in his microphone!

On a justifiably classic route that would become far more famous in years to come, 70013 brings 1T57 over the tops, near Dent. *Anon/M.L.S. collection*

It was indeed a glorious day for train watching. Bare legs dangled from walls, even disused platform edges and other vantage points, as the public turned out in force to wave and cheer us on our way. Morecambe secured the day's sunshine record of 13.2 hours, but it was no less summery elsewhere, even in those fells. Two thousand cars an hour were reported to have been entering Blackpool, but the few and narrow byways of Ais Gill were far more inconvenienced by perhaps a tenth of that.

We had been able to omit the booked water stop of five minutes at Blea Moor, but dropped 4mph in two minutes from that signal box up to entering the tunnel at 29mph. A photo stop lined up for Ais Gill was cut by five minutes, too. At least the journey continued to be remarkably free of engineering work for a Sunday and 70013 managed unhindered progress from Ais Gill to Carlisle in fifty-five and a half minutes. Top speeds of 75 at Ormside and 69 through Little Salkeld were not supported by sufficient velocity elsewhere to maintain the fifty-one-minute booking common to steam-hauled expresses of eight summers before. Their pass to stop status had us at a disadvantage, admittedly, probably facilitating even time dashes over the 48.4 miles in the many seasonal night-time expresses and odd daytime relief that spurned Appleby, too. 1T57 pulled into Citadel station thirty-four late.

That stop at Carlisle, more than halved to a quarter of an hour, took me unawares and still in my seat, unlike one journalist who was allegedly left behind. I should have been sharper and soon paid for my tardiness. Even a futile and largely obstructed walk through the ten coaches and back looking for a free window didn't justify a twenty-eight-minute gap in my log, almost to Culgaith! No. 44781, piloted by 44871, were running well. Emitting mostly a thin grey exemplary exhaust, the pair were clearly not to be trifled with, gaining five minutes to pass Appleby in just less than forty at 60mph, after much speeding in the mid-60s. An unfortunate lapse to 36mph by Griseburn, ending the first 1 in 100 stretch, kept the Appleby–Ais Gill average down to a shade under 50mph, but a lively enough 52 over the summit made amends. Quickly up to 70 beyond the crest, 1T57 swept around the curves approaching Garsdale at slightly less. Only a slack at Dent, to 32mph, prevented an on-time arrival at the Blea Moor water stop. This was extended to a photo opportunity too, but though descending to the ballast using the steps provided, I stayed at the train's rear, more peacefully obtaining an alternative view and one of the signal box, recalling no doubt the time spent therein, 'all in an April afternoon' more than two years before, and how so much more than the weather that day contrasted with this. We were away again at 16.21, breaking the thread of any such reverie.

Much less taxed in other departments than on the northbound run, I cheerfully accepted a spare 'high tea' salad as well as my own before Blackburn. The day's highest speed of 77mph came briefly approaching Settle, but the seventeen-minute lateness from Blea Moor was deviated from but a little through to Manchester. Our pair of 5MTs fell from 42 through Whalley to 37mph on the bank by Langho, prior to a short signal stop at Wilpshire. At Blackburn I walked forward again to tape our ascent to Waltons, being loath to let those classic uphill miles of

What could today pass for the U.K.'s biggest classic car show, is, as many will recognise, the traffic jam approaching Ais Gill on 11 August as practically all the linesiders homed in on the equally classic location to view or photograph 1T57. Wild Boar Fell to the north is in the background. *V.A. Sidlow*

which I'd become so fond and familiar slip by unrecorded, but window occupancy, as expected, prevented full absorption of the live event, to say the least. Through the early sunny evening we forged in the 30s, an urgent enough exhaust audible from one or both locos intermittently, until their exertions ceased at 31mph over the see-saw summit to which I never expected to return. Uneventful was the rest of the running with our double-header as the many familiar features on home ground were passed by, never to be seen again in quite the same way. Thoughts, until now largely distracted by goings on of the day spent steam-hauled through town and country, began to turn to the significance of those diminishing miles.

1T57 halved the loco-changing allowance at Victoria to one of only seven minutes. This involved 45110 coupling to our rear for the final (non-stop) stretch to Liverpool Lime Street. This time I couldn't be caught out by the slick operation! The 4-6-0 began slowly, very slowly, but more sure-footedly than the Pacific, from platform 12, no easier proposition than 14. It did feel as if the brake drag characteristics, real or imagined, had returned briefly. However, 45110 got away soon after to hold very similar rates along the flat as it had that morning. A check before Newton-le-Willows, then the last highlight in sound with an energetic attack on the short but steep length of railway between St Helens Jc. and Rainhill constituted the day's final recording.

As the lowering sun's rays of that beautiful summer's day played along and through the coach windows of our unnamed farewell train, they were metaphorically setting on so much more, a plain fact of which few passengers, as 1T57 rolled its last miles into the city, were not deeply conscious.

At a few seconds to 20.00, 45110 came to rest at the Lime Street buffers. After collecting my belongings I stood alone for some time opposite the familiar engine's smokebox, half lost to melancholy thought. That's all I would have said here, but there exists a certain tape recording that gives an independent view in part of a conversation held elsewhere on Lime Street between some

The last movement for 70013 after its part in the 1T57 tour was returning light from Carlisle to its new home at Bressingham Gardens, near Diss, where, by design or coincidence, 'Britannias' reigned in their infancy. The early part of its preservation there would be considered quite dormant, until the later awakening of the main line scene brought things to it unimaginable in 1968. Here, the Pacific crosses Dent Head viaduct en route to expected retirement on that lovely summer's afternoon. *N. Fields/M.L.S. collection*

As 1T57 passed under Green Lane bridge, Bolton behind its pair of 5s, 44871 and 44781 (both 10A), the author's thoughts may well have flashed back to his earliest spotting days there, just a mile from home, whilst being far from alone in having other memories evoked throughout that day. Green Lane is the location depicted. *Bill Harrison*

For those most closely involved and affected by the decline and ultimate demise of steam on B.R., the sun had set already on so much more than the 'farewell' tour, seen here on its last leg as 45110 passes Lea Green. The alternative steam attractions hinted at within were as yet virtually untried (industrials) and very underdeveloped (preservation). Industrial steam became important and fulfilling for some whilst the best places survived, as did world steam for much longer, but I think that few in August 1968, your author included, felt other than a kind of suspension when all that they'd known and allowed to dominate their lives ended. *V.A. Sidlow*

of the 20.55 Club and the 'Wellington Mouth'. The latter is asked if he's seen me. He had, voicing the opinion that I looked 'close to tears. Very, very sad'. There partly for the purpose of meeting me off the train were Vern (who'd made the recording, unknown to all), Hilary, Keith, Jim and probably 'Tosh' too. All acknowledged the mood below the surface, but there was cheerfulness in numbers and 'Wellington' effervesced in parting. 'Come to Bridgnorth!' he entreated lightly, as an indicator of where the immediate future lay for him, but neither Bridgnorth nor the preserved scene could satisfy him for long. It was B.R. that had him in its grip and as one of the era's reluctant adaptables to conventional post-1968 life, he'd probably be content to own that it eventually, if indirectly, killed him.

I still went home by train from Liverpool, probably too late to catch *Flying Scotsman*'s non-stop May East Coast Main Line run on BBC TV (in colour). Maybe I'd shunned it in anticipation of continued inaccurate representation. There was plenty of that next morning as people at work showed me four newspaper accounts of the 15 Guinea Special, two of which I'd dismissed as 'rubbish'. Ill-informed statements such as confusing the day's mileage with the number of passengers were mixed with over-emphasis on cost and the leaving behind of careless journalists at stops that had been shortened to reduce the lateness they also criticised! The *Daily Express*'s Alan Bennett at least combined dignity with some useful information in his account. 'WHAT A GLORIOUS WAY TO END IT ALL' read the headline. Yes, it had been indeed!

It's a quieter railway now than it used to be. The sounds that once emanated from the Bolton sheds and yards over Great Lever have gone for good; engine whistles, exhausts and other surprisingly varied loco and associated noises, wagons crashing together in rough shunts, even ordinary shunting when the wind was right, as well as rolling stock on fish-plated track. A quieter railway to me is a less interesting railway, but of course not just any kind of sound will do!

Nearly all the church bells have long since ceased to peal in Bolton. The rag and bone man no longer calls out unintelligibly for wares. Internal combustion engines don't backfire any more, but they are ten times in number. I wouldn't claim to actually pine for those vanished sounds, even those of the railway, but each cacophonic 'essential' of modern life in general that has replaced them brings a reminder of less frantic times. Who will mourn their eventual passing?

There are few railway enthusiasts who have never expressed a wish, however seriously, that they'd been born earlier, to some degree or other. I have said it, and wished it too, for reasons not too obscure, but I'm also glad after all that, despite certain practical disadvantages, I wasn't completely grown up when all that is described herein and the railway years leading up to it took place. Its falling upon youthful senses and perceptions not then dulled by life and age is something I am well conscious of having made a difference. I am also aware that what we were able and privileged to experience looks set to endure in many hearts with undiminished affection for a long time to come.

Appendix I
Abbreviations and Railway Terms

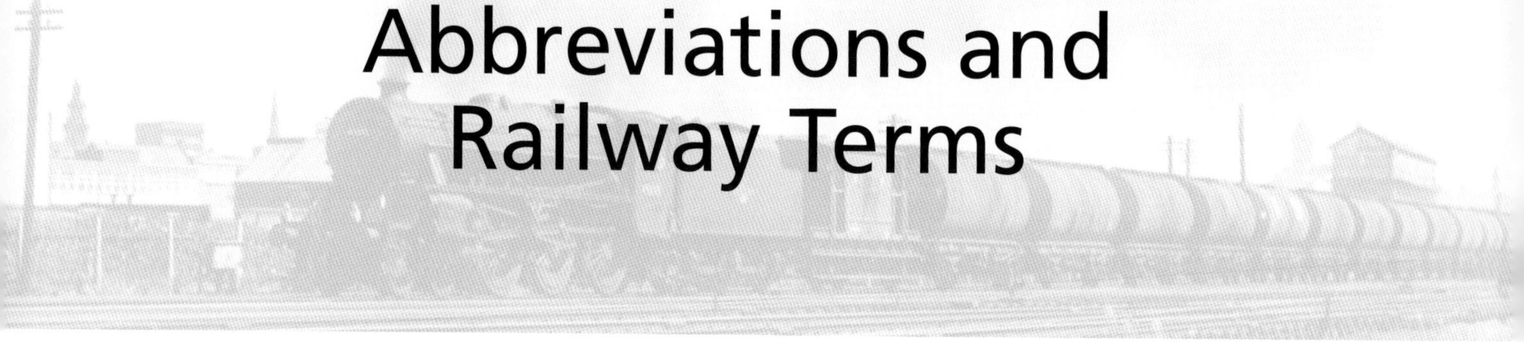

Steam Locomotive Classes

Ivatt 4	L.M.S. Ivatt 4MT 2-6-0
Piggy(ies)	(ditto)
Black 5	L.M.S. Stanier 5MT 4-6-0
5MT	(ditto)
Class 5	(ditto)
8F	L.M.S. Stanier 8F 2-8-0
75XXX	B.R. Standard 4MT 4-6-0
Standard 5	B.R. Standard 5MT 4-6-0
Caprotti 5	Caprotti Valve Gear version of above
Brit/Britannia	B.R. Standard 7MT 4-6-2
WD 2-8-0	Austerity 8F 2-8-0
9F	B.R. Standard 9F 2-10-0

Diesel Locomotive Classes

Type 1 – Clayton Bo-Bo (later class 17)
Type 2 – Sulzer Bo-Bo (later class 25)
Type 3 – English Elec. Co-Co (later class 37)
Type 4 – English Elec. 1Co-Co1 (later class 40)
Brush 4 – Brush/Sulzer Co-Co (later class 47)
Peak – Sulzer 1Co-Co1 (later class 45)
(NB: Certain other diesel and electric locos appear without further clarification needed.)

A.S.L.E.F.	Associated Society of Locomotive Enginemen and Firemen
Adex	Additional Day Excursion
Ballast Engine	Loco-hauling train engaged in track ballast and P. Way work.
Block	Signalling block section. Instruments in signal box appertaining to.
Bobby	Signalman
Brake	Abbreviation for brake van.
B.R.	British Railways.
B.T.E.G.	British Transport Enthusiast Guild.
Circuit	Traffic message circulated simultaneously to number of signal boxes on a specific 'circuit'.
C.S.	Carriage Sidings.
C.L.C.	Cheshire Lines Committee (Rly Co.)
Covhops	Covered Hoppers (for grain, powders and chemicals, etc.).
Derv	Diesel.
Diagram	Scheduled work for one locomotive between leaving motive power depot and returning.
Distant	Yellow signal arm caution or clear.
Down	Down line, direction of travel.
Dmu	Diesel Multiple Unit.
E.B.V.	Engine and brake van.
E.C.S.	Empty Coaching Stock.
E.L.	East Lancs, lines (at Preston).

Emu	Electric Multiple Unit.
Even Time	60mph average.
FO	Fridays Only.
F.O.C.	Free of Charge.
G.C.	Great Central.
Grice	To travel over track for the first time, i.e. specific route.
I.C.I.	Imperial Chemical Industries.
L.C.G.B.	Locomotive Club of Great Britain.
LE	Locomotive without any train.
Light	(ditto)
Limited Load	B.R. Passenger train timing category with set limit on train weight.
L.M.R.	London Midland Region of B.R.
L.M.S.	London Midland & Scottish Rly.
L.N.W.R.	London & North Western Rly.
L.P.	Long playing record.
L. & Y.	Lancashire & Yorkshire (Rly).
MO	Mondays Only.
Mpd	Motive Power Depot.
MSO	Mondays and Saturdays Only.
MSX	Mondays and Saturdays Excepted.
MWFO	Mondays, Wednesdays and Fridays Only.
MX	Mondays Excepted.
N.E.R.	North Eastern Region.
N1 Notice	Special Traffic Notice dealing with Western Lines of L.M.R.
N2 Notice	Special Traffic Notice dealing with Central Lines of L.M.R.
Off	Clear aspect of signal.
O.S.	Ordnance Survey (map).
Peg	Slang for signal.
Pilot	Assisting engine or shunting engine at specific location, depending on context.
P.S.	Power Station.
P.W. Slowing	Speed restriction imposed by Permanent Way Engineers.
P. Way	Permanent way.
P. Way Work	Work carried out on above.
R.C.T.S	Railway Correspondence & Travel Society.
Relief	Enginemen/Signalmen's relief by new crew/personnel, or a relief (additional) train, depending on context.
R.O.F.	Royal Ordnance Factory.
R.S.F.	Running Shed Foreman (loco).
S.L.S.	Stephenson Locomotive Society.
SO	Saturdays Only.
S.T.Ns.	Special Traffic Notices.
SuX	Sundays Excepted.
SX	Saturdays Excepted.
Target	Non-Working Timetabled loco duty.
Trip	(ditto)
Up	Up line; direction of travel.
W.C.M.L.	West Coast Main Line.
W.T.T.	Working Timetable (not Public).

Appendix II
Railway Place Names Lesser Known in the Twenty-first Century

Agecroft Jc	Bolton–Manchester line, 1½ miles south of Clifton Jc.	Byng Street Sdgs	Former carriage and dmu Sdg. Immediately north of Bolton station on Blackburn line. Became temporary diesel stabling point June 1968.
Ancoats	Manchester goods yard, between Ashburys and Ardwick.		
Ardwick	Manchester station and yard just west of Ashburys.	Canklow	Midland Railway mpd 2 miles south of Rotherham Masborough station.
Arpley	Warrington goods yard on low level LNWR lines.		
Ashton Moss	Yards and Sidings just west of Guide Bridge.	Clayton Bridge	Station between Park and Droylsden on Manchester Vic.–Stalybridge line.
'A' Side or Siding	Between Bolton East Jc. and Burnden Jc. on Down side. (see Diagram 2, Appendix V)	Constable Lane	Box on LH side, 2¾ miles west of Salwick.
		Copy Pit	Summit of Burnley–Todmorden line.
Astley Green	Colliery Sidings on Chat Moss, 2 miles east of Glazebury.	Cowlairs Works	Glasgow.
Avenue Sidings	Midland Main Line just south of Hasland.	Croes Newydd	Mpd for Wrexham GWR.
		Crow Nest Jc	Convergence of Bolton, and Manchester Vic. via Atherto–Wigan lines.
'B' Side or Siding	Bolton East Jc. facing Bury line. AKA Rose Hill. (see Diagram 2, Appendix V)		
		Dallam	Mpd 1 mile north of Warrington on WCML.
Bay Horse	Closed station north of Preston between Scorton and Galgate.	De Trafford Jc	Box west of Hindley North controlling Wigan avoiding (Whelley) lines.
Bradley Fold	2½ miles east of Bolton on Bury line.		
Bradshawgate	First box on Blackburn line north of Bolton, within Bolton.	Dewsnap	Large yard on electrified line between Guide Bridge and Hyde M Jc.
Brewery Sidings	Other side of main line opposite Newton Heath mpd, Manchester.	Dobbs Brow Jc	Box on Manchester Vic.–Wigan via Atherton line where Horwich Fork Jc. line diverged.
Brindle Heath	Sidings both sides of Agecroft Jc.–Pendleton Broad St line.		
Broadfield	Station before Castleton on Bury–Rochdale line.	East Jc	Bolton East Jc. (often abbreviated in text). (see Diagram 2, Appendix V)
Burnden Jc	Box controlling entrance to Bolton mpd. Also nearby sidings.	Eastfield	Mpd in Glasgow.
		Farington	Closed station and two boxes on WCML between Leyland and Preston.
Bullfield	East and West boxes, first out of Bolton on Lostock Jc. line, & Sdgs.		
Bushbury	LNWR Motive Power Depot, Wolverhampton.	Giggleswick	Station and sidings between

	Settle Jc. and Clapham.	Ribble	Sidings immediately south of Ribble bridge (WCML) at Preston.
Gowhole	Marshalling yard between New Mills and Chinley.	Rose Hill Siding	As per 'B' Side, Bolton.
Grassington	Terminus of branch north of Skipton.	Rose Hill Jc	Box at easternmost point of Bolton East Jc./Burnden Jc./Rose Hill Jc. triangle, Bolton.
Great Rocks Jc	Box and sidings a mile south of Peak Forest.	Shotwick	Iron Ore Siding in south west corner of the Wirral.
Green Ayre	Midland station and mpd in Lancaster.	Skelton Jc	Three-way junction just east of Altrincham.
Green Lane	This reference is to bridge over Bolton–Manchester line before Moses Gate.	Smithy Bridge	Closed station and loops east of Rochdale on Calder Valley line
Halliwell	Sidings on Astley Bridge branch just north of Bolton off Blackburn line.	Sough/Sough Tunnel	Half mile south of Spring Vale on Blackburn–Bolton line.
Haslams	Sidings between Bolton East Jc. and Burnden Jc. (see Diagram 2, Appendix V)	Spencer's Sidings	On Grassington branch, north of Skipton.
Healey Mills	'New' (1963) super-marshalling yard near Horbury & Ossett on L & Y.	Spink Hill	On GC lines, ten miles west of Worksop.
Heap Bridge	Paper Mill with BR connection between Bury and Broadfield.	Spring Vale	Closed station just south of Darwen on Blackburn–Bolton line.
Heaton Norris Jc	Junction immediately north of Stockport viaduct.	Stansfield Hall	Immediately east of Todmorden on connection to Burnley line.
Hindlow	3 miles south east of Buxton.	Stoke Gifford	Marshalling yard at present site of Bristol Parkway station.
Lea Green	1¼ miles east of Rainhill.	Summit	Box, tunnel and summit of line between Littleborough and Walsden.
Long Meg	Box and sidings on Settle & Carlisle line near Lazonby & Kirkoswald.	Tank Yard	Near summit of Miles Platting bank from Manchester Victoria.
Millerhill	Marshalling yard on North British metals south-east of Edinburgh.	Tinsley	'New' super-marshalling yard south of Rotherham.
Mold Jc	Goods Yard just west of Saltney Jc., Chester.	Todd Lane Jc	Convergence of lines from Preston EL and Lostock Hall.
Orlando Bridge	Footbridge and separate traffic bridge immediately east of Bolton Stn.	Tunstead	Box and sidings south of Peak Forest before Buxton line diverges.
O.B.	Footbridge and separate traffic bridge immediately east of Bolton Stn.	Tyseley	GWR mpd in Birmingham.
		Wallerscote	ICI Sidings off main line just south of Oakleigh (Northwich).
Oakleigh	ICI Sidings south of Northwich.	Waltons Sidings	Summit of Bolton–Blackburn line north of Entwistle.
Partington	3 miles west of Skelton Jc. on the CLC line.	Whitebirk	Power station between Rishton and Blackburn.
Peel Hall	Between Walkden High Level and Atherton Central.	Windsor Bridge	Three signal boxes just north of Salford on Bolton line.
Pepper Hill	Box and Down loop north of Clifton Jc.	Wyre Dock	Fleetwood.
Portsmouth	This reference is to closed station on westbound climb to Copy Pit.		
Portwood	Goods Yard close to Stockport Tiviot Dale.		
Queen's Road	Carriage Sidings, Cheetham Hill, north Manchester.		
Red Bank	Carriage Sidings, closer to Manchester Vic. than above, on LH Thorpes Bridge route.		

Appendix III
Summary of Trips Made in 1968

DATE	LOCATION/DESTINATION	DURATION
Wed 3/1	Bradley Fold	Evening
Sat 6/1	Manchester Vic., Sheffield, Preston*	Afternoon & evening
Mon 8/1	Kearsley	Morning
Fri 12/1	Preston, Manchester Vic.	Afternoon
Sat 13/1	Northwich, Preston*	Full day
Sat 20/1	Peak Forest, Stockport, Preston*	Full day
Sat 27/1	Skelton Jc., Preston*	Full day with late afternoon break
Sat 3/2	Skelton Jc., Woodley, Preston*	Full day
Sat 10/2	Hindley, Littleborough, Preston*	Full day
Sun 11/2	Skelton Jc.	Morning and afternoon
Sat 17/2	Peak Forest, Edale, Preston*	Full day
Fri 23/2	Footplate run: Bolton–Rochdale–Ancoats–Bolton	Full evening
Sat 24/2	Manchester Vic., Peak Forest, Preston*	Midday–late evening
Sat 2/3	Chinley, Peak Forest, Ashwood Dale, Preston*	Full Day
Sat 9/3	Bradley Fold, Waltons Sdgs, Bolton, Manchester Vic.	Full Day
Sat 16/3	Woodlands Road, Chorley*, Manchester Vic.	Morning & evening separately
Sun 17/3	Turton	Morning
Wed 20/3	Manchester Vic.*	Evening
Sat 23/3	Skelton Jc.	Up to mid-afternoon
Mon 25/3	Manchester Vic.*	Evening
Sat 30/3	Liverpool via Exchange, Speke Jc., Runcorn, Sutton Weaver	Full day
Wed 3/4	Manchester Vic.*	Evening
Sat 6/4	Latchford, Runcorn, Northwich, Warrington	Full day
Tues 9/4	Bradley Fold West	Evening
Fri 12/4	Preston, Manchester Vic.*	Morning & evening separately
Sat 13/4	Manchester Vic.*, Westhoughton, Halliwell, Spring Vale, Manchester Vic., Chorley*	Full day
Mon 15/4	Preston, Blackpool, Colne	Full day
Tues 16/4	Manchester Vic., Clayton Bridge, Blackpool South	To late afternoon
Sat 20/4	Manchester Vic. (1Z77 Railtour chase), Manchester Vic.–Bolton*	Full day
Tues 23/4	Spring Vale	Evening
Sat 27/4	Woodley, Preston*	Full day
Mon 29/4	Manchester Vic.*	Evening
Fri 3/5–Sat 4/5	Manchester Vic., Heysham, Manchester Vic., Woodley, Preston*	Overnight & full day
Wed 8/5	Broadfield	Evening
Sat 11/5	Westhoughton, Bradley Fold, Waltons Sidings, Blackpool South*	Full day
Tues 14/5	Hoddlesden Jc.	Evening
Wed 15/5	Darwen & Hoddlesden Jc.	Evening
Sat 18/5	Todmorden, Lydgate, Bamber Bridge, Lostock Hall, Skew Bridge	Full day
Mon 20/5	Broadfield	Evening
Sat 25/5	Skipton, Hoddlesden Jc., Preston, Blackpool South*	Full day
Mon 27/5	Hoddlesden Jc.	Evening
Sat 1/6	Newton Heath, Brewery area, Blackpool South*	Full day

Appendix III — Summary of Trips Made in 1968

DATE	LOCATION/DESTINATION	DURATION
Mon 3/6	Preston	Evening
Wed 5/6	Broadfield	Evening
Fri 7/6	Footplate run: Bolton–Rochdale–Ancoats–Bolton	Full evening
Mon 10/6	Hoddlesden Jc.	Evening
Wed 12/6	Broadfield	Evening
Fri 14/6–Sat 15/6	Manchester Vic. & Exch, Carnforth, Oxenholme, Preston, Kirkham*	Overnight & full day
Mon 17/6	Preston Docks	Evening
Sat 22/6	Newton Heath, Brewery area, Blackpool South*	Full day
Sun 23/6	Todmorden, Lydgate	Up to mid-afternoon
Sat 29/6	Agecroft, Manchester Vic., Castleton, Bolton, Manchester Exch, Patricroft	Full day
Mon 1/7	Ulverston, Dalton	Full day
Tues 2/7	Preston, Carnforth, Lancaster	Up to teatime
Wed 3/7	Preston, Carnforth, Lancaster	Up to early evening
Thur 4/7	Preston, Carnforth, Kendal	Up to early evening
Fri 5/7	Preston, Rose Grove, Colne, Stockport	Full day
Mon 8/7	Rose Grove	Up to early evening
Tues 9/7	Rose Grove, Hoghton	Full day
Fri 12/7	Rose Grove, Hoghton	Full day
Sat 13/7	Waltons Sidings, Blackpool South*	Afternoon–late evening
Wed 17/7	Hoghton, Blackburn	Evening
Fri 19/7–Sat 20/7	Accrington, Stockport	Overnight
Sat 20/7	Preston, Blackpool South	Mid-afternoon–late evening
Sun 21/7	Westhoughton	Short afternoon
Wed 24/7	Blackburn	Evening
Sat 27/7	Preston, Preston Docks, Manchester Vic., Lostock Hall, Blackpool South*	Full day
Mon 29/7	Hoghton	Evening
Wed 31/7	Waltons Sidings	Evening
Fri 2/8–Sat 3/8	Waltons Sidings, Entwistle	Overnight
Sat 3/8	Preston, Blackpool South*	Evening
Sun 4/8	Railtours chase by car. Various locations	Full day
Sun 11/8	Travelling on 1T57, 15 Guinea Special	Full day

Note: Locations with asterisk denote that this was the destination of a steam run on either the 'Belfast Boat Express' or the 20.50 Preston–Blackpool only.

Appendix IV
Explanation of Train Reporting Numbers

The four-character Reporting Number system (as in the 'reporting' by signal boxes of a train's progress to Control Offices), established by mid-1961 and still in use today, gave every train on B.R. a unique number on the day carried, e.g. 1J42. The first numeric character denoted the classification of the train, i.e. zero for light engine, 1 and 2 passenger trains (express and others), 3 for parcels, loaded or empty and finally 4 to 9 were for goods trains in descending order of vacuum brake-fitted vehicles, 4 being fully fitted. The second character denoted the district or area of the train's destination, as follows, and applicable to 1968 and the contents of this book:

- A – London Euston.
- C – Manchester Exchange from Western (ex L.N.W.R. lines)
- E – Eastern Region destinations.
- F – Wigan, Warrington and Liverpool.
- H – South Manchester & Stoke areas.
- J – North Manchester area.
- K – Crewe and Liverpool Lime Street.
- L – Local to L.M.R.
- M – to L.M.R. from other Regions or within L.M.R.
- N – North Eastern destinations.
- P – Preston, Fylde & district.
- S – Scottish Region destinations.
- T – Local to L.M.R.
- V – Western Region destinations.
- Z – Inter-Regional (special trains only).

The last two characters denoted the unique number of the train in question. Loaded parcels trains had numbers 00 to 29, whereas 30 to 49 were used for empty parcels stock within the class 3 category. One would occasionally find one that defied the general area guidelines. The only exceptions to a reporting number being unique to a single train on a given day occurred within frequent and repeated passenger trains between the same two points being designated the same number. 'L' and 'T' became much more widely used from mid-1967 when 'Z' replaced 'X' for inter-regional special trains, the latter then being used for royal trains only.

Opposite top: A forlorn sight that had become all too familiar in the last years is epitomised in this view of 9K after closure and the removal of locos. Gaunt, yet welcoming to any loco seeking a resting place, but none would enter that building again. *Bart van der Leeuw*

Bottom: As the shed emptied, their erstwhile contents were towed away to places such as this. This, unmistakeable as Woodham Bros., Barry, was at the time no different to any other major scrapyard purchasing steam locos from B.R., except that the ranks of the condemned had been growing steadily for years. Someone, somewhere, must first lay claim to having said 'Can't we get one of these going again?' But none of this was dreamed of as 1T57 rolled the last few yards to the Lime Street buffer stops. *David A.J. Shirres*

Appendix IV   Explanation of Train Reporting Numbers

243

Appendix V
Maps and Diagrams

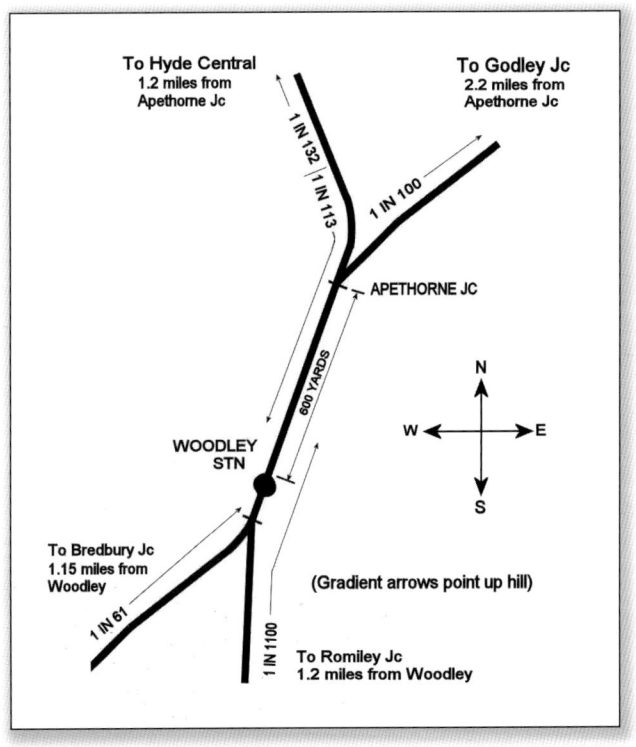

Opposite: Bolton Shed Layout.

Left: A reference map of Woodley and Apethorne Jc.

Bottom: Bolton East Jc. circa 1967.

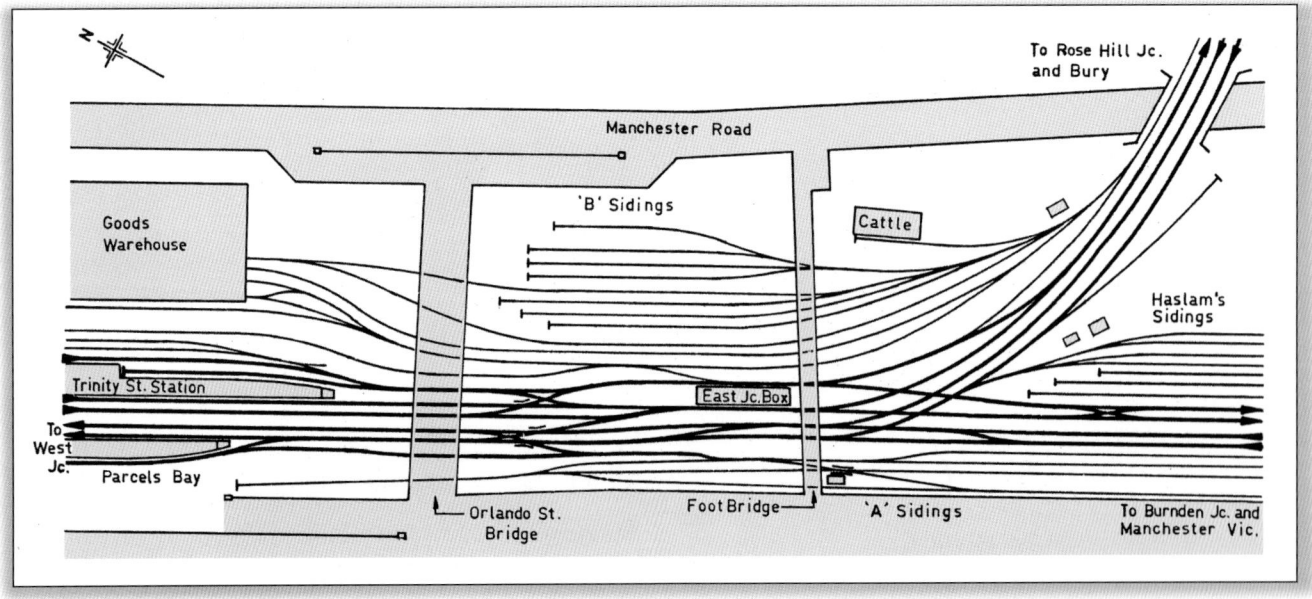

APPENDIX V   MAPS AND DIAGRAMS

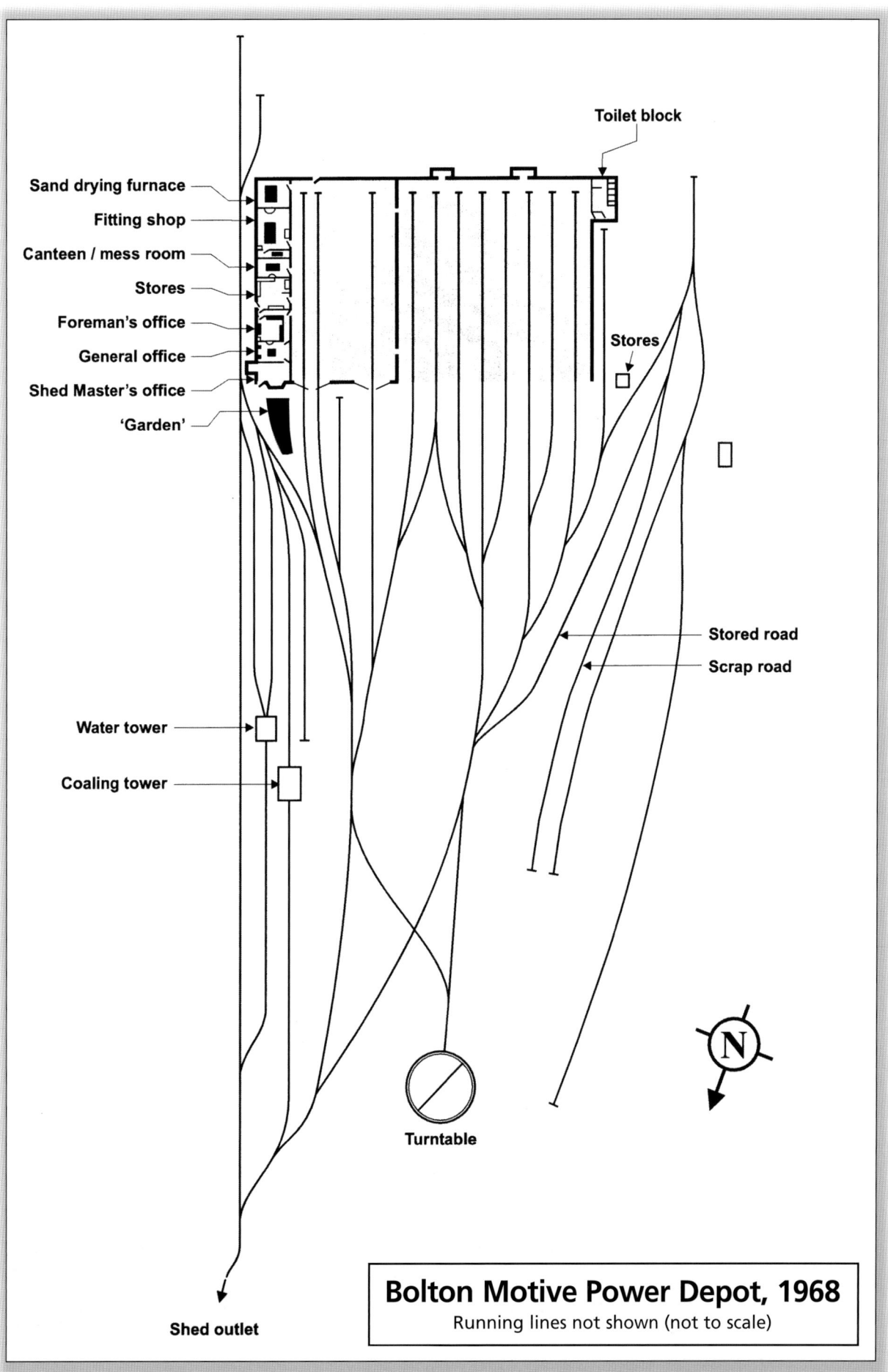

British Railways Steam 1968

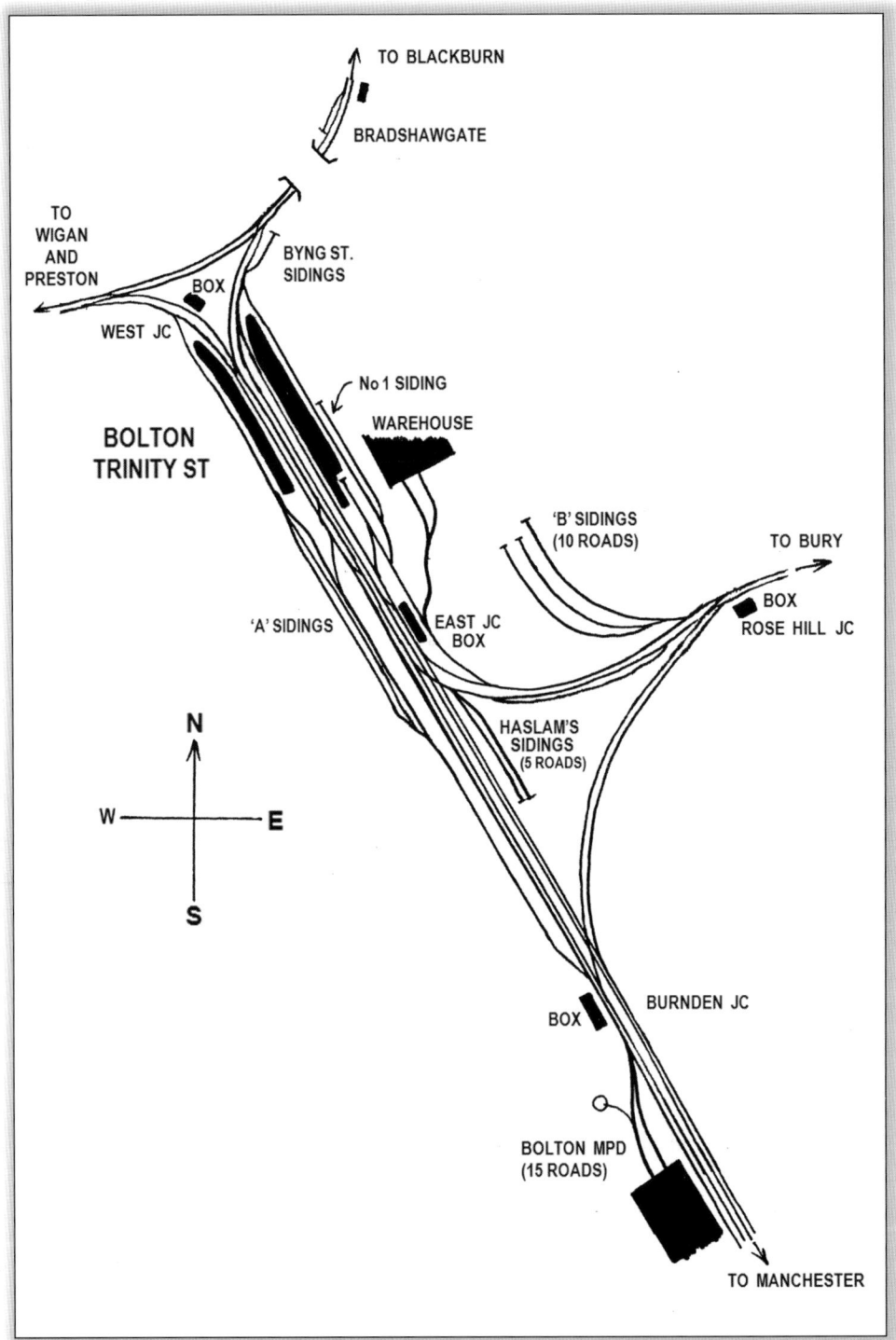

Simplified diagram of Bolton station and surrounding area, 1968.

Index

Individual trains are indexed by starting point with departure time in brackets.
Principal subjects in CAPITALS are followed by subsidiary or related subjects also in alphabetical order until the next principal subject or individual line.

20.55 CLUB
    Formation of 29, 41, 51, 58, 62-63, 113
    In general.......................128, 160, 202, 225, 233-234
    Official greeting/catch phrases 214

Abram-Halliwell (09.20) 14, 15
Ancoats-Carlisle (20.00) 48
Announcers...184
Apethorne Jc...105, map 244
Astley Green Signal Box 172
Avenue Sidings-Garston (06.27) 45

BANKING
    Brewery Sidings..141
    Great Rocks-Peak Forest.......................................36
    Miles Platting...46
    Oxenholme-Grayrigg..152
    Stansfield Hall-Copy Pit..................................128-129
Barrow-Carnforth goods (13.50) 178
Barrow-Manchester parcels (07.40)..........................8, 12
Barrow-Preston parcels (20.28)............................183, 218
BELFAST BOAT EXPRESS
    Delayed by derailment 29
    End of Steam...112-121
    Fatality at Farnworth 161
    Focal point of trips 29
    Image 53
    In general...................8, 14, 51, 70, 73, 79, 104, 140
    Increased popularity with enthusiasts.........20, 29, 110
    Late start (M/C Vic. SO) 46, 51
    Local observations (not Bolton Station) 35, 41
    LOCOMOTIVES (selected) on 'Boat Train'
        Non-Carnforth-based......41, 50-51, 73, 82, 100, 102
        Unidentified 35
        Unsettled power 41
        45025...51, 60, 2
        45342 (intermittent) 112-120
        45394...105
        45435...110
        Punctuality..15
        Runs described – performance
        (chiefly south of Preston)........20, 29, 31, 35, 39,
        42, 47-49, 53, 60, 63, 66, 71, 73, 77-78, 82,
        83, 85, 88, 94, 99, 100, 104-105, 109,
        111-114, 119-120
Bickershaw Colliery 199
Birkenhead-Ilkeston (09.35)...45

Blackpool-Manchester parcels (03.05) 13
Blackpool-Manches ter parcels (13.50).......8, 14, 24, 100
Blackpool-Manchester parcels (21.45) 13
Blackpool North mpd..96-97
Bloemfontein 212
Bloomfield Road Signal Box..212
BOLTON EAST Jc. SIGNAL BOX
    Description..19
    Hours worked 19
    Phone console (new)...79
    Self leaving 24
BOLTON EAST Jc. SIGNALMEN
    Blackburn, M...73
    Dewberry, G..87
    Hofton, A. 60, 87
    Middlewood, R. 19
    Plant, A..79
    Shepherd, T...100
    Thomasson, S. 21, 41
    Winnard, J...19
    Wood, H...21
    Trainbookers/booking 41, 79, 7, 196, 221
    Visits by self (post-employment)..............79, 100, 126,
        140, 144, 157, 196, 199, 221
Bolton Evening News 110, 167, 169
Bolton-Guide Bridge parcels (20.55)................14, 24, 35,
    79, 123, 140
BOLTON MOTIVE POWER DEPOT & LOCOS
    After closure 204
    Allocation list/strength of .87, 120, 135-136, 165, 177
    Availability 55-56
    Byng Street 210
    Cleaning..8, 20-21, 40, 47-48, 50, 60, 63, 73, 85, 88,
        104, 128, 138, 167
    Coaling tower..173
    Contents (nature of) 55, 135
    Depot records 15, 199
    Diesel presence 82
    Driving (unofficial)..50, 147
    End of steam at......................141, 160, 165-169, 174
    ENGINEMEN & STAFF
        Conversation between crews 60
        Byrne, J...25
        Faulkner, W..89
        Frost, M..168
        Greenfield, F...25
        Hesketh, P..70

ENGINEMEN & STAFF (continued...)
  Horrocks, R. 60, 124, 146-147, 165
  Hulton A. 19, 70
  Leigh, O. 52, 53, 60, 165
  Markland, J. 89
  Meadowcroft, E. 25
  Platt, P.C. 21
  Sammon, T. 168
  Welsby, H. 76
  L & Y saddletank visit 105
  Painting (detail) 33, 35, 94, 128, 165
  Railtour involvement 74, 102, 108
  Scrap line 56
  Scrapping on site 56, 82, 146
  Turns/jobs worked 14, 15, 122-123
  Women at depot 165-166
  Work levels/assessment of 15, 56, 122-123

BOLTON MOTIVE POWER DEPOT
  REGULAR WORKINGS – not all
  complete turns, in some cases, but parts thereof
  Abram-Bolton (11.20) 123
  Agecroft-Dewsnap (10.00) 168
  Ancoats-Heysham (22.30)
    – men only – 13, 61, 123, 147, 149
  Ardwick-Moses Gate (15.25) 123
  Ashton Moss-Agecroft (00.36) 123
  Ashton Moss-Agecroft (05.17) 123
  Ashton Moss-Agecroft (13.25) 123
  Bamfurlong-Halliwell (08.58) 15, 51, 89-90, 125
  Bolton Ballast 15, 123
  Bolton-Bamfurlong 15
  Bolton-Bedford parcels (20.20)
    – men only – 14, 24, 48, 60-61, 73, 78, 86,
                                                    123, 124, 135
  Bolton-Healey Mills (22.16) 14, 60, 123, 149
  Bolton-Moston (04.00) 15
  Bolton-Moston (18.05) 14, 17, 86, 124, 135, 146, 149
  Bolton-Moston (19.37) 19, 22, 35
  Bolton Station Pilot 14, 24, 40, 73, 87
  Brewery-Bolton (18.33) 124
  Brewery-Horwich (07.40) 14, 18, 24
  Brindle Heath-Agecroft-Moston trips 15
  Brindle Heath-Horwich (12.07) 14, 24, 27
  'B' Side Pilot 24, 79
  'Carnforth Engine' 167
  Castleton Pilot 15, 168
  Colne-Ashton Moss parcels (17.45) 14, 24, 41, 48,
                73, 76, 79, 104, 123, 125, 135-136, 140, 211
  Continuous Pilot 15
  Halliwell-Healey Mills (12.35) 14, 19, 24, 52,
                                                    70, 123, 126
  Halliwell-Healey Mills (14.40) 123

Halliwell Pilot 16
Healey Mills-Bolton (03.05) 14, 123
Heap Bridge trip 15
Heysham-Ardwick (18.45) 14, 46, 53, 70, 92, 123
                                                    (to Brewery), 126
Horwich-Moston 14, 18, 22, 24, 48
Kearsley Pilot 15, 18, 21
Manchester-Colne news (03.45) 14, 41, 123, 137
Mottram-Philips Park (22.52) 123
Patricroft-Crumpsall 15, 73
Rawtenstall Pilot 15
Rawtenstall–Rochdale parcels (18.16) 123
Red Bank-Manchester Vic ECS (03.05) 123
Special trips 15
Bolton-Rochdale line closure 135
Bolton-Wigan parcels (20.05) 24, 48, 73, 78, 140
Bolton Youth Orchestra 29, 48, 56, 125, 158, 211
Bradshawgate Signal Box 70
Brewery-Blackburn (03.55) 14
Brewery-Blackburn (23.28) 13, 140, 220
Brewery-Blackpool (03.35/40) 14, 18
Brewery-Burnley (05.25) 12, 14, 16, 18, 21, 70
Brewery-Burnley (07.45) 12
Brewery-Carlisle (08.30) 12, 18, 24
Brewery-Ribble (23.20) 13
British Rail Image 53
British Transport Enthusiasts Guild 40, 82, 110, 111, 204
Bullfield West Signal Box 41
Burnley-Moston (16.40) 14, 24, 73, 78, 79, 112,
                                            124, 128, 135, 136, 140,
                                                    146, 149, 210
Burnley-Moston (19.05) 12, 14, 24, 41, 48, 73, 79,
                                            104-105, 125, 136, 140, 147,
                                                149, 158, 191, 199, 204,
                                                    209, 211, 218, 219
Burnley-Wyre Dock (10.50) 201
Buxton mpd 35, 49, 63, 67
Buxton Sidings 65
Buxton-Sproughton Sidings (12.45) 107

Caldon Low Quarry 57
Carlisle-Moston (04.05) 12, 24
Carlisle Kingmoor mpd 8, 9
Carlisle-Red Bank Empty Vans (08.05 or 17.36) 12, 74,
                                                    140, 146, 149
Castleton Curve 22, 79
Castleton-Workington (05.25) 14
Chorley Pilot 185
Clarence (Shunter) 157
Clitheroe-Shap (09.15) 26
Colne-Preston parcels (19.14) 198, 205, 211
Colne-Red Bank empty vans (13.25) 14, 70, 92,
                                                    126, 138, 158, 202

Colne Station 194
Cowlairs Works 35

Daily Express report (11 August)..............................234
Daily Mirror report 218
Darwen-Heysham Tanks 130, 138, 198
Dent ('The Final Hours') 122, 128, 183, 197
DERAILMENTS
    Bay Horse...29
    Bolton..74, 78
    Great Rocks 37
    Dewsnap-Buxton (08.29) 35, 117
    Dewsnap-Gowhole (08.10) 116
DMUs
    Late running & failure 104, 178, 180, 219
    Lights (none)..214
    Dove Holes Tunnel 35, 57
    Edge Hill mpd 49, 67, 120
    End of steam (reflective & detail).....209-210, 217-221

ENGINEMEN (Non 9K)
    Fothergill, E...114
    Morale of...104
    Sullivan, J...48, 112
ENTHUSIASTS
    Behaviour 113, 118-119, 140, 160, 204, 214
    'Founder member' types 112
    Telephoning mpds 36, 52, 53, 87, 127, 130, 147,
                                                 205, 211, 227
    Tickets (without).................53, 98-100, 160, 206, 208
    Tight connections involving steam 31, 155, 160,
                                                        203-204
    Trespassing..107, 226
Entwistle Signal Box......................................70, 107, 126
EXCURSION TRAFFIC
    Belle Vue...87
    Blackburn & Preston holidays 207
    Bolton holidays 167, 168
    Colne holidays 191, 196, 205
    Faster 1968...87, 96
    Football specials 79
    Fylde 94, 96
    Grand National 79
    Party specials 149, 205
    Reduction in..94
    Whit weekend 145-146

FAMILY
    Brother 147, 205
    Parents 199, 210
Farington-Brewery (01.43)..13
Farington-Carlton (21.45) 197, 205, 210, 217

Fleetwood mpd..97
Folly Lane (Runcorn)..80
Footplate rides.......................60-61, 140, 147, 168, 211
FREIGHT (selected, special)
    En masse 53, 54, 128, 161
    Individual (as objectives) 149, 151-152
    Individual (unanticipated) 56
    Out of gauge loads 19
    Van specials 18, 41, 60, 69, 125

'Ghost Train, The'..48, 73
Giggleswick Tripper 183
Glasgow-Manchester (08.25) 8
Gowhole-Northwich (09.05)..45
GRADIENTS QUOTED
    Ancoats-Philips Park 61
    Ashwood Dale 65
    Bradley Fold 61
    Bradshawgate 90
    Broadfield Bank..61
    Chapel-en-le-Frith LNWR....................................102
    Chorley Bank 60, 92, 114
    Darwen Station 128
    Droylsden Station Jc.-Ashton Moss Jc....................108
    Folly Lane (Runcorn) 80
    Hoddlesden Jc. 128, 138, 139, 206
    Hoghton Bank 98, 130, 197
    Lancaster Bank...114
    Leyland 60
    Linnyshaw Moss (from Kearsley)...........................21
    Liverpool Lime St. -Edge Hill 228
    Mill Hill-Rishton 199
    Newton Heath 142
    Northwich-Hartford..30
    Padiham-Rose Grove West 188
    Peak Forest 35
    Preston-Kirkham 127
    Red Bank (M/C Vic.)......................................35, 89
    Skelton Jc. 42, 49
    Spring Vale...92
    Stansfield Hall-Lydgate 129, 162
    Todmorden (main line) 129
    Waltons Sidings (from north) 70, 206
    Westhoughton 125, 209
    Woodley & environs map 244
Grassington Branch 136
Guards' productivity disputes..............77, 158, 161, 165

Halifax-Manchester (04.38) 11, 70
Heaton Mersey mpd 49, 67, 120

Heysham-Burnden (16.50) 14, 22
   (Heysham-Moston hereon), 24, 50, 73, 78, 124,128,
       135, 140, 146, 149, 157, 167
Heysham-Manchester parcels (09.30)....................12, 18
Heysham-Ribble Sidings (14.30) 183
Heysham-Stourton (12.08).................................183, 184
Heysham-Warrington (15.05)............................181, 184
Hoghton Signal Box 217-218
HORWICH WORKS
   Diesel shunters.......................................18, 87, 120
   Ex works electric multiple unit..............................157

I.C.I. limestone trains...30
I.C.I. Woodlands Road..73
Industrial steam locos 196, 214, 216

Job (self) post B.R. 18, 33, 77, 178
Johnson H.C. 77, 144
JOURNEYS WITH STEAM
   (see also 'Belfast Boat Express')
   45156 Accrington-Stockport..........................206-207
   44802 Ancoats-Bolton 61
   45134 Ancoats-Bolton 147
   45268 Blackpool N-Colne 98
   45269 Bolton-M/C Vic.-Castleton Curve-Bolton LE 168
   44802 Bolton-Rochdale..61
   45134 Bolton-Rochdale..147
   44781/44871 Carlisle-Manchester 231-232
   45156 Colne-Stockport 194-195
   45110 Liverpool Lime St.-Manchester Vic..............228
   70013 Manchester-Carlisle..............................230, 231
   45110 Manchester-Liverpool Lime St. 232
   45149 Preston-Blackpool South 96
   45444 Preston-Blackpool South 99
   44816 Preston-Blackpool South 127-128
   44816 Preston-Blackpool South 138
   45212 Preston-Blackpool South 144-145
   45388 Preston-Blackpool South 160
   45305 Preston-Blackpool South 203-204
   45388 Preston-Blackpool South 207-208
   45388 Preston-Blackpool South 212-214
   45212 Preston-Blackpool South 221
   44971 Preston-Kirkham 155
   45076 Preston-Manchester 27
   48026 Westhoughton-Halliwell................................90

Keighley mpd...137
Kitson Wood Tunnel...161

Lancashire Life Magazine 120
Leeds-Halifax (03.32) 11, 70
Liverpool Exchange-Preston (09.00)......................70, 79

LOCOMOTIVES (GENERAL)
   Condemned at other depots than own....................79
   Disposal of (specific locos).......15-16, 33, 48, 56, 104,
       138, 149, 155-156, 169
   Exhaust sounds – peculiarities, etc..............62, 70, 76,
       142-143, 196, 197
   Failures..112
   Priming 155
   Shopping proposals...68
   Slipping (excessive)..92, 139
   Steam totals in service...11
LOCOMOTIVE TRANSFERS
   Large movements 67, 120, 174, 177
   Last to Bolton 120
   Moves north (30/6/68) 174, 177
   Observed in transit............................118, 169, 183
LOCOMOTIVES BY CLASS
   Ivatt 4MT..11, 32, 109
   Black...5 11
   Black...8 11
   B.R.5MT...11, 172, 174
   B.R. 4MT..11
   B.R.9F..11, 55
   Working after condemned date 50-51
LOCOMOTIVES – DIESEL
   D400 class 96, 185
   Failures..112
   Shunters 56

Manchester-Blackpool parcels (03.05) 13
Manchester-Blackpool parcels (09.15)...............8, 14, 18
Manchester-Blackpool parcels (09.30) 14
Manchester-Blackpool parcels (16.30) 12
Manchester-Blackpool parcels (18.05) 73
Manchester-Colne parcels (05.00) 14
Manchester-Heysham News (20.30) 46
Manchester-Wigan (01.00)..151
Metal Box Co..89
Morale (self) 77, 112, 170, 172, 232, 234
MOTIVE POWER DEPOTS (GENERAL)
   Closure dates uncertainty................................68, 111
   Ejected from 228
   Permits..40
Motorways...22, 188
Mottram-Partington (10.27)...............................107, 117
Mottram-Widnes (09.00)..45
MUSIC
   Classical engagements 77
   Popular/contemporary 60, 104, 169, 205

Newspaper reports..218, 234

INDEX

NEWTON HEATH MPD
    Closure 177
    Contents 142, 158
    'Newton Heath Look' 26
    Last day 168
Normanton mpd 11
Northwich mpd 31, 49, 63, 67, 85
Notebook inadequacy 33, 155

Oldham Clegg Street-Blackburn parcels ...14, 73, 79, 140
Overnights & overnight travel 113, 151, 154, 207, 216

Padiham coal trains 188, 200
Patricroft mpd 67, 78, 85, 120, 170, 174, 177
Peak Forest....................................35-37, 56-58, 64-65
Preston-Barrow parcels (09.58)...............................178
Preston-Blackpool South (12.44) 88, 96, 138
Preston-Blackpool South (20.50)........125, 134, 144-145,
                            147, 154, 203-204, 207-208,
                                 212, 214, 221
Preston-Colne parcels (02.50)..................................198
Preston Docks Railway 154, 156, 211
Preston-Healey Mills (18.45).....................157, 197, 201,
                                    205, 211, 217
Preston-Liverpool (21.25) 70, 126, 134, 135, 221
Preston-Manchester (12.17) 14, 15, 18, 25-26, 41, 61,
                                    70, 87, 109-110
Privilege travel..20, 25

Railway Magazine.........................56, 158, 209-210, 216
RAILTOURS for ENTHUSIASTS
    Banned by B.R. 11, 73
    Ban lifted 73
    B.R./L.C.G.B. 'Flying Scotsman'
        East Coast non-stop................................158, 234
    B.R.15 Guinea Tour.......................209, 210, 228-234
    B.R./L.M.R (4 August)...223
    B.R. Scottish Region.....................................92, 134
    G.C. Enterprises..............................74, 75, 76, 223
    L.C.G.B. 83, 162, 223
    M.R.T.S./S.V.R. 100-103, 104, 108, 216
    R.C.T.S. 104, 151, 223
    Roch Valley Rly. Soc...208
    S.L.S..138, 223
    Unknown (28 April & 2 June)........................109, 145
    Warwickshire Rly. Soc..............................129, 130, 134
    William Deacon's Bank 74
Raymond, Sir Stanley 11, 77
Ribble-Carnforth/Heysham (10.05)............183, 184, 185
Ribble-Heysham (11.50) 181, 184
River Weaver 30
Rochdale-Stockport parcels (21.43) 147

Rollason D.T.J................................56, 74, 203, 214, 234
ROSE GROVE
    Introduction to..185-186
    Traffic listed..200
    Traffic patterns, Monday, 8 July..........................196
    Up grid (yard)...196
ROSE GROVE MPD
    5MTs, work for 197
    Dead engines movement 156
    Grassington branch engine 199, 201
    Motive power monitor 187-188
Relieving work only..227
Rose Grove-Ribble (13.40)..200
Rose Grove-Wyre Dock (13.10) 188, 200
Rose Grove-Colne empty vans (08.15).......................198
Rotherwood-Garston (00.10) 45, 107
Rotherwood-Garston (08.20) 107
Runcorn Folly Lane-Spink Hill (12.25).............49, 75, 84,
                                    107, 117-118

St Simon & St Jude's Church Choir 29, 60, 87, 120
SCRAPYARDS/FIRMS
    Buttigieg's, Newport..155
    Cashmore's, Great Bridge 156
    Cashmore's, Newport 15, 155
    Cohen's, Kettering 149
    Drapers, Hull 104, 120
    Hatton's, Bolton 56
    Woodham's, Barry 33
Scunthorpe-Warrington (05.21).................................107
Shap-Clitheroe (cement empties)................................26
Shrewsbury-Bolton parcels 15, 18
SIGNALMEN (Not Bolton East Jc.)
    Carroll (at Waltons Sidings)........................70, 126, 202
    Chinley Station South Jc......................................66
    Hoghton Signal Box 217
Sinderland Crossing 45
Skelton Jc. (introduction to) 42
Skipton mpd 137
Sough Tunnel...70
Speke Jc. mpd 9, 49, 67, 79, 86, 155
Spring Vale 70, 92, 104
Steam ban on passenger work 110
Stockport-Bolton through service 195
Stockport Edgeley mpd.........................9, 37, 49, 67, 120

TAPE RECORDING
    Commentary...66, 151
    Composition/content 217, 227
    Difficult conditions 17, 74, 64-65, 125, 230
    Dominating photography.........................17, 30, 64
    Missed opportunities 140, 158, 188

TAPE RECORDING (continued...)
- Police enquiry 107
- Tape usage 45, 88
- Very long recordings 149, 188

TICKETS (see also 'Privilege')
- Day returns 203
- Farewell to steam tour, 11 August 210
- New design (experiment) 149
- Runabout (Lancashire) 178

TIMINGS
- Diesel 127, 146
- Limited load 112

Tinsley-Edge Hill (06.45) 45
Topley Pike Signal Box 65
Trafford Park mpd 11, 49, 63, 67
Trainspotting 134

TRIP COMMENT
- Desperate action taken 49, 53
- Distorted appreciation of 53
- Flexibility within trips 82-83
- Low success rate of 61-62, 81, 137-138, 154

Tunstead-Runcorn (12.00) 36, 56, 64, 81, 84
Turton Signal Box 70

Ulverston Tripper 183, 184

Waltons Sidings Signal Box 70
Warsop-Edge Hill (05.04) 49, 107
Wath-Garston (12.47) 107

WEATHER
- Blizzards 82
- Bolton holidays 182, 198
- Frost (late) 113
- Hot spell 138, 149
- Snow 7, 18, 30, 48, 50, 82
- Wind 7, 74

Wigan-Manchester (05.45) 35, 70, 89
Windermere Tripper 152, 184
Woodley 49, 105-106, 114-115
Working timetables 127, 146, 172
Workington mpd 11
World Steam Publication 181
Wyre Dock-Moston (21.15) 13

ALSO FROM CRÉCY PUBLISHING

Atlas of Rail Station Closures

It is often said that it was Dr Richard Beeching, Chairman of British Railways in the 1960s, who was responsible for scrapping the vast majority of the UK rail network. However, closures, replacements, re-alignments and modifications to the network had been taking place from the very earliest days of the railways. This exhaustively researched and original work deals with all the closures which were made throughout the railway age in Britain.

A valuable new work of railway reference, the *Atlas of Railway Station Closures* maps all the standard gauge railway lines built in Britain and lists the dates when each line and every station on those lines was closed. The company, BR Region or later organisation owning the station at the time of the closure is listed, as well as the last pre-grouping owner. The name of the station used is, in every instance, that applied at the time of its closure

Encompassing a wealth of invaluable information organised and presented in an easily accessible format, the *Atlas of Railway Station Closures* includes comprehensive cartographic mapping of the entire railway network of Britain showing its railway station closures; a complete easy to use index and gazetteer listing the date of each closure; and a photographic section illustrating some of these lost stations. An invaluable and comprehensive record and a fascinating insight into the history and development of Britain's railway network, the *Atlas of Railway Station Closures* is a must have reference for the bookshelves of any railway enthusiast, local historian and anyone with an interest in Britain's industrial heritage.

ISBN: 9780860936770

128 pages, hardback. £25

Southern Steam Swansong

Paul Cooper

It was during the 1964 Autumn half term that a young Paul Cooper picked up a copy of Modern Railways at Kings Cross. Inside was a story announcing the £15 million Bournemouth electrification scheme, due for completion in early 1967. He knew that would represent the elimination of a 100% steam service in a little over two years and so he resolved to record as much of the action as he could, before it was gone forever.

Over the next three years, Paul fulfilled that promise by travelling all over the Southern Region, photographing not just the special services of the era, but moreover the daily workings and the scenes in the stations, sidings and workshops where steam locomotives were seeing out their final years in service.

Now, to mark 50 years since the last steam services ran in the UK, Paul has teamed-up with Crécy Publishing to bring many of these glorious photographs into publication for the first time. In addition to Paul's own photographs, *Southern Steam Swansong* also includes images from other photographers, including in particular a selection from a recently uncovered cache of previously unknown large format colour Ektachrome images, taken by Ken Vernon and all recorded on a German-made Rolleiflex camera.

In all, *Southern Steam Swansong* contains over 250 photographs, of which 187 are in colour and around 90% have never been published before. These stunning images are supported by detailed captions which tell the story not just of the images themselves, but of the people, places and machinery that were part of the Southern Railway in these years of transition from a steam railway to the diesel and electric era.

ISBN: 9781909328679

176 pages. Hardback. £27.50

Holding the Line
How Britain's Railways Were Saved

Richard Faulkner and Chris Austin

At its zenith, there were 21,000 route miles of railway in Britain. Today the country's railways deliver more passenger miles than they did at their greatest extent despite a drastic reduction in the size of the network. Those cuts were the result of a campaign by a number of individuals who believed, erroneously as the passing of time has shown, that railways were a thing of the past and an impediment to progress.

Although the process of railway closures started early, it gained momentum in the 1950s and in the harrowing years following the publication of the Beeching report. However, as the original research by the authors of this book reveals, it could have been much worse and there were plans to reduce the size of the network even more drastically, to the point where only a few lines would have survived.

An understanding of what happened in the past is vital to understanding how today's railways struggle to meet the demands imposed on them. Trimming at the margins remains an attractive option for some policy makers who do not comprehend what happened in the past and the risk remains that previous errors may be revisited. Now available in paperback for the first time, this book shows how close Britain's railways came to being eviscerated and how the dangers of closure by stealth still exist, even today.

ISBN: 9780860936763

344 pages, paperback. £9.95

LOST LINES
Railway Treasures
Nigel Welbourn

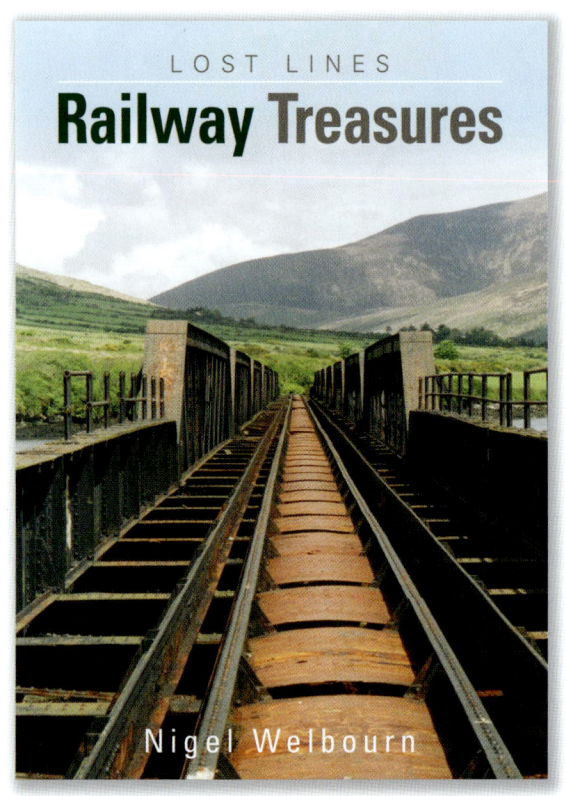

Many readers will be familiar with Nigel Welbourn's long-running and best selling *Lost Lines* series in 15 volumes, each covering a part of the country. In this brand new book, he takes an overview of what has been lost from a national perspective. The book spans a period from the first line lost to passengers – part of the Stockton & Darlington Railway in 1836 – to the closure of the line from Spalding in March 1982.

Railway Treasures takes us on a journey through a huge variety of closed lines, including those abandoned by the 'Big Four' post 1923, as well as those lost in the savage cuts of the Beeching era. It offers an intriguing perspective on what remains of many lines and stations, from the largest structures to tiny relics of past glories.

None of the book's 300 photographs have been published before and it includes a treasure trove of maps, tickets and other items of railway ephemera. This book will delight not only railway enthusiasts but will appeal to a much wider cadre of readers with an interest in the British countryside and our transport and industrial heritage.

ISBN: 9781909328822
128 pages, hardback. £24.95